HOW THE WORLD BECAME A BOOK
IN SHAKESPEARE'S ENGLAND

CW01500213

Human beings build their worlds using metaphors. Just as computer technology has inaugurated a massive metaphorical transformation in the present era, in which we can "reboot" social causes or "program" human behavior, books spawned new metaphorical worlds in newly print-savvy early modern England. Pamphleteers appealed to books to stage political attacks, preachers formulated theological claims using metaphors of page and binding, and scientists claimed to leaf through the "Book of Nature." Jonathan P. Lamb shows how, far from offering a mere linguistic tool, this astonishingly broad lexicon taught entire cultures how to imagine, giving early modern writers – from Shakespeare to Cavendish, and from the famous to the anonymous – the language to describe and reshape the worlds around them. This book reveals how, at a scale beyond anything scholars have imagined, bookish language shaped religious, political, racial, scientific, and literary questions that remain alive today.

JONATHAN P. LAMB is Professor of English at the University of Kansas and an award-winning scholar and teacher of Shakespeare, Renaissance literature, and book history. He is the author of *Shakespeare in the Marketplace of Words* (2017) and many articles and is a leading expert in the use of digital scholarly methods to study literature and culture.

"Ever since writing was invented it has been used as a metaphor by human beings for themselves and who they are, or for the world and how they live in it. This is especially true at times of media change, such as the printed book in Renaissance Europe. Jonathan P. Lamb provides an enthusiastic and insightful survey of how Shakespeare and other writers describe the world as a book."

Brian Cummings FBA, Anniversary Professor of English,
University of York

"Lamb has written a fascinating study of early modern England's 'bookish lexicon'. Encyclopedic in scope and filled with engaging examples, How the World Became a Book in Shakespeare's England shows us, as no other book has before, how the materiality of texts became a habit of mind and a way of imagining the world. This is a book that will be read and re-read by anyone interested in Renaissance books and their readers."

Zachary Lesser, Edward W. Kane Professor of English,
University of Pennsylvania

"An astonishing achievement. This is a work about book history and philology, about modernity, metaphor, and mythology; it is about mediation and imagination, about how we think and the concepts we use to think with. Lamb guides the reader through his vast intellectual territory with verve and wit. The result is entertainingly readable and endlessly illuminating."

Laurie Maguire, Professor of English Literature,
Magdalen College Oxford

"If the world were indeed a book you'd want it to be written by Jonathan P. Lamb, with his simultaneous attention to large themes and individual details, his whip-smart humour, and his commitment to the affordances of literary study. His humane, interrogative, and generative study is a true manifesto for the discipline."

Emma Smith, Professor of Shakespeare Studies,
Hertford College Oxford

"Lamb reveals the ways books were alive in the mind and in discourse: books provided a language for conceiving of, and writing about, love, literature, nature, race, and the world. Lamb's book is teeming with examples from writers familiar and little known, and Lamb writes with verve, wit and clarity."

Adam Smyth, Professor of English and the History of the Book,
Balliol College, Oxford University

HOW THE WORLD BECAME A BOOK IN SHAKESPEARE'S ENGLAND

JONATHAN P. LAMB

University of Kansas

CAMBRIDGE
UNIVERSITY PRESS

Shaftesbury Road, Cambridge CB2 8EA, United Kingdom

One Liberty Plaza, 20th Floor, New York, NY 10006, USA

477 Williamstown Road, Port Melbourne, VIC 3207, Australia

314–321, 3rd Floor, Plot 3, Splendor Forum, Jasola District Centre, New Delhi – 110025, India

103 Penang Road, #05–06/07, Visioncrest Commercial, Singapore 238467

Cambridge University Press is part of Cambridge University Press & Assessment, a department of the University of Cambridge.

We share the University's mission to contribute to society through the pursuit of education, learning and research at the highest international levels of excellence.

www.cambridge.org
Information on this title: www.cambridge.org/9781009460415

DOI: 10.1017/9781009460378

First published 2025

Printed in the United Kingdom by CPI Group Ltd, Croydon CR0 4YY

A catalogue record for this publication is available from the British Library

Library of Congress Cataloging-in-Publication Data
NAMES: Lamb, Jonathan P., 1980– author
TITLE: How the world became a book in Shakespeare's England / Jonathan P. Lamb, University of Kansas.
DESCRIPTION: Cambridge ; New York, NY : Cambridge University Press, 2025. | Includes bibliographical references and index.
IDENTIFIERS: LCCN 2025000339 | ISBN 9781009460415 hardback | ISBN 9781009460408 paperback | ISBN 9781009460378 ebook
SUBJECTS: LCSH: English language – Early modern, 1500–1700 – Style | English language – Early modern, 1500–1700 – Terms and phrases | Metaphor | Books – Terminology
CLASSIFICATION: LCC PE877 .L35 2025
LC record available at https://lccn.loc.gov/2025000339

ISBN 978-1-009-46041-5 Hardback

For April, Charlotte, and Henry,
my favorite people in the world

Contents

Color plates are to be found between pages 150 and 151

Figures and Plates

Figures

viii

Plates

Preface

Books have infiltrated the English language. When we agree with each other, we say *we are on the same page*. When one idea closely relates to another, we say they are *bound up together*, two books stitched into one volume. We call capital letters *upper-case* and small letters *lower-case* because, when pieces of type were set by hand to print books, the typecase containing capital letters was positioned above (i.e., *upper*) the one containing small letters. When we are feeling unwell or unlike our usual selves, we say we are *out of sorts*. Though the etymology of this phrase is uncertain, it probably refers to a single piece of type (a "sort") that has been put into the wrong place in the typecase. When the next person to set type reaches for what they think will be a "c," they get an "e," so that instead of "cat in the hat," the page reads "eat in the hat."

Many bookish phrases have lost their evident bookishness. Actors complain of being *type-cast*. We warn against *stereotyping* or *marginalizing* others. We joke about posters featuring typefaces called Comic Sans and Papyrus, rarely pausing to mention that *sans serif* refers to the absence of marks at the end of each character's stroke and *papyrus* refers to an ancient plant-based writing surface similar to paper. And when a person who has been making bad or harmful choices begins making good ones instead, we say they have *turned over a new leaf*. The *leaf* in this phrase refers to a sheet of paper in a book (with a *page* on each side); turning over the leaf means flipping from one page to the next.

In the two centuries after the introduction of printing to Europe, "turn over a new leaf" was trending. It sparked with meaning precisely because it summoned a book to the imagination. Gervase Markham observes how difficult it is for good servingmen to cut off associations with people of ill repute (a "crue of [...] clusterfystes"). These servingmen find themselves "loathing to lyue in fellowshyp with such vnseruiceable people" and thus resolve "to turne ouer a new leafe."[1] In an English version of Plutarch's

---

[1] Gervase Markham, *A Health to the Gentlemanly Profession of Seruingmen; or, The Seruingmans Comforts* (London, 1598), sig. F1r. STC 17140.

Moralia, the translator suggests that "every sinfull and wicked person" should ask themselves, "how should I cast off the remorse of conscience from me? and from hencefoorth begin to turne over a new leafe, & lead another life[?]"² In an English translation of Mateo Alemán's picaresque novel *The rogue: or The life of Guzman de Alfarache* (1623), the titular character describes how, "Beaten with the rod of affliction, I began to be humbled, and was fully resolued to turne ouer a new leafe, and betake my selfe to a better course of life."³ Across three genres, writers and translators figure moral reformation as turning the page of a book, and they do so in moral terms familiar even today, invoking loathing, sin, and injustice. "Turning over a new leaf" marks personal narratives as redemptive, giving language for the rehabilitation of those to have made grievous choices. The phrase's rhetorical power derives from the way it does not merely *reflect* the redemption of the self but *presents the self as capable of redemption*.

Most sixteenth- and seventeenth-century uses of "turn over a new leaf" appear in sermons and other religious texts. Devout English writers unsurprisingly found themselves drawn to the leaf as a metaphor of redemption, but their knowing invocation of a book leaf goes further still. In a sermon on the book of Deuteronomy (translated by Arthur Golding), Jean Calvin imagines God as a divine corrector: "when God visiteth vs and sendeth vs any corrections, to humble vs and to abate our ouergreat vnthankfulnes and frowardnes: let vs turne ouer a newe leafe and returne againe vnto him."⁴ In another sermon, Thomas Bankes warns Christians against polluting themselves, unless "by repentance they take vp in time, and turne ouer a new leafe."⁵ Less grimly, Henry Smith exhorts congregants to "reioyce and remember: thou hast learned to bee merry, now learne to bee wise: nowe therefore turne ouer a new leafe, and take a new Lesson."⁶ For someone who believes in the doctrine of divine election – as Calvin, Bankes, and Smith do – God has already declared who will repent and when. The future is already ordained or appointed. In this awkward nexus between theology and the rhetorical situation of preaching, "turn over a new leaf" gives these preachers a way to talk about personal reformation – they would use the term "repentance" – without diluting their belief

---

² Plutarch, *The Philosophie, Commonlie Called, the Morals* (London, 1603), sig. Zz5v. STC 20063.

³ Mateo Alemán, *The Rogue: or The Life of Guzman de Alfarache* (London, 1623), sig. Y6r. STC 289.

⁴ Jean Calvin, *The Sermons of M. Iohn Caluin Vpon the Fifth Booke of Moses Called Deuteronomie* (London, 1583), sig. A3v. STC 4442.

⁵ Thomas Bankes, *A Verie Godly, Learned, and Fruitfull Sermon against the Bad Spirits of Malignitie, Malice, and Vnmercifulnesse* (London, 1586), sig. A7v. STC 1365.

⁶ Henry Smith, *Two Sermons, of Ionahs Punishment* (London, 1607), sig. D4r. STC 22754.

in divine election. What is written (or printed) on the next page is already set down; the believer must simply "turn over a new leaf" and actualize the repentance God has already set in motion.

How the World Became a Book in Shakespeare's England is about the language surrounding books in early modern England. "Turn over a new leaf" was just one of many bookish figures to which sixteenth- and seventeenth-century writers appealed. Today, this robust figurative lexicon has crusted and calcified, but these writers enthusiastically wielded it to describe their world and their position in it. This language is not merely metaphorical, however. It gave expression to and therefore shaped questions that remain with us today. As the chapters of this book explore, writers used the language of books to formulate ideas that would be central to the modern era – but they did so in distinctly *premodern* ways that resonate in a postmodern world. Much of the public discourse about early modern England still focuses on the "impact" of the printing press, which was introduced to Europe in the late fifteenth century. But I will argue that the *technological* innovation of printing was just a prelude to the *rhetorical* and *conceptual* innovations books make possible. Following the currents of recent book historical scholarship, which continues to move away from the fixity, objectivity, and totality of books and toward an ecology of their creation, dissemination, and use, I show how the very idea of "the book" took shape in (and in turn shaped) English culture.

I must warn you that this book contains *a lot* of examples. To argue for the widespread and generative use of the language of books across two centuries of English writing, I spent more than two years with a team of student researchers finding and collecting as many examples as possible. Using the Early English Books Online Text Creation Partnership (EEBO-TCP) corpus along with other resources, the team collected over 5,000 quotable examples of the bookish lexicon at work. Although I do not quote all 5,000, and although I will guide the way, reading this book (to say nothing of writing it) means repeatedly working through diverse, rich, and sometimes difficult language. There will be opportunities for close analysis, but the broad argument of this book requires ordering a wide range of examples and studying them as a bicycle rider studies houses, trees, and fields along the way.

The phrase "Shakespeare's England" in this book's title is shorthand for a lengthier explanation. As Chapter 1 will discuss, the various terms used to describe sixteenth- and seventeenth-century England ("early modern," "Renaissance," and "premodern") bear value-laden relations to modernity. Each of these terms comes loaded with associations and inclinations, and each does distinct rhetorical work as a marker. Consider, for instance, that there are not many housing developments called "Medieval Apartments," but plenty called "Renaissance"; the latter term suggests cultural capital, social mobility, and renovated bathrooms. "Shakespeare's England" is no exception: as a Shakespeare scholar, I am invested (sometimes literally) in the value of this particular writer's name as an umbrella term. To be sure, England is not Shakespeare's except as a retroactive conceptual label, but that is precisely why I use his name here: as a heuristic principle or finding aid.[7] Shakespeare's name helps coordinate the broad range of writers, genres, and material texts in this book under a rubric other than that of modernity. Although I rarely refer to "Shakespeare's England" in this book, therefore, I use it in the title as a way of drawing a historical radius around Shakespeare's writing career at the end of the sixteenth century and the beginning of the seventeenth century.

Each chapter of *How the World Became a Book in Shakespeare's England* explores how the terms, metaphors, and concepts arising from books achieved broad cultural significance and widespread use. The book lexicon prompted the reimagination of relationships between people, of attitudes toward the nonhuman world, and of concepts such as media and literature. Chapter 1 articulates the book's main intervention and contribution, ending with a brief discussion of the phrases "is a book" and "like a book." Premodern writers who said something "is" or is "like a book" forged the very conceptual connection that *How the World Became a Book* traces through English culture. Chapter 2 works backwards from the glossary of terms in Joseph Moxon's 1683 printer's manual and a 1684 poem that uses those terms extensively to show how the less technical, more widespread set of terms collected in this book demonstrate considerable rhetorical and conceptual flexibility. Two key terms, "bookish" and "set forth," begin my exploration of how the language of books gave people a way to describe their culture and situate themselves within it.

Chapter 3 explores the "The Metaphors We Read With." Here we find books rhetorically manufacturing a new kind of consciousness, as the affordances of text technologies provide a way to describe human experience. This chapter shows that, whether it is poets claiming love "is printed on my

---

[7] I am indebted to Jeffrey Masten's explanation of "Shakespeare's Time" in his book's title: Shakespeare's texts are "a preeminent site for *methodological* articulation, expansion, and revolution for early modern philological, textual, bibliographical, editorial, and sex/gender work." See *Queer Philologies: Sex, Language, and Affect in Shakespeare's Time*, Material Texts (Philadelphia: University of Pennsylvania Press, 2016), 33–34.

heart," or physicians claiming a man's sickness is his "comma" and not his "period," or a botanist saying an animal is a plant "bound up in one volume," the symbols of the book reshaped the intellectual and linguistic makeup of English culture. Chapter 4 takes up the question of book size, including format (folio, quarto, etc.) as well as the adjectives applied to books (big, large, little, etc.). The rhetoric of book size gave people a way to talk about information. Chapter 5 explores the stakes of touching, tasting, smelling, and hearing books. Writers connected bookish words with sensory language to conceptualize the process of mediation.

Chapters 6 and 7 extend the project's inquiry to the global limits by offering focused accounts of single terms. Chapter 6 takes up the best-known bookish metaphor: the book of nature. Tracing the phrase "book of nature" and its attendant metaphors through early modern English writing, I show how its Christian use did not fully disappear when the metaphor suddenly flipped to work in service of the modern scientific method. The "book of nature" gave people a language for knowledge in a rapidly changing epistemology. Chapter 7 builds on recent scholarship demonstrating that print technology was foundational to concepts of racial identity and whiteness in particular. I explore how writers appealed to the phrase "the art of printing" to describe racial sameness and otherness as a set of ethnic, geographical, and bodily differences. Press technology itself gave people a way to talk about race, which in turn framed racial concepts for later writers.

Though a work of literary and cultural scholarship, this book seeks to highlight the resonance, even relevance, of Shakespeare's England to the present. Both cultures feature a heightened media consciousness, in which producers and consumers use the terminologies of media to make sense of the world. Chapter 1 sets out the high stakes, scholarly intervention, and methods of this book in detail. I invite you, therefore, to turn over a new leaf.

Acknowledgments

Three University of Kansas (KU) General Research Fund grants helped make this project possible. They helped convene a team of brilliant undergraduate and graduate student researchers to find and collect as many examples as possible. A Midcareer Fellowship from the KU Hall Center for the Humanities provided time, space, atmosphere, morning coffee, and afternoon tea to write most of the book. A KU Department of English Shirley Cundiff and Jordan L. Haines Faculty Fellowship provided a course release to complete the book. For this relief, much thanks.

Likewise, libraries made this project possible. Before and after it closed for renovation, the Folger Shakespeare Library has been a home away from home for me and many others, supporting and stimulating our work with its programs, collections, and above all its superb staff. Special thanks to Mike Witmore and Owen Williams. The University of Kansas Kenneth Spencer Research Library has been an actual home for me for many years; its mostly quiet halls and incomparable staff have made it the perfect place to teach, learn, and study. Exuberant thanks to Beth Whittaker and Elspeth Healey. I am also profoundly grateful to Emily Hockley and everyone else at Cambridge University Press, who helped conjure this book into existence. Thanks too to the anonymous readers of the press, whose rigorous feedback made the book better in every way.

I belong to a community of incredible scholars. Thanks to the many dozens of people who have read, listened to, critiqued, and interrogated this work. I am especially grateful to Doug Eskew, Greg Foran, Alan Galey, Miles Grier, Megan Heffernan, Jonathan Hope, M. J. Kidnie, Elizabeth Kolkovich, Zack Lesser, Laurie Maguire, Arthur Marotti, Bernadette Myers, Vim Pasupathi, Dan Shore, Maggie Simon, Ian Smith, Scott Trudell, and Georgina Wilson. Some of you read whole chapters; some asked great questions in key conversations. Whitney Sperrazza read and offered rigorous, formative feedback on every chapter. Whitney, I am truly grateful for your friendship and intellect.

At Kansas, I continue to be rich in friends. Student researchers Tina Kaiser, Nellie Kassebaum, Demetra McBrayer, Suzanne Tanner, and Mikaela Warner enthusiastically accepted a rather peculiar challenge: find thousands of examples. Their ingenuity and creativity made this book what it is. Lydia Benda helped bring the book to completion. I am grateful for the support and friendship of colleagues: Giselle Anatol, David Bergeron, Marta Caminero, Darren Canady, Katie Conrad, Phil Drake, Randy Fuller, Richard Godbeer, Peter Grund, Caroline Jewers, Anna Neill, Elaine Nelson, Pritha Prasad, Ann Rowland, Misty Schieberle, Geraldo Sousa, and Steven Wang. Many of you heard more about this book than you could ever ask or imagine. A very special thanks to Tim Jackson, Laura Mielke, and Dave Tell; your friendship means the world to me. Finally, my deepest love and gratitude go to Charlotte, Henry, and April Lamb, to whom I dedicate this book. I cannot imagine life without you, nor do I want to. (Also, April: don't tell the kids, but you are my actual favorite person.)

A Note on Texts and Citations

This book attempts to show the familiarity of Renaissance England within its often-baffling strangeness. As scholars of book history and language have taken pains to demonstrate over the last few decades, modernization often distorts the variety, fecundity, and material textuality of early modern English. For example, wordplay legible in early modern spelling is often erased in modernized spelling. For these reasons, I have not modernized the texts I cite. Two exceptions to this practice are (1) the use of "s" in place of the long-s and (2) the expansion of macrons that stand for additional letters, as when "ō" stands for "on" or "om." In the latter cases, I include the additional letter in square brackets. Where a word's early spelling is so different from its modern one that readers may not recognize it, I offer a modernized term in square brackets.

Many of the texts cited here come from transcriptions of Early English Books Online (EEBO) image sets. In most cases, these images are digital scans of Early English Books microfilms, which were in turn photographed from library copies. To cite from EEBO is thus to cite a transcription of an image of a microfilm of a book. In keeping with my eagerness for readers to come to grips with the material realities of the past, I have cited the short, unmodernized title and the Short Title Catalog (STC) or Wing number for each book cited. In cases where additional title page information is relevant to the argument, I supply it.

CHAPTER I

An Introduction Is Like a Book

The answer to the riddle in Figure 1.1 is, of course, a book: "for the paper is white as snow, and the inke is as blacke as a crow, and the leaues more pliant then a wand."[1] The book you are holding presumably does not have a "silken lace" tied around it. I certainly hope you are not experiencing an ambivalent "sad cheare," not when we are only on page 1. But you get the idea. A book has a set of material properties familiar to anyone who has seen or handled one, let alone read it. And the more familiar books of all types become, the more precise and nuanced one's bookish references can be. A familiarity with pagination conventions, for instance, makes my reference to "page 1" elicit no surprise, even though I have already been writing to you for several pages.

Unless, that is, you are reading this book in digital form. In this case, your device's settings will determine the color of letters and background you see. Perhaps, like me, you prefer screen reading in "dark mode," and thus your letters are "white as snow," the background "blacke as any crow." You cannot turn "plyant" leaves. If you are reading these words in a portable document format (PDF) file or web browser, you cannot turn leaves at all: you must *scroll* through a remediated form of the book, remembering how the codex (a set of stacked pages bound on one side) replaced the scroll as the dominant text technology in the West.[2] Or perhaps you are reading this on a *tablet*, originally the term for a stiff sheet made of clay or waxed wood and used for writing.[3] If you think this is a useful point, be sure to mark it with your *stylus*, the term for the sharp instrument used for making and erasing letters on the wax tablet.[4]

---

[1] Anonymous, *The Booke of Meery. Riddles* (London, 1629), sig. B3r. STC 3323.
[2] The standard account remains Colin H. Roberts, T. C. Skeat, and Colin H. Roberts, *The Birth of the Codex* (London: Published for the British Academy by the Oxford University Press, 1983).
[3] *OED* s.v. "tablet n."
[4] *OED* s.v. "style n."

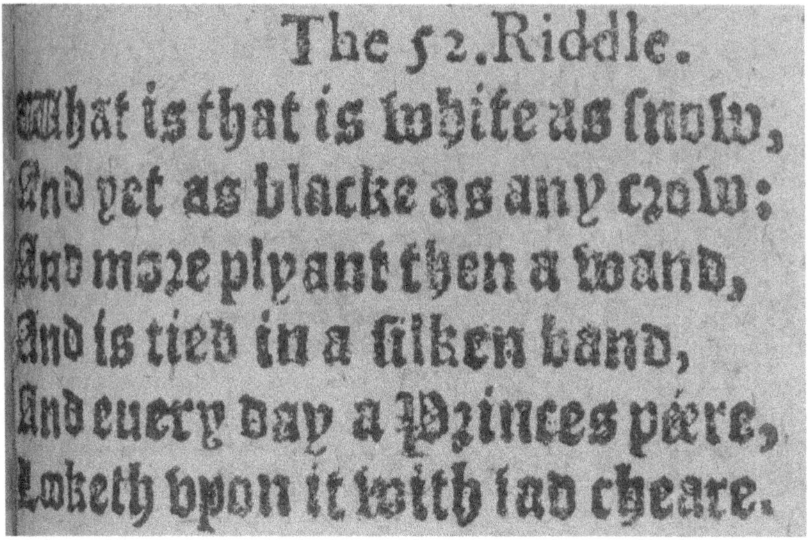

The 52.Riddle.

What is that is white as snow,
And yet as blacke as any crow:
And more plyant then a wand,
And is tied in a silken band,
And every day a Princes pære,
Loketh vpon it with sad cheare.

Figure 1.1   Detail of *The Booke of Meery. Riddles* (London, 1629), sig. B3r, RB 82977, The Huntington Library, San Marino, California.

Your plight, dear hypothetical digital reader, draws me to the broad point of this chapter and the animating spirit of the entire book: the lexicon arising from text technologies shapes how we think about and describe the world. There is not merely a "rhetoric of the page," as Laurie Maguire has brilliantly described, but a rhetoric of every aspect of the book, "invit[ing] readers to respond imaginatively."[5] Just as digital technologies have recently required the use of new terms, many of which are old terms, so too has a set of words and phrases clustered around books. We already encountered a few of these in the Preface. These vocabularies of the book have expanded and morphed over centuries, particularly in the time period often called "early modern" (ca. 1500–1700). One difference is key, however: while terms such as *scroll* and *tablet* have thus far been taken from one text technology and straightforwardly applied to a new one, the language of books has been used expansively in a bewildering variety of situations.[6] Think of the way "turn over a new leaf" creates narratives of selfhood in both religious and secular contexts. As Andrew Piper writes,

---

[5] Laurie Maguire, *The Rhetoric of the Page* (Oxford: Oxford University Press, 2020), 5.

[6] Already, of course, may terms have migrated out of their initial digital usage into other areas. One now speaks of having "bandwidth" for time commitments, of "unsubscribing" from a friendship, and of "rebooting" the cause of social justice. Future scholars will write *How the World Became a Computer*, noting how these terms preceded computers.

"the materiality of the book" provides "contours ... to the imagination itself."[7] Books shape language; language shapes the world.

Sixteenth- and seventeenth-century England abounded in bookish words. Although someone familiar with Shakespeare's plays might assume that the era's dominant figures came from the theater – "all the world's a stage," after all – books furnished a flexible and widespread figurative repertoire to English writers.[8] Playwrights and poets used the bookish lexicon to make new kinds of art. Pamphleteers appealed to books to stage political attacks. Preachers, as we have seen, formulated theological arguments using metaphors of page and binding. Scientists claimed to leaf through the Book of Nature. Always rhetorically situated and rarely systematic, this lexicon did not merely offer a linguistic tool; it created a broad conceptual resource for writers and readers. In this book, I argue that books gave early modern writers the language to describe and reshape the world around them – even as most of this language was inherited from earlier traditions and media or imported from other cultures and languages. At a scale and range far beyond what scholars have explored, this language expressed and, in turn, gave form to religious, political, racial, scientific, and literary questions that remain alive today.

This book applies what scholars know about books as objects to books as symbols, figures, and implements of the imagination. This first chapter's task is to stake out the contribution and intervention of the entire book, a task complicated by the many moving parts an argument like mine entails. The first moving part is to consider the broad context in which bookish VOCABULARIES have signified in human cultures and to articulate how this book extends and critiques orthodox accounts of the "book as symbol." The second part necessarily deals with printing technologies (or TYPOGRA-PHIES), which have justifiably occupied significant attention in those orthodox accounts of the book's place in culture. The printing press has often been recruited to support what thinkers such as Derrida and Foucault have theorized about the "totality" of the book. These first two sections therefore sketch out the broad field of knowledge in which my study positions itself.

In these broad scholarly contexts, new ECOLOGIES of the book have arisen in recent book history and textual scholarship focused on early modern

---

[7] Andrew Piper, *Dreaming in Books: The Making of the Bibliographic Imagination in the Romantic Age* (Chicago: University of Chicago Press, 2009), 2.

[8] See Lynda G. Christian, *Theatrum Mundi: The History of an Idea*, Harvard Dissertations in Comparative Literature (New York: Garland, 1987); William Egginton, *How the World Became a Stage: Presence, Theatricality, and the Question of Modernity* (Albany: SUNY Press, 2003); and William N. West, *Common Understandings, Poetic Confusion: Playhouses & Playgoers in Elizabethan England* (Chicago: University of Chicago Press, 2021).

England. These ecologies decompose the "totality" of the book and instead emphasize the precarity, fragmentation, and social embeddedness of books, particularly in the sixteenth and seventeenth centuries. These centuries are often understood as the inauguration of the modern era, tightly linked with the printing press and the book as a symbol of totality. The stakes of *How the World Became a Book* therefore concern books' place in the MODERNITIES to which they have been linked. My overall project is to *demodernize* our understanding of books' symbolic value. To accomplish this multifaceted feat, I draw on the rich and ever-generative method of scholarly PHILOLOGIES for studying language at scale. In the hope of avoiding any "sad cheare," the chapter concludes with a brief discussion of the phrases "is a book" and "like a book" to show premodern English writers performing BIBLIOGRAPHIES – literally, book writings, or writings of the book.

Vocabularies

> The World's a Book in Folio, printed all
> With God's great Works in letters Capitall:
> Each Creature is a Page; and each Effect,
> A faire Character, void of all defect.[9]

I am hardly the first to argue for books' special symbolic place in human cultures generally, or in early modern England specifically. As a range of scholars from P. Gabrielle Foreman to Leah Price and from Brian Cummings to Jacques Derrida and the German philologist Ernst Robert Curtius have explored, the history of the book is the study not merely of material artifacts – how they are constructed, circulated, used, and archived – but also the study of how those artifacts signify in and profoundly shape human experience.[10] To return to the example stated earlier, scholars of late Roman culture have shown how Christianity became identified with the codex as opposed to the scroll.[11] Christians did not merely

---

[9] Guillaume Du Bartas, *Du Bartas His Deuine Weekes and Workes*, trans. Josuah Sylvester (London, 1611), sig. C3v. STC 21651. For an extended discussion of these lines, see Chapter 6.

[10] See P. Gabrielle Foreman, "Slavery, Black Visual Culture, and the Promises and Problems of Print in the Work of David Drake, Theaster Gates, and Glenn Ligon," in *Against a Sharp White Background: Infrastructures of African American Print*, ed. Brigitte Fielder and Jonathan Senchyne (Madison: University of Wisconsin Press, 2019), 29–61; Leah Price, *What We Talk about When We Talk about Books* (New York: Basic Books, 2019); Brian Cummings, *Bibliophobia: The End and the Beginning of the Book* (Oxford: Oxford University Press, 2022).

[11] See Roberts, Skeat, and Roberts, *The Birth of the Codex*. See also Walter J. Ong, *Orality and Literacy: The Technologizing of the Word* (London: Routledge, 2002); M. T. Clanchy, *From Memory to Written Record: England, 1066–1307*, 3rd ed. (Malden, MA: Wiley-Blackwell, 2013).

use the codex form as a means of textual transmission, though of course that is true. Rather, their use of the codex entailed a symbolic, imaginative, sensory, and rhetorical absorption of and assimilation to the codex form. The book acquired symbolic value, which in turn organized culture.

The example of the codex's ascendancy is instructive precisely because it falls far outside the chronological and geographical scope of this book. It reminds us that books and other text technologies have held symbolic value in most human cultures, for better and worse.[12] For instance, the "book of nature" metaphor, the subject of Chapter 6, circulated widely in classical and medieval cultures, informing the figure's explosive use in the seventeenth century. In one of the best-known pieces of scholarship on the book as symbol (a book chapter titled "The Book as Symbol," if you can believe it), Curtius observes that "the use of writing and the book in figurative language occurs in all periods of world literature."[13] For Curtius, a culture that maintains an interdependent relationship with books – what he calls "life relations" – will inevitably use books as figures for thought and expression because they so deeply invest in the symbolic value of the book. Cummings extends Curtius's account, observing how "even in its textual [i.e., physical] form, the book becomes more than itself, a visual representation not only of the contents within but of the idea of the book altogether."[14] Bookish language (e.g., the "book of nature") indexes the bookishness of a culture.

It works the other way around too, and here we come closer to the present study's concern with early modern England. If the vocabularies of books *express* a culture's relationship with books, they also *produce* that relationship. That is, if Curtius and those in his wake are right that different cultures are bookish in different ways, to varying degrees, then we must also ask how cultures become bookish and how that bookishness develops over time. Happily, scholarship on early modern England

---

[12] For instance, indigenous peoples of North America viewed the printed books of European colonials with ambivalence and had a distinctive relationship with text technologies. See Hugh Amory and David D. Hall, eds., *The Colonial Book in the Atlantic World*, History of the Book in America (Cambridge: Cambridge University Press, 2000); Phillip H. Round, *Removable Type: Histories of the Book in Indian Country, 1663–1880* (Chapel Hill: University of North Carolina Press, 2010); Matt Cohen, *The Networked Wilderness: Communicating in Early New England* (Minneapolis: University of Minnesota Press, 2010); Kelly Wisecup, *Assembled for Use: Indigenous Compilation and the Archives of Early Native American Literatures*, The Henry Roe Cloud Series on American Indians and Modernity (New Haven: Yale University Press, 2021).

[13] Ernst Robert Curtius, *European Literature and the Latin Middle Ages*, Bollingen Series 36 (Princeton: Princeton University Press, 1967), 303.

[14] Brian Cummings, "The Book as Symbol," in *The Book: A Global History*, ed. Michael F. Suarez and H. R. Woudhuysen (Oxford: Oxford University Press, 2013), 95. See also Cummings's remarkably capacious account of book-fear and book-wonder: *Bibliophobia*.

has long begun addressing these questions by showing how, in particular moments, the culture's bookishness enhanced. James Kearney has argued that the Reformation "sparked ... a crisis in representation and language," in which material books became objects both to cling to (the Bible) and repudiate (because iconoclastic), thus requiring a reimagining of the book's symbolic value.[15] Sarah Wall-Randell has demonstrated how "immaterial books" can "tell us far more than can 'material' traces about the many and diverse ways in which early modern writers and readers thought about books." The "immaterial potential" of books make them "useful objects for the early modern imagination."[16] More specifically focused on book metaphors, Charlotte Scott has argued that "the metaphoric function that both the book and the stage were able to provide for the world was supported by their dual ability to accommodate and represent the self," while Frederick Kiefer has shown how "metaphoric books" in early modern plays "can reveal nothing less than certain directions in Renaissance culture."[17] More recently, Rachel Stenner has focused on printing technology to show how "writers in the late medieval and early modern periods created imaginative depictions of the print trade as a means of analysing their evolving media ecology and understanding of their place within it."[18] These and other scholars have begun to articulate how early modern English culture's relationship with books took shape.

I extend this scholarly inquiry in several important ways. First, as the Preface already warned, I present many examples of bookish language from early modern England. Ranging across these examples to assemble an unprecedented level of detail from the cultural record, I will show how books became imprinted on the English cultural imagination. While scholars since Curtius have understandably sought bookish language in exemplary or canonical writings such as those of Luther, Shakespeare, Montaigne, Dante, and Milton, I reject exemplarity in favor of expansiveness.[19] Shakespeare's bookishness appears here, but so does that of obscure preachers, anonymous poets, and cranky politicians. Second, I expand the

---

[15] James Kearney, *The Incarnate Text: Imagining the Book in Reformation England*, Material Texts (Philadelphia: University of Pennsylvania Press, 2009), 2.

[16] Sarah Wall-Randell, *The Immaterial Book: Reading and Romance in Early Modern England* (Ann Arbor: The University of Michigan Press, 2013), 3.

[17] Charlotte Scott, *Shakespeare and the Idea of the Book*, Oxford Shakespeare Topics (Oxford: Oxford University Press, 2007), 2; Frederick Kiefer, *Writing on the Renaissance Stage: Written Words, Printed Pages, Metaphoric Books* (Newark: Associated University Presses, 1996), 12.

[18] Rachel Stenner, *The Typographic Imaginary in Early Modern English Literature*, Material Readings in Early Modern Culture (New York: Routledge, 2019), 1.

[19] I have emulated Maguire's *The Rhetoric of the Page* as a model of expansiveness.

scope of inquiry from metaphors to all bookish language. In this respect, I follow Harry Newman's "challenge [to] the binary opposition between the figurative and the material," emphasizing instead the "complex linguistic, material and historical networks" of text technologies.[20] For instance, the key phrase of Chapter 7, "the art of printing," refers to printing technology itself, just as the language of book size in Chapter 4 often refers to actual big or small books. Third, as I will elaborate in the later sections, the bookishness of the world surged in the sixteenth and seventeenth centuries. Even if Piper is right that "becoming bookish" in the nineteenth century "necessitated significant reorganizations of both social and individual identities" and Christina Lupton is right that eighteenth-century writers "flaunt with great energy the way [their] texts are produced and circulated as paper, print, and commodity," I contend that both shifts were already occurring, with differences, centuries before.[21] Finally, as far as possible given the number of examples, I strive to interpret those examples as rhetorically situated utterances. While the scholars mentioned earlier have sensitively contextualized and thoughtfully traced how the discourse of material objects "worked itself into the semantics of the period, wending its way through discourses beyond the literary, into pedagogy, anatomy, law, [and] finance," other scholars have been less careful. Indeed, a major problem of Curtius's influential chapter is that he skips from choice examples to "life relationship" without asking the very question at the heart of this book: what are writers doing with the language of books?[22]

The stakes of these bookish vocabularies are alarmingly high because books and the intellectual formation they make possible have exerted a profound, if imperfectly understood, influence on culture. For much of the last few centuries of Western culture (and beyond), books have helped constitute what Charles Taylor calls a "social imaginary," a primary way "people imagine their social existence, how they fit together with others, how things go on between them and their fellows, the expectation that are normally met, and the deeper normative notions and images that underlie

---

[20] Harry Newman, *Impressive Shakespeare: Identity, Authority and the Imprint in Shakespearean Drama* (New York: Routledge, 2019), 10. See also Helen Smith, "'A Man in Print?' Shakespeare and the Representation of the Press," in *Shakespeare's Book: Essays in Reading, Writing and Reception*, ed. Richard Meek, Jane Rickard, and Richard Wilson (Manchester: Manchester University Press, 2008), 59–78.

[21] Piper, *Dreaming in Books*, 3; Christina Lupton, *Knowing Books: The Consciousness of Mediation in Eighteenth-Century Britain*, Material Texts (Philadelphia: University of Pennsylvania Press, 2012), 4.

[22] For another example, in *Divine Art, Infernal Machine*, Eisenstein collects many examples of writers responding to the printing press and printed books but takes those examples at face value and does not regard them as rhetorically situated and motivated statements.

these expectations."[23] The cultural identification with the book as a symbol has become more noticeable as it has waned in recent decades. Writing in the late 1990s, the French scholar Régis Debray argued that the advent of digital technologies would decenter the book, not just from reading habits but from an entire cultural imaginary, irrespective of the number of books one reads (or does not read). Debray helpfully articulates the importance of the codex as a "symbolic matrix, the affective and mental schematization in whose dependence we bind ourselves […] to the world of meaning."[24] The material specificity of the codex is "an existential code unto itself, a unifying factor of a culture."[25] For Debray, books have a social symbolic function separate from (but also emerging from) their use as a technology of inscription.

Despite Debray's assumption of a single common culture and universal literacy, his claim that digital technologies will displace the "symbolic matrix" of the book has proven oddly prophetic in the twenty-first century. One result of this displacement is that we see anew that the codex has been a unifying symbol only for some people, some of the time. Just to pick the easiest of examples, if you were born a woman in the 1400s or an enslaved black African in 1840, you would not have characterized the book as a "unifying factor of culture." Coming to terms with the past entails a clear response to the way books, as a chief symbol of Western culture, have been used to exclude or discriminate (or worse).

The pervasiveness and apparent normativity of books have led some scholars to offer maximalist interpretations of their place in the world. For instance, one of the key premises of Jacques Derrida's thought is that "the idea of the book is the idea of a totality, finite or infinite, of the signifier." For Derrida, this totality makes the idea of the book "profoundly alien to the sense of writing [*écriture*]," which Juliet Fleming glosses as the term for Derrida's conviction that "a thing never exists *as such* but always and only in its relation to and difference from other things."[26] This means that the book-as-totality stands against the writing that, for Derrida, underpins all meaning.[27] Hans Blumenberg, no bosom buddy of Derrida, nevertheless agrees that the book's

---

[23] Charles Taylor, *Modern Social Imaginaries*, Public Planet Books (Durham: Duke University Press, 2004), 23.

[24] Régis Debray, "The Book as Symbolic Object," in *The Future of the Book*, ed. Geoffrey Nunberg (Berkeley: University of California Press, 1996), 141.

[25] Debray, 141.

[26] Jacques Derrida, *Of Grammatology*, trans. Gayatri Chakravorty Spivak, Fortieth-Anniversary Edition (Baltimore: Johns Hopkins University Press, 2016), 19; Juliet Fleming, *Cultural Graphology: Writing after Derrida* (Chicago: The University of Chicago Press, 2016), 8.

[27] Derrida dials up the rhetoric, calling the book "the encyclopedic protection of theology and of logocentrism against the disruption of writing, against its aphoristic energy." See *Of Grammatology*, 19.

power is its "production of totality," so that when humans come to experience the world as a book that can be read, that experience can only take the form of a "totality."[28] In the accounts of both these famous thinkers, a book can symbolize in culture only as a coherent whole, a totalizing symbol, and an autonomous and violent artifact. Later in this chapter, I will dispute both these claims by situating them in recent scholarship on the history of the book. For now, my point is that the vocabularies of the book index central questions of human cultures: what is knowledge? What kind of thing is the self, and how does it relate to others? How does consciousness operate? How do form and medium relate to content and concept? These may not necessarily be bookish questions, but they have long been given bookish answers.

Typographies

> O *Printing!* how hast thou disturb'd the Peace of Mankind! that Lead, when moulded into Bullets, is not so mortal as when founded into Letters![29]

Next, we must deal with the Gutenberg in the room. When Andrew Marvell wrote the line above, published in 1672, he could look back on more than two centuries to conclude that *"Printing"* had "disturb'd the Peace of Mankind." The account already known to Marvell and his contemporaries is downright mythical today: printing with movable type was introduced to Europe in the mid fifteenth century by a man named Johannes Gutenberg.[30] In short, the process of printing involves assembling pieces of type (each with the form of a letter and usually made of lead, hence Marvell's joke), covering that type in ink, and pressing the ink onto paper.[31] This "art of printing," otherwise known as typography (literally, "type writing") eventually spread around Europe (see Chapter 7). The social acceleration arising from the printing press is a major reason this book focuses on early modern England.[32]

Marvell's claim of printing's disruptive power sounds like an argument for the press as an "agent of change." Pieces of type are more violent than bullets! The letter killeth! His grand political statement is not

---

[28] Hans Blumenberg, *The Readability of the World*, trans. Robert Savage and David Roberts, Signale/Transfer : German Thought in Translation (Ithaca: Cornell University Press, 2022), 9.

[29] Andrew Marvell, *The Rehearsal Transpros'd* (London, 1672), sig. B2v. Wing M878.

[30] See Andrew Pettegree's accessible account in *The Book in the Renaissance* (New Haven: Yale University Press, 2010), 21–42.

[31] This is a drastic overreduction of the process, of course. See Philip Gaskell, *A New Introduction to Bibliography* (Oxford: Clarendon Press, 1972).

[32] See Hartmut Rosa, *Social Acceleration: A New Theory of Modernity*, New Directions in Critical Theory (New York: Columbia University Press, 2013).

so straightforward as it might seem, however, and it gives rise to a crucial point concerning narratives about typography. Marvell's irony becomes apparent with more context: this line comes from a printed book, a piece of "controversial" literature attacking Marvell's opponent, Samuel Parker. Moreover, Marvell himself had witnessed firsthand the rapid expansion of printed texts circulating in London in the 1640s and was in many ways a beneficiary of that expansion.[33] If printing is more deadly than bullets, Marvell wielded the weapon well. Instead of a naïve belief in the transformative power of printing, his line reminds us that this power, if it exists, thrives because a culture of the book supports it. Printing's capacity for harm is in fact the product of the rhetorical effort of writers like Marvell.

For the last few decades of the twentieth century, scholarship on printing and printed books occurred in an erudite ping-pong match pitting technological determinism against technological instrumentalism.[34] Marvell's bullets hint at the most extreme versions of these two positions: do guns kill people, or do people kill people using guns? Determinism, often associated in book history with the work of Marshall McLuhan and Elizabeth Eisenstein, tends to emphasize the transformations not just made possible but caused by the printing press. Eisenstein famously proclaimed the press inaugurated a "communications revolution," while McLuhan much more modestly argued that "the typographic explosion extended the minds and voices of men to reconstitute the human dialogue on a world scale that has bridged the ages."[35]

Instrumentalism, on the other hand, emphasizes the human and cultural agency in transformations associated with technology. In book history, Adrian Johns's trenchant critique of Eisenstein is the most canonical instance, but there are many others, including Michael Warner's argument that "the assumption that technology is prior to culture results in a kind of retrodetermination whereby the political history of a technology is converted into the unfolding nature of that technology."[36] Writing about early modern England, David McKitterick fairly stresses how printing throughout

---

[33] See Jesse M. Lander, *Inventing Polemic: Religion, Print, and Literary Culture in Early Modern England* (Cambridge: Cambridge University Press, 2006).

[34] Perhaps the best-known intervention in the determinism/instrumentalism squabble is Neil Postman, *Amusing Ourselves to Death: Public Discourse in the Age of Show Business* (New York: Penguin Books, 1986).

[35] Elizabeth L. Eisenstein, *The Printing Press as an Agent of Change: Communications and Cultural Transformations in Early Modern Europe* (Cambridge: Cambridge University Press, 1979), xi, 25, 30, 39; Marshall McLuhan, *Understanding Media: The Extensions of Man*, 1st MIT Press ed. (Cambridge: MIT Press, 1994), 170; Marshall McLuhan, *The Gutenberg Galaxy; the Making of Typographic Man* (Toronto: University of Toronto Press, 1962).

[36] Michael Warner, *The Letters of the Republic: Publication and the Public Sphere in Eighteenth-Century America* (Cambridge: Harvard University Press, 1990), 9.

the period was "a process liable and subject to change as a result both of its own mechanisms and of the assumptions and expectations of those who exploit its technological possibilities to greater and lesser extent."[37] Even recent attempts to moderate the extremes, including McKitterick's appeal both to printing's "mechanisms" and to its "exploit[ers]," do so in a manner still framed by opposing views about technology in culture.

I wade into this quagmire to articulate how *How the World Became a Book* pertains to printing. Most of the language of books I present in this study is not specific to the press or printed books. The leaf one turns over can be paper or parchment, marked by hand or machine (or both). Moreover, even though most of the evidence presented here appeared in printed materials from early modern England (see the "philologies" section below), it emerges from long classical and medieval traditions that existed long before William Caxton set up the first press in England in 1476. The "book of nature" metaphor goes back millennia, for example.[38] Except where I am concerned specifically with printing (in Chapters 2 and 7) or where the writers I cite appeal to it, I treat the concept of books as broadly and flexibly as possible.[39] This scope reflects my broader inquiry about books and bookishness. I resist what Bonnie Mak has described as an effort to "demarcate the printed book" that has "fractured the broader history of the codex and communication technologies."[40]

That said, however, it is difficult to deny printing any role in the increased prominence of books in the English cultural imagination. It is true that media determinists in the vein of McLuhan and Eisenstein have overdrawn their claims about the impact of printing, just as twentieth-century bibliographers and those in their wake have uncritically taken up the language of printing in a way that reinforces its social normativity.[41] But it seems equally reactionary to deny what D. F. McKenzie (himself no determinist) describes as early modern writers' "exhilarating acknowledgement of [printing's] resources, a craftmanly pleasure in the exploration of [printed books'] materiality, and the provision of a skilled service" to an increasing number

---

[37] David McKitterick, *Print, Manuscript and the Search for Order, 1450–1830* (Cambridge: Cambridge University Press, 2003), 4.

[38] See Jesse M. Gellrich, *The Idea of the Book in the Middle Ages: Language Theory, Mythology, and Fiction* (Ithaca: Cornell University Press, 1985); Blumenberg, *The Readability of the World*.

[39] Importantly, even the language of printing and impressions is broader than the printing press and can refer to coins, seals, and more. See Newman, *Impressive Shakespeare*.

[40] Bonnie Mak, *How the Page Matters*, Studies in Book and Print Culture Series (Toronto: University of Toronto Press, 2011), 6.

[41] See Masten, *Queer Philologies*.

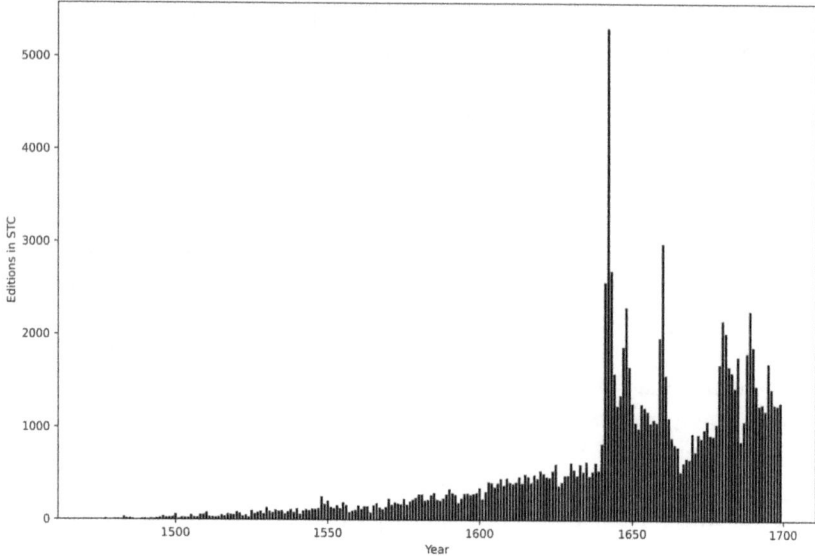

Figure 1.2   Editions in the English Short Title Catalogue (ESTC).

of readers.[42] Rather than depending on contested features of printing, such as Eisenstein's "fixity" or McLuhan's triad of "continuity, uniformity, and repeatability," I rely on the sheer increase in the number and prevalence of books and other text technologies in sixteenth- and seventeenth-century England. Again, this increase is not limited to printed books, since scholars have persuasively shown that the rising number of printed books in England was matched, if not exceeded, by a rise in manuscripts and other non-codex books.[43] Figure 1.2 shows the number of editions per year listed in the English Short Title Catalogue before 1700. Given loss rates, this chart likely reflects an undercount, but it also underscores the abundance and prevalence of books throughout the period. Even before the spike in 1642, editions with print runs in the hundreds and even thousands meant that

---

[42] D. F. McKenzie, *Making Meaning: "Printers of the Mind" and Other Essays*, ed. Peter D. McDonald and Michael F. Suarez (University of Massachusetts Press, 2002), 258. See also Alexandra Halasz, *The Marketplace of Print: Pamphlets and the Public Sphere in Early Modern England*, Cambridge Studies in Renaissance Literature and Culture 17 (Cambridge: Cambridge University Press, 1997); Lander, *Inventing Polemic*.

[43] See Harold Love, *Scribal Publication in Seventeenth-Century England* (Oxford: Clarendon, 1993); Arthur F. Marotti, *Manuscript, Print, and the English Renaissance Lyric* (Ithaca: Cornell University Press, 1995); Arthur F. Marotti and Michael D. Bristol, eds., *Print, Manuscript, & Performance: The Changing Relations of the Media in Early Modern England* (Columbus: Ohio State University Press, 2000).

more and more books were available for purchase, circulation, reading – and the imagination. Thus, if printing underlies this project, it does so as a major factor in early modern England's media consciousness. The chapters of this book maintain the conviction that Lupton's brilliant claim about the eighteenth century – "that acceptance of a new medium can coexist with a high level of critical consciousness about its presence" – was already true for many sixteenth- and seventeenth-century writers.[44]

Ecologies

> Yea this mans brow, like to a title leafe,
> Foretells the nature of a tragicke volume,
> So lookes the strond, whereon the imperious floud,
> Hath left a witnest vsurpation.[45]

Early in Shakespeare's *The second part of Henrie the fourth* (1600), the Earl of Northumberland sees the messenger Morton enter and knows he brings bad news. The Earl describes Morton's face ("brow") as a "title leafe" or title page, which in Shakespeare's time served to advertise a book's genre ("foretell" its "nature").[46] Figure 1.3 shows the title page of the very book from which this line comes, for instance. It tells us to expect Henry's death, the coronation of his son, and additional entertainment from John Falstaff and "swaggering Pistoll." Morton's face, like this title page, sets the expectations of those who see it.

Northumberland is not finished, however. Having introduced the figure of the title page to say he knows bad news is coming, the Earl adds another comparison: the "strond" is the sandy, wrinkly area uncovered during the sea's low tide. Having usurped the land, just as Northumberland believes Henry IV usurped the throne of Richard II, the sea retreats and leaves the wrinkled "witness" of its imperiousness. Morton's face, like the sand, is wrinkled with sorrow, and those wrinkles explain what makes the messenger's face appear like the title page of a tragedy. The dark lines of a furrowed brow resemble the dark lines of the furrowed sand resemble the dark lines of the title page.

---

[44] Lupton, *Knowing Books*, xi. See also Asa Briggs and Peter Burke, *A Social History of the Media: From Gutenberg to the Internet*, 2nd ed. (Cambridge: Polity, 2005); Lisa Gitelman, *Always Already New: Media, History, and the Data of Culture* (Cambridge, Mass: MIT Press, 2006); John Guillory, "Genesis of the Media Concept," *Critical Inquiry* 36, no. 2 (2010): 321–62, https://doi.org/10.1086/648528.

[45] William Shakespeare, *The Second Part of Henrie the Fourth* (London, 1600), sig. A3r. STC 22288.

[46] See Whitney Trettien, "Title Pages," in *Book Parts*, ed. Dennis Duncan and Adam Smyth (Oxford: Oxford University Press, 2019), 39–49.

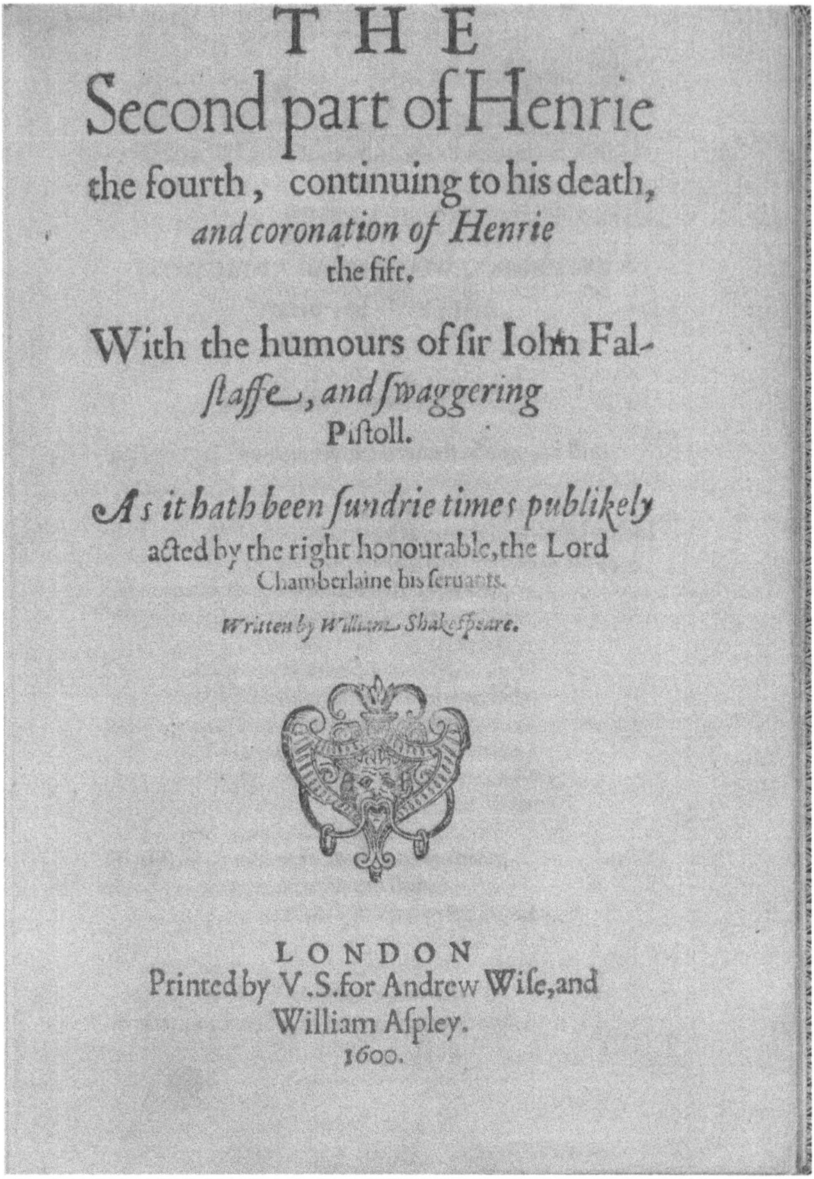

THE
Second part of Henrie

the fourth, continuing to his death,
and coronation of Henrie
the fift.

With the humours of sir Iohn Fal-
staffe, and *swaggering*
Pistoll.

As it hath been sundrie times publikely
acted by the right honourable, the Lord
Chamberlaine his seruants.

Written by William Shakespeare.

LONDON
Printed by V.S.for Andrew Wise,and
William Aspley.
1600.

Figure 1.3 William Shakespeare, *THE Second part of Henrie the fourth* (1600), sig. A1r,
STC 22288, image 113289, Folger Shakespeare Library.

The point is not to disentangle this vivid double image, but rather to call attention to its entangledness. Even by itself, the bookish metaphor is mixed up in the semantics and economics of the early modern title page. Still further, the comparisons of a man's face to a "title leafe" and the "strond" mutually explain and complicate one another. The book comparison emerges from a fecund set of imaginative possibilities that were hardly unique to Shakespeare, even if Shakespeare could powerfully draw them out. To study what writers do with the language of books – and what the language of books does to writers – means confronting the rich cultural entanglements of that language. And those entanglements arise, as Northumberland's line illustrates and as I will argue in this section, from the semantic richness of books themselves.

Recent scholarship in book history has stressed an ecology of books. Not limited to biology, ecology can refer to the study of the "interrelationship between any system and its environment."[47] An ecology of the book is therefore not (or not just) a playful metaphor but refers to the study of text technologies and their relationship to one another and to their environments. Although a few scholars have appealed to this particular term to designate how they approach material texts, most book historical scholarship is implicitly pursuing just such an ecology.[48] In the characteristically vivid phrasing of Johanna Drucker, the signal contribution of this recent scholarship is that "a *book is conceived as a distributed object* […] *a set of intersecting events, material conditions, and activities.*" A book is never just a book but one of many "event spaces within an ecology of changing conditions."[49]

In early modern studies, decades of work in textual studies and new materialism have led to the widespread acceptance of many key book historical insights, spurring in turn this new ecological study. Chief among these insights is, in Heidi Brayman, Jesse Lander, and Zachary Lesser's words, that "early modern literary works exist always and only in their material instantiations," though we may as well expand this to include works of all kinds.[50] Taking this conclusion as a premise for further study, scholars have begun to

---

[47] *OED* s.v. "ecology n. 1c."
[48] For instance, see Joshua Calhoun, *The Nature of the Page: Poetry, Papermaking, and the Ecology of Texts in Renaissance England*, Material Texts (Philadelphia: University of Pennsylvania Press, 2020). The term "media ecologies" is more popular, in part because it links book history with the jazzier and more capacious field of media studies.
[49] Johanna Drucker, "Distributed and Conditional Documents: Conceptualizing Bibliographical Alterities," *MATLIT: Materialidades Da Literatura* 2, no. 1 (November 8, 2014): 12. Emphasis in original. See also Johanna Drucker, "Performative Materiality and Theoretical Approaches to Interface," *Digital Humanities Quarterly* 007, no. 1 (July 1, 2013).
[50] Heidi Brayman Hackel, Zachary Lesser, and Jesse Lander, eds., *The Book in History, the Book as History: New Intersections of the Material Text: Essays in Honor of David Scott Kastan*, The Beinecke Series in the History of the Book (New Haven: Beinecke Rare Book & Manuscript Library, 2016), 12.

ask, for example, how material concerns affected the collection and definition of poetry, how printed texts emulate theatrical performance, how women writers used the materiality of writing as a knowledge practice, how book owners used scissors and glue to fashion bespoke texts, and how "literal representation (typography) and literary representation (fictionality) go hand in hand."[51] Growing "beyond the book," these and many other projects critically study the "interrelationship" between text objects and the environment of their production, circulation, and even destruction.[52]

This new textual ecology has necessarily revised approaches to printing and printed books. Rather than "monologic or logocentric," Pauline Reid writes, an early modern printed book was in fact a "fragile, fragmented material object ... culturally coded as both a thing and a medium."[53] Scholars such as Lisa Maruca and Rachel Stenner have paid revitalized attention to print houses to show, in Maruca's words, how "those who worked within the many professions of the print trade ... understood books and other print products to be the result of *collaboration* of many hands and the process of textual production to include not only writing but also the work— and workers—of technology."[54] Maruca does not use the word "ecology," but the shoe fits. Adam Smyth offers an elegant summary of the situation:

[51] Maguire, *The Rhetoric of the Page*, 22. See also Claire M. L. Bourne, *Typographies of Performance in Early Modern England* (Oxford: Oxford University Press, 2020); Megan Heffernan, *Making the Miscellany: Poetry, Print, and the History of the Book in Early Modern England* (Philadelphia: University of Pennsylvania Press, 2021); Whitney Trettien, *Cut/Copy/Paste: Fragments from the History of Bookwork* (Minneapolis: University of Minnesota Press, 2022); Whitney Sperrazza, *Anatomical Forms: The Science of the Body in Early Modern Women's Poetry* (Philadelphia: University of Pennsylvania Press, 2025).

[52] Lisa Maruca and Kate Ozment, "What Is Critical Bibliography?," *Criticism* 64, no. 3/4 (Summer/ Fall ///Summer/Fall 2022): 231, https://doi.org/10.1353/crt.2022.a899716. Several recent monographs and collections model these new ecologies. See Adam Smyth, *Material Texts in Early Modern England* (Cambridge: Cambridge University Press, 2018); Alexandra Gillespie and Deidre Lynch, eds., *The Unfinished Book* (Oxford: Oxford University Press, 2020), https://doi.org/10.1093/oxfordhb/9780198830801.001.0001; Zachary Lesser, *Ghosts, Holes, Rips and Scrapes: Shakespeare in 1619, Bibliography in the Longue Durée* (Philadelphia: University of Pennsylvania Press, 2021); Claire M. L. Bourne, ed., *Shakespeare/Text: Contemporary Readings in Textual Studies, Editing and Performance* (London: Bloomsbury, 2021); Adam Smyth, *The Oxford Handbook of the History of the Book in Early Modern England* (Oxford: Oxford University Press, 2023); Jonathan Sawday, *Blanks, Print, Space, and Void in English Renaissance Literature: An Archaeology of Absence* (Oxford: Oxford University Press, 2023). Compare the older but still important model in John Barnard, D. F. McKenzie, and Maureen Bell, eds., *The Cambridge History of the Book in Britain. Vol. 4: 1557–1695*, vol. 4 (Cambridge: Cambridge University Press, 2008).

[53] Pauline Reid, *Reading by Design: The Visual Interfaces of the English Renaissance Book* (Toronto: University of Toronto Press, 2019), 3–4. See also Jeffrey Todd Knight, *Bound to Read: Compilations, Collections, and the Making of Renaissance Literature*, 1st ed., Material Texts (Philadelphia: University of Pennsylvania Press, 2013).

[54] Lisa Maruca, *The Work of Print: Authorship and the English Text Trades, 1660–1760*, Literary Conjugations (Seattle: University of Washington Press, 2007), 17–18. See also Stenner, *The Typographic Imaginary in Early Modern English Literature*.

[A] book is no less ideological than a text, the network of signs that is its physical form, no less demanding of interpretation. So we should read material form rather as we read literary form: attentively and exactly, with an awareness of how bibliographical codes shift across a volume; ... with an awareness of the traditions and conventions underpinning the physical book, and the ways in which those traditions and conventions are sustained or resisted; with the knowledge that the conventional bibliographical or literary critical terms and priorities might exclude or trivialize some material features; with a sense of the labour and the various agents behind the material object; with attention to what is being signified and by what means.[55]

Like Smyth, the scholar known as Randall McLeod/Random Cloud/ Random Clod has focused on undermining appeals to the "continuity, uniformity, and repeatability" of printing for his entire career.[56] As I have written elsewhere, textual scholars now treat books as literary scholars have long treated language.[57]

How the World Became a Book in Shakespeare's England carries this ecology of the book into language. If books are and always have been "distributed objects," then we must not let their crucial place in the English cultural imaginary languish in an outdated model that treats them as mere bounded wholes. Curtius, Derrida, Blumenberg, and many others declared that books hold symbolic value in a culture, but they assumed books function in cultures primarily as unities, containers, and conduits. Scholars' newfound and critical awareness of the ecologies of books calls these assumptions into question. Indeed, Juliet Fleming has appealed to Derrida's own notion of writing (*écriture*) to look beyond widespread assumptions "that each printed book is a totality, whose ideal form is somehow established at the end of the production process, beyond which point it can only be compromised by further material alteration; and that the printed book is the best stronghold

---

[55] Smyth, *Material Texts in Early Modern England*, 12. Along different lines but in the same direction, Joseph A. Dane has queried concepts such as "print culture" and evidence. See Joseph A. Dane, *The Myth of Print Culture: Essays on Evidence, Textuality, and Bibliographical Method*, Studies in Book and Print Culture (Toronto: University of Toronto Press, 2003); Joseph A. Dane, *Out of Sorts: On Typography and Print Culture* (Philadelphia: University of Pennsylvania Press, 2011); Joseph A. Dane, *Blind Impressions: Methods and Mythologies in Book History* (Philadelphia: University of Pennsylvania Press, 2013).

[56] See, for instance, Randall McLeod, "Information on Information," *Text* 5 (1991): 241–81. Part of the point of Prof. Cloud's variant name spellings is to embody the extreme variability and instability of early modern texts. He has also published as R. Macgeddon in "An Epilogue: Hammered," in *Negotiating the Jacobean Printed Book*, ed. Pete Langman (London: Routledge, 2016), 137–99.

[57] Jonathan P. Lamb, *Shakespeare in the Marketplace of Words* (Cambridge: Cambridge University Press, 2017). See also Allison K. Deutermann and András Kiséry, eds., *Formal Matters: Reading the Materials of English Renaissance Literature* (Manchester: Manchester University Press, 2013).

for the information it contains."[58] The recent book history scholarship to which I am appealing here has amply demonstrated how these assumptions would not compute for early modern English readers and writers. As Fleming writes elsewhere, "while the advent of printing technology ... is usually understood to be coterminous with, if not identical to, an increase in intellectual and technological abstraction" – totality, once again – "to the early modern English it may rather have represented a mode of materializing thought more densely."[59] These new ecologies reform how we regard not only material texts from early modern England but the language and symbolic codes to which those texts give rise.

In this book, I study how this new and more critical view of early modern books works itself out in and through language. The figure of the "Book of Nature," as we will see in Chapter 6, does not always or primarily refer to a *totality* of archived knowledge but rather provides a way of describing a collected repertoire of knowledge.[60] Even when writers appeal to books as bounded wholes, as they often do when appealing to the size of books (see Chapter 4), they are usually *refuting* the assumption that "the printed book is the best stronghold for the information it contains."[61] And as Chapter 3 will discuss, the title page affords a set of uses unrelated to the totality of the book, which Shakespeare appropriates for dramatic effect in Morton's wrinkly "title leafe" of a face. Overall, I argue that books impressed themselves on English culture far less as stable, autonomous, and self-contained carriers of data than as messy, collaborative, fragile, and ideologically loaded objects of media consciousness.

Modernities

VVe liue in a printing age, wherein there is no man either so vainely, or factiously, or filthily disposed, but there are crept out of all sorts vnauthorized authors, to fill and fit his humor, and if a mans deuotion serue him not to goe to the Church of GOD, he neede but repayre to a Stationers shop and reade a sermon of the diuels: I loath to speake it, euery rednosed rimester is an author, euery drunken mans dreame is a booke, and he whose talent of little wit is hardly worth a farthing, yet layeth about him so outragiously, as

---

[58] Fleming, *Cultural Graphology*, 98.
[59] Juliet Fleming, *Graffiti and the Writing Arts of Early Modern England*, Material Texts (Philadelphia: University of Pennsylvania Press, 2001), 44.
[60] Diana Taylor, *The Archive and the Repertoire: Performing Cultural Memory in the Americas* (Durham: Duke University Press, 2003).
[61] Fleming, *Cultural Graphology*, 98.

if all Helicon had run through his pen, in a word, scarce a cat can looke out of a gutter, but out starts a half peny Chronicler[.][62]

A major question underlying this study is how we should approach the bookishness (or the becoming bookish) of sixteenth- and seventeenth-century English culture without, on the one hand, lumping it into a form of nascent modernity or, on the other, ignoring undeniable connections with the modern. We cannot deny that many writers of this period, from early to late, felt themselves to be living in a new kind of world. Some used the word "modern" to describe this world as it compares to the "ancient" one. Still others, like the writer quoted above ("R. W.," possibly Robert Wilson), spoke of this new age as having something to do with books. R. W. declares his a "printing age," in which "vnauthorized authors" meet demand for reading material ("euery drunken mans dreame") with ample supply ("euery rednosed rimester is an author"). No-talent writers behave as if they are vehicles for the Muses (associated with the springs of Mount Helicon), while cheap books ("half peny Chronicler[s]") abound so greatly that they seem to appear out of street gutters. Here is a vivid picture of the proliferation that signals a media consciousness much earlier than conventional scholarly narratives would suggest. You would think R. W. was describing a digital social media platform.

If this text comes from *early modern* England, then it does not apparently conform to most definitions of "modernity" or "the modern era." Modernity is both deeply familiar and notoriously difficult to define. Early uses of "modern" simply meant "new" or "recent" as opposed to "ancient," and the word still conveys recency or a break from tradition, like the related term "modernism."[63] Scholars use the term as a marker of a particular historical period, even when they debate the span of that period. Ann Blair and Nicholas Popper describe how so-called Whig histories of steady progress "created a sense that over the period from roughly 1450 to the end of the eighteenth-century— bracketed by the invention of the printing press or Columbus's voyage on one end, and Enlightenment and French Revolution on the other—modern subjectivity, institutions, and social structures came into being."[64] Blair and Popper, along with many other scholars of history, culture, literature, and technology, resist such a narrative. Some push the modern era forward to the late eighteenth and nineteenth centuries, while others emphasize that "the

---

[62] R. W., *Martine Mar-Sixtus* (London, 1591), sig. A3v. STC 24913.

[63] See *OED* s.v. "modern adj." See Margreta de Grazia, "The Modern Divide: From Either Side," *Journal of Medieval and Early Modern Studies* 37, no. 3 (September 1, 2007): 453–67.

[64] Ann Blair and Nicholas Popper, eds., *New Horizons in Early Modern Scholarship* (Baltimore: Johns Hopkins University Press, 2021), 3.

elements of emergent modernity detectable in these years [1450–1900] now seem contingent and precarious rather than inexorable, universal, and irreversible."[65] Still others find supposedly "modern" social and cultural formations on the other side of what William Kuskin calls "the firewall of 1500."[66] Amid these contested start and end dates, the seventeenth and eighteenth centuries are loosely viewed as the beginning of the "modern" era in Europe, with the mid twentieth century sometimes cited as the end.[67]

What exactly *is* modernity, though? Chronological parameters of the period arise from understandings of what it means to be "modern." Steven B. Smith offers a helpful list of modernity's associated features:

> the sovereign individual as the unique locus of moral responsibility, the separation of state and civil society as distinct realms of authority, the secularization of society or at least the lessening of the public role of religion, the elevation of science and scientific forms of rationality as the standard for knowledge, and a political regime based on the recognition of rights as the sole basis of its legitimacy.[68]

We could add to this list of selfhood, statehood, secularity, science, and rights. Achille Mbembe has powerfully argued that racialized dehumanization underpins and makes possible these social formations: "the Black Man is in effect the ghost of modernity."[69] Hartmut Rosa has argued that "social acceleration is the key to understanding modernity and the modernization process."[70] Paul Connerton looks to economics, defining modernity as "the objective transformation of the social fabric unleashed by the advent of the capitalist world market which tears down feudal and ancestral limitations on a global scale, and psychologically the enlargement of life chances through the gradual freeing from fixed status hierarchies."[71] None of these necessarily excludes the other, of course, and that is part of the

---

[65] Blair and Popper, 4.

[66] William Kuskin, *Recursive Origins: Writing at the Transition to Modernity* (Notre Dame: University of Notre Dame Press, 2013), 44. In the case of the supposedly modern category of race, see Kim F. Hall, *Things of Darkness: Economies of Race and Gender in Early Modern England* (Ithaca: Cornell University Press, 1995); Geraldine Heng, *The Invention of Race in the European Middle Ages* (Cambridge: Cambridge University Press, 2018).

[67] A slightly dated but capacious sampling is Victor E. Taylor and Charles E. Winquist, eds., *Postmodernism: Critical Concepts*, 4 vols., Routledge Critical Concepts (New York: Routledge, 1998).

[68] Steven B. Smith, *Modernity and Its Discontents: Making and Unmaking the Bourgeois from Machiavelli to Bellow* (New Haven: Yale University Press, 2016), ix. See also Marshall Berman, *All That Is Solid Melts into Air: The Experience of Modernity* (New York: Simon & Schuster, 1982); David Harvey, *The Condition of Postmodernity: An Enquiry into the Origins of Cultural Change* (Oxford: Blackwell, 1989).

[69] Achille Mbembe, *Critique of Black Reason*, trans. Laurent Dubois (Durham: Duke University Press, 2017), 129.

[70] Rosa, *Social Acceleration*, xii.

[71] Paul Connerton, *How Modernity Forgets* (Cambridge: Cambridge University Press, 2009), 4.

point: instead of a "monolithic, unified, and singular" modernity – remember "totality" above! – we now have "a world of multiple competing modernities engaged in relentless transmission and conflict."[72] A once totalizing narrative of the modern has given way to a messier and more accurate (not to mention more interesting) account of modernity.

Critical accounts of modernity, like critiques of modern assumptions about books, observe that its apparent grand totality hardly seems plausible or even possible. Margreta de Grazia has argued that modernity's "existence as a period concept has depended" on the way "modern" suggests the "possibility of a spontaneously generated *new*, with no connection to the past."[73] The "modern" works like a cudgel for artificially separating oneself from dependence on the past; to shift metaphors, it is a broom that sweeps away the modern man's footsteps from the snow behind him. Going still further, Bruno Latour has memorably argued that "we have never been modern" because modernity depends on a false separation of Nature and Society (or Culture), humans and nonhumans, all the while encouraging nature–culture hybrids to flourish. Scientific instruments, for instance, seem to offer human knowers (Society) an objective understanding of nonhuman species (Nature), but the instruments themselves hybridize nature and society and depend on a chain of associations to produce knowledge. As Latour writes, moderns feel themselves "pushed by time's arrow in such a way that *behind them* lies an archaic past unhappily combining Facts and Values, and *before them* lies a more or less radiant future in which the distinction between Facts and Values will finally be sharp and clear."[74] Latour calls this era of unsustainable Nature–Society separation the "modern parenthesis," which began in the late seventeenth century and from which we are only beginning to emerge.[75]

The stakes of the term "early modern" are therefore just as high as those of the vocabularies of books, and for related reasons. De Grazia articulates the point by reference to academic specializations: "whether you work on one side or the other of the medieval/modern divide determines nothing less than relevance."[76] Two terms used for the years 1500–1700, "early

[72] Blair and Popper, *New Horizons in Early Modern Scholarship*, 5.
[73] de Grazia, "The Modern Divide," 454.
[74] Bruno Latour, *An Inquiry into Modes of Existence: An Anthropology of the Moderns* (Cambridge: Harvard University Press, 2013), 8. See also *We Have Never Been Modern* (Cambridge: Harvard University Press, 1993).
[75] Bruno Latour, "Why Has Critique Run Out of Steam? From Matters of Fact to Matters of Concern," *Critical Inquiry* 30, no. 2 (January 1, 2004): 236.
[76] de Grazia, "The Modern Divide," 453. De Grazia wryly notes how "whatever the subject in question (subjectivity, representation, racism, nationalism, capitalism, empire, new science), it is readily and commonly supposed that the modern *here* and *now* has a special rapport with the early modern *there* and *then*" (458).

modern" and "Renaissance," hook that period to the emergence of the modern features listed above. Another increasingly popular term, "premodern," defines the period against the modernity it seeks to preempt.[77] Any study of sixteenth- and seventeenth-century England must contend with the "modern parenthesis." This is especially the case if the study pertains to books and printing, since printing so frequently links arms with modernity (and vice versa) in scholarly narratives.[78]

I dwell so long on the question of modernity to highlight its urgency: we live in a world variously described as postmodern, nonmodern, or late modern. We live on the latter side of Latour's parenthesis, in which a modern epistemological project that once seemed so inevitable and irrevocable has been seriously called into question, even by its adherents. We must, in Vanessa Machado de Oliveira's shocking phrase, hospice modernity.[79] A central conviction motivating this book is that one of the best ways to come to terms with our side of the "modern parenthesis" is to study the other. I therefore aim to *demodernize* books' symbolic value in sixteenth- and seventeenth-century English culture without losing track of the undeniable fact that people throughout this period felt themselves mixed up in large-scale changes wrought by, among other things, books.[80] In detaching books' symbolic relationship with modernity and instead exploring how the book signified in sixteenth- and seventeenth-century England "in accordance with its own discursive expression," I suggest models for thinking bookishly in the twenty-first century.[81]

In practice, what does it mean to decompose narratives of books and modernity? How might we avoid making the mistake de Grazia warns against – reflexively "crediting some new aspect of modernity to the early modern" – while remaining alive to the complex entanglements of the premodern and the modern?[82] We might look to the quotation that opened this

---

[77] See Bruce W. Holsinger, *The Premodern Condition: Medievalism and the Making of Theory* (Chicago: University of Chicago Press, 2005).

[78] For instance, Siskin and Warner argue that "Enlightenment is an event in the history of mediation," linked in turn with printing. See Clifford Siskin and William Warner, eds., *This Is Enlightenment* (Chicago: The University of Chicago Press, 2010).

[79] Vanessa Machado de Oliveira, *Hospicing Modernity: Facing Humanity's Wrongs and the Implications for Social Activism* (Berkeley: North Atlantic Books, 2021).

[80] It is not lost on me that, as Smith and others have noted, "modern" gained widespread currency in England as part of a bookish dispute known as the "battle of the books." See Smith, *Modernity and Its Discontents*, 1–6. I take the urge to "demodernize" from De Grazia's superb *Hamlet Without Hamlet* (Cambridge: Cambridge University Press, 2007). De Grazia demodernizes Shakespeare's supposedly modern play.

[81] Rayna Kalas, *Frame, Glass, Verse: The Technology of Poetic Invention in the English Renaissance* (Ithaca: Cornell University Press, 2007), 16.

[82] de Grazia, "The Modern Divide," 463.

section for guidance. Does R. W.'s cantankerous description of his "printing age" reflect a nascent modernity? He hints at capitalism, but he paints a picture of *failed* supply and demand. He hints at modern authorship, but only by its inverse, "vnauthorized authors." He hints at a modern public sphere, but he frames the books growing in gutters as Latourian hybrids, startled to life by stray cats. R. W.'s books resemble Reid's description of printed books as "fragile, fragmented material object[s]" much better than Derrida's "totality of the signifier" or Debray's "symbolic matrix" even if we, looking back through the modern parenthesis, might perceive some through-lines.[83]

Following R. W.'s lead, in this book I explore the sixteenth- and seventeenth-century English language of books without assuming a modern future. I use the terms "early modern," "premodern," and "Renaissance" interchangeably to emphasize the multiple temporal models built into those frames. The titular phrase "Shakespeare's England" likewise gestures at Shakespeare's ambivalent status as "icon of modernity" to some and talisman of the premodern past to others.[84] Moreover, as previous sections of this chapter have already explored, I extend an ecology of books precisely because it resists the impulse to modernize indecorously. Some of this book's chapters draw explicit and even linear connections to the modern era, but most do the harder and messier work of asking what ideas were like before they were modern – if they ever were.

Philologies

> As trauellers haue many ostes, but fewe frie[n]ds: so they that cursorily read all things hand ouer head, do runne ouer much, and remember little.[85]

The line above comes from the "Reading of bookes" section in Francis Meres's *Palladis tamia Wits treasury* (1598), a book better known for its mention of "mellifluous & hony-tongued *Shakespeare*" and its tantalizing reference to the now-lost play *"Loue labours wonne."*[86] Meres has a lot to say about books, which get their own section before the one on reading from which I quote. Like most of the witty sayings in *Palladis tamia*, this one takes the "as … so …" linguistic form.[87] Like travelers who have few friends even though they have many hosts, those who read hastily and

---

[83] Reid, *Reading by Design*, 3–4.
[84] Kuskin, *Recursive Origins*, 7.
[85] Francis Meres, *Palladis Tamia Wits Treasury* (London, 1598), sig. Mm3r. STC 17834.
[86] Meres, sig. Oo1v-Oo2r. STC 17834.
[87] See Catherine Nicholson, "Algorithm and Analogy: Distant Reading in 1598," *PMLA* 132, no. 3 (2017): 643–50.

recklessly ("hand ouer head") may cast their eyes over many words but retain few of them.[88]

As I teased in the Preface, this book features many, many examples. Such an abundance of evidence, which ranges from familiar and canonical instances to obscure and anonymous ones, puts me at risk of becoming Meres's traveler-reader, covering "much" but remembering "little." These examples span over 200 years of English writing, from William Caxton to William Congreve. They cover the spectrum of genres, from poem to polemic to scientific treatise. They address as much of the language of books as possible. This task calls for a rigorous, critical scholarly method to order and interpret so many examples, a method that can turn hosts into friends. That method is philology.

"Philology" means a love (philo-) of words (-logos). The poet John Skelton personifies it as "Dame Phylology" to claim she "gave me a gyfte in my neste when I lay, / To lerne all langage and hyt to speke aptlye."[89] Over the twentieth century and into the twenty-first, philology has come to refer not merely to a general love of or skill with language (implied in Skelton's use) but to a lively and contested branch of knowledge concerned with language and texts. In European contexts, the word refers to historical linguistics, the study of language change over time.[90] It is easy to see how that institutionally specific meaning, which calcified a century ago, links with broader and far grander definitions offered more recently: Roman Jakobson supposedly called philology "the art of reading slowly," while Hans Gumbrecht calls it "a configuration of scholarly skills that are geared toward historical text curatorship."[91] Edward Said defines it as the study of texts "whose meaning is to be unceasingly decoded by acts of reading and interpretation grounded in the shapes of words as bearers of reality, a reality hidden, misleading, resistant, and difficult," while Jerome McGann (not to be outdone) calls it the "science of archival memory" whose task is "to preserve, monitor, investigate, and augment our cultural inheritance."[92]

---

[88]   *OED* s.v. "hand over head adv. n. & adj."

[89]   *OED* s.v. "philology n."

[90]   *OED* s.v., "philology n." See also Sheldon Pollock, "Future Philology? The Fate of a Soft Science in a Hard World," *Critical Inquiry* 35, no. 4 (2009): 931–61, https://doi.org/10.1086/599594; Jonathan P. Lamb, "Computational Philology," *Memoria Di Shakespeare. A Journal of Shakespearean Studies* 7 (December 31, 2020), https://doi.org/10.13133/2283-8759/17248.

[91]   Quoted in Jan Ziolkowski, "'What Is Philology': Introduction," *Comparative Literature Studies* 27, no. 1 (1990): 6; Hans Ulrich Gumbrecht, *The Powers of Philology: Dynamics of Textual Scholarship* (Urbana: University of Illinois Press, 2003), 2.

[92]   Edward W. Said, *Humanism and Democratic Criticism*, Columbia Themes in Philosophy (New York: Columbia University Press, 2004), 58; Jerome McGann, "Philology in a New Key," *Critical Inquiry* 39, no. 2 (January 1, 2013): 338 and 334, https://doi.org/10.1086/668528.

Despite recent accusations otherwise, philology is how we retain a living relationship with the cultural past.[93]

Like much of the work on which it draws, *How the World Became a Book* is therefore proudly philological in both stance and method.[94] However illuminating the definitions above – I did warn you there would be a lot of examples – Michelle Warren's speaks most brilliantly to the present study: philology is both "a set of techniques for producing language histories and edited texts from all periods" and "a general attitude toward the construct-edness of textuality in a transhistorical perspective."[95] Method and stance. This book pursues a philology of the language of books in premodern English culture because philology is best situated both to decompose the book's symbolic place in culture and to sever its affiliation with the totali-ties of the modern. I therefore offer a philology of the book, rather than a cultural history, a textual study, an anthropology of thought, or a literary analysis of exemplary texts.

Admittedly, philology has fallen on hard times. Its use in the preser-vation of vernacular languages has created unfortunate associations with European nationalism.[96] Nonetheless, recent scholarship has revised and expanded philology's scope, a project to which I too am committed. Masten's *Queer Philologies* offers a helpful model. Masten first advances a philological practice that "investigates the etymology, circulation, transfor-mation, and constitutive power of some 'key words' within early modern lexicons and discourses of sex and gender," but then he pulls the rug out from under us, insisting "that this discipline [i.e., philology] can be read

---

[93] John Guillory, *Professing Criticism: Essays on the Organization of Literary Study* (Chicago: University of Chicago Press, 2022), 168–98.

[94] Role models in this vein include Brad Pasanek, *Metaphors of Mind: An Eighteenth-Century Dictionary* (Baltimore: Johns Hopkins University Press, 2015); Hugh Craig and Brett Greatley-Hirsch, *Style, Computers, and Early Modern Drama: Beyond Authorship* (Cambridge: Cambridge University Press, 2017); Daniel Shore, *Cyberformalism* (Baltimore: Johns Hopkins University Press, 2018); Andrew Piper, *Enumerations: Data and Literary Study* (Chicago: The University of Chicago Press, 2018); Maguire, *The Rhetoric of the Page*; Bourne, *Typographies of Performance in Early Modern England*; Jenny C. Mann, *The Trials of Orpheus: Poetry, Science, and the Early Modern Sublime* (Princeton: Princeton University Press, 2021); Urvashi Chakravarty, *Fictions of Consent: Slavery, Servitude, and Free Service in Early Modern England* (Philadelphia: University of Pennsylvania Press, 2022). As far as I recall, only one of these scholars (Shore) assumes the label "philology," but I take them all to be doing philological work.

[95] Michelle R. Warren, "Introduction: Relating Philology, Practicing Humanism," *PMLA* 125, no. 2 (2010): 283.

[96] Marc Nichanian and Narine Jallatyan, "Philology from the Point of View of Its Victims," *Boundary 2* 48, no. 1 (February 1, 2021): 177–206, https://doi.org/10.1215/01903659-8821473; Eduardo Ramos, "Philology and Racist Appropriations of the Medieval," *Literature Compass* 20, no. 7–9 (2023): e12734, https://doi.org/10.1111/lic3.12734.

and practiced in a way that will highlight its own normativizing categories and elisions."[97] In the same spirit, Daniel Shore has called for a "more promiscuous philology" that "look[s] not only at words but through them … to the categories they occupy."[98] Shore, who like me searches digital datasets to craft "qualitative philological narratives," emphasizes the "fragility" of philology: "its responsiveness to the singular, its unwillingness to rule out the possibility that the one text that is always, constitutively missing from an archive has the potential to transform an entire story, revise or discredit a claim, dispense with some explanations and suggest new ones, or upset accounts of origin, influence, and diffusion."[99] Philology is indeed a useful set of techniques for studying the cultural past, but it also requires and makes possible a persistent self-critique of its methods and stance.

What does this self-critique look like for *How the World Became a Book in Shakespeare's England*? The most obvious "normativizing categor[y] and elision" is my use of the Early English Books Online Text Creation Partnership (EEBO-TCP) data to gather examples of the language of books for philological study. Although the EEBO-TCP repository contains over 2 billion words transcribed from over 60,000 books, it offers a small and highly selective subset of the cultural record from premodern England.[100] As a fraction of the more than 146,000 "image sets" of printed books in Early English Books Online, which are in turn a fraction of extant books printed in English, which are in turn a fraction of the books actually printed in the period (the vast majority of which were written by men whose social position made possible both learning to write and publishing), which are in turn a fraction of all materials written during the period, the TCP dataset is hardly comprehensive. Indeed, it skews heavily in favor of middle- and upper-class male writers and against women, heterodox writers, and those who could not write, as well as books not in English. Most writers I cite in

---

[97] Masten, *Queer Philologies*, 15 and 23.

[98] Shore, *Cyberformalism*, xi.

[99] Shore, 58.

[100] On EEBO, see Diana Kichuk, "Metamorphosis: Remediation in Early English Books Online (EEBO)," *Literary and Linguistic Computing* 22, no. 3 (June 18, 2007): 291–303, https://doi .org/10.1093/llc/fqm018; Ian Gadd, "The Use and Misuse of Early English Books Online," *Literature Compass* 6, no. 3 (2009): 680–92, https://doi.org/10.1111/j.1741-4113.2009.00632.x; Michael Gavin, "How to Think about EEBO," *Textual Cultures* 11, no. 1–2 (2017): 70–105, https:// doi.org/10.14434/textual.v11i1-2.23570. On archival visibility and invisibility, see Imtiaz H. Habib, *Black Lives in the English Archives, 1500–1677: Imprints of the Invisible* (Aldershot: Ashgate, 2008); Marisa J. Fuentes, *Dispossessed Lives: Enslaved Women, Violence, and the Archive*, Early American Studies (Philadelphia: University of Pennsylvania Press, 2016); Michelle Caswell, *Urgent Archives: Enacting Liberatory Memory Work*, 1st ed., Routledge Studies in Archives (Milton: Taylor & Francis, 2021), https://doi.org/10.4324/9781003001355.

this book are male, and most of the books were printed in England. The best I can do in the face of this critical limitation is to remain resolutely awake to what it means for the philological narratives I pursue: the cultural imaginaries I trace here will always fall along some range of "normative."

Another, related problem is what we might call the representational fallacy, in which a certain number of examples are said to (but cannot possibly) stand in for an entire culture. The presumably apocryphal statement made by (or to?) the eminent historian Keith Thomas illustrates this fallacy: "if I am not persuaded by your third example, I will not be persuaded by your fifteenth." But here we reach the very necessity that makes the self-aware, scaled, and sticky philology of this book such a virtue. The many writers I cite here do not *stand in for* their culture; they *constitute* it by using the language of books to do things in the world. Five-thousand examples may not represent all premodern English culture (not least because they leave out most women, children, and those who cannot read or write), but they do allow us to sketch a cultural imaginary far more complex and engaging than analyzing a few exemplary writers would permit. Philology is at once a method for "producing language histories" and a stance toward culture.[101] It seeks not representatives but citizens of premodern England.

Bibliographies

The heart is a booke, legible enough, and intelligible in it selfe; but we have so interlined that booke with impertinent knowledge, and so clasped up that booke, for feare of reading our owne history, our owne sins, as that we are the greatest strangers, and the least conversant with the examination of our owne hearts.[102]

To summarize, this book offers PHILOLOGIES of the TYPOGRAPHIES and broader ECOLOGIES of the bookish VOCABULARIES of early modern England while avoiding the impulse to impose unwarranted MODERNITIES. Instead of debating how sixteenth- and seventeenth-century England became *modern*, I show how it became *bookish* in and through the expressive, conceptual repertoire of books.[103] The world became a book when the language of books gave people a way to talk about it.

---

[101] Matt Cohen has recently called for a "destituent" philological stance. See "Textual Scholarship in the Situation," *Textual Cultures: Texts, Contexts, Interpretation* 15, no. 2 (2022): 1–29. See also Derrick R. Spires, "On Liberation Bibliography: The 2021 BSA Annual Meeting Keynote," *The Papers of the Bibliographical Society of America* 116, no. 1 (2022): 1–20, https://doi.org/10.1086/717066.

[102] John Donne, *LXXX Sermons* (London, 1640), sig. Vuurv. STC 7038.

[103] I suppose it is time to acknowledge the shade thrown in my title. See Stephen Greenblatt, *The Swerve: How the World Became Modern*, 1st ed. (New York: W.W. Norton, 2011).

As a palate cleanser for the chapters to come, this brief final section will combine the concerns of this introduction by focusing on the phrases "like a book" and "is a book." These humble figures identify parts of human experience and culture with books and thus forge the very conceptual connection this entire project will explore. Even a sampling of English writers claiming something is or is like a book illustrates (1) the non-totalizing way books signify in premodern England, (2) the fact that printing technology does not necessarily dominate the bookish lexicon, (3) the ecological purchase of books on writers' imaginations, (4) the way bookish figures resemble but are not identical to modern categories, and (5) the value of a philology of bookish language. "Bibliography" literally means "book writing"; here and in the chapters that follow we have a set of premodern bibliographies – writings not *of* but *with* books.[104]

When John Donne claims, in the quotation that began this section, that the "heart is a booke," he at once activates and complicates the resemblance of the human heart (already a metaphor for the center of personhood) to a book.[105] This book is not simply a bounded whole or vessel of information. It is an interactive device. Donne claims that we should know how to read it (it is both "legible" and "intelligible"), but we have impertinently written in it while refusing to examine it. He does not specify whether this book began as a manuscript or a printed book, and that is part of the point. The distinction is not relevant to Donne's figurative work, especially since a printed book that has been "interlined" becomes a print–manuscript hybrid. The marked up, "clasped up" book gives Donne an evocative image of the dissonance that accompanies an unexamined heart. The congregant who hears or reads this sermon must become both the book and its reader.

Donne's vivid metaphor extends the conventional comparison of the conscience to a book in which one's actions are recorded. Many writers of the period cite John Crysostrom's "conscientia codex est in quo quotidiana peccata conscribuntur" ("conscience is a book in which daily sins are written") as the source of this bookish comparison, and many expand on it. In a sermon, William Fisher quotes the proverbial statement, then exhorts his audience to "keepe this boke well & cleare fro[m] the blots and blemishes of sinne."[106] Mathew Stoneham expands on the line to claim

---

[104] *OED* s.v. "bibliography n."

[105] For a long history of this metaphor of selfhood, see Eric Jager, *The Book of the Heart* (Chicago: University of Chicago Press, 2000).

[106] William Fisher, *A Godly Sermon Preached at Paules Crosse the 31. Day of October 1591* (London, 1592), sig. Cr. STC 10919.

that "the conscience it selfe performeth the office of an Accuser, Iudge, Tormentor, against our selues."[107] Immanuel Bourne adds to the book of conscience "our good actions as well as our euill," looking ahead to the day of judgment, when "both these shall be brought to light when the bookes shall bee opened."[108] Like Donne, Peter Barker imagines a closed-up book of conscience but takes a gloomier view:

> conscience is a booke, and God hath giuen euery man one to carry in his bosome, which though hee be vnwilling to open, yet at last he must needes vnclaspe it, it is a monitor, and at last it will complaine, it is a watch, and at last it will giue warning: it is our Domesticall Chaplaine, & wil not always stop his mouth, bu[t] cry out of the fullnes and foulenes of iniquitie, of the ripenes and rottennes of sinne, let a man haue so large and able a gorge that he can swallow and digest sinne as the Estridge [i.e., Ostridge] doth yron, and vpon digestion sleepe, and with Epimenides take a nappe of 47. yeares long, yet many times euen in sleeping, Conscience which he would restrayne and imprison will put him in minde of his sinne.[109]

Barker imagines the conscience as a clasped up book that will eventually "cry out," even if one can "swallow and digest" as much "sinne" as an Ostridge can eat iron (they were believed to be able to eat great quantities) and sleep as long as the mythical Epimenides, who fell asleep when he was supposed to be caring for sheep. To paraphrase the immortal words of Hank Williams, your cheatin' book of conscience will tell on you.

These and many other writers who appeal to and expand upon the conscience as a book use the book to speak about human personhood as a record of moral action.[110] References to blemishes and blots suggest a manuscript book, consistent with a recording of lived experience. The book can

[107] Mathew Stoneham, *A Treatise on the First Psalme* (London, 1610), sig. D3r. STC 23289.

[108] Immanuel Bourne, *The Anatomie of Conscience or a Threefold Reuelation of Those Three Most Secret Bookes: 1. The Booke of Gods Prescience. 2. The Booke of Mans Conscience. 3. The Booke of Life* (London, 1623), sig. C3v. STC 3416.

[109] Peter Barker, *A Iudicious and Painefull Exposition Vpon the Ten Commandements* (London, 1624), sig. H3r-v. STC 1425.

[110] Other examples include Thomas Adams, *A Commentary or, Exposition Vpon the Diuine Second Epistle Generall, Written by the Blessed Apostle St. Peter* (London, 1633), sig. Ooooo4r. STC 108. Jeremiah Dyke, *Tvvo Treatises the One of Good Conscicnce; Shewing the Nature, Meanes, Markes, Benefits, and Necessitie Thereof. The Other The Mischiefe and Misery of Scandalls, Both Taken and Given* (London, 1635), sig. A3r. STC 7428. Anthony Cade, *A Sermon Necessarie for These Times Shewing the Nature of Conscience* (London, 1639), sig. B3r. STC 4330. *Thrēnoikos The House of Mourning: Furnished with Directions for Preparations to Meditations of Consolations at the Houre of Death* (London, 1640), sig. Cc3v. STC 24049. G. D., *Rex Meus Est Deus, or, A Sermon Preached at the Common Place in Christs-Church in the City of Norwich* (London, 1643), sig. B2v. Wing D2061. John Stalham, *The Reviler Rebuked: Or, A Re-Inforcement of the Charge against the Quakers* (London, 1657), sig. Kk1v. Wing S5186.

be clasped up, overwritten, or forcibly opened. What is written in it can accuse, judge, and torment. This commonplace image contrasts sharply with the Cartesian comparison of the human person to a blank slate or *tabula rasa* (*table rase* in French). In this more familiar, indeed modern view of the self, which Rene Descartes and then John Locke popularized in Europe, the human person is born empty of all impressions and is formed by sensory data they receive.[111] Importantly, these two images of book and blank tablet are not *opposites*. Indeed, both use bookish technologies to talk about the formation of the self – one moralist, the other empiricist. But whereas the *tabula rasa* fits on a trajectory toward a "heads on a stick" modernity, the messier and unexpectedly bodily language of the book of conscience resists such an easy trajectory toward the modern. It provides a language for describing inwardness ("clasped vp"), but also a mechanism for mediating inwardness to others (reading). It provides a way to think about knowledge as both moral and conceptual but not fully disembodied or immaterial. It even provides a language for justice that also requires self-reflection. The inky book of conscience speaks more pertinently to a postmodern culture than Descartes's blank iPad ever could.

How the World Became a Book in Shakespeare's England records many examples as it traces paths through premodern English culture. To be sure, there are many possible paths even in a single phrase, but we cannot walk them all. Plenty of writers compared things other than the conscience to a book, for instance. Francis Davison writes that:

> euery widdowes heart is like a booke,
> Where her ioyes past imprinted doe remaine,
> But when her iudgements eye therein doth looke
> She doth not wish they were to come againe.[112]

According to Davison, widows recall the joys of marriage but do not, on further inspection, want them back. Thomas Dekker's character Gazetto cynically tell a husband, "th'art a foole, to grieue that thy wife is taken away by the King to his priuate bed-chamber, Now like a booke call'd in, shee'l sell better then euer she did."[113] The joke, which is not funny, is that when the wife sleeps with the King, her social status will raise as a banned

[111] See Galen Strawson, *Locke on Personal Identity: Consciousness and Concernment*, Princeton Monographs in Philosophy (Princeton: Princeton University Press, 2011).
[112] Francis Davison, *A Poetical Rapsodie Containing: Diuerse Sonnets, Odes, Elegies, Madrigals, Epigrams, Pastorals, Eglogues, with Other Poems, Both in Rime and Measured Verse* (London, 1611), sig. B6r. STC 6375.
[113] Thomas Dekker, *A Tragi-Comedy: Called, Match Mee in London* (London, 1631), sig. H2v-H3r. STC 6529.

book's value raises when it has been "call'd in" by the authorities. Less offensive but still latently sexualized is Shakespeare's Hector, who says to Achilles: "O like a booke of sport thou'lt read me ore: / But ther's more in me then thou vnderstandst[.]"[114] Following these pathways would require further philologies of bookish language, but like a book, an introduction must eventually end, if only because its reader loses patience.

[114] William Shakespeare, *The Historie of Troylus and Cresseida* (London, 1609), sig. I4r. STC 22331.

CHAPTER 2

The Lexicon of Print

> In my country, and in my daies, learning and bookishnes, doth much
> mend purses, but minds nothing at all.
> —Michel de Montaigne, trans. John Florio[1]

When Montaigne complains of the way learning fills purses with money
but not minds with knowledge, he is thinking of premodern France,
his own "country." He goes on to tell how learning "over-burthens and
swelleth" empty minds, leaving them "a raw and indigested masse." Only
the "well borne minde" can use learning as a "profitable accessory." But
John Florio's translation offers another, emphatically English word that has
no equivalent in Montaigne's French: "bookishnes."[2] If "learning" only
implies the use of books, "bookishnes" guarantees it. Florio inserts this
term fully aware of its ability to conjure for his English readers the image
of someone overly committed to their books. Indeed, Florio's understated,
almost casual use of the word suggests that it belongs to a repertoire of
such terms – a repertoire of use, which this book seeks explore. But what
are the limits of this repertoire, and what does exploring it involve?

This chapter establishes historical parameters for the study of bookish
language in early modern England. Happily, because "historical parameters" is such an unwieldy term, the imposition of rough date limits also
provides a set of intellectual parameters for the story. Although, as the previous chapter indicated, the concern of this book does not fall exclusively
on printed books and print technology, there are a number of generative
reasons to focus on the period of time between the introduction of the

---

[1] Michel de Montaigne, *Essays* (London, 1613), sig. Aaa3v. STC 18042.
[2] The French text reads, "En mon pays, et de mon temps, la doctrine amande assez les bourses,
rarement les ames." See Michel de Montaigne, "Les Essais de Montaigne with Page Images from
the Bordeaux Copy," accessed December 12, 2022, https://artflsrv03.uchicago.edu/philologic4/
montessaisvilley/navigate/1/5/9/.

printing press to England in the late fifteenth century and, to be quite precise, the year 1683.

The earlier date is easier to explain: because I am studying the transformation of the English cultural imagination after the introduction of the printing press, the book's many examples necessarily come from the so-called "print era" following the establishment of the press in England. This is not to occlude the circulation of texts in manuscript or other media, of course, nor am I suggesting that England was somehow *not* bookish before printing. Scholars have persuasively demonstrated that manuscript texts proliferated in the sixteenth and seventeenth centuries, even as printing technology expanded.[3] Indeed, as the previous chapter's discussion of the phrase "like a book" indicates, a "book" was not restricted to print or manuscript (nor even to a textual object). Rather, the point of this project is to show how the increased production and circulation of books and other text technologies expanded the bookish imagination of early English readers and writers. More books and readers meant more people thinking about their books, and with them too.

The later date of 1683 requires a bit more explanation. Starting in that year, the map-maker, printer, globemaker, and royal hydrographer Joseph Moxon published one of the earliest printing manuals in any language as part of his series *Mechanick Exercises: Or, the Doctrine of Handy-works.* The volume on printing, which carries the additional title *Applied to the Art of Printing* (a phrase to which we will return in Chapter 7), describes the printing process from press construction to letter-cutting to the compositor's trade to the preparation of books for the market. Moxon's manual served as the basis of printing manuals for at least a century afterward, and many twentieth- and twenty-first century bibliographers resort to *Mechanick Exercises* for descriptions and images of the technical operations of the press.[4] For the purposes of this book, Moxon shows us what bookish language is *not*: his glossary of printing terms, fascinating and lively in its own right, makes explicit a technical terminology of printing that had previously circulated orally in printing houses.

Beginning at the end, therefore, this chapter argues first that Moxon's lexicon of print marks a fitting stopping point for our inquiry because it signals the beginning of modern England. The manual, and in particular its glossary, participates in the Royal Society's attempt to explicate and

---

[3] Love, *Scribal Publication in Seventeenth-Century England*; Marotti, *Manuscript, Print, and the English Renaissance Lyric*; Marotti and Bristol, *Print, Manuscript, & Performance*.

[4] See, for instance, Gaskell, *A New Introduction to Bibliography*.

organize all forms of knowledge, an attempt long understood as part of a widespread epistemic shift to modernity.[5] More practically, for my purposes, Moxon's glossary also clarifies what terms we should and should not regard as part of the bookishness of premodern England. To explore the limits of the technical terminology of printing, the second section of this chapter turns to a poem by the clergyman John Dunton (1628–76) titled "The most Ingenious Art of Printing SPIRITVALIZ'D." The poem, printed posthumously by Dunton's son in 1684, extensively analogizes human life as a printed book using the whole suite of technical printing terms – the same ones made available in Moxon's glossary. I reproduce the entire poem, then argue that, although downright charming, the poem exposes the limits of the technical lexicon of print. Here again, the shift to modernity is evident as the clear separation of embodied human experience from technological apparatus – nature from culture, as Bruno Latour's influential account of modernity terms it.[6]

With the endpoint established, we can then look backward from 1683 to ask what bookish terms premodern English writers and readers actually used. Here the situation gets messy, and that is precisely the point: rather than an organized set of printing terms, such as we see in Moxon and Dunton, the language of the book thrives in premodern England as an ever-shifting, often conflicting, sometimes boring, but nevertheless broadly circulated set of words, phrases, metaphors, figures of speech, and conceits. The third section of the chapter explores the term "bookish" itself, which reaches beyond the simile of "like a book" and figures whatever it modifies as directly *of the book*. "Bookish" builds a bridge from Moxon and Dunton to the broader lexicon of books by showing how that lexicon extends far beyond the technology of printing. A philological history of "bookish" sketches a broad cultural history of bookishness. Finally, the fourth section turns to another very common term, "set forth." I show how this phrase gradually acquired not only the meaning "to publish" but, more specifically, "to print and publish." I show how four major writers – Philip Sidney, William Shakespeare, Margaret Cavendish, and John Milton – use the term in ways alive to its associations with printing.

---

[5] See Steven Shapin, *Leviathan and the Air-Pump: Hobbes, Boyle, and the Experimental Life: Including a Translation of Thomas Hobbes, Dialogus Physicus de Natura Aeris by Simon Schaffer* (Princeton: Princeton University Press, 1985); Steven Shapin, *A Social History of Truth: Civility and Science in Seventeenth-Century England*, Science and Its Conceptual Foundations (Chicago: University of Chicago Press, 1994).

[6] Latour, *We Have Never Been Modern*.

Joseph Moxon at the Beginning of Modernity

A familiar name among bibliographers, Joseph Moxon wrote the first extensive printing manual in English – and in any language, depending on how one defines a manual.[7] Moxon printed and published *Mechanick Exercises* serially. Beginning with smithing, then joinery, then other trades, these books attempted to make the trades or "handy-works" legible to a broader public. Moxon likely began work on the volumes on printing in 1683 and continued into 1684, when they were advertised as nearly complete.[8] After an opening general issue on "Printing" (with sections on "Letter," "Cases," and "the Galley," for instance) and the press itself (with sections on the various parts of the wooden press), there followed an issue on "Letter-Cutting" featuring a discussion of the cutting of letter punches and the design of type-faces. Then, Moxon offers a detailed account of "Mold-Making, Sinking the Matrices, Casting and Dressing of Printing-Letters," followed by equally detailed sections on the compositor's and pressman's trades, the last of which contains additional shorter sections on the warehouse keeper and the "Customs used in a Printing-house."[9] Finally, a "Dictionary" of printing terms, which is the focus of this section, serves as an index as well as a glossary. The sum of these parts – subsequently published as one collection – is a fairly comprehensive account of the printing process, illustrated with plates showing the technologies and techniques of printing.

Recent scholarship has explored the social and rhetorical dynamics of *Mechanick Exercises*, with particular emphasis on Moxon's relationship with the Royal Society, the group formed in 1660 and chartered in 1662 with the titular objective of the "improvement of natural knowledge." Rachel Stenner argues that this and other early books about books create "a set of imaginative parameters through which they ask their readers to engage with typography as a subject."[10] While for Stenner this engagement involves a broad-based exploration of "the social relations

---

[7] See Adrian Johns, *The Nature of the Book: Print and Knowledge in the Making* (Chicago: University of Chicago Press, 1998), 79–108; Stenner, *The Typographic Imaginary in Early Modern English Literature*, 32–55.

[8] Joseph Moxon, *Mechanick Exercises on the Whole Art of Printing (1683–4)*, ed. Herbert Davis and Harry Carter (New York: Dover, 1978), xlix. The sequence of the issues is not especially easy or important to apprehend: Moxon labels volume numbers, section numbers, issue numbers, and then paginates continuously.

[9] Joseph Moxon, *Mechanick Exercises, or, The Doctrine of Handy-Works* (London, 1677), sigs. Tr, Oor, and Aaa4v.

[10] Stenner, *The Typographic Imaginary in Early Modern English Literature*, 34–35.

of the print trade," for Lisa Maruca, Moxon's persistent emphasis on the "body of print … as a working body, a laborer whose physical construction of print" helps construct the meaning of a printed book, is directly tied to his relationship with the Royal Society.[11] Maruca shows how, in detailing the mechanics of the press and the production of printed books, Moxon "struggle[s] to fulfill the demands of competing ideologies": on the one hand, the Royal Society's philosophical and experimental focus and, on the other, the bodily, laborious, craft-based world of the worker.[12] Jocelyn Hargrave extends Maruca's analysis to argue that Moxon's "self-positioning between the professional [i.e., the trades] and philosophical [i.e., the Royal Society] worlds enables [*Mechanick Exercises*] to address each."[13] Hargrave interprets Moxon's manual alongside his changing relationship with the Royal Society: elected in 1678 and then expelled in 1682 for failing to pay his fees, Moxon nevertheless "aligned with the Society's own philosophical research interests in the mechanical arts."[14]

These scholars show how Moxon links his detailed description of the "art of printing" with the epistemic shifts of the day, particularly the Royal Society's attempts to systematize technical knowledge. Although this link is nowhere more explicit than in Moxon's "Dictionary," scholars have not yet paid it much attention. Extending the work of Maruca and Hargrave, therefore, I want to explore this printing dictionary, which sets down many terms and phrases that were not previously circulated beyond print shops. I risk making a modernity mountain out of a molehill to explore how Moxon's lexicographical attempts to make printing knowledge explicit, even accessible, belong more to the modern world to come than to what came before. My argument is that the dictionary distills Moxon's scientistic impulses and places Moxon's entire project on a trajectory with later, more famous documents of Enlightenment modernity such as Diderot's *Encyclopedie* (1751).

Even Moxon hints that he knows he is doing something new and forward-looking. He declares the purpose of the glossary in large typeface on the first page: "a DICTIONARY, Alphabetically explaining the abstruse VVords and Phrases that are used in Typography. VVhich also may serve as an Index to direct to the most material Concerns contained

---

[11] Maruca, *The Work of Print*, 32.
[12] Maruca, 38.
[13] Jocelyn Hargrave, "Joseph Moxon: A Re-Fashioned Appraisal," *Script & Print: Bulletin of the Bibliographical Society of Australia and New Zealand* 39, no. 3 (2015): 175.
[14] Hargrave, 172.

in this Volumn" (see Figure 2.1).[15] Such an objective conforms to Maruca's insightful claim that *Mechanick Exercises* transforms "somatic ways of knowing into print information" and that this transformation "made guild techniques the business (in both senses) of the literate and educated classes, allowing them to buttress their power—and personal finances—by increasing their knowledge of once mysterious techniques."[16] The dictionary literally publishes (one might say *sets forth*) terms used in the print house but never before printed, and it coordinates them with the descriptions throughout the manual. Before the list, however, Moxon introduces a bit of further explanation (see Figure 2.1). Moxon imagines a key to all mechanical mythologies, as it were: a "perfect" or complete dictionary that will domesticate terms of the trade that seem "Alien" and "barbarous." Interestingly, he frames the problem as a bookish limitation, blaming the absence of a complete dictionary on the "want of a proper Repository to store them in." That is, there is no book form to contain all the terms of the trades – until the encyclopedia, of course, which arose to fill precisely the need Moxon describes and which was also staged as a way to mediate the "alien" and "barbarous" aspects of unfamiliar cultures into the normalized language of white European modernity.[17] Of course, Moxon could not know the particular future he was predicting, but he surely knew he was articulating the need for information architectures that can sustain the explication of "all Trades and Faculties whatsoever."

To read Moxon's dictionary is to read an organized abstraction of the print trade's living language. The dictionary mixes terms more familiar to students of book history, such as "galley," "frisket," and "tympan" with a huge number of terms emerging from the everyday speech and action of the print house and surrounding spaces. Moxon defines "*Beat Fat*," for instance, as "If a *Press-man Takes* too much *Inck* with his *Balls*, he *Beats Fat*." Then he adds that "The *Black English Faced Letter* is generally *Beaten Fat*" – that is, the type requires more ink on the balls. By contrast, "*Beat Lean*, is to *Take* but little *Inck*, and often: all *Small Letter* must be *Beaten Lean*."[18] Even these apparently descriptive terms read like residue of an oral

---

[15] Moxon, *Mechanick Exercises*, sig. Ccc2r.

[16] Maruca, *The Work of Print*, 37–38.

[17] See Clorinda Donato and Robert M. Maniquis, eds., *The Encyclopédie and the Age of Revolution* (Boston: G.K. Hall, 1992); Marian Hobson, Kate E. Tunstall, and Caroline Warman, *Diderot and Rousseau: Networks of Enlightenment*, SVEC, 2011:04 (Oxford: Voltaire Foundation, 2011); Hans Ulrich Gumbrecht, *Prose of the World: Denis Diderot and the Periphery of Enlightenment*, English edition (Stanford: Stanford University Press, 2021).

[18] Moxon, *Mechanick Exercises*, sig. Ccc3r.

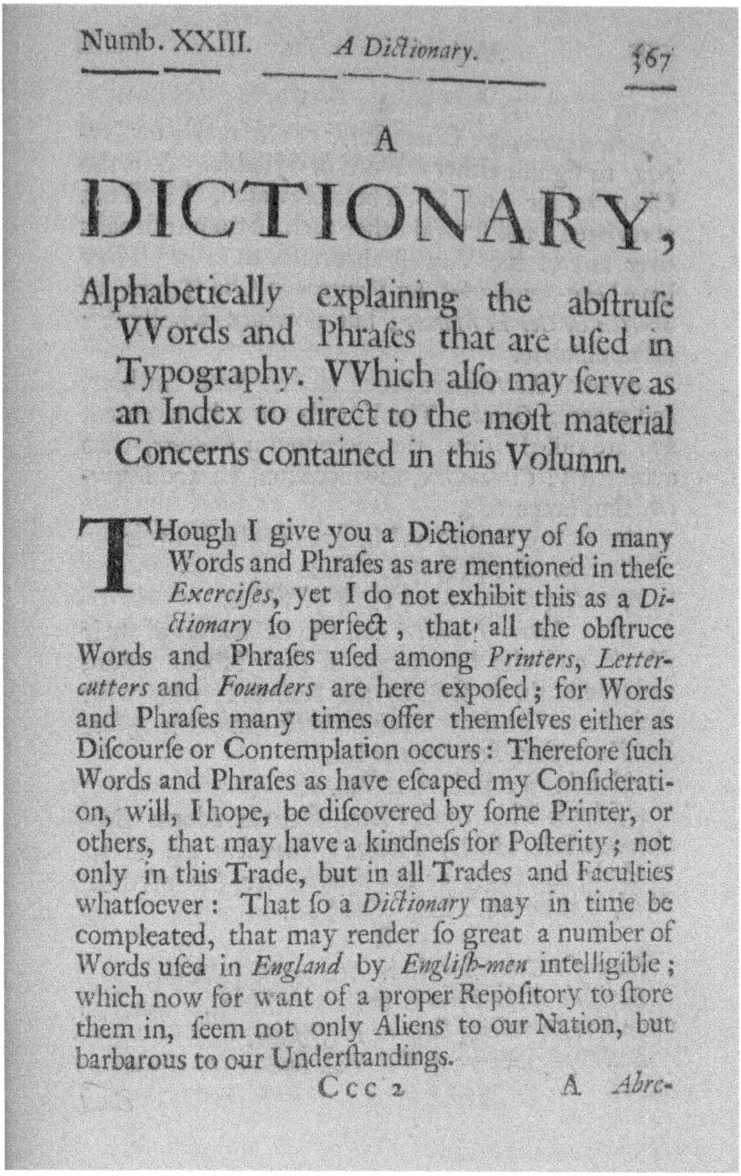

Numb. XXIII.   *A Dictionary.*   567

A

DICTIONARY,

Alphabetically explaining the abſtruſe
VVords and Phraſes that are uſed in
Typography. VVhich alſo may ſerve as
an Index to direct to the moſt material
Concerns contained in this Volumn.

THough I give you a Dictionary of ſo many
Words and Phraſes as are mentioned in theſe
Exerciſes, yet I do not exhibit this as a *Dictionary* ſo perfect , that all the obſtruce
Words and Phraſes uſed among *Printers, Letter-
cutters* and *Founders* are here expoſed; for Words
and Phraſes many times offer themſelves either as
Diſcourſe or Contemplation occurs : Therefore ſuch
Words and Phraſes as have eſcaped my Conſiderati-
on, will, I hope, be diſcovered by ſome Printer, or
others, that may have a kindneſs for Poſterity; not
only in this Trade, but in all Trades and Faculties
whatſoever : That ſo a *Dictionary* may in time be
compleated, that may render ſo great a number of
Words uſed in *England* by *Engliſh-men* intelligible;
which now for want of a proper Repoſitory to ſtore
them in, ſeem not only Aliens to our Nation, but
barbarous to our Underſtandings.

Ccc 2   A *Abre-*

Figure 2.1   Joseph Moxon, *Mechanick Exercises, or, The Doctrine of Handy-Works*
(London, 1677), sig. Ccc2r, RB 138367, The Huntington Library,
San Marino, California.

performance, with press operators saying to one another that they "beat fat" or "lean," but many other terms Moxon ascribes specifically to oral performance: "*Froze out*" refers to the time "In Winter when the Paper is Froze, and the *Letter* Froze, so as the Workmen cannot Work. They say, *They are Froze out.*"[19] The entry for "*Off*" describes when "A *Press-man* usually says, *I am off*, meaning he has *Wrought off* his *Token*, his *Heap*, his *Form*" – that is, he has worked through the allotted amount of paper.[20] Compositors, meanwhile, have a set of options for indicating the state of the cases:

> *Case is full*, viz. a *Case* full of *Letter*, wanting no Sorts.
> *Case is Low.* When a *Case* grows empty, *Compositers* say the *Case is Low.*
> *Case Stands still.* When the *Compositer* is not at Work at his *Case*, it is said, *The Case stands still.*[21]

From Moxon's definitions, one gets a sense of the noise of the print shop – with phrases and prompts carrying industrially specific meanings spoken (or shouted) across the space. Importantly, most of the terms in Moxon's dictionary did not appear in print previously, and when they did, it was without reference to printing.[22] The glossary thus does not merely demonstrate how the language of the body works its way into the language of typography, as Maruca has argued about the whole *Mechanick Exercises* (Figure 2.2). It also makes explicit and indeed *archival* what had circulated for generations as a matter of oral, embodied *repertoire*.[23] Not coincidentally for my purposes, this move from repertoire to archive has long been associated with European modernity.[24]

Although, as Maruca and Stenner have demonstrated, Moxon's manual differs significantly from later printing manuals, it nevertheless shares with those books a fully realized attempt to externalize and describe systematically the production of printed books. In so doing, Moxon links his work

---

[19] Moxon, sig. Ddd3r.
[20] Moxon, sig. Eee3r-v.
[21] Moxon, sig. Ccc4r.
[22] See specific lemmata at *Lexicons of Early Modern English*, ed. Ian Lancashire (Toronto: University of Toronto Press, 2018). http://leme.library.utoronto.ca.
[23] Taylor, *The Archive and the Repertoire*. Other discussions of Moxon include Elizabeth L. Eisenstein, *Divine Art, Infernal Machine: The Reception of Printing in the West from First Impressions to the Sense of an Ending*, Material Texts (Philadelphia: University of Pennsylvania Press, 2011), 78–79; Masten, *Queer Philologies*, 57–60; Cait Coker, "Gendered Spheres: Theorizing Space in the English Printing House," *The Seventeenth Century* 33, no. 3 (July 7, 2018): 323–36, https://doi.org/10.1080/0 268117X.2017.1340850.
[24] A host of scholarship has explored this shift. See Ong, *Orality and Literacy*; Taylor, *The Archive and the Repertoire*; Clanchy, *From Memory to Written Record*.

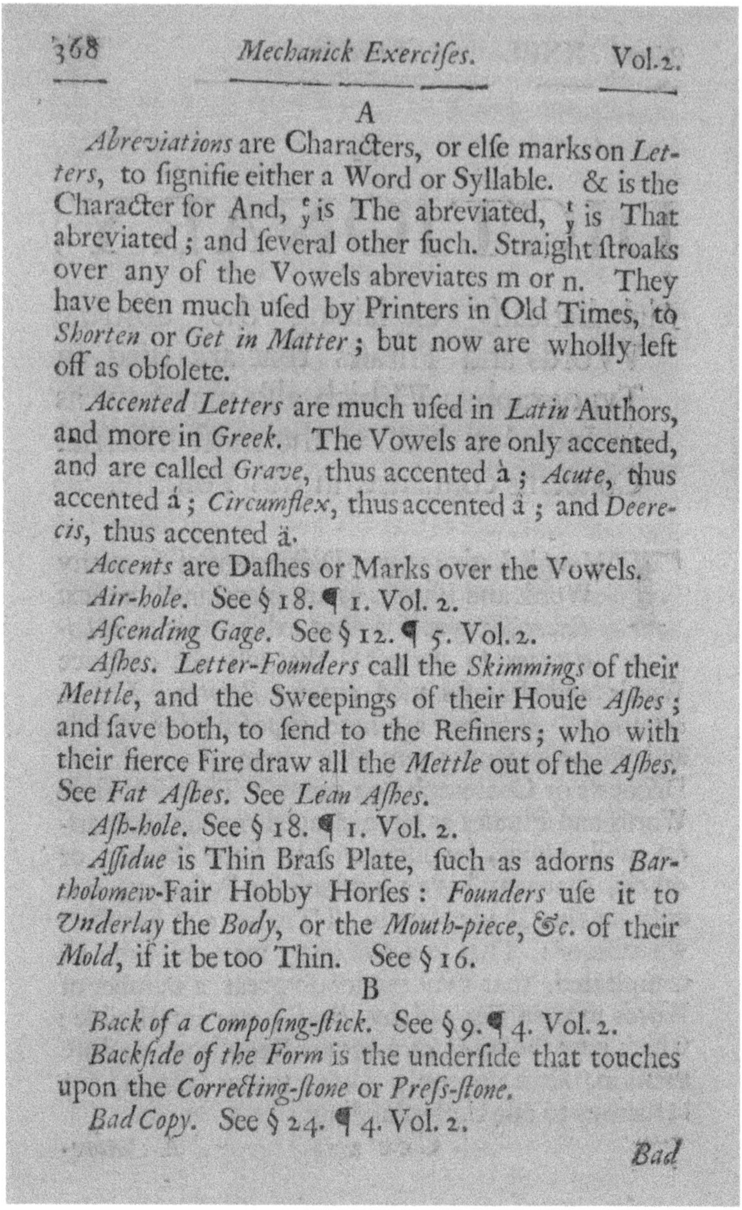

A

Abreviations are Characters, or elſe marks on *Letters*, to ſignifie either a Word or Syllable. & is the Character for And, ꝥ is The abreviated, ẏ is That abreviated ; and ſeveral other ſuch. Straight ſtroaks over any of the Vowels abreviates m or n. They have been much uſed by Printers in Old Times, to *Shorten* or *Get in Matter* ; but now are wholly left off as obſolete.

Accented Letters are much uſed in *Latin* Authors, and more in *Greek.* The Vowels are only accented, and are called *Grave*, thus accented à ; *Acute*, thus accented á ; *Circumflex*, thus accented â ; and *Deerecis*, thus accented ä.

Accents are Daſhes or Marks over the Vowels.

Air-hole. See § 18. ¶ 1. Vol. 2.

Aſcending Gage. See § 12. ¶ 5. Vol. 2.

Aſhes. Letter-Founders call the *Skimmings* of their *Mettle*, and the Sweepings of their Houſe *Aſhes* ; and ſave both, to ſend to the Refiners; who with their fierce Fire draw all the *Mettle* out of the *Aſhes.* See *Fat Aſhes.* See *Lean Aſhes.*

Aſh-hole. See § 18. ¶ 1. Vol. 2.

Aſſidue is Thin Braſs Plate, ſuch as adorns *Bartholomew*-Fair Hobby Horſes : *Founders* uſe it to *Underlay* the *Body*, or the *Mouth-piece, &c.* of their *Mold*, if it be too Thin. See § 16.

B

Back of a Compoſing-ſtick. See § 9. ¶ 4. Vol. 2.

Backſide of the Form is the underſide that touches upon the *Correcting-ſtone* or *Preſs-ſtone.*

Bad Copy. See § 24. ¶ 4. Vol. 2.

Bad

Figure 2.2 Joseph Moxon, *Mechanick Exercises, or, The Doctrine of Handy-Works* (London, 1677), sig. Ccc2v, RB 138367, The Huntington Library, San Marino, California.

as a medium of the trades with the Royal Society's stated program. Indeed, at least two advertisements for *Mechanick Exercises* in the *London Gazette* mention Moxon's lexicographical accomplishment. In the initial marketing push for the whole series in 1678, the *Gazette* (edited by the then Royal Society President Joseph Williamson) explicitly links the Society's scientistic goals with Moxon's dictionary:

> Forasmuch as all Natural Knowledge was Originally produced (and still eminently depends) upon Experiments, and all or most Experiments are couched among the Handy-crafts; and also that Handy-works themselves may be improved: there was begun (by *Joseph Moxon* […]) Monthly Exercises, upon the Mechanicks. […] These Arts are described in Workmens Phrases, and their several Terms explained.[25]

The advertisement draws a clear line from the Royal Society's goals to its experimental practice to the "Handy-works" and then to the "several Terms" of those trades. Likewise, the 1684 *Gazette* advertisement for the volumes on printing draws attention to the dictionary:

> this volume treats of Typography, or the whole Art of Printing in all its Branches. With an Alphabetical Dictionary explaining all the abstruse Terms used in each Art.[26]

That the dictionary twice receives mention in advertisements seems intriguing; that it receives such mention in the *London Gazette* is downright significant. Moxon's attempt to make the lexicon of the printing repertoire legible as an archive is linked explicitly with and marketed to the institution most closely associated with the rise of modern scientific inquiry.

We do not have to try too hard to see how, in terms of the language of books, Moxon's dictionary marks a shift to modernity. Consider Foucault's statement in *The Order of Things* that:

> from the seventeenth century, one began to ask how a sign could be linked to what it signified. A question to which the classical [i.e., post-Renaissance] period was to reply by the analysis of representation; and to which modern thought [i.e., post-1700] was to reply by the analysis of meaning and signification. But given the fact itself, language was never to be anything more than a particular case of representation (for the Classics) or of signification (for us). The profound kinship of language with the world was thus dissolved.[27]

---

[25] Quoted in Moxon, *Mechanick Exercises on the Whole Art of Printing (1683–4)*, xlvi.
[26] Quoted in Moxon, xlix.
[27] Michel Foucault, *The Order of Things; an Archaeology of the Human Sciences* (New York: Vintage Books, 1973), 43.

In Foucault's influential account, modernity begins to emerge when the Renaissance episteme of resemblance – words are *like* things – gives way to an episteme of signification – words *signify* things – and eventually to a study of language for its own sake. We are thus left, in the seventeenth century, with a series of binaries and an understanding of knowledge as a table.[28] Moxon's dictionary participates in this shift, first, by making what had been understood as resemblance (the older episteme, in which the "head" of a piece of type resembled the position of a human head) available for analysis and, second, lines up a series of binaries: words and their signification in the form of a dictionary, one might even say a table. Moxon converts a premodern lexicon of resemblance into a modern lexicon of signification.

At the risk of the reputational damage that comes from invoking two famous French thinkers in successive paragraphs, Moxon's dictionary also fits the template of Bruno Latour's account of the modern constitution. In Latour's more recent and arguably just as influential account, the modern constitution supposedly enforces a hard separation between nature and culture, but continually encourages the proliferation of nature–culture hybrids that remain, as it were, out of sight.[29] For Latour, we have never been modern because the pure separation of nature and culture has never been achieved, and hybrids continue to accumulate beneath the surface. Thus, for Latour, the Royal Society's attempt to privilege the cultivated and philosophical mind over the natural world that thus becomes the object of that mind's knowledge may seem successful, but merely produces nature–culture hybrids that persist through the duration of modernity.[30] In a slightly different account than the Foucaultian one above, here we might consider the way Moxon's dictionary attempts to enforce just such a separation by aligning the lexicon of print with the purifying philosophical agenda of the Royal Society, even as printing itself was always and would continue to be a messy, inky nature–culture hybrid.[31]

However convincing these connections with well-worn accounts of modernity (not to mention similar political and scientific histories), the point remains that Moxon's dictionary does something no one had done

---

[28] To clarify, knowledge-as-table is part of the Classical episteme, which in Foucault's account bridges from the Renaissance to the Modern epistemes.

[29] Latour, *We Have Never Been Modern*.

[30] Latour, 20–22.

[31] Recent book history scholarship attests to this point, including Leah Price, "From The History of a Book to a 'History of the Book,'" *Representations* 108, no. 1 (November 1, 2009): 120–38; Lupton, *Knowing Books*; Knight, *Bound to Read*; Price, *What We Talk About When We Talk About Books*.

in over two centuries of printing: it makes the technical language of print explicit and public. In arguing for these connections, I am really aiming to think about what came *before* 1683, *before* the knowledge of books became a table. Before Moxon, the language of printing and books in England flowed along a variety of lexical pathways and across routinized linguistic forms. Rarely systematized and never organized, bookish words reached far beyond the technical, technological language of the press and the industrialized language of the book trade. And if, as I have been arguing, Moxon marks the turn to modernity, then the rest of the terms I take up in this book offer a distinctly *premodern* cultural and literary history. Instead of a table, premodern bookish language functioned more like...well, like a book: an iterable, motile assemblage that is at once a material thing and a mechanism for expression, able to be reconfigured and repurposed for a variety of occasions and needs.

Printing in Poetry

To illustrate still more vividly what premodern bookish language was *not* and why, I turn to a poem published in 1684 but written earlier: John Dunton's "The most Ingenious Art of Printing *SPIRITVALIZ'D*," published by his son, also named John.[32] The year 1684 is not insignificant, of course, because the poem appeared in print only after Moxon's *Mechanick Exercises* laid open the technological and lexicographical work of the printing shop. The poem, which I reproduce below in its entirety, uses many of the very terms that Moxon takes pains to define and illustrate. In impressive, even charming detail, Dunton compares the Christian life to the printing process – like Moxon, from type sorts to the warehouse. Also like Moxon, I want to suggest, Dunton's poem takes us to the limit of the concerns of this study. The poem's technologically specific, willfully heavy-handed use of printing terms shows how the book-as-conceit reaches its fullest and most explicit and therefore most pervasive point. Instead of using the bookish conceit to express something about human life, Dunton uses human life to talk about printing (see Figures 2.3–2.6).

The material circumstances of this poem's publication illustrate how *bookish* England had become by 1684 and, in our time, how drastically the scholarly understanding of "print culture" has recently shifted. Published

---

[32] John Dunton, *The Pilgrims Guide from the Cradle to His Death-Bed with His Glorious Passage from Thence to the New-Jerusalem* (London, 1684), sigs. L4r-5v. Wing D2632.

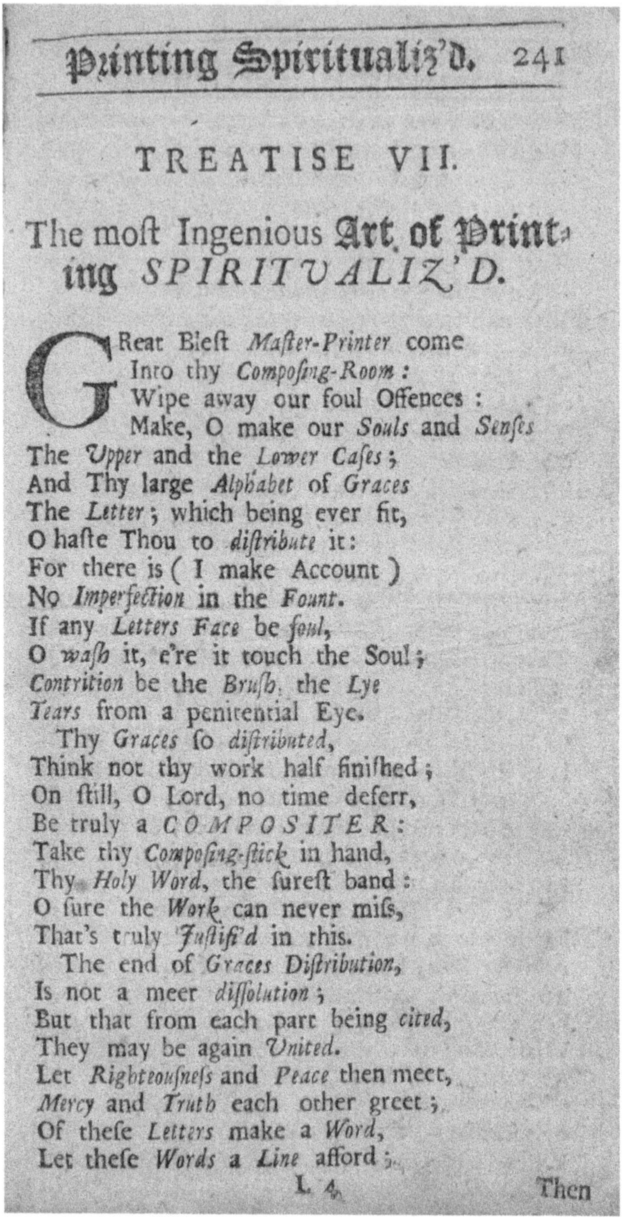

TREATISE VII.

The moſt Ingenious 𝕬𝖗𝖙 𝖔𝖋 𝕻𝖗𝖎𝖓𝖙-
𝖎𝖓𝖌 *SPIRITVALIZ'D.*

Reat Bleſt *Maſter-Printer* come
Into thy *Compoſing-Room :*
Wipe away our foul Offences :
Make, O make our *Souls* and *Senſes*
The *Vpper* and the *Lower Caſes* ;
And Thy large *Alphabet* of *Graces*
The *Letter* ; which being ever fit,
O haſte Thou to *diſtribute* it :
For there is (I make Account)
No *Imperfection* in the *Fount.*
If any *Letters Face* be *foul,*
O *waſh* it, e're it touch the Soul ;
Contrition be the *Bruſh*, the *Lye*
Tears from a penitential Eye.
    Thy *Graces* ſo *diſtributed,*
Think not thy work half finiſhed ;
On ſtill, O Lord, no time deferr,
Be truly a *C O M P O S I T E R :*
Take thy *Compoſing-ſtick* in hand,
Thy *Holy Word,* the ſureſt band :
O ſure the *Work* can never miſs,
That's truly *Juſtiſt'd* in this.
    The end of *Graces Diſtribution,*
Is not a meer *diſſolution* ;
But that from each part being *cited,*
They may be again *Vnited.*
Let *Righteouſneſs* and *Peace* then meet,
Mercy and *Truth* each other greet ;
Of theſe *Letters* make a *Word,*
Let theſe *Words* a *Line* afford ;
                    L 4   Then

Figures 2.3–2.6   John Dunton, *The Pilgrims Guide from the Cradle to His Death-Bed with His Glorious Passage from Thence to the New-Jerusalem* (London, 1684), sigs. L4r-5v, Case Y 1565.D924, Newberry Library, Chicago, Illinois.

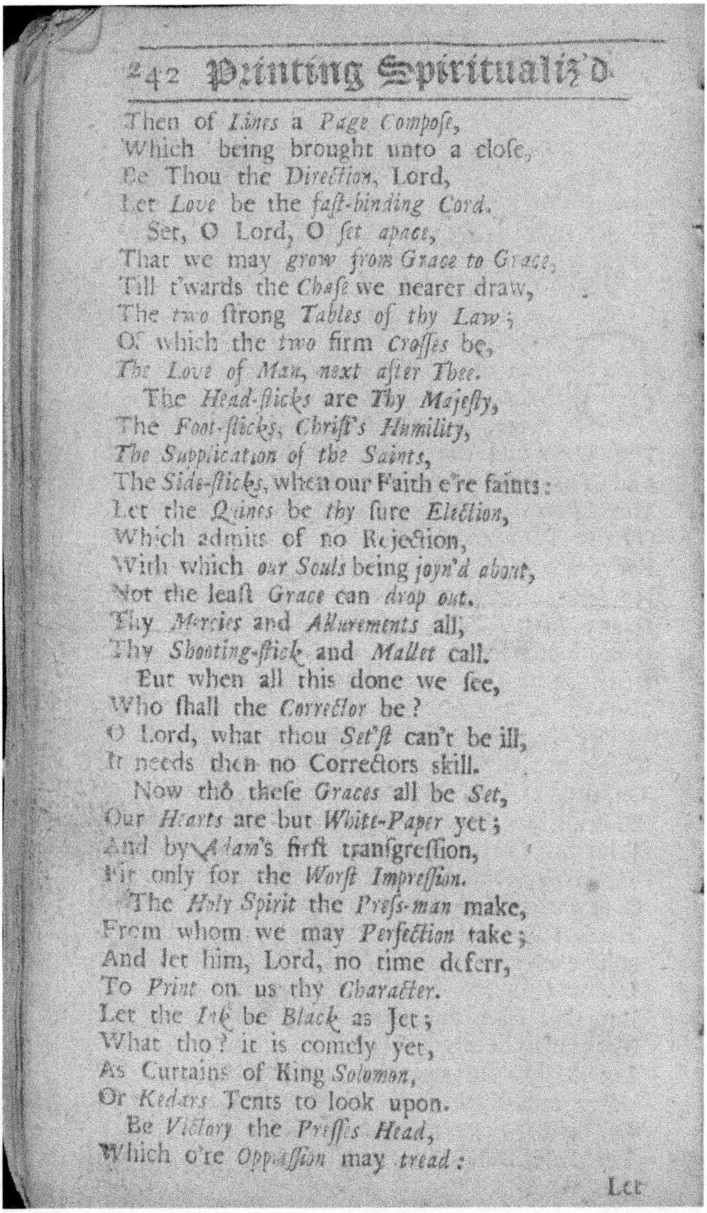

242 **Printing Spiritualiz'd**

Then of *Lines* a *Page Compose*,
Which being brought unto a close,
Be Thou the *Direction*, Lord,
Let *Love* be the *fast-binding Cord*.

Set, O Lord, O *set apace*,
That we may *grow from Grace to Grace*,
Till t'wards the *Chase* we nearer draw,
The *two* strong *Tables* of thy *Law*;
Of which the *two* firm *Crosses* be,
The *Love* of *Man*, next after *Thee*.

The *Head-sticks* are *Thy Majesty*,
The *Foot-sticks*, *Christ's Humility*,
The *Supplication* of the *Saints*,
The *Side-sticks*, when our Faith e're faints:
Let the *Quines* be *thy* sure *Election*,
Which admits of no Rejection,
With which *our Souls* being *joyn'd about*,
Not the least *Grace* can *drop out*.
Thy *Mercies* and *Allurements* all,
Thy *Shooting-stick* and *Mallet* call.

But when all this done we see,
Who shall the *Corrector* be?
O Lord, what thou *Set'st* can't be ill,
It needs then no Correctors skill.

Now tho' these *Graces* all be *Set*,
Our *Hearts* are but *Whitt-Paper* yet;
And by *Adam's* first transgression,
Fit only for the *Worst Impression*.
The *Holy Spirit* the *Press-man* make,
From whom we may *Perfection* take;
And let him, Lord, no time deferr,
To *Print* on us thy *Character*.
Let the *Ink* be *Black* as Jet;
What tho'? it is comely yet,
As Curtains of King *Solomon*,
Or *Kedars* Tents to look upon.
Be *Victory* the *Press's Head*,
Which o're *Oppression* may *tread*:

Let

Figures 2.3–2.6 (cont.)

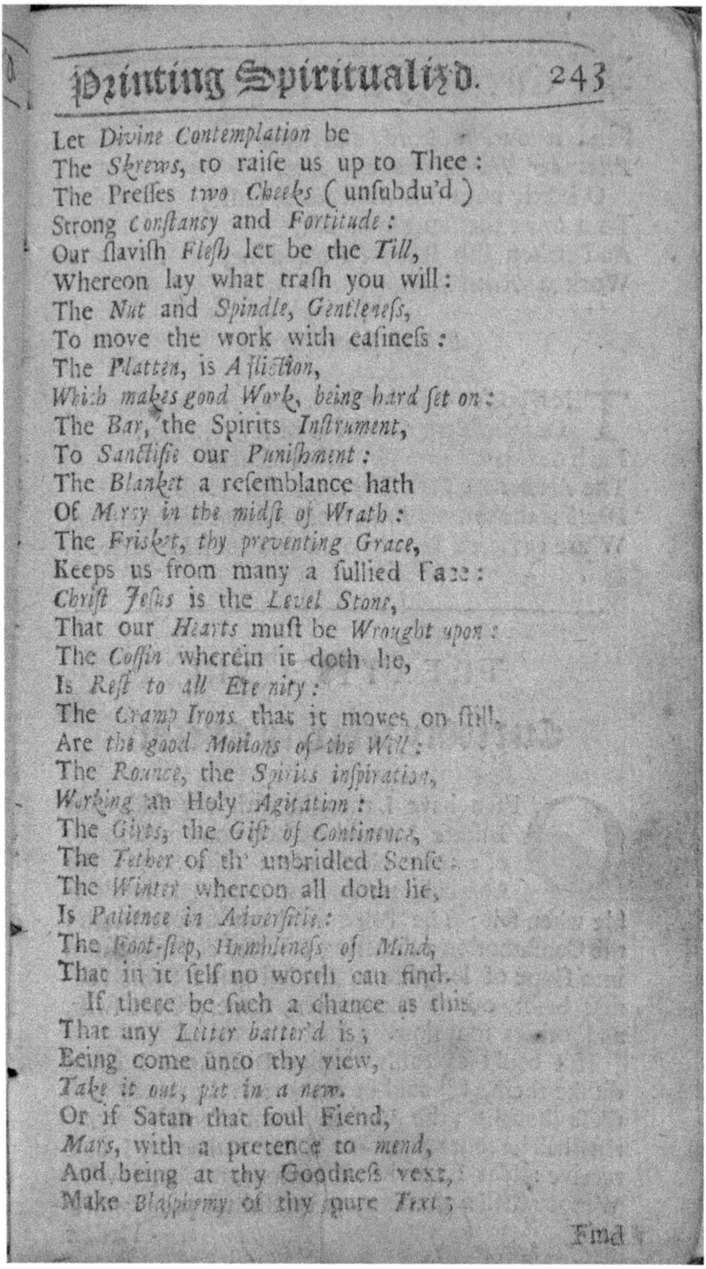

𝔓𝔯𝔦𝔫𝔱𝔦𝔫𝔤 𝔖𝔭𝔦𝔯𝔦𝔱𝔲𝔞𝔩𝔦𝔷𝔡.   243

Let *Divine Contemplation* be
The *Skrews*, to raife us up to Thee:
The Preſſes *two Cheeks* (unſubdu'd)
Strong *Conſtancy* and *Fortitude*:
Our ſlaviſh *Fleſh* let be the *Till*,
Whereon lay what traſh you will:
The *Nut* and *Spindle*, *Gentleneſs*,
To move the work with eaſineſs:
The *Platten*, is *Affliction*,
Which makes good Work, being hard ſet on:
The *Bar*, the Spirits *Inſtrument*,
To *Sanctifie* our *Puniſhment*:
The *Blanket* a reſemblance hath
Of *Mercy in the midſt of Wrath*:
The *Frisket*, *thy preventing Grace*,
Keeps us from many a ſullied Face:
Chriſt Jeſus is the *Level Stone*,
That our *Hearts* muſt be *Wrought upon*:
The *Coffin* wherein it doth lie,
Is *Reſt to all Eternity*:
The *Cramp Irons* that it moves on ſtill,
Are *the good Motions of the Will*:
The *Rounce*, the *Spirits inſpiration*,
Working an Holy Agitation:
The *Gifts*, the *Gift of Continence*,
The *Tether* of th' unbridled *Senſe*:
The *Winter* whereon all doth lie,
Is *Patience in Adverſitie*:
The *Foot-ſtep*, *Humbleneſs of Mind*,
That in it ſelf no worth can find.
If there be ſuch a chance as this,
That any *Letter* batter'd is;
Being come unto thy view,
Take it out, put in a new.
Or if Satan that foul Fiend,
Mars, with a pretence to *mend*,
And being at thy Goodneſs vext,
Make *Blaſphemy* of thy pure *Text*;

                        Find

Figures 2.3–2.6   (cont.)

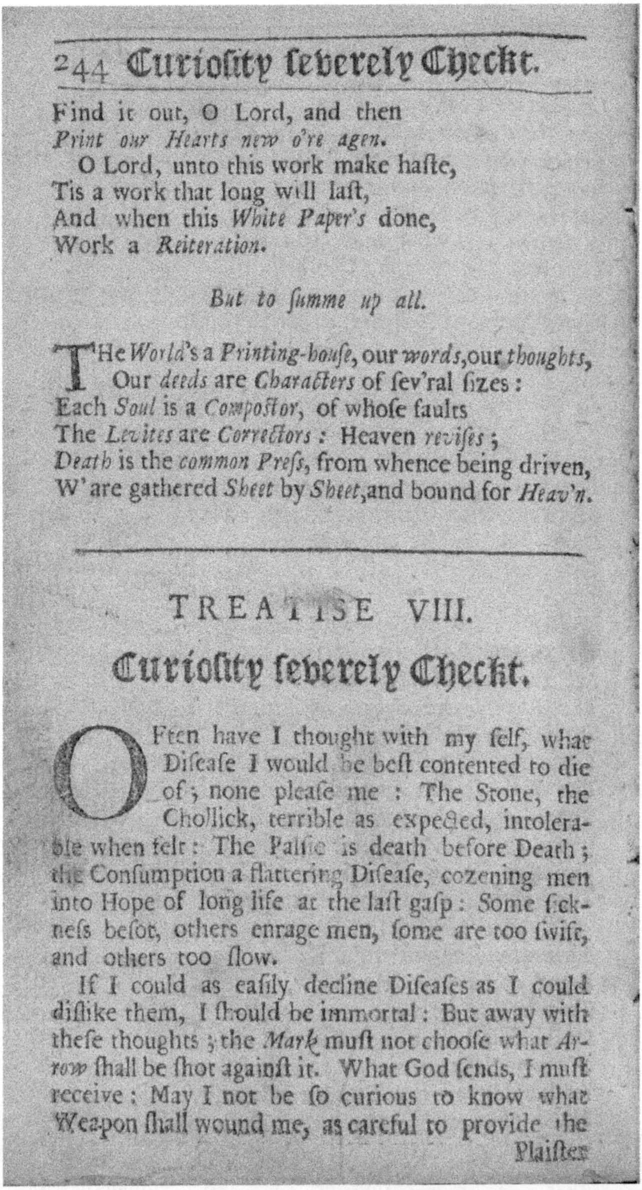

244 **Curiosity severely Checkt.**

Find it out, O Lord, and then
Print our Hearts new o're agen.
  O Lord, unto this work make haste,
Tis a work that long will last,
And when this *White Paper's* done,
Work a *Reiteration.*

But to summe up all.

THe *World's* a *Printing-house*, our *words*, our *thoughts*,
    Our *deeds* are *Characters* of sev'ral sizes :
Each *Soul* is a *Compostor*, of whose faults
The *Levites* are *Correctors* : Heaven *revises* ;
Death is the *common Press*, from whence being driven,
W' are gathered *Sheet* by *Sheet*, and bound for *Heav'n.*

TREATISE VIII.

Curiosity severely Checkt.

OFten have I thought with my self, what
Disease I would be best contented to die
of ; none please me : The Stone, the
Chollick, terrible as expected, intolera-
ble when felt : The Palsie is death before Death ;
the Consumption a flattering Disease, cozening men
into Hope of long life at the last gasp : Some sickness besot, others enrage men, some are too swift,
and others too slow.
  If I could as easily decline Diseases as I could
dislike them, I should be immortal : But away with
these thoughts ; the *Mark* must not choose what *Ar-*
row shall be shot against it. What God sends, I must
receive ; May I not be so curious to know what
Weapon shall wound me, as careful to provide the
                                             Plaistes

Figures 2.3–2.6   (cont.)

in a series of "treatises" at the end of a devotional book titled *The pilgrims guide from the cradle to his death-bed*, this poem has escaped mainstream literary critical attention. Other treatises in the volume include "Several *Sins, or the Devils Brats* describ'd in their proper Colours" and "The best *Bed-maker* in time of *Sickness*." Before his death in 1676, Dunton had worked as a rector in the village of Aston Clinton. His son John, who had taken up work as a printer, became a kind of literary executor for his father, publishing the elder John's writings in the decade following his death. *The pilgrims guide* features mostly prose with some verse interspersed, mostly in the form of shorter lyrics and epigraphs. The elder Dunton's best-seller was *the Sick-mans Passing-Bell*, which is included in *The pilgrims guide* and published in subsequent, standalone editions. If ever a book could be said to signal what we now mean by the term "print culture," *The pilgrims guide* is a good candidate: rather than the secular, self-contained, authorized, fixed "work" that earlier scholarship emphasized, this one features religious and religious-adjacent verse, printing work in the family, posthumous attribution of authorship, miscellaneous assemblage of various texts covering multiple genres, and, of course, a poem featuring an extended comparison of human spiritual life to the printing press itself.[33] Perhaps the best piece of evidence for this claim is that neither Dunton wrote the final sextet that "summe[s] up all." One Dunton or the other appropriates it word-for-word and without attribution from Francis Quarles's *Divine fancies* (1633), where it appears under the title "*On a Printing-House.*"[34]

The poem makes extensive use of the technical terms of printing technology, and in doing so, it accords with Moxon's use of the lexicon of print. Although the book's title page suggests that the elder John Dunton wrote the poem, it would not be utterly surprising if evidence emerged that his printer son John had written or cowritten it. In keeping with the goal of spiritualizing the "art of printing," the poem as it is printed italicizes printing *and* spiritual terms. Thus, the couplet "*Christ Jesus* is the *Level Stone*, / That our *Hearts* must be *Wrought upon*" offers a neat

---

[33] On the changing status of "print culture," see Harold Love, "Early Modern Print Culture: Assessing the Models," *Parergon* 20, no. 1 (2003): 45–64, https://doi.org/10.1353/pgn.2003.0071; Dane, *The Myth of Print Culture*; Alexandra Gillespie, *Print Culture and the Medieval Author: Chaucer, Lydgate, and Their Books, 1473–1557*, Oxford English Monographs (Oxford: Oxford University Press, 2006); Sabrina A. Baron, Eric N. Lindquist, and Eleanor F. Shevlin, eds., *Agent of Change: Print Culture Studies after Elizabeth L. Eisenstein*, Studies in Print Culture and the History of the Book (Amherst: University of Massachusetts Press, 2007); Solveig C. Robinson, *The Book in Society: An Introduction to Print Culture* (Peterborough, Ont.: Broadview Press, 2014).

[34] Francis Quarles, *Divine Fancies Digested into Epigrammes, Meditations, and Observations* (London, 1633), sig. Y2v.

symmetry between "*Christ Jesus*" and "*Hearts*" on the one hand and "*Level Stone*" and "*Wrought upon*" on the other. We have already encountered the printing term "wrought" in Moxon, in reference to the work of the press operator who "*Wrought off* his *Token*" of paper. "*Stone*" refers to the stone in the press coffin itself, which Moxon insists "must be exactly straight and smooth" – hence, in Dunton, "*level.*"[35] Importantly, however, this and many of the other printing terms in the poem require a familiarity with the repertoires of their usage. To grasp the image of Christ as the "*level stone*" requires not only theological knowledge concerning Jesus's righteousness but also, and more to the point, technical knowledge of how the press stone acts as a firm base against which the "*Platten*" presses moistened paper against inked type to make a printed sheet. Other figurations in the poem function similarly. Even if someone knows that a compositor assembles type sorts, for instance, the request to God to "Be Thou the *Direction*" and to "Let *Love* be the *fast-binding Cord*" requires more advanced knowledge. The "*Direction*," now often known as the catchword, Moxon defines as "the word that stands alone on the Right Hand in the bottom *Line* of a *Page*" to direct the assembly of the book, and the "*cord*" is the string used to tie up the block of type once it has been composed.

The most important and admittedly rather obvious feature of the poem is the direction of its metaphorical emphasis. Instead of primarily using the printing press to illustrate or express something about spirituality, the poem uses the tropes of spirituality to catalog the parts of the printing press. The poem's title is significant: it promises the "art of printing" as the thing being spiritualized, rather than the Christian life materialized in printing technology. To be sure, the poem still effects a comparison of the two in an extended conceit, but the emphasis constantly falls on reconciling the spiritual life to the printing press, not the other way around. Dunton seems intent on using every word his printing lexicon contains, and he reaches wherever necessary to find a spiritual analogue for a printing term. For instance, he names the "*Frisket*" (the frame that holds the paper in place in the press and keeps the margins clean) God's "*preventing Grace*" that "Keeps us from many a sullied Face." As an image of the Christian experience of grace, this is an ingenious comparison, but Dunton does not seem too concerned with how this image of grace relates to his earlier comparison of the type fount to God's "large *Alphabet* of *Graces*." Such an explanation of how one image relates to another seems unnecessary to the poem, and that is exactly my point: this is not so much

---

[35] Moxon, *Mechanick Exercises*, sig. L3r.

a systematic theology of the press as it is a systematic lexicon of the press by way of theology.

To press this point still further, consider moreover how God and the human person (one side of the comparison) change throughout the poem but the printing press (the other side) remains only itself. For a brief moment at the beginning of the poem, humans seem to be type sorts located in the "*Vpper* and the *Lower Cases*," which are said to correspond to "*Souls* and *Senses*." Then, with God as the "*COMPOSITER*," the poem figures humans as the composed type, locked with furniture into the chase. So far, so good. But then, mid-poem, we hear that "Our *Hearts* are but *White-Paper* yet" on whom God the press-man prints his "*Character*" in black ink. From that moment in the poem on, humans become the paper sheets impressed with ink and subject to anti-demonic stop-press correction. No longer type locked in the chase, we are pieces of paper that, as Quarles's final summary says, "are gathered *Sheet* by *Sheet*, and bound." To be sure, the overall purpose of Dunton's metaphor seems to be that humans are a text God prints, and that in the course of printing, that text is first to be found in type sorts, then in composed type, then in printed sheets, and finally in a bound book. Again, however, this is exactly my point: Dunton is imagining the human person by way of printing technology; ultimately, the poem presents the press's operations with far greater resolution than it does the human.

Here we must do a bit of heavy lifting to suggest how Dunton's poem is more modern than it is premodern. In many ways, the poem seems to evoke a kind of Renaissance "world picture" that was popular in mid-twentieth-century scholarship on the period.[36] Dunton lines up resemblances between the Christian life and the printing press and emphasizes how the operations of one resemble the operations of the other. Resemblance, the reader will remember, is also Foucault's key term for describing the Renaissance episteme or knowledge system. It therefore seems as though Dunton looks backward to the Renaissance rather than forward to modernity. Considering what we have just seen about how the humanity/press analogy plays out, however, "resemblance" does not seem like quite the right term, because "resemblance" is not what Dunton portrays. Rather, the technical lexicon of the printing press overbears the press's resemblance to human life, and once again, we have a table of knowledge. The bookish words are just on the verge of ceasing to intersect with what they are supposed to represent; according

---

[36] Two well-known treatments of the "world picture" are E. M. W. Tillyard, *The Elizabethan World Picture* (London: Chatto & Windus, 1943); C. S. Lewis, *A Preface to Paradise Lost* (New York: Oxford University Press, 1961).

to most accounts, this means modernity is imminent. To put the claim more pragmatically, as we now transition to a discussion of words this book *does* attend to, Dunton uses the lexicon of print to build a conceit that ultimately concerns the lexicon and technological apparatus of print. The other writers cited in this study, by contrast, use bookish words to build conceits that concern something other than themselves.

What We Talk about When We Talk about Bookishness

So far, this chapter has sketched what the language of books in the English Renaissance was not: it was not tied exclusively to print technology, not connected with any particular scientific program, and not elaborately systematic. To fill in the outline, we must look earlier and more broadly than the lexicon of the press. What terms did readers and writers actually use to think about – and think with – books? The rest of *How the World Became a Book* offers an answer, and this section appeals to the term "bookish" to bridge backward from Moxon and Dunton to the rich premodern discourse of the book. The word "bookish" makes for a prime example of the rhetorical and conceptual flexibility of this discourse.

If the first two sections of this chapter set out historical parameters, the final two sections set out methodological ones. While the present section attempts to find patterns amid a consistent semantic range of a particular term ("bookish"), the next one shows how another term ("set forth") acquired a new meaning, which in turn loads subsequent instances. In this first case, narrowing our focus to a single term broadens the scope of inquiry to reveal not only how the widespread language of the book is not about print technology *per se*, but also how the language of books that worked its way through sixteenth- and seventeenth-century English culture was far more capacious, flexible, and frankly interesting than Dunton's and Moxon's lexicon. A philological study of "bookish" sketches a broad cultural history of bookishness itself in premodern England.

Despite their apparent similarities, the word "bookish" and the phrase "like a book," which we explored in Chapter 1, have very different uses for premodern English writers. By its very syntax, the simile forges an explicit comparison, but "bookish" presents something like identity. *OED* tells us that the suffix "-ish" modifies things with the sense "of the nature of, tending to," so that "freakish" means "of the nature of or tending to a freak."[37] What

---

[37] *OED* s.v. "-ish," 2.

the *OED* presents as a synonymous pair – "nature of" and "tending to" – in fact reveal the power of "-ish." As any number of words formed by "-ish" can tell us, the suffix implies a spectrum of possibility from a list of shared qualities to an assertion of identity. "Clownish" suggests at once that someone *has the qualities of* a clown and that they *are or are becoming* a clown. The stakes are still higher for terms like "whorish" or "mannish" or "goatish," for the suggestion of identity does greater harm. No one who has been called "whorish" dismisses the term as a mere simile. "Bookish" differs further still, because the book is an object, so calling someone "bookish" is not to say that they are a book but have the nature of books. When Thomas Drant translates Horace as calling philosophers a "bookish broode," for instance, he does so because he says they "teache [...] by sleighte" or cunning rather than "skille."[38] Drant's use of "bookish," which does not have an equivalent in Horace's Latin, underlines the studied deceit of philosophers: "bookish" suggests not that they are like books, nor that they are books, but that they have acquired an identity by association with books. They are identified *with* books without being identified *as* books. As with "freakish" and other such words, this quality gives "bookish" considerable rhetorical power.

At stake in the use of "bookish" is the relationship of books to the rest of the world. Every instance of the term makes an implicit claim about whether, how, and why books matter. This is apparent in Drant's use of the term to disparage philosophers on the grounds that they – philosophers, and by extension the books they read – teach subtlety at the expense of skill. In one of his prose fiction narratives, John Lyly asserts that "those that giue themselues to be bookish are oftentimes so blockish that they forget thrist [sic]" (i.e., they forget to drink water).[39] Later in the same text, Lyly claims it is "as great a shame to be valiant and courtly without learning, as to be studious and bookish without valure" (i.e., valor).[40] Lyly, who himself has no business insulting people for loving books, later has a character in *Campaspe* (Melippus) say "bookish men are so blockish, & so great clearkes such simple courtiers" that he refuses to introduce scholars to the king.[41] For better and worse, each of these begins with the premise that identification with books can take one away from what we might call worldly concerns: the needs of the body, the demands of gender, or the

---

[38] Horace, *A Medicinable Morall, That Is, the Two Bookes of Horace His Satyres* (London, 1566), sig. B5v. STC 13805.

[39] John Lyly, *Euphues and His England* (London, 1580), sig. Ciiiv. STC 17070.

[40] Lyly, sig. Ciiiir. STC 17070.

[41] John Lyly, *A Moste Excellent Comedie of Alexander, Campaspe, and Diogenes* (London, 1584), sig. A4r. STC 17047.5.

necessities of courtliness. Edwin Sandys uses the term to create a very different distinction when, in a preface to a book of sermons, he opposes the "the bookish humor of co[m]mon writers, & idle discoursers" with "the writing of necessarie and needefull workes."[42] Lyly's "bookish" admits a possible tension between world and book, while Sandys's sets one kind of writer against another. Both use the same term to do it.

In contrast to the print-centered language of Moxon and Dunton, "bookish" remains agnostic about the type of book in question. Manuscript or print matters little when books operate at the level of personality. In his essay "Of Censuring," for instance, William Cornwallis admits, "I am determined to speake of bookes next, to whom if you wold not say I were too bookish, I shuld giue the first place of all thinges here."[43] Later, he boasts that his "occupation has beene vehemently bookish" to make the point that "Writing is the draught of reading, and by this I have disburthened my head, and taken account of my profiting."[44] In both cases, "bookish" conveys the way books have made Cornwallis a certain kind of person. For him, the acquisition of a state in which it is possible to identify him with books – a state we might redundantly label "bookishness" – creates the precondition for the "profiting" of writerly production. It is crucial to note that Cornwallis does not use "bookish" as a negative signifier, unlike many of the writers we will meet shortly. Likewise, William Vaughan does not oppose learning when he describes "young men" who, "hauing gotten but a taste of learning, become so headie with a fond fantasie of that little which they haue, that they tire and lie downe in the midst of their bookish pride."[45] These young men suffer from not too great an identification with books, but too little. The actual, physical books with which a person is identified matter less than the fact of their identification. Vaughan's young men may have read few books at all to acquire their "bookish pride." Likewise, George Langford tells of one Chrisippus, who was "so Bookish, that hee had perished with hunger, had not his Mayd Melissa thrust meat into his mouth."[46]

As it often does today, "bookish" served as a common insult in premodern England, suggesting that an overcommitment to books makes one

---

[42] Edwin Sandys, *Sermons Made by the Most Reuerende Father in God, Edwin, Archbishop of Yorke, Primate of England and Metropolitane* (London, 1585), sig. ¶2r. STC 21713.

[43] William Cornwallis Sir, *Essayes* (London, 1600), sig. H2v. STC 5775.

[44] Cornwallis, sig. N7v. STC 5775.

[45] William Vaughan, *The Golden-Groue Moralized* (London, 1600), sig. Y4r. STC 24610.

[46] George Langford, *Search the Scriptures. Or, An Enquirie after Veritie* (London, 1623), sig. Gv. STC 15194.

otherwise inadequate. The range of these insults, as instructive as they are impressive, shows the ease with which writers saw the world by relation to books. Richard Harvey complains about corrupt Christians who "make the bookish vnwary Minister a cloake for their conueyances, and a shadowe for their skarres."[47] These companions commit harm while they minister studies. Elsewhere, Harvey declares someone "very bookishly and literally wise, not reasonably and discoursiuely," creating a distinction between two types of wisdom.[48] Robert Greene imagines a soldier accusing another of being "farre more bookish than wise, especially in martiall affaires." In "gazing at a starre" (and apparently not a book!), the person "stumble[s] at a stone."[49] John Harrington reports that "faulconers and hunters" would say that "bookish fellowes" such as Philip Sidney "could iudge of no sports, but within the verge of the faire fields of Helicon, Pindus, and Pernasus" (i.e., Grecian mountains associated with the muses).[50] Thomas Heywood refers to a "bookish Priest," Roger Fenton to "bookish Clerks," and Edward Hoby to "bookish Disputants" whose "arguing hath made vs wait so long for our dinner."[51] George Wither's couplet – "Although a little learning be not bad, / Those that are bookish are the soonest mad" – would offer the perfect summary of the situation, if Thomas Cooper had not done it more succinctly: "we must liue, and therefore we cannot be bookish."[52]

This rhetorical opposition between bookishness and active, productive living gave writers a way to critique bad leaders or soldiers and compliment good ones. John Speed writes how the future King Henry II, "grown now from a Child, thought it best a while to leaue Mercury, (for it is said hee was Bookish) and to follow Mars," the Roman god of war.[53] Although "hee" probably refers to Mercury, it could also refer to the youthful Henry; both are associated with bookishness. An English translation of Livy describes how many people in Syracuse spread the rumor that Scipio "was over

---

[47] Richard Harvey, *A Theologicall Discourse of the Lamb of God and His Enemies* (London, 1590), sig. xr. STC 12915.

[48] Richard Harvey, *Philadelphus, or a Defence of Brutes, and the Brutans History* (London, 1593), sig. B2r. STC 12913.

[49] Robert Greene, *Greenes Farewell to Folly* (London, 1591), sig. Cv. STC 12241.

[50] John Harington, *A Nevv Discourse of a Stale Subiect, Called the Metamorphosis of Aiax* (London, 1596), sig. vr. STC 12779.5.

[51] Thomas Heywood, *Troia Britanica: Or, Great Britaines Troy* (London, 1609), sig. T3v; Roger Fenton, *A Treatise of Vsurie Diuided into Three Bookes* (London, 1611), sig. Q4r; Edward Hoby, *A Curry-Combe for a Coxe-Combe* (London, 1615), sig. S4r. STC 13366; STC 10806; STC 13540.

[52] George Wither, *Abuses Stript, and Whipt. Or Satirical Essayes* (London, 1613), sig. P3r; Thomas Cooper, *The Conuerts First Loue Discerned Iustified, Left and Recouered* (London, 1610), sig. A2v. STC 25892; STC 5697.5.

[53] John Speed, *The History of Great Britaine* (London, 1611), sig. Eeeeer. STC 23045.

bookish, and set his mind too much upon reading."[54] Another Roman history describes Julian as acting like a "bookish smattering Grecian," while a book about Germany claims that its monarch is a "Hermit [...] too bookish to raigne long."[55] A history of England tells of those who would not "permit a Bookish vnexperienced souldior to read vnto them a Lecture of warlike proceedings," and a published travel journal describes how the Earl of Essex alleged "that the Lord Mountioy had small experience in martiall affaires [...], adding that he was too bookish [...] to imbrace so great a businesse."[56] More familiarly, Shakespeare's Richard Plantagenet declares he will "make him yeeld the Crowne, / Whose bookish Rule, hath pull'd faire England downe."[57] And early in *Othello*, Iago criticizes Cassio's promotion to Lieutenant by claiming "Bookish Theoricke" makes up Cassio's military knowledge: "Meere pratle (without practise)."[58] In a bitter irony, later in the play Iago claims that Othello's "vnbookish ielousie must conserue / Poore Cassio's smiles, gestures, and light beauiours / Quite in the wrong."[59] In Iago's mind (and perhaps in early modern English culture broadly), you're loathed if you're bookish and loathed if you're not.

Over the course of the sixteenth and especially seventeenth centuries, "bookish" acquired a new and rich range of uses. One commonly finds things and qualities labeled with the term that previously described people. For instance, John King anticipated later complaints of information overload when he opined that "The number of bookes written in these daies without number, I say not more then the worlde can holde, (for it even emptieth it selfe of reason and moderation to giue place to this bookish folly, and serveth vnder the vanitie thereof) but more than well vse."[60] Thomas Jackson agrees, quoting a "wise Preacher" who asserted that "There is none end of making of bookes, and much reading is a wearines of the flesh [...,] which is most true in this bookish age, wherein as one saith, It would require a mans whole life, but to read ouer the titles or

---

[54] Livy, *The Romane Historie* (London, 1600), sig. Qqiiv. STC 16613.

[55] Ammianus Marcellinus, *The Roman Historie Containing Such Acts and Occurrents as Passed under Constantius, Iulianus, Iovianus, Valentinianus, and Valens, Emperours* (London, 1609), sig. Niiir; Wentworth Smith, *The Hector of Germany. Or The Palsgraue, Prime Elector A New Play, an Honourable History* (London, 1615), sig. A4r. STC 17311; STC 22871.

[56] William Martyn, *The Historie, and Liues, of the Kings of England from VVilliam the Conqueror, Vnto the End of the Raigne of King Henrie the Eight* (London, 1615), sig. Y4r; Fynes Moryson, *An Itinerary* (London, 1617), Ff3r. STC 17527; STC 18205.

[57] William Shakespeare, *Mr. William Shakespeares Comedies, Histories, & Tragedies* (London, 1623), sig. M3v. STC 22273.

[58] Shakespeare, Ff3v. STC 22273.

[59] Shakespeare, vvr. STC 22273.

[60] John King, *Lectures Vpon Ionas Deliuered at Yorke* (Oxford, 1599), sig. *3r. STC 14977.

inscriptions."[61] Too many books evidently transforms the whole "age," at least according to Jackson – and me.

Even as the semantic range of "bookish" broadened, so did writers grow keen to use the term in situations of direct address and exhortation. In *The compleat gentleman*, Henry Peacham warns his reader:

> affect not as some doe, that bookish Ambition, to be stored with bookes and haue well furnished Libraries, yet keepe their heads emptie of knowledge: to desire to haue many bookes, and neuer to vse them, is like a childe that will haue a candle burning by him, all while he is sleeping.[62]

For Peacham, the problem is not books but unread books; people who own but do not read them are insufficiently bookish. John Reading encourages his readers to have "Hope in God [...] wher in the most illiterate Christian exceleth the most bookish Philosopher."[63] William Vaughan tells Bible readers to be humble, because "bookish learning, selfe-conceit, and pampering cheere haue beene the chiefe obstacles, that carnall Courtiers, presumptuous Papists, and pompous people could neuer attaine to the right knowledge of the Scriptures, nor arriue aright at the hauen of truth."[64] In *The elder brother*, John Fletcher's Brisac exhorts his studious son Charles that:

> To manage worldly businesse, you must part with
> This bookish contemplation, and prepare
> Your selfe for action; to thrive in this age,
> Is held the palme of learning; you must study
> To know what part of my land's good for th' plough,
> And what for pasture, how to buy and sell
> To the best advantage, how to cure my Oxen
> When they're oregrowne with labour.[65]

Anticipating modern fathers encouraging their children to major in "worldly businesse" in college, Brisac articulates his conviction that land management is the purpose of learning. Richard Younge encourages his readers by arguing that "they that give themselves to be so bookish, are often times so blockish, that they forget God who made them."[66] Similarly, John Dury assures his readers that God will "bring those that

---

[61] Thomas Jackson, *Dauids Pastorall Poeme: Or Sheepeheards Song* (London, 1603), sig. ¶4v. STC 14299.

[62] Henry Peacham, *The Compleat Gentleman* (London, 1622), sig. Iv. STC 19502.

[63] John Reading, *Dauids Soliloquie Containing Many Comforts for Afflicted Mindes* (London, 1627). STC 20788.

[64] William Vaughan, *The Arraignment of Slander Periury Blasphemy, and Other Malicious Sinnes* (London, 1630), sig. Lr. STC 24623.

[65] John Fletcher, *The Elder Brother a Comedie* (London, 1637), sig. Cr. STC 11066.

[66] Richard Younge, *Sinne Stigmatizd: Or, The Art to Know Savingly, Believe Rightly, Live Religiously* (London, 1639), sig. N5r. STC 26112.

seeke wisdome in the simplicity of the word, to understand the depths of Gods counsell which are hid from the great Rabbies of the world, and men rather addicted to bookish learning (to tell us what this or that Author saith) then to search after the wisedome & demonstration of the spirit of & power."[67] These writers do not have to work too hard to convert "bookish" from offense into advice. The term comes preloaded with an opposition between utility and study, profit and idleness, action and contemplation, "true" knowledge and useless knowledge. However facile these binaries, they remain rhetorically potent even in our own time.

Despite these and many more instances of "bookish" as a negative signifier, however, many premodern writers used the term in a positive sense. Indeed, reading across hundreds of instances of the term offers a salutary reminder that many people thought bookishness worthwhile. Richard Mulcaster refers to the Latin language as the one "commonlie best known to our bookish peple," while others use the term as a synonym for "literate."[68] Intriguingly, most writers appeal to the same basic identification of persons with books as those who hurl the term to offend. Poets and poetry therefore fare well: George Puttenham writes of a poet who is an "honest ciuill Courtier somewhat bookish."[69] Joshua Sylvester translates the French poet Du Bartas referring to the muses as "bookish maids."[70] And Nathaniel Baxter refers to pastoral poets as "bookish shepheards."[71]

Other writers rallied around bookish learning more generally, often winking at the conventional negative use of "bookish" explored above. The preacher Arthur Dent claims he has no time to judge his own sermons, so he decides to "Let them that are bookish, and heare so many Sermons, iudge of such matters."[72] Thomas Westerne states that Socrates was "Bookish [...] because as hee loued learning, and therefore liued learning, so he would dye learning."[73] Thomas Taylor tells fathers not to dislike their sons' studiousness: "how is the Kingdome of God in the family,

[67] John Dury, *A Motion Tending to the Publick Good of This Age and of Posteritie* (London, 1642), sig. D3v. Wing D2874.

[68] Richard Mulcaster, *The First Part of the Elementarie* (London, 1582), sig. Xr. STC 18250. For "bookish" as "literate," see Thomas Deloney, *Thomas of Reading. Or, The Sixe Worthy Yeomen of the West* (London, 1612), sig. B4v. STC 6569: "I pray you [...], seing you are bookish, will you do so much as to read a loue letter that is sent me."

[69] George Puttenham, *The Arte of English Poesie* (London, 1589), sig. Dv. STC 20519.5.

[70] Guillaume Du Bartas, *The First Day of the Worldes Creation* (London, 1595), sig. Ev. STC 21658.

[71] Nathaniel Baxter, *Sir Philip Sydneys Ouránia That Is, Endimions Song and Tragedie* (London, 1606), sig. D2r. STC 1598.

[72] Arthur Dent, *The Plaine Mans Path-Way to Heauen Wherein Euery Man May Clearely See, Whether He Shall Be Saued or Damned* (London, 1606), sig. S7r. STC 6629.

[73] Thomas Westerne, *The Flaming Bush. Or, An Embleme of the True Church* (London, 1624), sig. F6v. STC 25284.

when the husband checketh his wife, because shee is the Spouse of Christ;
the father frowneth on his sonne, because hee is bookish, and diligent in
reading, and good exercises[?]"[74] More passionately and explicitly, Joseph
Hall defends bookishness against its detractors. Some people, he argues,

> scoffe at the foolishnesse of preaching, scorne the forward bookishnesse of
> others, fearing nothing but a surfet of Manna, and hating to know more,
> than their neighbours, than their fore-fathers; and thus are led on muffled
> vp in an vnfelt ignorance, to their graue, yeah, (without the mercy of God)
> to their hell.[75]

Willful ignorance carries high spiritual stakes. Hall also criticizes the Roman
church for its alleged opposition to learning: "neither haue the Doctors of
the Romish Church (vpon whom the implicite faith of the Laitie is sus-
pended) found it any ill policie, to cherish this dislike of bookishnesse in the
great: for whiles the candle is out, it is safe for them to play their tricks in
the darke[.]"[76] Along the same lines, Edwin Sandys argues that "by reason of
this bookish age, [the leaders of the Roman church] haue not that helpe of
ignorance which in times past they had: they cast about gently to soake and
settle them in mens perswasions and consciences another way."[77]

Sandys's phrase, "bookish age," deserves a bit more attention, not least
because he seems to be thinking of the scale at which the press produces
books. Like many of the Protestants we have met and will meet in this book,
he sees printing as an instrument for reforming the church. More broadly,
though, Sandys carries bookishness beyond the description of a particular
personality and situates it in a larger social matrix. He thinks about what is
at stake in a world increasingly identified with books. Nor is Sandys alone:
among plenty of others, Robert Harris laments, "tis a thousand pities, that
in this bookish age, this Book of Conscience is least studied."[78] Although he
draws a different conclusion than Sandys, for whom bookishness requires
the Roman church to find other ways to persuade people, Harris too is
coming to terms with an age that identifies with its books. Decades earlier,
in his first educational treatise, Richard Mulcaster appeals to bookishness
as both the goal and liability of schooling. In what may seem a profound
irony for a writer committed to teaching, Mulcaster spends a whole chapter

[74] Thomas Taylor, *Christs Victorie over the Dragon* (London, 1633), sig. Kk6r. STC 23823.
[75] Joseph Hall, *The Vvorks of Ioseph Hall Doctor in Diuinitie, and Deane of Worcester* (London, 1625),
sig. Vv6r. STC 12635b.
[76] Hall, sig. Mmm3r. STC 12635b.
[77] Edwin Sandys, *Europæ Speculum. Or, A Vievv or Survey of the State of Religion in the Vvesterne Parts
of the World* (The Hague, 1629), sig. Diiv. STC 21718.
[78] Robert Harris, *Tvvo Sermons: The One Preached before the Iudges of Assize at Oxford. The Other to the
Vniuersitie* (London, 1628), sig. B2v. STC 12853.

addressing "The meanes to restraine the ouerflowing multitude of scholers." Because teaching every child to become a scholar would bankrupt many trades – "defeating other trades of their necessarie travellours" – Mulcaster advocates for everyone to be taught to read and write, but for only a few to study beyond that. More scholars would cause "to great a spring of bookish people" for the common good.[79] He advises parents to "surrender their interest to the generall consideration of their common countrie, and thinke that it is not best to haue their children bookish, notwithstanding their owne desire, be it neuer so earnestly bent." In advising parents to balance their desires for their children with the needs of the commonwealth, Mulcaster nods at the same need to situate the bookishness of the age that Sandys and Harris respond to. These writers appeal to "bookish" not to insult or praise but to come to terms with the inevitability and apparent ubiquity of books in their culture.

Two poems conclude our exploration of "bookish." Together, they emblematize premodern England's increasingly reflexive awareness of its own relationship with books. In Samuel Rowlands's 1608 epigram, identification with books collides hard with marriage (see Figures 2.7 and 2.8).[80] More sexist than funny, the joke is that new almanacs appear yearly, and thus the scholar would get a new wife every year. But lurking around Rowlands's unsavory humor is a sense that the poem arises from and addresses itself to a culture already identified with "bookish busines." Only in such a culture does this epigram have purchase. Indeed, the proposed resolution to the poem's basic premise – a scholar too committed to his books for his marriage's good – is that the wife proposes identifying not *with* but *as* a book, the only thing the poem attributes with agency ("papers cause"). Likewise, in the second poem, John Gadbury's 1662 prefatory poem to John Heydon, bookishness collides with the limitations of the body:

> *MOst* studious friend! *thy constant* Bookish cares,
> *Will on thy* head *full soon pull* silver hairs:
> *They'l keep thee waking, while the world's at rest,*
> *And bring thy* smoother face *unto the test*
> *Of* Age and Wrinkles; *make thy* Spring-like brow,
> *To feel the force of [Kronos's] crooked Plough*
> *Before thy time*[.][81]

---

[79] Richard Mulcaster, *Positions Vvherin Those Primitiue Circumstances Be Examined, Which Are Necessarie for the Training vp of Children, Either for Skill in Their Booke, or Health in Their Bodie* (London, 1581), sig. Siiir. STC 18253.

[80] Samuel Rowlands, *Humors Looking Glasse* (London, 1608), sig. Dr-v. STC 21386.

[81] John Heydon, *The Harmony of the World Being a Discourse Wherein the Phænomena of Nature Are Consonantly Salved and Adapted to Inferiour Intellects* (London, 1662), sig. d4r. Wing H1668.

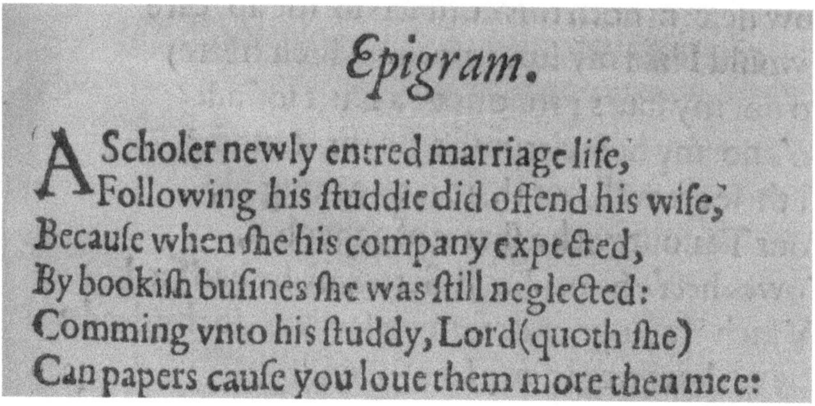

Epigram.

A Scholer newly entred marriage life,
Following his ſtuddie did offend his wife,
Becauſe when ſhe his company expeɛted,
By bookiſh buſines ſhe was ſtill negleɛted:
Comming vnto his ſtuddy, Lord(quoth ſhe)
Can papers cauſe you loue them more then mee?

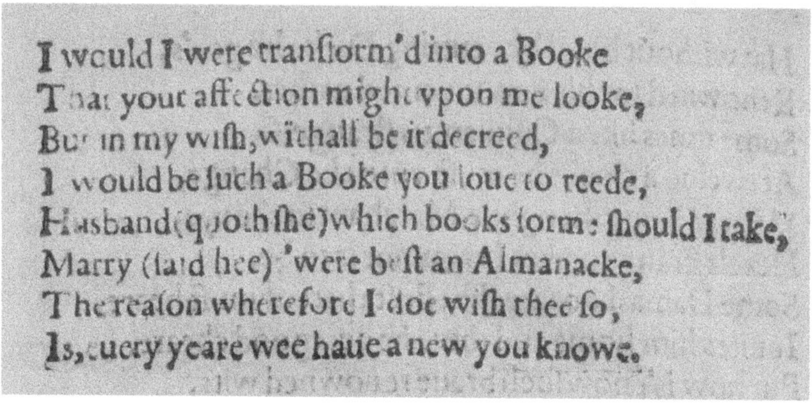

I would I were tranſtorm'd into a Booke
That your affeɛtion might vpon me looke,
But in my wiſh, withall be it decreed,
I would be ſuch a Booke you loue to reede,
Husband(quoth ſhe)which books form: ſhould I take,
Marry (ſaid hee) 'were beſt an Almanacke,
The reaſon wherefore I doe wiſh thee ſo,
Is, euery yeare wee haue a new you knowe.

Figures 2.7 and 2.8   Detail of Samuel Rowlands, *Humors Looking Glasse* (London, 1608),
sigs. Dr-v, RB 31783, The Huntington Library, San Marino, California.

Heydon's "cares," here figured by association with books and the labor they
require, will age his body prematurely. Gadbury goes on to ask if it is the
"Common Good *that makes thee labour thus*," echoing Mulcaster's attempt
to balance commitment to books with the needs of the commonwealth.

Like many of the instances of the term I have explored here, it might
be tempting to regard these as quotidian uses of a word that, by the seventeenth century, was familiar. Unlike words such as "blood" or "language,"
which Roland Greene describes as having "a disciplinary purchase" in the
Renaissance, the word "bookish" draws a sketch or tells a story of disciplin-
arity itself. Bookishness is the only thing that makes the intellectual discourses of the Renaissance meaningful and distinct. Instead of functioning

as a "powerful carrier [...] of often ambiguous or contradictory mean-ings," as Greene writes of certain key words, the power of "bookish" is its odd consistency.[82] Writers who wield it, weaponlike, to offend and writers who use it to articulate their scholarly "cares" and "busines" appeal to the same relationship with books.

"Set Forth" for All to See

The semantic range – or rather, the lack of range – of "bookish" becomes discernible by gathering as many examples as possible. There is no clear vector in the uses of "bookish" from one meaning to another, so the story we can tell with it requires a kind of scatter-plot method, by which we seek and interpret patterns in a messy cluster of examples. I am therefore not necessarily tracking semantic change, as a historical linguist might, nor am I attempting to make an argument about the representational sig-nificance of a term, as for example William Empson did with "honest" in Shakespeare's *Othello*.[83] I am instead considering what writers used the word "bookish" to do, and what that rhetorical work tells us – a kind of philological regression.

Other cases, however, require a different approach. "Bookish" endured no major changes across the sixteenth and seventeenth centuries, but "set forth" did. The collective uses of this surprisingly common phrase invite us to identify the shifting usage of the term, interpret that shift, and then look closely at particularly resonant uses of "set forth" in light of the shift. Instead of a scatter plot, we need a line graph. In this final section of the chapter, I model another method for reading across many examples to argue that in the sixteenth century, "set forth" acquired a durable asso-ciation with publication in print. The phrase's frequent appearance on printed title pages lodged its general meaning of "to make public" securely in the print medium. Then, having demonstrated how this association came to exist, I turn to four writers' use of "set forth" to show how the term subsequently carried its association with printing into the late sixteenth and seventeenth centuries. Just as "bookish" helped track the increasing

---

[82] Roland Greene, *Five Words: Critical Semantics in the Age of Shakespeare and Cervantes* (Chicago: University of Chicago Press, 2013), 6–7.

[83] On semantic change, see for instance Elizabeth Closs Traugott and Richard B. Dasher, *Regularity in Semantic Change*, Cambridge Studies in Linguistics 96 (Cambridge: Cambridge University Press, 2002); Andreas H. Jucker and Irma Taavitsainen, eds., *Historical Pragmatics*, Handbooks of Pragmatics, v. 8 (Berlin: De Gruyter Mouton, 2010). On Empson, see William Empson, *The Structure of Complex Words* (London: Chatto & Windus, 1951).

bookishness of the English cultural imagination, "set forth" reveals the imaginative gravitational pull of printing.

The popularity of "set forth" among premodern English writers arose from its simplicity and utility. The *OED* tells us the phrase began with the sense of "to thrust forth" or "to send forward" as on a journey.[84] In *1 Henry 4*, Shakespeare uses the phrase in this way at least seven times. Poins declares, "we wil set forth before or after them, and appoint them a place of meeting," and Hotspur tells his wife, "To day will I set forth, to morrow you, / Will this content you Kate?"[85] The phrase quickly came to refer to various ways of *making public*, however. I italicize this phrase because it does not appear in the *OED*, but it underlies most definitions:

- "to arrange or dispose in a certain manner; to lay out" (1c)
- "to send out [...] for service; hence, to equip, to fit out [...]" (2a)
- "to promulgate, publish, issue" (4)
- "to publish (a literary work)" (5)
- "to express in words, give an account of, present a statement of [...]; to declare, expound, relate, narrate, state, describe" (6a)
- "to adorn, decorate" (7)
- "to further the progress or advancement of; to promote, advance" (8)
- "to praise, commend" (9)
- "to exhibit, display, show forth" (10)

These are not all of the *OED*'s definitions, but they suffice to show how meanings of "set forth" as this dictionary distinguishes them carry a sense of making public. Indeed, the definitions that do not feature some obvious connection with publicization feature citations that do. Definition 8, for instance, cites Thomas More's 1528 claim about a heretic: "to confesse … what he had done for the setting forth of that secte." More uses "set forth" to mean "advance," but the means of that advancement is increased public prominence. To promote a heresy is to call it to the attention of a widening audience.

Although "set forth" occurred across the range of genres, formats, and media in sixteenth-century England, it evidently found a warm welcome in what we might call the discourse around Protestantism. More's line about heresy above comes from a discussion of the Lutheran reforms,

---

[84] *OED*, s.v. "set, v.1" and "to set forth, 1a and 1b."
[85] William Shakespeare, *The History of Henrie the Fourth* (London, 1598), sigs. Biv and D2r. STC 22280.

for instance, and he used the phrase elsewhere too: in his book refuting William Tyndale's heresies, More argues that Tyndale's translation of the Bible exceeds the "infydelyte" of Muslims, because it has "purposely mysse translate[d] Chrystes holy gospel, to sette forth heresyes."[86] Elsewhere, More defends King Henry VIII's orthodoxy by claiming he "nothynge more detesteth then these pestilent bokes that Tyndale and suche other sende in to the realme, to sette forth theyr abominable heresyes wythall."[87] It seems fitting that in the very book More names, an English translation of the New Testament, Tyndale himself uses "set forth." In the story of Jesus turning water to wine, for instance, the master of the feast says to Jesus, "All men at the beginnynge / set forth good wyne / and when men be dronke / then that which is worse."[88] Here, the phrase means to "lay out" but carries a sense of publication or making public: the wine is available for all to drink. For Miles Coverdale, who partly based his Bible translation on Tyndale's, "set forth" acts as a keyword for the crucial activity of vernacular translation itself. In the preface epistle to Henry VIII, Coverdale offers a Protestant spin on Henry's title "Defender of the Faith" (given by the Pope) by arguing that Henry "in very dede shulde defende the Fayth, Yee [i.e., yea] euen the true fayth of Christ, no dreames, no fables, no heresie, no papisticall inuencions, but the vncorrupte fayth of Gods most holy worde, which to set forth [...] your hyghnes [...] applyeth all his studye and endeuoure."[89] The strategic ambiguity of "set forth" to mean both "translate" and "publish" helps Coverdale link his English Bible project directly with Henry's piety. The link becomes more explicit in Coverdale's preface to the reader, in which he explains why he "toke the more vpon me to set forth this speciall translacyon, not as a checker, not as a reprouer, or despyser of other mens translacyons" but because (to paraphrase Coverdale's argument) the more translations made public, the better the vernacular Bible can be.[90] Crucially, "set forth" gave More, Tyndale, and Coverdale – along with English translators of reformers such as Martin Luther, Philip Melanchthon, and John Calvin – an operator with which to describe the interrelated acts of translation, expression, and

---

[86] Thomas More, *The Co[n]Futacyon of Tyndales Answere Made by Syr Thomas More Knyght Lorde Chau[n]Cellour of Englonde* (London, 1532), sig. Aaiiv. STC 18079.

[87] More, sig. Ddiir. STC 18079.

[88] *The Newe Testament Dylygently Corrected and Compared with the Greke* (Antwerp, 1534), sig. Qiiiv. STC 2826.

[89] *Biblia the Byble, That Is, the Holy Scrypture of the Olde and New Testament, Faithfully Translated in to Englyshe* (London, 1535), sig. +iir. STC 2063.3.

[90] Ibid., sig. +v. STC 2063.3. Coverdale makes abundant use of "set forth" in his translation.

transmission.[91] Similarly, the *Book of Common Prayer* uses the phrase in a summary claim justifying its own existence as a liturgical guide for the whole English church: the ceremonies retained in the book "be neyther darke nor dumme ceremonies, but are so set forth that euery man may vnderstande what they dooe meane, and to what vse they do serue."[92] In the crucible of English Protestantism, much depended on the "public" of publication, those to whom writings are set forth.

In this political context, a new trend emerged over the course of the period. All sorts of title pages began to feature "set forth" to refer to the action of bringing into existence not just a text or a book but a *printed book*. This regular appearance on title pages loaded the phrase with an association with printing that it would never shake off.[93] The phrase helps name a particular public as the audience of a sermon by the popular preacher Arthur Dent: *the plaine mans path-way to heauen wherein euery man may clearely see, whether he shall be saued or damned: set forth dialogue-wise, for the better vnderstanding of the simple.*[94] Similarly, Richard Bernard's *A double catechisme one more large, following the order of the common authorized catechisme, and an exposition thereof: now this second time published: the other shorter for the weaker sort: both set forth for the benefit of Christian friends and wel-willers* bridges its two distinct audiences into a single group of "friends."[95] The title page of a 1607 edition of Hugh Latimer's sermons describes them as *newly imprinted with others not heeretofore set forth in print*, one of many instances linking the term explicitly with printing.[96] Editions of William Lily's much-reprinted Latin textbook, *A short introduction of grammar, generally to be vsed: compiled and set forth for the bringing vp of all those that intend to attaine the knowledge of the Latine tongue*, distinguish writing (*"compiled"*) from print publication (*"set forth"*) to

[91] See, for instance, many uses in Martin Luther, *The Last Wil and Last Confession of Martyn Luthers Faith* (Wesel, 1543); Anonymous, *The Confessyon of the Fayth of the Germaynes Exhibited to the Moste Victorious Emperour Charles the. v* (London, 1536); Jean Calvin, *An Abridgement of the Institution of Christian Religion Written by M. Ihon Caluin* (London, 1585). STC 16984, STC 908, and STC 4429.

[92] Anonymous, *The Booke of the Common Prayer and Administracion of the Sacramentes, and Other Rites and Ceremonies of the Churche: After the vse of the Churche of England* (London, 1549), sig. U9r. STC 16270a.

[93] Although I will not catalog all instances here, the ProQuest EEBO search interface allows search for phrases that appear only on title pages.

[94] Dent, *The Plaine Mans Path-Way to Heauen Wherein Euery Man May Clearely See, Whether He Shall Be Saued or Damned*. STC 6628.5.

[95] Richard Bernard, *A Double Catechisme One More Large, Following the Order of the Common Authorized Catechisme, and an Exposition Thereof* (Cambridge, 1607). STC 1936.

[96] Hugh Latimer, *Fruitfull Sermons Preached by the Right Reuerend Father, and Constant Martyr of Iesus Christ, M. Hugh Latimer* (London, 1607). STC 15282.

express the book's purpose and public.[97] The title page of King James's *apologie for the oath of allegiance* explains that it was *first set forth without a name* but is now attributed to the king.[98]

These examples illustrate the larger use of "set forth" to describe the print publication of books. Other title pages feature the phrase as a way of connecting the printed book with its larger communicative purpose. In Richard Kilby's book *The burthen of a loaden conscience: or the miserie of sinne set forth by the confession of a miserable sinner*, it is not the book that has been "set forth" but the "miserie of sinne."[99] Note the grammar, however: it is the confession – the expression and affirmation of something in writing and here in printed text – that does the setting forth. The medium, not just the misery, is the message. In Joseph Hall's sermon, *Pharisaisme and Christianitie compared and set forth in a sermon at Paules Crosse, May 1. 1608*, "set forth" refers at once to the oral performance of the sermon at a specific place and time and to the printed form in which that performance is memorialized. A translation of Luther's infamous commentary on the book of Galatians describes how the book was *first collected and gathered word by word out of his preaching, and now out of Latine faithfully translated into English for the vnlearned. Wherein is set forth most excellently the glorious riches of Gods grace* [...].[100] The title page describes the process of remediation from voiced sermon to transcription to translation. Again, however, note the grammar: "wherein" refers to the printed book itself, which makes "Gods grace" publicly available to "the vnlearned."

The title page of one of the bestselling books in the period secured the association of "set forth" with print publication: *the vvhole boke of psalmes, collected into English metre by Thomas Sternhold, Iohn Hopkins, and others: conferred with the Ebrue, with apt notes to syng them wyth all* (see Figure 2.9).[101] As early as the partial translation published by John Day in 1560, the book's title page additionally claimed to be *Newly set fourth and*

97 William Lily, *A Short Introduction of Grammar* (London, 1607). STC 15626.
98 King of England James I, *An Apologie for the Oath of Allegiance* (London, 1609). STC 14401.
99 Richard Kilby, *The Burthen of a Loaden Conscience: Or the Miserie of Sinne Set Forth by the Confession of a Miserable Sinner* (Cambridge, 1608). STC 14950.
100 Martin Luther, *A Commentarie of M. Doctor Martin Luther Vpon the Epistle of S. Paul to the Galathians* (London, 1616). STC 16973.
101 Thomas Sternhold, *The Vvhole Boke of Psalmes, Collected into English Metre by Thomas Sternhold, Iohn Hopkins, and Others: conferred with the Ebrue, with Apt Notes to Syng Them Wyth All.; Newlye Set Foorth and Allowed to Bee Soong of the People Together, in Churches, before and after Moring and Euening Prayer: as Also before and after the Sermon, and Moreouer in Priuate Houses, for Their Godlye Solace and Comfort, Laying Apart All Vngodly Songes and Balades, Which Tend Onely to the Nourishing of Vice, and Corrupting of Youth.* (London, 1566). STC 2437. The title as listed for this 1566 edition is one of many variable titles under which these Psalm translations were published.

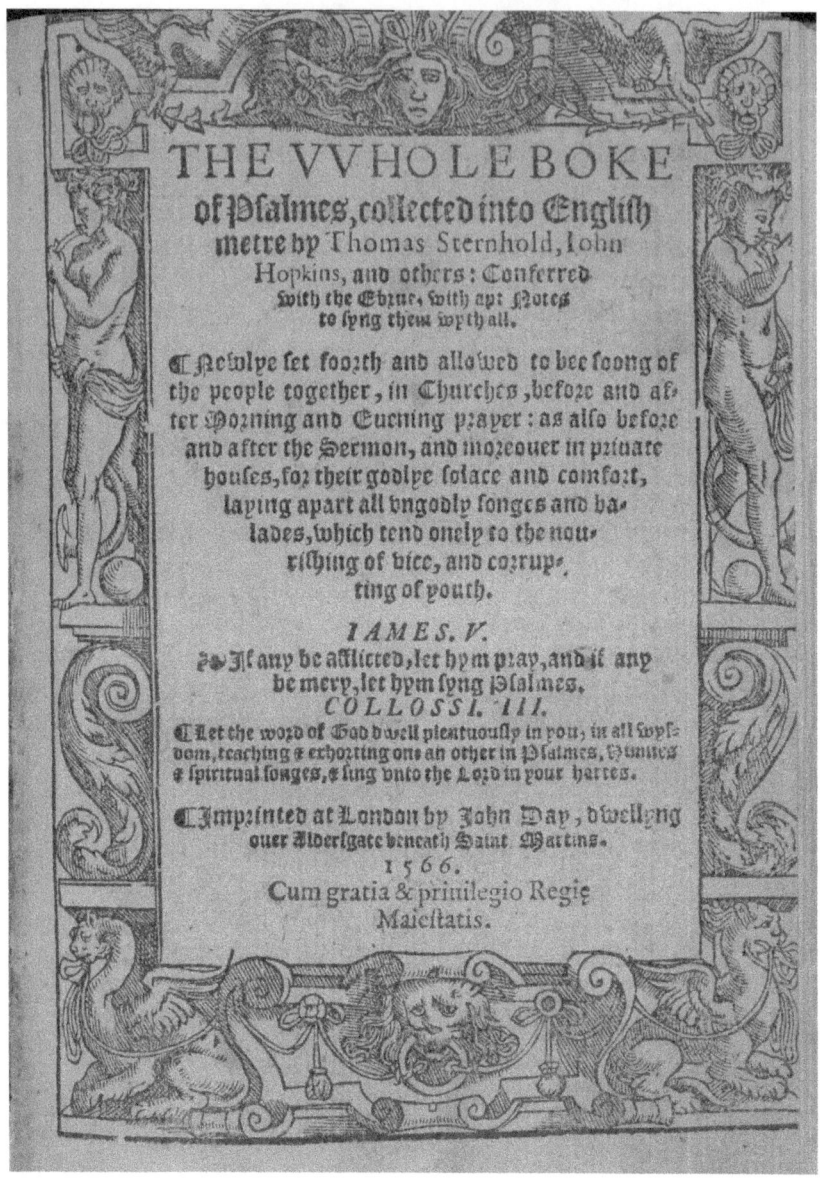

Figure 2.9 *The vvhole boke of psalmes, collected into English metre by Thomas Sternhold, Iohn Hopkins, and others* (London, 1566), sig. A1r, 438000:597, The Huntington Library, San Marino, California

allowed, according to the order appointed in the Quenes Maiesties iniunc-tions.[102] By the 1566 edition also printed by Day and pictured here, the title page claims the book is *newlye set foorth and allowed to be soong of the people together, in Churches* […]. Once more, the title page ties the act of setting forth, which could strictly refer to typesetting, printing, offering for sale, or making known that the book exists, to the public the book addresses. The book thus marks "set forth" as a general signifier for "published in print," with the additional suggestion that this publishing occurred to a specific set of people for a particular purpose. The inclusion of such an important keyword in a position of prominence would subsequently grow durable when, for decades to follow and through dozens and dozens of printed editions, the "Sternhold and Hopkins" Psalms (as they are still called) claimed to be *newlye set foorth*. Fittingly, this repetition functions as a kind of liturgy, in which the repeated phrase acquires over time a reflexive connection with the print medium by way of the printed book's emphasis on setting forth.

By the 1590s, a decade scholars have long identified as a crucial moment in premodern English culture's relationship with printed books, "set forth" carried this association with printing everywhere. A sense surrounds the term that there is a public to be addressed at a scale beyond the closet, the coterie, the court, or the congregation. Along these lines, D. F. McKenzie glosses "setting forth" as "a highly intelligent disposition of all the book's communicative modes, not just to present a text for the reader, but to present *a set of different texts for different readerships.*"[103] Even when specific instances do not invoke printing, the phrase's use on title pages made the category of a print public or readership thinkable in the first place and loaded any use of the term with the potential for associations with print-ing. Instead of invoking, that is, "set forth" *evokes* printing and the public constituency of printed books. The final step in our study of "set forth," therefore, is to follow the phrase through familiar, indeed canonical texts where it has gone largely unnoticed but where it makes a difference.

Philip Sidney twice drops the phrase in one of the most cited and cele-brated moments of *The defence of poesie* (ca. 1580, printed 1595). The phrase's semantic freight opens the passage to new significance. As he works his way toward a definition of poetry as a "speaking *Picture,* with this end to

---

[102] Thomas Sternhold, *Psalmes of Dauid in Englishe Metre* (London, 1560). STC 2427. The Stationers' Register indicates that Day acquired the license to print these Psalm translations in ca. 1559. See Edward Arber, ed., *A Transcript of the Registers of the Company of Stationers of London; 1554–1640 A.D.* (New York: Peter Smith, 1950), 1.42.

[103] McKenzie, *Making Meaning: "Printers of the Mind" and Other Essays*, 252–54. Emphasis mine.

teach and delight," Sidney compares the poet to "other sciences" such as astronomy, law, medicine, and grammar: "there is no Art deliuered vnto mankind that hath not the workes of nature for his principall obiect, without which they could not consist, and on which they so depend, as they become Actors & Plaiers, as it were of what nature will haue set forth."[104] Sidney offers three distinct claims about these fields of knowledge. They take nature as their "principall obiect" – that is, they model, examine, or imitate the natural world. Historians, for instance, say "what men haue done." Second, they consequently "could not consist" without nature's works as an object; without actions and events in the world, there would be neither history nor historians. Third, these sciences therefore "depend" on nature as actors depend upon a script. R. W. Maslen paraphrases the last part of Sidney's sentence as referring to what "Nature (as playwright) wishes the actors to perform on stage," but "set forth" does not merely indicate nature's "wishes," nor does it necessarily cast nature as a "playwright."[105] Rather, these "other sciences" become players of what nature has *made public as if in print*; they act out a script that is publicly available.

This point changes the stakes of Sidney's still-more-crucial claims to follow. Unlike other fields of knowledge, which are tied to the public text of nature's works, the poet has free range:

> only the Poet disdeining to be tied to any such subiectio[n], lifted vp with the vigor of his own inuention, doth grow in effect into an other nature: in making things either better then nature bringeth foorth, or quite a new, formes such as neuer were in nature: as the *Heroes, Demigods, Cyclops, Chymeras, Furies*, and such like; so as he goeth hand in hand with nature, not enclosed within the narrow warrant of her gifts, but freely raunging within the Zodiack of his owne wit. Nature neuer set foorth the earth in so rich Tapistry as diuerse Poets haue done, neither with so pleasaunt riuers, fruitfull trees, sweete smelling flowers, nor whatsoeuer els may make the too much loued earth more louely: her world is brasen, the Poets only deliuer a golden.

In this famous passage, Sidney's language gives an electric charge to Renaissance theories of poetry, arguing that poets both improve upon nature and possess nature's creative capacity.[106] Scholars have understandably focused on the powerful image of the poet "raunging within the Zodiack

---

[104] Philip Sidney *The Defence of Poesie* (London, 1595), sig. B4v-Cr. STC 22535.

[105] Philip Sidney, *An Apology for Poetry, (or, The Defence of Poesy)*, ed. Geoffrey Shepherd and R. W. Maslen, 3rd ed. (Manchester: Manchester University Press, 2002), 135.

[106] Only this early edition, published by William Ponsonby, contains the word "into" in "in effect into an other nature."

[i.e., all-inclusive circle] of his owne wit" and on the punchy contrast of the poets' "golden" world with nature's brass one ("brasen"). The key line, however, occurs between these two: "nature neuer set foorth the earth in so rich Tapistry as diuerse Poets haue done." The figurative tapestry – itself a speaking picture – allows us to compare the rivers, trees, and flowers of nature with the texts that poets have "set foorth." Consistent with Catherine Bates's argument that the *Defense* subverts its own claims about the usefulness of poetry, this second use of "set forth" shifts slightly to spell out how poets have outdone nature: by challenging nature's monopoly in a market of attention.[107] Sidney does not just suggest that poets can theoretically beat nature at its own game; he suggests that they are already actively competing with nature by making their work available to a larger public. This difference explains Sidney's use of "diuerse," since he seems to have in mind a real group of poets who have "deliuer[ed]" a golden world to a public.

Printing lurks in the background of Sidney's claims about poetry. Although he did not publish his writings in print, within a decade of his death, most of them had been printed and reprinted.[108] His use of "set forth" as the decisive term for how poets exceed nature nevertheless carries the notion of a *public* made available by printing. A similar usage occurs in Shakespeare's *Lucrece*, printed in 1594 and, unlike Sidney's *Defense*, authorized by the writer. Early in the poem, the speaker describes how Collatine "vnwisely" praises his wife Lucrece's beauty, causing Tarquin to be stirred with lust. (Tarquin subsequently rapes Lucrece, who kills herself after telling Collatine and others of the rape and demanding that they avenge her.) The speaker pauses for a stanza to reflect on the husband's praise:

> Beautie it selfe doth of it selfe perswade,
> The eies of men without an Orator,
> VVhat needeth then Apologies be made
> To set forth that which is so singuler?
> Or why is Colatine the publisher
> Of that rich iewell he should keepe vnknown,
> From theeuish eares because it is his owne?[109]

The stakes of this stanza could not be higher, given the poem's obvious and much-debated concern with questions of consent, agency, and

---

[107] Catherine Bates, *On Not Defending Poetry: Defence and Indefensibility in Sidney's Defence of Poesy* (Oxford: Oxford University Press, 2017).

[108] See H. R. Woudhuysen, *Sir Philip Sidney and the Circulation of Manuscripts, 1558–1640* (Oxford: Clarendon Press, 1996). STC 22345.

[109] William Shakespeare, *Lucrece* (London, 1594), sig. Bv.

culpability.[110] To what extent can we hold Collatine responsible for Tarquin's actions? Further still, does the poem suggest that Tarquin's rape is the result of Lucrece's beauty and that therefore this victim is responsible for the sexual violence against her?

A short paragraph cannot do justice to these profound questions, but we can consider how our new appreciation for "set forth" as a term associated with print publics fits into them. The stanza's careful framing uses rhetorical questions to make claims without making claims. The first four lines suggest that, because beauty needs no orator to persuade, there is no need to defend Collatine for his praise. The final three lines pivot, suggesting instead that Collatine should have kept Lucrece's beauty "vnknown" but also points a finger at those with "theeuish eares." The clear and troubling implication of both questions is that Lucrece's beauty would have stirred Tarquin's lust without Collatine's words. "Set forth" complicates this picture, however.[111] Along with "publisher," the term figures Collatine's primary mistake as more technological than rhetorical. In both of the stanza's questions, these terms locate the tension between the singularity of Lucrece's beauty and the (printed) multiplicity required by her husband's praise to suggest that Collatine should not be in the book business in the first place.

Decades later, in *Poems, and fancies* (1653), Margaret Cavendish uses the phrase for all its print-laden punch to convene an audience of public women readers. Not insignificantly, this book was Cavendish's first publication in print, and it would appear in two revised editions in the seventeenth century.[112] Although the 1653 edition exists in several variant states, they all contain the author's letter "TO ALL NOBLE, AND WORTHY LADIES."[113] The letter seems to begin on a defensive note: "*Noble, Worthy Ladies*, COndemne me not as a *dishonour* of your Sex, for setting forth this *Work*; for it is *harmelesse* and *free* from all *dishonesty*[.]" "Setting forth" sets the terms for Cavendish's constitution of women readership. It offers a frank acknowledgement of her printed, published "*Work*" as a poet and thus opens

---

[110] See, for instance, Catherine Belsey, "Tarquin Dispossessed: Expropriation and Consent in 'The Rape of Lucrece,'" *Shakespeare Quarterly* 52, no. 3 (2001): 315–35; Lisa S. Starks-Estes, *Violence, Trauma, and Virtus in Shakespeare's Roman Poems and Plays: Transforming Ovid* (New York: Palgrave Macmillan, 2014).

[111] Compare John Taylor's poem comparing "a Whore and a Booke," in which Taylor writes, "As *Whores* haue Panders, to emblaze their worth / So these [i.e., books] haue Stationers to set them forth." See *A Common Vvhore Vvith All These Graces Grac'd: Shee's Very Honest, Beautifull and Chaste* (London, 1622), sig. B6v.

[112] Liza Blake, "Textual and Editorial Introduction – Margaret Cavendish's Poems and Fancies," accessed December 12, 2022, http://library2.utm.utoronto.ca/poemsandfancies/textual-and-editorial-introduction/.

[113] Margaret Cavendish, *Poems, and Fancies* (London, 1653), sig. A3r-v. Wing N869.

the door for her subsequent claim that *"Poetry,* which is built upon *Fancy,* *Women* may claime, as a *worke* belonging most properly to themselves." With a wry twist on the established systems of literary patronage to which such letters conventionally appeal, Cavendish goes on to declare her desire for *"Fame,"* which she describes as "nothing but a *great noise,* and noise lives most in a *Multitude*; wherefore I wish my *Book* may set a worke every *Tongue."* Here the loop opened by "setting forth" closes with Cavendish's reminder of the bookishness of the book, and the effect she means it to have among these women readers. Cavendish set forth her printed book to be talked about by "every *Tongue,*" creating a massive female reading public.

Let us turn, in conclusion, to one final, underappreciated use of "set forth." In *Areopagitica* (1644), John Milton's now-famous defense of the freedom of the press, the phrase wears its connection with printing like a badge. Presumably, it is a coincidence that Milton invokes "set forth" at the beginning and end of the treatise, but it seems fitting nevertheless. First, in his opening praise of Parliament compared to other governing bodies, Milton assures them that:

> there can no greater testimony appear, then when your prudent spirit acknowledges and obeyes the voice of reason from what quarter soever it be heard speaking; and renders ye as willing to repeal any Act of your own setting forth, as any set forth by your Predecessors.[114]

Like Sidney's *Defense,* Milton's treatise takes the form of a classical oration, and as in Sidney's use of "set forth," this one occurs as part of the buildup to the main argument. Here, the term seems to mean "promulgated," but its association with print follows closely, as if reminding the Parliament that their public authority depends on the very print medium they are trying to suppress. Later in the treatise, as Milton runs (as I do) to a conclusion, he wades into a discussion of how God reforms the church "by degrees [...] so as our earthly eyes may best sustain it."[115] This being the case, Milton argues, the risk of false teaching and schism is a price worth paying for revelation, especially when there are ways of responding to wrong views more productive than pre-publication censorship:

> and if the men be erroneous who appear to be the leading schismaticks, what witholds us but our sloth, our self-will, and distrust in the right cause, that we doe not give them gentle meetings and gentle dismissions, that we debate not and examin the matter throughly with liberall aud frequent

---

[114] John Milton, *Areopagitica* (London, 1644), sig. A3. Wing M2092.
[115] Milton, sig. E4v-Fr. Wing M2092.

audience; if not for their sakes, yet for our own? seeing no man who hath tasted learning, but will confesse the many waies of profiting by those who not contented with stale receits are able to manage, and set forth new positions to the world.

It is no exaggeration to observe Milton's fully developed concept of an active, even *generous* public sphere in this passage.[116] If people express what we believe to be wrong views, he suggests, then we must meet with them and listen carefully. But note who exactly does the setting forth here: it is the very potential "schismaticks" who are not "contented with stale receits" – that is, with received knowledge – and thus "set forth new positions." For Milton, himself a setter forth of "new positions," the production of knowledge requires at once the publication at scale ("to the world"!) of fresh ideas and the willingness to contest those ideas at equal scale.

The purpose of these four short readings has been to explore how the semantic baggage of "set forth" works its way into various situations. My argument concerns the phrase's accumulation of associations with printing and print publics, and the subsequent application of the term's networks of use in particular instances. The following chapters of *How the World Became a Book* employ this extensive philology to follow words through premodern English culture. In some cases, writers use the language of books to talk how books change culture, as "bookish" allowed writers to confront their own bookishness. More often, however, the language of books gives writers a way to imagine and express something else, as "set forth" gave expression to an emerging sense of a print public. Unlike the lexicon of Moxon and Dunton, which looks ahead to modernity, the bookish language we will explore in this book remains resolutely and gloriously premodern.

---

[116] See Ben LaBreche, "*Areopagitica* and the Limits of Pluralism," *Milton Studies* 54, no. 1 (2013): 139–60, https://doi.org/10.1353/mlt.2013.0006.

CHAPTER 3

The Metaphors We Read With

In Shakespeare's *Loues labors lost* (1598), the attendant Boyet describes the face of Ferdinand, King of Navarre, who cannot hide his affection for the Princess of France: "his faces owne margent [i.e., margin] did coate [i.e., quote] such amazes, / That all eyes saw his eyes inchaunted with gazes."[1] In this couplet-bound metaphor, Boyet compares the King's face to the margin of a book page. Long before the 1590s, book printers and readers alike used margins to record cross-references, summaries, comments, and more.[2] Marginal space made possible and indeed provoked makers and users to "quote" and record in the margins, and thus to make that record available. To use a term from design theory that has migrated into literary scholarship, the material features of margins have distinct affordances.[3] They *afford* quotation, indexicality, and an accessible record of interaction. Boyet figuratively activates just these affordances: the King's margin/face quotes "amazes," or marks of great astonishment, that record his affection and make it publicly accessible (or *set it forth*), so that "all eyes" can see he is enchanted.

Boyet's line makes for a prime instance of a writer reading *with* the material features of books. Shakespeare is merely the best-known of many scores of premodern writers who incorporated the affordances of

[1] William Shakespeare, *A Pleasant Conceited Comedie Called, Loues Labors Lost* (London, 1598), sig. C3r. STC 22294.
[2] See Evelyn B. Tribble, *Margins and Marginality: The Printed Page in Early Modern England* (Charlottesville: University Press of Virginia, 1993); William H. Sherman, *Used Books: Marking Readers in Renaissance England* (Philadelphia: University of Pennsylvania Press, 2008); Katherine O. Acheson, ed., *Early Modern English Marginalia*, Material Readings in Early Modern Culture (New York: Routledge, 2018).
[3] See James J. Gibson, *The Ecological Approach to Visual Perception* (Boston: Houghton Mifflin, 1979); Caroline Levine, *Forms: Whole, Rhythm, Hierarchy, Network* (Princeton: Princeton University Press, 2015). Although Jeff Dolven and I independently arrived at affordances as a way to study book metaphors, I have benefitted from Dolven's superb chapter, "The Early Modern Book as Metaphor," in *The Oxford Handbook of the History of the Book in Early Modern England*, ed. Adam Smyth (Oxford: Oxford University Press, 2023), 531–48.

book technologies into language as metaphors. If the last three decades of scholarship on sixteenth- and seventeenth-century England have realized the call to study material texts (to look *at* not *through* them, in the influential phrasing of Margreta de Grazia and Peter Stallybrass), then this chapter on book metaphors extends that work from a focus on materiality to a concern with its propagation in figurative language.[4] This chapter – indeed, this entire book – thus begins where book history ends: where books come to function as elements of the imagination, as we began to explore in Chapter 2. A focus on writers reading *with* books permits us to ask how, in early modern England, the material technologies of books acquired the symbolic function they still powerfully possess today. I am therefore less interested in how, in D. F. McKenzie's famous words, material "forms effect meaning" and more interested in how they themselves become meaning.[5] That is, I am less invested in the materiality of the early modern text than in the material textuality of the early modern imagination.

This chapter argues that book technologies transformed premodern England by giving people something to read the world *with*. Books and related text technologies entailed a wide array of figurations, each with its own rhetorical and conceptual affordances. Writers thought *with* this array, for instance, when saying a person possesses virtues "bound up in a volume" or declaring an intention to "turn over a new leaf" or, as we have already seen, comparing a face to a book's "margent." Such a reflexive awareness of the book medium confirms and indeed backdates Christina Lupton's claim, referring to eighteenth-century writers, that "the acceptance of a new medium can coexist with a high level of critical consciousness about its presence."[6] The material features of books furnished the premodern English cultural imagination with figures to think *with*. We will spend most of this chapter getting acquainted with the furniture.

Heeding Ian Smith's recent call to move beyond de Grazia and Stallybrass's *at*-not-*through* mandate and the misreadings it can create, here

---

[4] See Margreta de Grazia and Peter Stallybrass, "The Materiality of the Shakespearean Text," *Shakespeare Quarterly* 44, no. 3 (1993): 255–83, https://doi.org/10.2307/2871419. Other scholars have borrowed or critiqued this phrasing, including Stephen Best and Sharon Marcus, "Surface Reading: An Introduction," *Representations* 108, no. 1 (2009): 1–21, https://doi.org/10.1525/rep.2009.108.1.1; Ian Smith, *Black Shakespeare: Reading and Misreading Race* (Cambridge: Cambridge University Press, 2022). A robust example of "looking at" appears in Mark Bland, "The Appearance of the Text in Early Modern England," *Text* 11 (January 1, 1998): 91–154.

[5] D. F. McKenzie, *Bibliography and the Sociology of Texts* (Cambridge: Cambridge University Press, 1999), 13.

[6] Lupton, *Knowing Books*, xi.

I employ an expansive scholarly reading: not "plural" or "desultory" reading, but perhaps, at the risk of being a bit too playful, a sticky philology that accumulates and sequences as many examples as possible.[7] A broad spectrum of writers – admittedly, predominantly white and male – refigured the book medium into the register of language. We will follow this language through anonymous recusants, defiant Quakers, cranky puritans, and, yes, canonical poets. This sticky philology thus keeps us awake to what Smith calls the "vagaries of human input and interpretation" and helps craft a more inclusive account of how the world became a book.[8]

This focus on writers reading *with* links the figurative language of books with the larger concerns of *How the World Became a Book*. As Chapter 1 discussed, this book aims to decompose the longstanding, persistent identification of the book with Enlightenment modernity, wherein the book's supposed totality and wholeness makes it an ideal (and idealizing) totem. I have already quoted Derrida's rather grandiose proclamation that "the idea of the book is the idea of a totality, finite or infinite, of the signifier" and Régis Debray's description of the codex "as [a] symbolic matrix, the affective and mental schematization in whose dependence we bind ourselves [...] to the world of meaning."[9] These writers wish, as I do, to move beyond the modern "symbolic matrix" of the book, but in doing so, they tend to speak as if books only, ever symbolized totality and self-containment. In these accounts, notwithstanding evidence that books have not always signified this way for readers, books remain modernity's ideological enforcer.

Reading premodern writers and readers thinking figuratively *with* books cuts against the idea of the book as a totalizing symbol. Premodern figurative language, as Rayna Kalas has demonstrated, is not simply "an artifact or concept that reflects reality by observing the mimetic conventions of pictorial representation" but rather "partakes of worldly reality."[10] That is, this language focused less on verbalizing concepts and more on crafting language itself as a thing – hence my focus here on the textuality of the imagination. For Renaissance writers, Kalas writes, "the principal question was not how words relate to things, but how the crafting of language related to the crafting of things"; figurative language thus functions as "a kind of technology rather than a kind of aesthetic experience."[11] Recent scholarship has explored the

---

[7] Daniel Shore advocates for "plural reading" in *Cyberformalism*. Brad Pasanek prefers "desultory reading" in *Metaphors of Mind*. See also Masten, *Queer Philologies*; Smith, *Black Shakespeare*, 35–40.

[8] Smith, *Black Shakespeare*, 38.

[9] Derrida, *Of Grammatology*, 19. Debray, "The Book as Symbolic Object," 141.

[10] Kalas, *Frame, Glass, Verse*, 1.

[11] Kalas, xvi and xiii.

persistence of this orientation toward figuration well into the seventeenth century.[12] At the same time, recent book history scholarship has put to the sword the assumption that books are (in Sarah Wall-Randell's fine phrasing) only ever "stable, rational, transparent containers for knowledge" – another version of the recruitment of books in the service of modernity. Without using exactly these terms, scholars such as Jeffrey Todd Knight and Whitney Trettien have worked against the very notion of book-as-totality on which critiques of the book as a symbol have been premised. A *premodern* "idea of the book" (to return to Derrida's phrase) simply cannot stand for "the idea of a totality [...] of the signifier" when the figurative language derived from books, as this chapter will explore, functions more like Derridean writing (*écriture*) than a totalizing signifier.

To put it all more plainly, the claim of this chapter is in its title: pre-moderns read the world with the bookish metaphors explored here. To grasp how book technology shaped culture, we must expansively study the figurative language of the book, which behaves as a technology for crafting and not just a surface decoration. The sticky philological practice of finding writers thinking *with* books thus makes available the multifarious materiality of the early modern imagination. For these writers and readers, the book symbolizes less as a totality and more as a set of possibilities for expression emerging from material texts. The first main section of this chapter shows how writers created metaphors by using and combining features of books such as title pages and paper. The second section follows metaphors of printing and binding through English culture to show how the bookish lexicon shapes the concepts it is recruited to express. The third section assembles the metaphorical and rhetorical repertoires of the alphabet and red letters (or rubrication) to show premoderns thinking about their world in terms of media and not the other way around.

The Book and Its Affordances

The present chapter's title riffs on the title of perhaps the best-known piece of metaphor scholarship, George Lakoff and Mark Johnson's *Metaphors We Live By*, which argues that "metaphors are fundamentally conceptual

[12] See, for instance, Fleming, *Cultural Graphology*; Margaret Simon, "Glossing Authorship: Printed Marginalia in Aemilia Lanyer's Salve Deus Rex Judaeorum," *Renaissance Papers*, 2017, 125–38; Dianne Mitchell, "The Absent Lady and the Renaissance Lyric as Letter," *English Literary Renaissance* 49, no. 3 (September 2019): 304–29, https://doi.org/10.1086/704507; Erin A. McCarthy, *Doubtful Readers: Print, Poetry, and the Reading Public in Early Modern England* (Oxford: Oxford University Press, 2020); Trettien, *Cut/Copy/Paste*.

in nature" and that "metaphorical language is secondary."[13] In the terms (and typography) of this conceptual metaphor theory, I am exploring the concept cluster emerging from the metaphor THE WORLD IS A BOOK. This metaphor involves the mapping of a concrete source (the book) onto an abstract target (the world) in such a way that the former explains the latter – and, for Lakoff and Johnson, *creates* it. When metaphor is "fundamentally conceptual," it's metaphors all the way down. Scholars who reject the conceptual account of metaphor, on the other hand, emphasize the linguistic and material (as opposed to conceptual) basis of metaphor. Roger White, for instance, notes the "characteristic linguistic simplicity" of the conceptual account of metaphor and argues instead that "*the* key to understanding the way metaphor works is to understand the way words have been combined in the metaphorical sentence" and thus to examine as many examples as possible.[14]

I have no horse in this race. Unlike White, I am not concerned with "understanding the way metaphor works," and unlike Lakoff and Johnson, I am not concerned with determining where metaphors come from and why. Simply to abstract the examples I have gathered as evidence of the concept THE WORLD IS A BOOK is not really to say very much because it does not answer the question of what writers do with that metaphor. A focus on writers reading *with* books thus steers us toward historical pragmatics and (thank heavens) away from cognitive science, calling our attention to the way books afford a range of figurative uses. For premodern writers, books are not dead metaphors, nor do they merely map onto the world; to claim so would merely rehearse the modernizing impulse to regard metaphor in terms of "the mimetic conventions of pictorial representation."[15] These metaphors remain very much alive, because the technology of the book provides writers with a multifarious rhetorical apparatus that readers could recognize as such. Thus, it is not only the case that, as Frederick Kiefer writes, "metaphoric books [...] allow people to organize conceptually the diversity and unruliness of everyday life, accommodating it within the form of a familiar artifact."[16] It is equally true that those metaphors

---

[13] George Lakoff and Mark Johnson, *Metaphors We Live By* (Chicago: University of Chicago Press, 2003), 272.

[14] Roger M. White, *The Structure of Metaphor: The Way the Language of Metaphor Works* (Oxford: Blackwell, 1996), 3. See Pasanek, *Metaphors of Mind*. Pasanek's footnotes are themselves an education in metaphor scholarship.

[15] Kalas, *Frame, Glass, Verse*, 1.

[16] Kiefer, *Writing on the Renaissance Stage*, 106. Kiefer offers a detailed and wide-ranging discussion of book metaphors on the stage.

make "everyday life" knowable and distinct in the first place. Book metaphors do not only make sense of the world; they help make it.

The title page provides a fitting prime instance. A phenomenon of the book trade, the title page endured a long and fascinating evolution across the sixteenth and seventeenth centuries. Title pages functioned as advertisements, reminders of stationer's copyright, signals of authorship and genre, conferrals of different kinds of value, and protection for an unbound book block.[17] When used for figuration, therefore, they afford liminality, publicity, and a contrast of surface and depth. In Wilkins and Shakespeare's *Pericles*, King Simonides tells his knights:

> Knights, to say you're welcome, were superfluous.
> [To] place vpon the volume of your deedes,
> As in a Title page, your worth in armes,
> Were more then you expect, or more then's fit,
> Since euery worth in shew commends it selfe[.][18]

Because these knights' "deedes" speak for themselves, they do not need the additional marketing of a title page. Thomas Overbury draws on the title page to make the opposite claim, describing the character of a "meere scholler" as "the Index of a man, and the Title-page of a Scholler, or a Puritane in morality, much in profession, nothing in practise."[19] As in *Pericles*, the title page supplies a distinction between content and cover, but here the scholar suffers from that distinction. Alexander Brome actualizes the same affordance in a poem "To a Gentleman that fell sick of the small Pox, when he should be married": "your affections are of riper age, / Then now to gaze on beauties *title-page*."[20] Elsewhere, the poem doubles down on this bookish surface/depth trope when it refers to the gentleman's smallpox scars as "red Letters" and encourages him to "let your *Mrs.* know, / They're but *Love-letters* written on your brow." In a shape poem on Jesus's circumcision, Eldred Revett appeals to the title page as a metaphor for "beginning" and "promise of contents," with the blood at the circumcision a promise of the blood at the

---

[17] See Thomas N. Corns, "The Early Modern Search Engine: Indices, Title Pages, Marginalia and Contents," in *The Renaissance Computer: Knowledge Technology in the First Age of Print* (London, England: Routledge. xi, 2000), 95–105; Trettien, "Title Pages."

[18] William Shakespeare, *The Late, and Much Admired Play, Called Pericles, Prince of Tyre* (London, 1609), sig. D1r. STC 22334.

[19] Thomas Overbury Sir, *Sir Thomas Ouerburie His Wife with New Elegies Vpon His (Now Knowne) Vntimely Death* (London, 1616), sig. F7r. STC 18909.

[20] Alexander Brome, *Songs and Other Poems* (London, 1664), sig. R2v. Wing B4853.

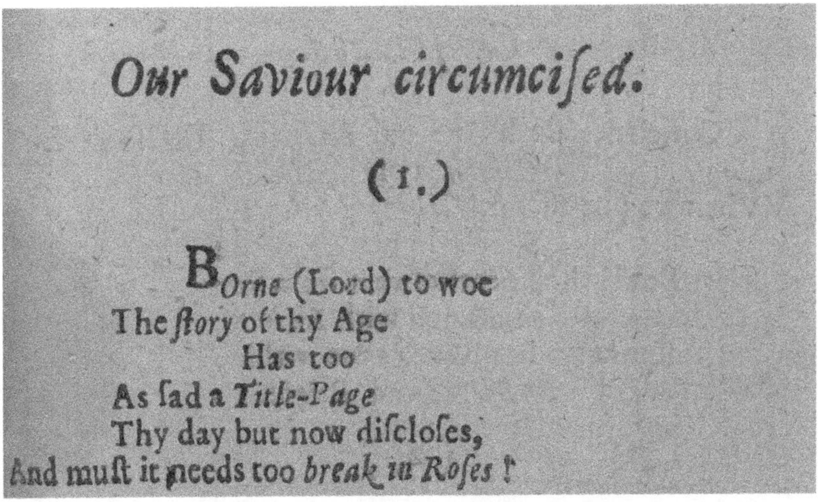

Our Saviour circumciſed.

(1.)

B*orne* (Lord) to woe
The *ſtory* of thy Age
Has too
As ſad a *Title-Page*
Thy day but now diſcloſes,
And muſt it needs too *break in Roſes*!

Figure 3.1 Detail of *Poems, by Eldred Revett* (London, 1657), sig. G11r, Houghton Library, Harvard University.

crucifixion (see Figure 3.1).[21] Likewise, in a sermon, Jeremy Taylor claims that "Repentance is a great volume of duty; and Godly sorrow is but the frontispiece or title page: it is the harbinger or first introduction to it."[22] The familiar book-trade functions of the title page make possible each of these figurative uses; that is, these writers create metaphors out of what title pages afford.

Typeface and paper generated figurative language too. English printing began with extensive use of black letter typeface, sometimes called Gothic or Textura. At the end of the sixteenth century and into the seventeenth, roman and italic typeface designs began to replace the densely inked (hence, "black") letters of blackface fonts.[23] Some references to black

21 Eldred Revett, *Poems* (London, 1657), sig. G11r. Wing R1195.

22 Jeremy Taylor, *XXVIII Sermons* (London, 1651), sig. E5r. Wing T405.

23 James Misson has recently called into question the narrative of a "victory" of roman over black letter type, describing English typography instead as a "multigraphy" that makes "typographical meaning inevitable through contrast." See James Misson, "Typography," in *The Oxford Handbook of the History of the Book in Early Modern England*, ed. Adam Smyth (Oxford: Oxford University Press, 2023), 319. See also Harry Carter, *A View of Early Typography up to about 1600* (Oxford: Oxford University Press, 1969); Peter Bain and Paul Shaw, *Blackletter: Type and National Identity* (New York: Princeton Architectural Press, 1998); Zachary Lesser, "Typographic Nostalgia: Play-Reading, Popularity, and the Meanings of Black Letter," in *The Book of the Play: Playwrights, Stationers, and Readers in Early Modern England*, ed. Marta Straznicky (Amherst: University of Massachusetts Press, 2006), 99–126; Margaret M. Smith, "Black Letter," in *The Oxford Companion to the Book*

letter played on its link with the past: in 1638, James Hamilton could refer to the 1584 Parliamentary acts "printed of old in black letter," and in 1669, Arthur Brett could say that "words in the old black Letter" imply "that they are out of use."[24] Intriguingly, however, some writers who made figurative use of black letter used it as an icon of abundance or ugliness. John Durant wrote that "There is never a black letter in all Gods face (especially as to his children) no, God is love, it is his Name, in love there is no unlovely letter," while in an epiphany hymn "svng as by the three kings," Richard Crashaw describes how the daytime darkness at Jesus's crucifixion will cause sinners "To'injoy his [God's] Blott; & as a large black letter / Vse it to spell Thy [Jesus's] beautyes better."[25]

The whiteness of paper, meanwhile, affords a figure for purity. Pierre Charron, translated by Samson Lennard, explains Aristotle's theories of the soul's formation "by reception and acquisition, comming from without by the senses, being of it selfe, as a white paper void of impression."[26] Likewise, Thomas Wilson notes that Pelagianism, which holds that original sin does not corrupt human nature, "sets forth [that belief] by a similitude of waxe fitte for any impression, of white paper, or a naked table ready to take any forme."[27] Sheets benefit from the capacity for puns: one anonymous writer complains that "Wanton Wives" will "adulterate as many pair of Sheets as they please," but marvels "that this Paper-cheat, should be palm'd on so many suburb bullyes[....]"[28] A character in Richard Brome's *A Jovial Crew* jokes how the Devil cozened a monk and let him live "soul-free, / Till he should finde him sleeping between sheets." The "wary Monk" reads to avoid sleeping, but "the foul Fiend took him napping with his nose / Betwixt the sheet-leaves of his

---

(Oxford: Oxford University Press, January 1, 2010), www.oxfordreference.com/display/10.1093/acref/9780198606536.001.0001/acref-9780198606536-e-0588.

[24] James Hamilton, *Whereas Some Have given out That by the Act of Councell, Which Explaineth the Confession of Faith Lately Commanded to Be Sworn by His Majestie, to Be Understood of the Confession of Faith* (Edinburgh, 1638), sig. E4r. STC 12728; Arthur Brett, *A Demonstration How the Latine Tongue May Be Learn't with Far Greater Ease and Speed Then Commonly It Is* (London, 1669), fol. 2. Wing B4395.

[25] John Durant, *Comfort & Counsell for Dejected Soules. Or a Treatise Concerning Spirituall Dejection* (London, 1650), sig. L5r. Wing D2673; Richard Crashaw, *Carmen Deo Nostro, Te Decet Hymnus Sacred Poems* (Paris, 1652), sig. Div. Wing C6830.

[26] Pierre Charron, *Of Wisdome* (London, 1608), sig. C6v. STC 5051.

[27] Thomas Wilson, *A Commentarie Vpon the Most Diuine Epistle of S. Paul to the Romanes* (London, 1614), sig. V1v. STC 25791. This Wilson is not the earlier rhetorician and logician of the same name.

[28] Anonymous, *Methinks the Poor Town Has Been Troubled Too Long, or, A Collection of the Several Songs Now in Mode Either at the Court or Theatres* (s.l., 1673), sig. A2r-v. Wing M1940. On the language of paper and ink, see Emma Depledge, "Paper / Ink," in *Shakespeare / Text*, ed. Claire M. L. Bourne (London: Bloomsbury, 2021), 383–401.

conjuring Book." Brome's character hits the point home: "there was the [...] double meaning on't."[29]

These figures operationalize the book as a metaphor in different ways, and thus the technologies of the book afford distinct kinds of conceptual work. My use of the term "afford" here nods at recent literary formalist work, which seeks to study forms in terms of what they make possible (that is, what they afford).[30] In the seventeenth century, writers grew rather inventive, combining various aspects of the book's material affordances into elaborate extended metaphors. Although these figures range from ingenious to belabored, they nonetheless show writers reading the world *with* the book.

Unsurprisingly, human life made an easy target for such combinatory metaphors. In a poem section on "Deaths certainty," Edward Buckler spells it out (see Figures 3.2 and 3.3).[31] This is not quite the exhaustive lexicon of the printing house we saw in John Dunton's poem in Chapter 2. Buckler uses the more familiar bookish features of binding, title page, and book size to figure forth the inevitability of death. Importantly, this is not a metaphysical conceit; that is, the aspects of human life figured here do not work in a perfect conceptual analogue to the technologies of the book. Rather, the poem makes the same point (i.e., people die) in multiple ways by way of bookish figuration. By comparison, several writers lovingly cite a 1620 sermon by Charles Fitz-Geffrey, who makes at least some attempt to fit the whole metaphor together:

> man, is as it were a Booke; his Birth is the Title-page, his Baptisme, the Epistle Dedicatorie; his grones and crying, the Epistle to the Reader, his Infancie and Child-hood is the Argument or Contents of the whole ensuing Tretise; his life and actions are the Subiect; his sinnes and errours are the Faults escaped; his Repentance is the correction. Now there are some large Volumes *In Folio*, some little ones *In Sixteenes;* some are fayrer bound, some playner; some in strong Velame, some in thin Paper; some whose Subiect is Piety and Godlinesse, some (and too many such) Pamphlets of Wantonnesse and Folly; but in the last Page of euery one, there stands a word, which is *Finis*, and this is the last word in euery Booke. Such is the life of man, some longer, some shorter, some stronger, some weaker, some fairer, some courser, some holy, some prophane; but Death comes in like *Finis* at the last, to close vp the whole[.][32]

[29] Richard Brome, *A Joviall Crew, or, The Merry Beggars Presented in a Comedie at Drury-Lane, in the Yeer 1641 / Written by Richard Brome* (London, 1652), sig. B1r-v. Wing B4873.
[30] See Levine, *Forms*.
[31] Edward Buckler, *A Buckler against the Fear of Death* (London, 1640), sig. Br-v. STC 4008.5.
[32] Charles Fitz-Geffry, *Deaths Sermon unto the Liuing* (London, 1620), sig. B4v-C1r. STC 10940.3. Writers who cite Fitz-Geffry include Richard Gove (Wing G1454, sig. Br), John Spencer (Wing S4960, sig. Ll4r), and Peter Bales (Wing B549, sig. C3r).

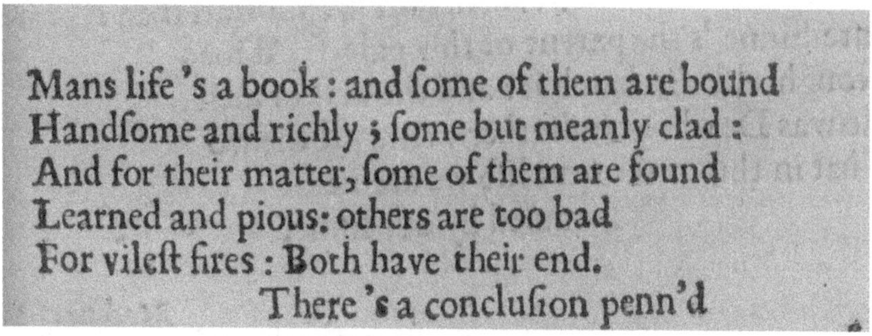

Mans life's a book : and fome of them are bound
Handfome and richly ; fome but meanly clad :
And for their matter, fome of them are found
Learned and pious: others are too bad
For vileft fires : Both have their end.
          There's a conclufion penn'd

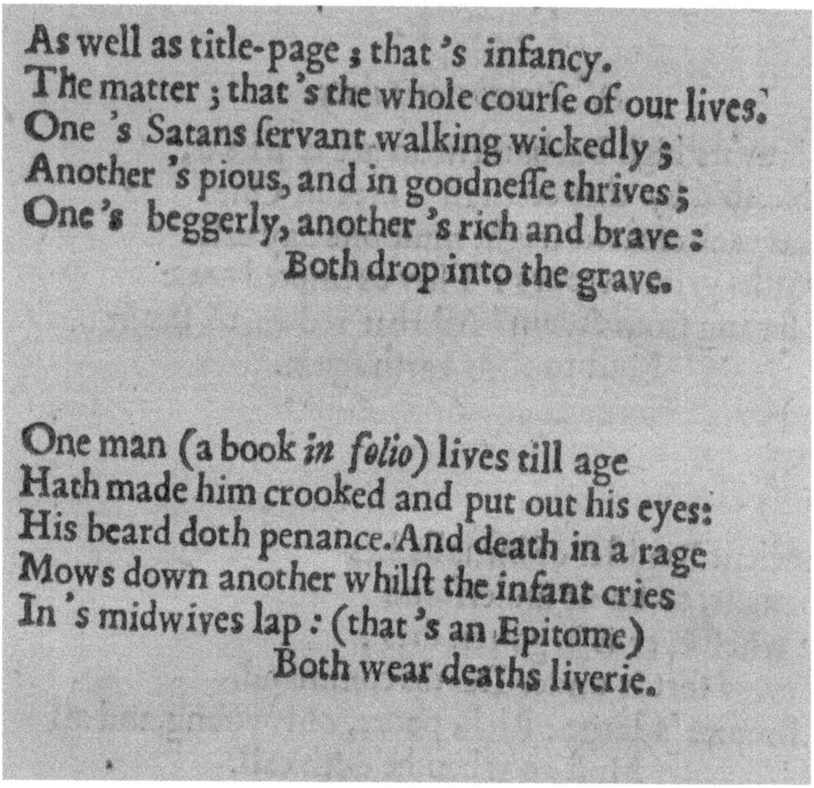

As well as title-page ; that's infancy.
The matter ; that's the whole courfe of our lives.
One's Satans fervant walking wickedly ;
Another's pious, and in goodneffe thrives ;
One's beggerly, another's rich and brave :
          Both drop into the grave.

One man (a book *in folio*) lives till age
Hath made him crooked and put out his eyes:
His beard doth penance. And death in a rage
Mows down another whilft the infant cries
In's midwives lap : (that's an Epitome)
          Both wear deaths liverie.

Figures 3.2 and 3.3   Detail of Edward Buckler, *A Buckler against the Fear of Death*
(London, 1640), sigs. Br-v, RB 60289, The Huntington Library, San Marino, California

As we saw with Dunton, here the book drives the conceptual work, not
the other way around. Fitz-Geffrey seems to have made the commitment
to compare humanity to a book, then sought aspects of human life to fit

to the material features of books: the growth from infancy to adulthood to the ordered sequence of pages, sin and repentance to the correction process, size and materials to bodies, and the concluding word "finis" to death itself. Nathaniel Morton apparently drew on Fitz-Geffrey to elegize John Cotton with a similarly elaborate metaphor in a book printed in Cambridge, Massachusetts and circulated in England:

> A living breathing Bible: Tables where
> Both Covenants at large engraven were;
> Gospel and Law in's Heart had each its Colume
> His Head an Index to the Sacred Volume.
> His very Name a Title Page; and next,
> His Life a Commentary on the Text.
> O what a Monument of glorious worth,
> When in a New Edition he comes forth
> Without Errata's, may we think hee'll be,
> In Leaves and Covers of Eternitie![33]

While Buckler and Fitz-Geffrey operationalize the book metaphor to articulate death's inevitability, Morton points back to the dead Cotton and ahead to the error-free Christian future. In all cases, the writers combine figurative uses of material features with knowable and distinct affordances. To shift the agency slightly, we might say the affordances of books entail figural combination.

Not all book metaphors were so busy. Writers selected and combined aspects of book technology to suit their ends. John Davies's satire from the perspective of paper, featuring the inspired title *A Scourge for Paper-Persecutors, OR Papers Complaint compil'd in ruthfull Rimes Against the Paper-spoylers of these Times* (1625), offers a different version of "man is a book." The paper persona complains:

> Though I (immaculate) be white as Snow,
> (Which Virgin Hue mine innocence doth shew)
> Yet these remorcelesse *Monsters* on me piles
> A massie heape of blockish senselesse *Stiles;*
> That I ne wot (God wot) which of the twaine
> Doe most torment me, heauy *Shame,* or *Paine.*[34]

Davies appeals to a black-ink-on-white-paper modality that was already gendered and racialized: here, the "Virgin Hue" of the innocent white paper is marked with the blot of bad writing. Along the same sexualizing

---

[33] Nathaniel Morton, *New-Englands Memoriall* (Cambridge (Mass.), 1669), sig. T1v. Wing M2827.
[34] John Davies, *A Scourge for Paper-Persecutors. Or Papers Complaint, Compil'd in Ruthfull Rimes, against the Paper-Spoylers of These Times* (London, 1625), sig. A3r. STC 6340.

lines, James Shirley's character Antonio in *The Cardinal* greedily describes his companion's beloved:

> Ther's a Lady for my humour,
> A pretty book of flesh and blood, and well
> Bound up, in a fair letter too; would I
> Had her with all the Errata.[35]

For Antonio, the woman's body is the book block, her clothes the binding. His desire for her "with all the Errata" (or errors in printing) probably means he wants her regardless of her imperfections, but it also carries a sexual charge: his desire is unchaste and indecorous. More conventionally, William Sampson's elegy for one Sir John Harper of Swarkeston proclaims that "To number out thy Birth, thy yeeres, and age,/ Each leafe would be a Chronicle, and each Page/ A volume! where our Patriouts might read/ Thy living actions though thou long since dead."[36] Not unlike the self-eternizing tropes of sonnets from the period, Sampson imagines a series of books within books. Samuel Rutherford likewise laments that "the booke of our ingagements to Christ is written full, Page and Margent within and without; its a huge book of many volumes."[37] One book becomes many in the course of the metaphor. So too the book gives Lewis Stuckley language for the record of the self: "though you now will not know your hearts; though you are so stately, as not to speak with them, or loth to examine the dirty Corners; yet God is coming with his Fan: the books must be opened, and every page of thy heart will be unfolded[.]"[38]

What is intriguing about these figures is not just the ease with which writers reached for book metaphors, but the way those metaphors so easily get out of hand, with the so-called target or tenor making such a mess of the source or vehicle that the distinction ceases to be meaningful. Richard Brome chases one symbolic book with another in an elegy: "TEach me (dread Fate) out of thy strong-clasp'd book, / Whose every Marble page as vast doth look / As th'immense Volume of Eternity, / Whereto for Index serves Mortality[.]"[39] Fate has a book with a strong clasp, here an affordance figuratively conveying the mystery and propriety of Fate's determinism. The marbled pages of this book – either an early reference to marbled

[35] James Shirley, *The Cardinal, a Tragedie* (London, 1652), sig. E4v. Wing S3461.
[36] William Sampson, *Virtus Post Funera Viuit or, Honour Tryumphing over Death* (London, 1636), sig. D1v-2r. STC 21687.
[37] Samuel Rutherford, *Christ Dying and Drawing Sinners to Himself* (London, 1647), sig. A3r. Wing 2373.
[38] Lewis Stuckley, *A Gospel-Glasse, Representing the Miscarriages of English Professors, Both in Their Personal and Relative Capacities* (London, 1667), sig. N7v. Wing S6088.
[39] Anonymous, *Lachrymæ Musarum The Tears of the Muses* (London, 1649), sig. C5r. Wing B4876.

paper or, more likely, another metaphor drawn from sculpture – entail comparison to another book altogether, the "Volume of Eternity." This second, "immense" volume has an index, a bookish affordance conveying the way "Mortality" points to and prefixes eternity. This is not to suggest that such messy metaphors must be inelegant, however. Quite the opposite. Thomas Butler squeezes the printing press for as much figurative potential as he can when riffing on Jeremiah 31:33:

> I *will put my Laws in their minds*; this is the heavenly resolution, to set up his Press in our Hearts, and print in us whole volumes, and from thence it shall be published to the world, what God hath done in the secret printing-house of the heart; and whatsoever comes out to the world, that is not of his printing and licensing, shall be suppressed by the Spirit, as not having the hand-writing that makes free; and none shall buy or sell but those that have his mark.[40]

What Jeremiah figures as manuscript (the 1611 Authorized Version renders it as "I will put my law in their inward parts, and write it in their hearts"), Butler imagines in terms of printing and the press. The affordances of the printing house – continuous output, a public to which that output is addressed, and the regulatory mechanisms of censorship – prompt Butler's impressive, if baffling, image of God as both printer and licensor.

One more fine example will round out this section. John Prime mounts a book metaphor to articulate the difference-within-sameness of the way the Christian God delivers groups of people:

> but there is no difference with God, to be with one or with many, to deliuer some fewe, or greater companies. All is one with the almighty. Some difference only may be this, which is in books printed of a large or a lesse letter, and paper, the matter not varying at all. When God tooke his people from the fierie furnace, and mierie clay, and from the vncessaunt toile of gathering strawe, when he brought all Israell out of bondage, and left not an hoof behind, here the presence of God is printed as it were in Royall paper and in Capital letters.[41]

Having affirmed that "there is no difference with God," Prime then backs up and accepts the minor difference that the scope and scale of some deliverances are bigger than others. To convey it, he appeals to the affordances of larger, Royal paper and capital letters – size and legibility – to hammer

---

[40] Thomas Butler, *The Little Bible of the Man or the Book of God Opened in Man by the Power of the Lamb* (London, 1649), sig. B7r. Wing B6339.
[41] John Prime, *The Consolations of David, Breefly Applied to Queene Elizabeth in a Sermon* (Oxford, 1588), sig. A8v. STC 20368.

home the point that the "matter" does not "vary" even if the materials do. As textual studies has persistently reminded us, however, the material features of a book (here, paper size and typography) shape and indeed effect the "matter" of a text. If Prime's goal was to emphasize the absence of difference, his metaphor only reminds us of its presence.

The Book at Scale

The bookish metaphors cited in the previous section feature interesting, funny, or at least obvious uses of the affordances of books and book technologies. Margin, typeface, page, paper, ink, binding, and more: singly or in combination, these facets of books' materiality supply writers with the stuff of metaphor, and those metaphors quickly scramble the modern "tenor/vehicle" divide. Even so, if we remained content to study just these intriguing but nevertheless peculiar examples, we would remain in a situation helpfully characterized by Andrew Piper: "the detailed attention to the particulars of language exiles us from an understanding of the representativeness of our own evidence."[42] For decades, Piper argues, literary scholars have been "replaying [the] epistemological crisis" of asking single pieces of exemplary evidence to stand in for cultural knowledge: "whether it is the anthropologist's notebook, the historian's archive, the media theoretician's screen, the art historian's collection, or the literary historian's book, each of these media is in its own way a flawed portal to understanding something larger than itself" because "they each fail, in a word, to *generalize*." We spend little time, Piper writes, "reflecting on the process [...] of how we move from the luminous detail to arguments about the larger social contexts in which those details are imbedded."[43]

Although Piper offers these claims as the basis for using computational models to study literary history, and although I think there are other, better reasons that exegetical close reading should remain indispensable to literary study, Piper's salutary claims about generalization nicely contextualize the arguments I am making about bookish metaphors. If one way out of the "epistemological crisis" of exemplarity is to scale up one's methodological apparatus to include regression formulae and dimension reduction techniques (thus making the "portal" less "flawed"), then another way out is philology: to identify key lines of evidence and scale up the inquiry along those lines, thus collapsing the distinction between the

---

[42] Piper, *Enumerations*, 7.
[43] Piper, 9.

"portal" of language and the "social contexts" for which they supposedly stand. What I half-jokingly have called a sticky philology of seeking and ordering many examples highlights vectors of figuration across early modern English culture. As we saw in Chapter 2, some such vectors produce coherent narratives of transformation or change while others tell a messier story, but neither kind generalizes in Piper's sense that they allow us to "move from the luminous detail to arguments about the larger social contexts." Rather, the accumulated details, by virtue of their accumulation, help populate the generalized social context we seek. The portal and the portrait are one.

The language cited here is not necessarily rooted in printing press technology, but printing enables them to scale up. Most of the examples below have roots in earlier cultures and in media other than printed books: the phrase "printed in" or "on" refers to the act of impression and imprinting and does not necessarily conjure up a printed book.[44] Likewise, to say something is "bound up in a volume" refers to the codex form, of which printed books are late instantiations. Nevertheless, as we saw with "set forth," printing technology expanded the range and availability of terms across time and distance. The sheer accumulation of books in the sixteenth and seventeenth centuries, by virtue of their accumulation, gives the language of printing and binding a wide breadth and a clear purchase in premodern England.

To print can refer to the creation of any impression in a surface: etching, sealing in wax, carving, and of course inking a substrate.[45] The term emerges complexly from the Latin word *imprimere* (to impress or imprint), and often connotes the imposition, permanence, and recognizability of a form or pattern.[46] Figuratively, therefore, printing affords *formative impression*, and figurative use of "print" is so common that the *OED* gives that usage its own entry: "to impress (an image, thought, saying, etc.) upon the heart, mind, memory, etc.; to fix in the mind."[47] The entry cites Chaucer's *Troilus and Criseyde* as its earliest instance: "every word which that she of hire herde, / She gan to prenten in hire herte faste." Even this instance, however, belies the apparent disembodiment of the *OED*'s straightforward definition. To "prenten in hire herte faste" is not merely to transmit idea into memory storage, but to do real formative work, as

---

[44] See Newman, *Impressive Shakespeare*.
[45] *OED* s.v. "print, v."
[46] *OED* s.v. "imprint, v."
[47] *OED* s.v. "print, v. 2b."

"faste" (firm, secure) hints.[48] "Every word" Criseyde hears she imposes and impresses upon the center of her person.

Later writers expand and elaborate this use of printing's affordances. As we might expect, these figures find their way easily into religious discourse in a variety of configurations. Joannes Thaddaeus writes that "the naturall Law in the first Creation was printed in every man"; Phineas Fletcher likewise that "Man therefore by consenting to the Devill, and revolting from God, lost that divine image which was printed in him, but received a new Character of Satan, being wholy conformed to that Prince of darkenesse"; John Craig writes that God's image "hath been printed in the infirmitie of our flesh"; and Erasmus affirms that "When thou receyuedst Baptysme, Goddes image was printed and grauen in thy soule."[49] For all four writers, the imposition of the *imago dei* onto humankind is expressed in the symbolic capacity of printing. Thomas Becon promises that if knowledge of Christ and oneself "were prynted in vs, all the plague wherwith the dyuell vexeth vs, should seme light, be it neuer so paynfull and pernicious."[50] For Becon, the printing of knowledge in the self changes one's orientation to later experiences; for Théodore Bèze's translator, by contrast, the apparently permanent printed mark may be removed: "a skarre that is seared, or a blot that is printed in vs by sinne, is not increased by such a publike confession as is made before the Church, but rather is cured vp and taken awaie."[51] Confession, a congregational eraser, removes the inky blot of sin. Even in reverse, printing affords a figure for a sustained impression.

Some writers use the phrase "printed in/on" to designate an impression on a surface, visible to others. In Shakespeare's *Much Ado About Nothing*, Hero's father Leonato wrongly believes the accusations against his daughter, asking:

> Wherfore? why doth not euery earthly thing.
> Cry shame vpon her? could she here deny
> The story that is printed in her bloud?[52]

---

[48] On the force required in printing, see Maruca, *The Work of Print*; MacGeddon [pseud. Randall McLeod], "An Epilogue: Hammered."

[49] Joannes Thaddaeus, *The Reconciler of the Bible* (London, 1655), sig. T1r. Wing T831; Phineas Fletcher, *The Way to Blessednes a Treatise or Commentary, on the First Psalme* (London, 1632), sig. E1v. STC 11085; John Craig, *The Mother and the Child A Short Catechisme or Briefe Summe of Religion* (London, 1611), sig. F5v. STC 5961.5; Desiderius Erasmus, *The First Tome or Volume of the Paraphrase of Erasmus Vpon the Newe Testamente* (London, 1548), sig. iiv. STC 2854.5.

[50] Thomas Becon, *A New Postil Conteinyng Most Godly and Learned Sermons* (London, 1566), sig. Eiir. STC 1736.

[51] Anonymous, *The Psalmes of Dauid Truly Opened and Explaned by Paraphrasis, According to the Right Sense of Euerie Psalme* (London, 1581), sig. f4r. STC 2034.

[52] William Shakespeare, *Much Adoe about Nothing* (London, 1600), sig. Gr. STC 22304.

Hero is blushing, and the red of her cheeks publishes a story she supposedly cannot deny, even though, in one of the play's many ironies, it is
modesty rather than guilt that causes her to blush. Similarly, in a book
titled *Penny-vvis[e] pound foolish* (1631), Thomas Dekker half-jokes that
the "Title of this Booke is Printed in many a mans face," and later Edward
Sherburne portrays Helen telling Paris, "Majesty is printed in thy Face."[53]
More seriously, John Calvin in translation emphasizes the embodiment
of the sacraments, asking, "Shal the body then wherein the mark of Iesus
Christ is printed, be polluted and defiled with so contrary, repugnaunt,
and so wicked abominations?"[54] These examples may not even strictly
count as metaphors, for in each case there lingers a sense that something is
actually impressed upon the person's face or body. We might even say that
the conceptual flexibility of printing is printed in these examples.

The chief figurative use of "printed in/on" in premodern England was
to characterize the formation of the human faculties. The examples cited
so far have hinted at this pattern, to be sure, but there are many more:
memory, mind, belly, and soul could receive impressions. Robert Crowley
quotes Erasmus, then calls the quotation "Wordes worthy to be printed
in memorie, and practised in the reading of all mennes wrytings."[55] The
translator of Joannes Jonstonus's *An history of the wonderful things of nature*
(1657) writes that before the French theologian Theodore Beza (or Bèze)
died, "when his mind was grown feeble, he forgat things present, but what
was printed in his Memory afore time, when he had his understanding."[56]
The poet Edmund Elviden writes of a man whose "griefes / were printed
in hys minde," and Arthur Golding translates Benedetto da Mantova's
assurance that the "certeinty" of God's promises "is printed aforehand in
our mindes."[57] Richard Ryce translates Hermann von Wied's double figure of inscription and impression: "the holyghoost that wrote these thinges
in the Apostles hartes / graunte that they also may be printed earnestly

---

[53] Thomas Dekker, *Penny-Vvis[e] Pound Foolish* (London, 1631), sig. A3r. STC 6516; Anonymous, *Salmacis, Lyrian & Sylvia, Forsaken Lydia, the Rape of Helen, a Comment Thereon, with Severall Other Poems and Translations* (London, 1651), sig. D5r. Wing S3223.

[54] Jean Calvin, *Foure Godlye Sermons Agaynst the Pollution of Idolatries Comforting Men in Persecutions, and Teachyng Them What Commodities Thei Shal Find in Christes Church* (London, 1561), sig. Biir-v. STC 4438.

[55] Robert Crowley, *A Setting Open of the Subtyle Sophistrie of Thomas VVatson Doctor of Diuinitie* (London, 1569), sig. Doiijr. STC 6093.

[56] Joannes Jonstonus, *An History of the Wonderful Things of Nature* (London, 1657), sig. Yyir. Wing J1017.

[57] Edmund Elviden, *The Most Excellent and Plesant Metaphoricall Historie of Pesistratus and Catanea* (London, 1570), sig. E7v. STC 7624; da Mantova Benedetto, *The Benefite That Christians Receiue by Iesus Christ Crucifyed* (London, 1573), sig. Giv. STC 19114.

in our mindes and woorkes."[58] More viscerally, Bernard Ochino specifies Jeremiah 31:33's "inward parts": "the lawe of god was prynted in theyr stomakes."[59] Thomas Twyne likewise asks God to "let the lines of thy law bee printed in the bowels of my bellie."[60] Lastly and most abstractly, the soul receives printing. Thomas Dekker writes of a foolish man who recalls a woman he once loved, "his deare and disconsolated Annabell." When his memory presents her in "the full volume of all her Uertues, being printed in his soule, he thus brake forth into a passionate reprehension of his new-conceiued folly."[61] And Robert Stapylton translates Pliny's address to the emperor to tell King Charles I that "the forme and figure of a Prince, are not expressed so lively and venerably in gold or silver, as in the hearts of men, wherein you are engraven to the life, your amiable lookes and cheere-full aspect being printed in the tongues, eyes and soules of all men."[62]

Writers figured printing on the heart, understood as the center and source of personhood, more than any other faculty.[63] The figure has a wide topical range, from amorous to religious to political to moral. In a 1527 dialogue poem between a lover and a bird, Thomas Feylde's lover proclaims:

> Her beaute pure
> And countenaunce demure.
> Is prynted sure
> In myne herte rote[.][64]

Feylde's image emphasizes the durability ("sure") and regularity ("rote") of the impression on his person. Thomas Becon expresses a desire that his book (*A pleasaunt newe nosegaye full of many godly and swete floures* [1543]) "not only to be borne in the handes or bosoms of all christen me[n] but also to be prynted and fast rooted in theyr hertes."[65] The move from bearing of the book on the body to the impression on the self articulates the deep moral formation Becon imagines for his readers. Richard Brasier likewise claims that if the "doctryne" of caring for the poor and weak "were prynted in all mennes heartes, the[n] shoulde we haue lesse tumulte

---

[58] Hermann von Wied, *The Right Institutio[n] of Baptisme* (Ipswich, 1548), sig. biir. STC 13210.

[59] Bernardino Ochino, *A Tragoedie or Dialoge of the Vniuste Vsurped Primacie of the Bishop of Rome, and of All the Iust Abolishyng of the Same* (London, 1549), sig. Piiir. STC 18770.

[60] Thomas Twyne, *The Garlande of Godly Flowers* (London, 1574), sig. Diiiv-4r. STC 24408.

[61] STC 6516.

[62] the Younger Pliny, *Pliny's Panegyricke: A Speech in Senate* (Oxford, 1645), sig. G4v. Wing P2579.

[63] See Jager, *The Book of the Heart*.

[64] Thomas Feylde, *Here Begynneth a Lytel Treatyse Called the Co[n] Traverse Bytwene a Louer and a Jaye* (London, 1527), sig. Bv. STC 10838.7.

[65] Thomas Becon, *A Pleasaunt Newe Nosegaye Full of Many Godly and Swete Floures* (London, 1543), sig. Biiiir. STC 1743.

and sedytyon."[66] Michael Cope makes the more straightforward Christian assertion that "He is a wise man which being taught in the worde of God, doeth set his whole delight therein, and through the knowledge that he hath thereof, the which is printed in his heart, he laboureth to gouerne himselfe wel both in his doings and sayings."[67] What Cope lacks in fireworks, he compensates for with a helpfully clear appeal to the figure of printing on the heart as that which impresses "knowledge" on the self and thus produces self-governance.

If the heart is the locus of the self, however, its very centrality makes it inscrutable. As premoderns were constantly reminded, the heart is the faculty from which human personhood flows, but it is also deceitful above all else and thus not fully knowable.[68] Metaphors of printing defang this basic epistemological problem. William Austin notes, for instance, that Socrates famously "seldome wrote any thing, saying that wisdome should be printed in mens hearts, not on beasts skins."[69] Even in this simple instance, the metaphor for the formation of the self does not merely relate some pre-existing self. Rather, it makes the self thinkable and distinct by attaching the affordances of printing to the abstract, nebulous, and often downright contradictory conception of the heart. Thomas North, translating Plutarch's *Lives*, makes the same move:

> for it is expressly set downe in his lawes they call Retra, that none of his lawes should be written. For he thought that which should chiefly make a cittie happie, and vertuous, ought throughly by education to be printed in mens heartes and manners, as to haue continuaunce for euer: which he tooke to be loue and good will, as a farre stronger knot to tye men with, then any other compulsary lawe. Which when men by vse and custome through good education doe take in their childhoode, it maketh euery man to be a lawe to himselfe.[70]

North makes explicit the sequence of self-formation, with education creating a durable impression that, in turn, becomes so customary that it

---

[66] Richard Brasier, *A Godly Wil and Confession of the Christian Faythe* (London, 1551), sig. Avr. STC 3552.7.

[67] Michael Cope, *A Godly and Learned Exposition Vppon the Prouerbes of Solomon* (London, 1580), sig, Aa3v. STC 5723.

[68] On the one hand, "The heart is deceitful above all things, and desperately wicked" (Jeremiah 17:9, Authorized Version). On the other hand, "of the abundance of the heart his mouth speaketh" (Luke 6:45).

[69] Samuel Rutherford, *The Divine Right of Church-Government and Excommunication: Or a Peacable Dispute for the Perfection of the Holy Scripture in Point of Ceremonies and Church Government* (London, 1646), sig. C3r. Wing C4288.

[70] Plutarch, *The Lives of the Noble Grecians and Romanes* (London, 1579), sig. Eiiv. STC 20066.

functions as an unwritten code. Ironically, these two printing metaphors sublimate the act of impression to the figurative register: both writers use printing to talk about the absence of written records. Other writers use the figurative register to reinforce or extend material impressions. James Gordon, a Jesuit writer defending Roman Catholic doctrine, argues that "the Tradition only of the Church which is not so much written in paper as is printed in the hartes of Christians, is a most certayne, and faithfull keeper of all the pointes of our diuine faith."[71] Silver-tongued preacher Henry Smith likewise asserts, "my sermon should be printed in your hearts, as this is printed in paper."[72]

Although the latter two writers in the previous paragraph (Gordon and Smith) use printing as an intensification of the formation made possible by written records, like the first two (Austin and North), they offer a concept of the heart as *that which receives impressions*, so that, like paper, the self functions as the bearer of those impressions. Peter Martyr activates all three primary affordances of printing (i.e., the imposition, permanence, and recognizability of a form) when he asks God to "to bestow (vpo[n] those that trust onely in thy goodnesse) thy blessed wil and sacred lawes to be printed and ingrauen within their heartes, to the intent they maye continually meditate and talke of the same, neyther let them be variable and inconstant touching the execution thereof."[73] For Martyr, the potency of the printing metaphor is not just that God will make an impression on people, but that this impression will not change ("be variable and inconstant") and will be publicly accessible ("continually … talke"). Finally, in Phineas Fletcher's *The Purple Island* (1633), Eclecta has this to say upon beholding her beloved Prince, just released from captivity: "thee, thee I see; thou, thou thus folded art [i.e., in my arms]: / For deep thy stamp is printed in my heart, / And thousand ne're-felt joyes stream in each melting part."[74] Eclecta's speech indexes the imaginative range of printing as a metaphor. Fletcher gives Eclecta no personality apart from the "stamp" of the Prince she loves. Like more explicitly sexualized appeals to printing, Fletcher figures Eclecta as that which receives an impression.

While printing affords formative impression, binding makes possible a different set of figurative uses. Sixteenth- and seventeenth-century English

---

[71] James Gordon, *A Treatise of the Vnvvritten Word of God, Commonly Called Traditions* (Saint-Omer, 1614), sig. D5v-6r. STC 13996.a.

[72] Henry Smith, *The Christians Sacrifice* (London, 1589), sig. A2r. STC 22658.

[73] Pietro Martire Vermigli, *Most Godly Prayers Compiled out of Dauids Psalmes* (London, 1569), sig. Hiiiir-v. STC 24671.

[74] Phineas Fletcher, *The Purple Island, or, The Isle of Man* (Cambridge, 1633), sig. Zr. STC 11082.5.

readers and writers did not take binding for granted, partly because many books were sold unbound throughout the period and partly because a book's binding could serve as a mark of ownership, prestige, or genre.[75] Memorably, the abusive husband of Chaucer's Wife of Bath has a book containing all sorts of stories of "wickid wyuys" (i.e., wicked wives):

> And alle thyse were bounden in on volume
> And euery day and nyght was his custume
> When he hadde leyser and ony vacacion
> Fro al other wordly occupacion
> To redyn on this book of wickid wyuys[.][76]

The generic consistency of this volume makes it all the more meaning-ful when the wife tears a page from the book. Moreover, as Jeffrey Todd Knight and others have explored, book binding functioned as an aspect of reading: readers could bind page gatherings and text blocks (i.e., the block of paper formed by a stacked set of gatherings) into combinations that suited them. Binding thus affords *combination* and *collocation*, and figures of binding activate those affordances, even into the present time, when we speak of one thing being "bound up with" another.

Binding metaphors combine like concepts just as material bindings combine like texts. One character in Philip Massinger's *The maid of honour* (1632) lists the features of another, then says:

> all these bound up
> Together in one Volume, give me leave
> With admiration to looke upon 'em,
> But not presume in my owne flattering hopes,
> I may or can injoy 'em[.][77]

A 1647 pamphlet advocating toleration tells of opponents who "[bind] in one volume a whole bundle of invectives."[78] Nathanael Culverwel warns against excessive admiration of great men, "for when we heare of so goodly an essence that hath all excellencies bound up in one vast volume, we wonder what that should be: and admiration is at the best but [...] a stupified kind of knowledge."[79] Cristobel Fonseca argues that the life

[75] See Julia Miller, *Books Will Speak Plain: A Handbook for Identifying and Describing Historical Bindings* (Ann Arbor, Mich.: The Legacy Press, 2010); Knight, *Bound to Read*.
[76] Geoffrey Chaucer, *wHan That Apprill with His Shouris Sote* (London, 1477). STC 5082 and 5069.
[77] Philip Massinger, *The Maid of Honour* (London, 1632), sig. C4r. STC 17638.5.
[78] John Goodwin, *Independencie Gods Veritie: Or, The Necessitie of Toleration* (London, 1647), sig. A2r. Wing G1173. The text has "binding" here.
[79] Nathanael Culverwel, *Spiritual Opticks, or, A Glasse Discovering the Weaknesse and Imperfection of a Christians Knowledge in This Life* (Cambridge, 1651), sig. B4v. Wing C7573.

of a soldier involves "misery" and "iniquity" "bound up altogether in an huge volume."[80] Edward Reyner describes marriage as "a great bundle of Benefits [...] bound up together [...] in one volume[.]"[81] Other writers would say that cities are "Republicks bound up in a lesser volume," that "Sin and Punishment are bound up as it were in the same volume," that the Bible contains (only half-figuratively) "Truths bound up in this sacred Volume," that a writer's patron has "Excellencies which singly adorn'd your Ancestors, are all Centred, and comprehended in you, not abridg'd, but bound up in one Fair Volume," and that an animal is "several Plants bound up into one Volume."[82] In these and other cases, writers appeal to the metaphor of binding to express the collocation of similar ideas or concepts. The final example emphasizes not that plants combine to create animals but that animals have a level of complexity that combines that of plants.

Binding metaphors can also yoke unlike things, just as bindings could combine unlike books. In a book of characters, John Stephens describes "A Gossip" as "the worst part of both sexes, bound vp in one volume."[83] Richard Baker translates a French writer pitting public prosperity against private: "the publicke prosperities would be lesse deare unto me if yours were not bound up in one volume with them."[84] Edward Knott argues that the so-called "Harmonie of Confessions" of faith written and published in Geneva "did consist only in bindeing vp in one Uolume disagreeing Confessions."[85] An anonymous writer accuses another of mixing heresy into orthodoxy: the heresy is "bound up in the volume of our Authors Truth."[86] Vincent Alsop accuses opponents of making arguments based on varying causes: "heterogeneous causes should be bound up together

[80] Cristóbal de Fonseca, *Theion Enōtikon, A Discourse of Holy Love, by Which the Soul Is United unto God* (London, 1652), sig. H5v. Wing F1405B.

[81] Edward Reyner, *Considerations Concerning Marriage the Honour, Duties, Benefits, Troubles of It* (London, 1657), sig. D7v. Wing R1221.

[82] John Robinson, *Tempora Mutantur A Treatise, Theological, Moral, and Historical* (London, 1664), sig. A7v. Wing R32B; Anthony Farindon, *LXXX Sermons* (London, 1672), sig. Aaaaaa4r. Wing F429; Anonymous, *A Supplement to The Morning-Exercise at Cripple-Gate, or, Several More Cases of Conscience Practically Resolved by Sundry Ministers* (London, 1676), sig. Y1v. Wing A3240; Madeleine de Scudéry, *Clelia, an Excellent New Romance* (London, 1678), sig. A4r. Wing S2156; Nehemiah Grew, *The Anatomy of Plants* (London, 1682), prefatory material. Wing G1945.

[83] John Stephens, *Essayes and Characters, Ironicall, and Instructiue* (London, 1615), sig. Bb3v. STC 23250.

[84] Jean-Louis Guez Balzac seigneur de, *Nevv Epistles of Mounsieur de Balzac* (London, 1638), sig. C2r. STC 12454.

[85] Edward Knott, *Infidelity Vnmasked, or, The Confutation of a Booke Published by Mr. William Chillingworth* (Ghent, 1652), sig. Cccc4r. Wing W2929.

[86] Anonymous, *Biddle Dispossest, or, His Scripture Perverting Catechism Reformed by Scripture* (London, 1654), sig. D11r. Wing B2884.

in the same Volume, and Covers."[87] Finally, in a sermon, the clergyman Thomas Browne argued that "in the volume of Gods booke," mercy and fear "are euer, thus bound vp together."[88]

Like and unlike things could thus be "bound up in a volume" together. Another, much different, use of binding figures emerged in the seventeenth century, in which binding serves to enhance the coherence or intensity of a thing. Another Massinger character invokes the warlike Pallas Athena to describe a battle as "Pallas bound vp in a little volume."[89] Miles Sandys vividly describes dissimulation as "the poysoning of Mans Vnderstanding, the Feeder of humors, the whole Volume of it is bound up in the Vellome Cover of Deceit; its actions are worse then Ravenous Beasts or Birds, the one doe prey but upon the dead Bodies, the other upon the living Soules."[90] In both these cases, the figurative volume is not just a miniaturized version of the thing described, but rather distills and maximizes that thing. Likewise, John Monson describes humans as "the Master peece of nature, and comprehension of all other beings, and perfections, close bound up in a little volume," John Stalham describes all the promises of the Bible as being "bound up in one Volume of Jesus Christ," and Henry Hammond describes a "band of iniquity" as a "complication of wickedness bound up all in one volume."[91] These and other such instances appeal to book-binding's collocational affordance for their figurative punch. Just as a book's binding unifies and sequences the gatherings of a codex, so too do these figures lend coherence to the ideas they supposedly convey.

If the examples cited here, along with others we might cite, make up a vector of figuration that more capaciously represents the social context of premodern England than a single exemplary citation could, then what becomes of those exemplary instances? Given what we have seen about binding metaphors – that binding has affordances, which writers appropriate figuratively in various ways – what needs to be said about this particularly powerful passage from a John Donne Easter sermon about the

[87] Vincent Alsop, *Melius Inquirendum* (London, 1678), sig. B5v. Wing A2914.
[88] Thomas Browne, *The Copie of the Sermon Preached before the Vniversitie at S. Maries in Oxford* (Oxford, 1634), sig. F3v. STC 3912.
[89] Philip Massinger, *The Picture a Tragaecomaedie* (London, 1630), sig. E4r-v. STC 17640.
[90] Miles Sandys Sir, *Prudence the First of the Foure Cardinall Virtues* (London, 1634), sig. I4v. STC 21732.
[91] John Monson Sir, *A Short Essay of Afflictions* (London, 1647), sig. H6v-H7r. Wing M2464; John Stalham, *Vindiciæ Redemptionis. In the Fanning and Sifting of Samuel Oates His Exposition upon Mat. 13. 44.* (London, 1647), P2v. Wing S5187; Henry Hammond, *Some Profitable Directions Both for Priest & People in Two Sermons Preached before These Evil Times* (London, 1657), sig. E4r-v. Wing H605.

> *Refurrection.* When I confider what I was in my parents loynes (a fubftance unworthy of a word, unworthy of a thought) when I confider what I am now, (a Volume of difeafes bound up together, a dry cynder, if I look for naturall, for radicall moifture, and yet a Spunge, a bottle of overflowing Rheumes, if I confider accidentall, an aged childe, a gray-headed Infant, and but the ghoft of mine own youth) When I confider what I fhall be at laft, by the hand of death, in my grave, (firft, but Putrifaction, and then, not fo much as Putrifaction, I fhall not be able to fend forth fo much as an ill ayre, not any ayre at all, but fhall be all infipid, taftleffe, favourleffe duft; for a while, all wormes, and after a while, not fo much as wormes, fordid, fenfleffe, namelesse duft) When I confider the paft, and prefent, and future ftate of this body, in this world, I am able to conceive, able to expreffe the worft that can befall it in nature, and the worft that can be inflicted upon it by man, or fortune; But the leaft degree of glory that God hath prepared for that body in heaven, I am not able to expreffe, not able to conceive.

Figure 3.4   Detail of John Donne, *LXXX Sermons* (London, 1640), sig. V5r,
RB 321564, The Huntington Library, San Marino, California.

resurrection (see Figure 3.4).[92] Donne's parentheticals tell part of the story, as he progresses from a list of what he was before conception to a list of what he is now to a third list of what his body will become after death, all in the interest of a contrast with his inability to conceive what embodiment will involve after resurrection. With the summative phrase, "when I consider the past, and present, and future state of this body [....]," he pins these parentheticals together to assert what he knows, then turns to express what he does not. The vividness of the second parenthetical, however, seems indispensable to this passage. Donne calls himself a "Volume of diseases bound up together," a phrase that suggests he has in mind a combination of like things, but the list that follows offers us a series of radically unlike things: a "dry cynder" and yet a "Spunge" of "overflowing Rheumes" (i.e., secretions), an old child, an infant with gray hairs, and a ghost that is yet young. The binding metaphor offers a compelling figure for what it means to have a body now: a set of contradictions located in one body. He does not even need to make explicit that the resurrection body will not collect such contradictions. What Donne frames as a contrast between his knowledge of one body and ignorance of another gives way to a deeper contrast between the volume of diseases and the new body he is "not able to conceive."

What then do we do with such an exemplary instance? Donne too fits on the vector of figuration made possible by binding. Like the other writers cited, he plays upon the ability of bindings to combine and hold together like and unlike things. That he seems to generate an interesting evocation

[92] Donne, *LXXX Sermons*, sig. V5r. STC 7038.

of the binding metaphor may be a function of the scholarly attention I have given him: no one else got such a long quotation! Then again, no other writer seemed to merit such attention. This conundrum returns us to Piper's complaint about literary study's representational problem. I am interpreting Donne's use of the metaphor – admittedly, it is my favorite example in this chapter – not as a stand-in for knowledge of the cultural imagination but as a product of and contributor to the larger figurative vector of binding. The "portal" of language *is* the cultural picture we seek. Donne's apparently exemplary use of the binding metaphor belongs to (because it emerges from) past uses of that metaphor, which make possible the expressive possibilities Donne activates.[93] By following these vectors, we learn more about premodern English culture than a smaller set of examples, however ingenious, could teach us.[94]

Understanding Man: Extensions of the Alphabet

The figurative vectors of bookish features take us many directions. Indeed, the chapters of the present book follow these vectors where they lead, cumulatively offering an account of the premodern bookish imagination. The material affordances of books entail figurative uses in language, which in turn shape human thought and expression. It is not merely the case that a technology produces cultural change, but rather that technologies work their way into a cultural imaginary, yielding a complex set of expressive possibilities that are not located in technology *per se*. Studying the figurative language of books therefore offers a way to address how books produce cultural change without subscribing to a narrative of media or technological determinism, the view whereby technology itself is the "agent of change" in a society.[95]

One of the hallmarks of media determinism is the assumption that people undergoing media transformations remain somehow unaware of the changes happening around them. Most prominently, Marshall McLuhan, the poster child and patron saint of media determinism, offered a grand thesis about the relationship between technological and cultural changes: beginning with the invention of the alphabet and greatly accelerating with

---

[93] For a version of this claim rooted in construction grammar, Paul Hopper, "Emergent Grammar," in *The New Psychology of Language: Cognitive and Functional Approaches to Language Structure*, ed. Michael Tomasello, vols. 1 and 2 (Mahwah, N. J: L. Erlbaum, 1998), 155–75.

[94] See Pasanek, *Metaphors of Mind*, 1: "to represent the past for my present reader, I have drawn thousands of metaphors...."

[95] See Chapter 1 and Baron, Lindquist, and Shevlin, *Agent of Change*.

the introduction of printing technology, the human visual sense came to dominate the oral or aural one. By changing the way human beings perceive – to a primarily visual orientation, resulting in the need to codify and transmit "every kind of learning" into visual form – printing produced the most prominent features of the modern world: democracy, science, capitalism, cold and impersonal bureaucracy, you name it.[96]

Essential to McLuhan's influential thesis is an understanding of media as an "extension of man," a conception made explicit in the title of one of his best-known books, *Understanding Media: Extensions of Man*.[97] For McLuhan, all media extend humankind's senses (e.g., sight, touch), faculties (e.g., memory, voice), or other media (e.g., early television extends the newspaper, which in turn extends the press). Crucially, like subsequent work following in its wake, McLuhan's definition and the grand thesis of social change it supports require the humans being transformed to be passive recipients of media change. Discussing "print," McLuhan writes that "an extension [of man] appears to be an amplification of an organ, a sense or a function, that inspires the central nervous system to a self-protective gesture of numbing of the extended area, at least so far as direct inspection and awareness are concerned."[98] This conviction leads McLuhan to assert wrongly that, in the early centuries of the printing press, few writers had much to say about printing. If media technology is the agent, people remain mostly unconscious of that agency, like a patient etherized upon a table.

But the patient was always awake. Premodern writers remained profoundly conscious of the media around them. This last section shows how the very letters on the page gave rise to a whole range of expressive possibilities. We see these possibilities even in the figurative language emerging from technologies not restricted to the printed codex but greatly expanded and developed by printing technology. Here, we will look to the alphabet,

---

[96] McLuhan, *The Gutenberg Galaxy; the Making of Typographic Man*, 155.

[97] Even if much media studies scholarship has moved beyond this book because of its strenuous media determinism, its grip on other disciplines and modes of inquiry, not to mention popular concepts of media, remains strong.

[98] McLuhan, *Understanding Media*, 172. Even McLuhan's metonymic handle, "print," suggests a single, immanent force, when in fact printing consists of a huge and complex array of mechanical, environmental, economic, cultural, and social factors including, of course, human beings who use and misuse printed texts alongside other kinds of media. Cite people critiquing tech determinism. Cf. Erika Mary Boeckeler, *Playful Letters: A Study in Early Modern Alphabetics*, Impressions: Studies in the Art, Culture, and Future of Books (Iowa City: University of Iowa Press, 2017), 11: "the new cultural history has strongly questioned the essentialism behind arguments that see the press as an agent of change or that see radical discontinuity between the regime of speech and manuscript and the regime of print. In this more recent view, use and performance, change and continuity better capture a world of coexistent media."

the hornbook, and red letters (or rubrication) to show how premodern writers extended media to define, describe, and delimit the world around them. This formulation inverts McLuhan's highly influential definition of media as "extensions of man," showing instead the way writers viewed the world and its people as extensions of media. If we look at "men" and see how media extends them, then we will necessarily gravitate toward a narrative of revolution and transformation, punctuated always by the introduction of new media technologies. But if we begin with media and see how writers extend them, then we may indeed create a more complex but better story that, in the case of the printing press, does not tautologically produce modernity even if it plays a part in the modern world. We see, instead, how writers and readers came to terms with technologies both familiar and new by thinking *with* those technologies about everything else.

Recent scholarship on the alphabet and letters has focused on the way "letters ... achieve their expressive power through playfulness."[99] Laurence de Looze, Erika Boeckeler, Patricia Crain, and others show how the alphabet has (in de Looze's words) "expressed how people ... see the world ... while at the same time the world, and even the cosmos, has been seen as a kind of alphabet."[100] These scholars have demonstrated the energetic reflexivity with which cultures have interacted with letters and the alphabet, from Albrect Dürer's letter shapes to Nathaniel Hawthorne's scarlet letter to the children's television show Sesame Street's song, "The Letter of the Day." In so doing, this scholarship has extended upon Johanna Drucker's attempt to "examine the body of literature within which the history and historiography of the alphabet has been established and transmitted."[101] At the same time, however, this scholarship has stressed what Jeffrey Masten describes as the "alterity and ... historical contingency" of the alphabet itself, a "structure ... that is at once contested, re/formed, persistent, changing, ideologically marked."[102] As Masten's history of Q vividly demonstrates, an alphabet is always so much more than a set of letters.

---

[99] Boeckeler, *Playful Letters*, 5.
[100] Laurence De Looze, *The Letter and the Cosmos: How the Alphabet Has Shaped the Western View of the World* (Toronto: University of Toronto Press, 2016), 5. See also Johanna Drucker, *The Alphabetic Labyrinth: The Letters in History and Imagination* (New York: Thames and Hudson, 1995); Patricia Crain, *The Story of A: The Alphabetization of America from The New England Primer to The Scarlet Letter* (Stanford: Stanford University Press, 2000); Johanna Drucker, *Inventing the Alphabet: The Origins of Letters from Antiquity to the Present* (Chicago: University of Chicago Press, 2022).
[101] Drucker, *The Alphabetic Labyrinth*, 21.
[102] Masten, *Queer Philologies*, 21–22.

In following the figurative language of letters across the alphabet, hornbooks, and rubrication, I expand upon this scholarship's exploration of exemplary writers or artists playing upon letters. Alphabetical self-consciousness did not begin and end with the likes of Dürer or Shakespeare. Rather, writers across the social spectrum adapted and played upon the affordances of letters. They did not merely write *about* letters but *with* them. Sometimes they did so with rhetorical or theological purposes, sometimes to stimulate mirth or insult. Letters gave writers a way to conceptualize and express social difference, temporal change, metaphysical claims, and erotic affections. If the world of printing ever was the monotone, regularized, un-self-aware, and sensually deprived one Marshall McLuhan imagined, it was not Shakespeare's England.

The alphabet's foundational role in education and literacy, not to mention its relative consistency across European languages, made it a ready figure. It would be wrong to label many uses of the alphabet strictly as *metaphor*, but they remain figurative. In the so-called Bishops' Bible, Archbishop Matthew Parker argues that it is not enough for people to study the Bible with "suche diligence, that they could number precisely, not only euery verse, but euery word and sillable, how oft euery letter of the alphabete was repeated in the whole scriptures."[103] Parker refers to the actual alphabet, but the image conveys Parker's point that those who count every letter have missed a more important aspect of the scriptures. Uncannily anticipating modern self-help books, Thomas Elyot reports advice to a hot-tempered person: "Whan any occasion happeneth [...] whiche maie prouoke the to angre: before that thou dooest or saiest any thynge, remember to reherce all the letters in the greke alphabete [...]."[104] For one who is angry, letters have less value as the building blocks of speech and writing and more value as an elemental sequence. Similarly, an anonymous book of characters, which claims to "transform" human personalities into a kind of allegory of animals and plants, describes the Lion with high praise, but then notes that lions (i.e., whoever is represented by lions – possibly the nobility) cannot read:

> yet they cannot a letter of the booke, not so much as the Christ-crosse Row. Onely in the Greeke Alphabet their memorie serues but to carry away the last letter (ω) which they will tone foorth with such a throat as no cryer in Westminster-hall can put you forth such a one. And no maruell they can

---

[103] Anonymous, *The. Holie. Bible. Conteynyng the Olde Testament and the Newe* (London, 1568), sig. *2v. STC 2099.
[104] Thomas Elyot, *A Preseruatiue Agaynste Deth* (London, 1545), sig. E1r. STC 7674.

reade no better, since they hate the vowels; the A because it is too childish, the E too feminine, the I stands not with their maiestie, for the O they are too stout to blinch or say oh at any thing, and for the V they hold it rusticitie.[105]

As with Elyot's angry friend, the Greek alphabet exists for the lions to recite aloud, ending with "omega" at top volume. They cannot even read the letters in the "Christ-crosse Row," the English alphabet printed in a row on a hornbook and preceded by a cross shape (see Figure 3.5).[106] These noble lions will not even deign to use vowels ("V" here equals "U").[107] The reference is probably not to ancient Hebrew writings, which did not include vowels, but rather to the illiterate nobility. Vowels are for sissies. Finally, a 1615 letter-writing manual provides an example of a university student writing to his uncle/benefactor:

> GOod Vnkle you writ vnto me, to know what fruit I haue made of my study: to tell you truth, in reading ouer my Alphabet, I found in all the Crosse Rowe, the worst letter was, O: especially when I, went before it, and V: followed after it: for there finding that I o u, and can not yet come out of your debt, I cannot be agrieued, that you are discontented, that I o u, and can not help it [...].[108]

This is probably not the first "IOU"/"I owe you" joke in history, but it is a funny one. Again, the alphabet serves as a figure for elemental learning and thus as a springboard for the joke. This writer, awake to the intersections of oral and written letters, is not too stout for "O."

Due to its position as a primary medium, the alphabet could easily function as a figure of summation, basic principles of order, and elemental knowledge. Introducing his book on grief, Sir William Leighton refers to his sufferings as "the Alphabet of Calamities" to convey the summative quality of his sorrows.[109] In an English translation by William Barker, Giovanni Gelli figures the Greek alphabet as a vessel when he complains that some Greek-reading snobs "say, that he that knoweth not Gréeke, knowes nothing, as if the spirites of Aristotle and of Plato [...] were shut in an alphabet of Gréeke, as in a glasse[.]"[110] In James Shirley's *The humorous*

---

[105] Anonymous, *A Strange Metamorphosis of Man, Transformed into a Vvildernesse Deciphered in Characters* (London, 1634), sig. B2v. STC 3587. This text has been attributed to Richard Brathwaite.
[106] *OED* s.vv. "Crist-cross-row n." and "Christ-cross n."
[107] *OED* s.v. "U n1."
[108] R.M., *A President for Young Pen-Men. Or The Letter-Writer* (London, 1615), sig. B2r. STC 20584.
[109] William Leighton Sir, *The Teares or Lamentations of a Sorrowfull Soule* (London, 1613), sig. *3v. STC 15433.
[110] Giovanni Battista Gelli, *The Fearfull Fansies of the Florentine Couper* (London, 1568), sig. F3r. STC 11710.

courtier, the foolish lord Depazzi is accused of hyberbolizing and thinks it means something sexual:

> Hiperbolize, whats that? I ha not that word
> Yet in my Alphabet, I hope Madam you
> Hold a better opinion of me then to imagine
> I would hiperbolize with your Lady-ship;
> That were immodest.[111]

Again, the alphabet stands for basic learning, as it does when Miles Coverdale claims that Jesus's call to deny oneself "is oure Alphabet."[112] Likewise, Jean Talpin argues that one who does not love God and neighbor "ought not to aspire to the reputacion of a christian as hauing no place there, séeing he hath not obserued those two lawes, as the first letters of his christian Alphabet," and Antonio del Corro that "the varietie and abundaunce, of all things shoulde be as it were an alphabet to induce [people] to the knowledge & contemplation of [God's] might, power, eternitie, & diuinitie."[113] Talpin and Corro reach for the alphabet to craft an image of what is (or should be) basic to Christians.

Writers thus come to use the alphabet as a figure for the essence or fundamentals of knowledge, for better and worse. Joseph Hall describes a good courtier as one whose "Alphabet is his Princes disposition; which once learned, hee plies with diligent seruice, not with flatterie; not commending euery action as good, nor the best too much [...]."[114] Thomas Jackson, evidently not a fan of gods represented on stage, imagines a vivid, dystopian world in which all poetry has been lost:

> WEre all the workes of auncient Poets vtterly lost, and no tradition or print of their inuentions left, so as the art of Poetrie were to begin anew, and the Theater to bee raysed from the ground; the most curious wits in this or neere adioyning Countries might for many generations to come beat their braines, and sift their fancies, vntill they had runne ouer all the formes and compositions which the whole Alphabet of their fantasmes could affoord, before they could euer dreame of bringing the gods in visible shape vpon the Stage.[115]

---

[111] James Shirley, *The Humorous Courtier A Comedy* (London, 1640), sig. C4r. STC 22447.
[112] Anonymous, *Certain Most Godly, Fruitful, and Comfortable Letters of Such True Saintes and Holy Martyrs of God* (London, 1564), sig. D2r. STC 5886.
[113] Jean Talpin, *A Forme of Christian Pollicie* (London, 1574), sig. I3v. STC 10793a; Antonio del Corro, *A Supplication Exhibited to the Most Mightie Prince Philip King of Spain &c* (London, 1577), sig. G1r. STC 5791.
[114] Joseph Hall, *Epistles, the Second Volume* (London, 1608), sig. H5v. STC 12663.2.
[115] Thomas Jackson, *The Eternall Truth of Scriptures, and Christian Beleefe, Thereon Vvholly Depending, Manifested by It Owne Light* (London, 1613), sig. I1r. STC 14308.

Although Hall and Jackson use the alphabet for very different ends, they equally depend upon its currency as the very essence of knowledge. The alphabet nicely suits this usage, because just as it makes up words but is not identical to them, a "Princes disposition" and the imaginations of the "most curious wits" make up but are not identical to the knowledge in question. In "The Second Anniversary," John Donne uses basic alphabetical knowledge to characterize imperfect human knowledge:

> We see in Authors, too stiffe to recant.
> A hundred controuersies of an Ant.
> And yet one watches, starues, freeses, and sweats,
> To know but Catechismes and Alphabets
> Of vnconcerning things, matters of fact;
> How others on our stage their parts did Act;
> What Caesar did, yea, and what Cicero said.
> Why grasse is greene, or why our blood is red,
> Are mysteries which none haue reach'd vnto.
> In this low forme, poore soule what wilt thou doe?[116]

In the "low forme" of human knowledge, one is limited to the minutiae of "matters of fact" acquired by the careful study of "Catechismses and Alphabets." Yoked with the question-and-answer rote learning of the catechism, the alphabet conveys precisely how mundane these decidedly unmysterious forms of knowledge can be.

Beyond these appeals to actual alphabets, writers used metaphors of the alphabet, drawing on the affordances we have already listed. Thomas Bilson describes how "Cranes flie after one like an Alphabet of letters" – one after another in ordered sequence.[117] William Perkins compares a diverse company of men "to the Alphabet, in which are vowels, halfe vowels, and mutes: vowels are olde men, learned, wise, expert: halfe vowels, are young men and women, who are then onely to speake when they are asked; mutes, are the same parties, who beeing not occasioned, are in silence to heare their betters."[118] Likewise, a translation of Livy states that messengers bearing various kinds of tidings ("joyfull or woful") make up "an alphabet of faces," while Dinant in John Fletcher and Philip Massinger's *The Little French Lawyer* exclaims, "This may be a rascall, but 'tis a mad rascall, / What

---

[116]   John Donne, *The First Anniuersarie An Anatomie of the Vvorld* (London, 1612), sig. G2r. STC 7023.
[117]   Thomas Bilson, *The Perpetual Gouernement of Christes Church* (London, 1593), sig. Q3r. STC 3065.
[118]   William Perkins, *A Direction for the Government of the Tongue According to Gods Word* (Cambridge, 1593), sig. E3v-r. STC 19688. William Westerman borrows this conceit in *Two Sermons of Assise* (London, 1600), sig. D2r. STC 25282.

an Alphabet of faces he puts on[!]" and Lucippe in Fletcher's *The Mad Lover* similarly says, "Look what an Alphabet of faces he runs through."[119] Thomas Wright appeals to the same affordance of ordered diversity when he assures his reader that Christ "passed ouer all the alphabet of mortification most exactly for thy sake."[120] And Walter Colman offers a concise image for death: "the Sunne that shines most glorious hath its set, / So deaths th' Omega of our Alphabet."[121]

These metaphors can be quite lively, even downright charming or dramatic. One Thomas Browne's contribution to a book of funeral elegies begins:

> ANd is he dead? Immortall creature! thou
> Whom the proud heaue[n]s sport to immantle now!
> Was Death ambitious? must he seaze on thee
> In th' Alphabet of thy mortality?[122]

Browne uses the elementary position of the alphabet to convey the untimeliness of the subject's death. Nicholas Breton piously prays that "Christs Crosse be my speed, and the Holy Ghost: for feare the Diuell should be in the letters of the Alphabet, as hee is too often when hee teacheth od fellowes play tricks with their Creditors, who in stead of payments, write IOV. and so scoffe many an honest man out of his goods."[123] This is probably not the second "IOU"/"I owe you" joke in history, but Breton is not trying to be funny. The conceit depends upon the homology of "Christs Crosse" as the cross of Jesus's crucifixion and the cross that begins the alphabet on a hornbook (see Figure 3.5), opening the door to a riff on the devil's "IOU." Francis Quarles alludes to Shakespeare's *Richard III* in appealing to the alphabet's associations with a complete sequence:

> Feare not, what thou ador'st; begin to moue,
> Chriscrosse sore-runs the Alphabet of loue:
> Tis halfe perfected, what is once begun;
> She is a woman; and she must be wonne.[124]

---

[119] Livy, *The Romane Historie*, sig. Pp3v. STC 16613; Francis Beaumont and John Fletcher, *Comedies and Tragedies* (London, 1647), sigs. I2v and B2v. Wing B1581.

[120] Thomas Wright, *A Treatise, Shewing the Possibilitie, and Conueniencie of the Reall Presence of Our Sauiour in the Blessed Sacrament* (London, 1596), sig. E4v. STC 26043.5.

[121] Walter Colman, *La Dance Machabre or Death's Duell* (London, 1632), sig. C1v. STC 5569.

[122] Anonymous, *Funerall Elegies, Vpon the Most Vntimely Death of the Honourable and Most Hopefull, Mr. Iohn Stanhope* (London, 1624), sig. G2v. STC 23225.

[123] Nicholas Breton, *The Court and Country* (London, 1618), sig. C1r. STC 3641.

[124] Francis Quarles, *Argalus and Parthenia* (London, 1629), sig. B3r. STC 20526.

As with Breton's line, the association of the criss-cross (or Christ's Cross) with the alphabet finds its way into the metaphor. The same is true, finally, when Michael Drayton's poetic speaker lays it on thick to his lover:

> Thine eyes taught mee the Alphabet of loue,
> To con my Cros-rowe ere I learn'd to spell:
> For I was apt a scholler like to proue,
> Gaue mee sweet lookes when as I learned well.[125]

Drayton's "Alphabet of loue" activates premodern England's widespread familiarity with the alphabet as the foundation of literacy and knowledge. This foundation is not some abstract principle, however, but a cultural phenomenon arising from material artifacts and situations: the hornbook on which students learned the alphabet, the Christ-cross-row on which that alphabet was printed, and even the possibility of praise from one's tutor. A whole humanist pedagogy underlies Drayton's goofy lines.

Drayton brings us to the hornbook itself, a pillar of humanist education (see Figure 3.5). As the above hints indicate, hornbooks served to instruct children in reading. They typically featured a leaf of paper or parchment printed with the alphabet (usually preceded by a cross – hence, the crisscross-row), the Lord's Prayer, sometimes the ten digits, and sometimes other texts such as the Apostle's Creed. The leaf was mounted on a wood handle and covered with a thin sheet of horn, from which the hornbook takes its name.[126] If one media technology made the alphabet what the writers above understood it to be (i.e., basic learning, the makeup of knowledge, an ordered sequence), it was the hornbook. But writers also used the affordances of the hornbook itself as a figurative resource.

Writers of the period testify to the hornbook as both foundational learning and a foundation for learning. In a grammar book, Ezekias Woodward argues that "the matter of the elementary (the Hornbook) though it be small in shew, yet it is great for processe [....] [I]t would promote the common good not a little, if an able man had the ordering the child at this first staire or step; for a firme ground here, at this low point, raiseth the work mightily, and makes all stand firme."[127] John Trapp more concisely asserts that "the deepest Doctour was once in his hornbook," and Fletcher and

---

[125] Michael Drayton, *Ideas Mirrour* (London, 1594), sig. C2r. STC 7203.

[126] See Andrew White Tuer, *History of the Horn-Book* (New York: Arno Press, 1979).

[127] Ezekias Woodward, *A Light to Grammar, and All Other Arts and Sciences* (London, 1641), sig. D7v–D8r. Wing W3497.

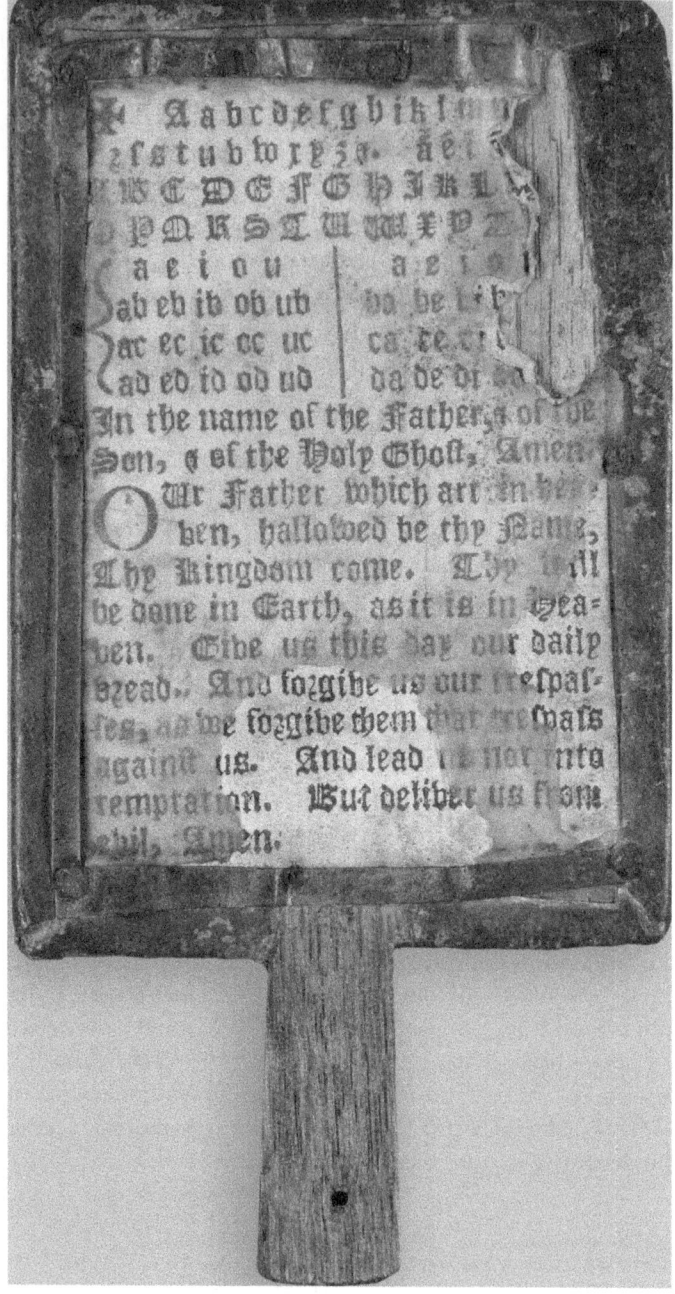

Figure 3.5   A Horn Book (ca. 1625), STC 21.6, image 170177,
Folger Shakespeare Library.

Massinger's Andrew in *The Elder Brother* complains that his friend wants to "bring me back from my Grammar to my Hornbook," a regression to a more elemental form of learning.[128] Likewise, when Shakespeare's Don Armado asks Holofernes if he is "lettred" (i.e., if he can read), Armado's page Moth jumps in to respond, "Yes yes, he teaches boyes the Horne-booke."[129] The exchange culminates, as hornbook references often do, with a joke about a cuckhold's horn. And Thomas Dekker vividly complains about the necessity of prefaces to the reader, who "must be honyed, and come-ouer with Gentle Reader, Courteous Reader, and Learned Reader, though he haue no more Gentilitie in him than Adam had (that was but a gardner) no more Ciuilitie than a Tartar, and no more Learning than the most errand Stinkard, that (except his owne name) could neuer finde any thing in the Horne-booke."[130] Stinkards do not know their ABCs, let alone their IOUs.

It should not surprise us that Dekker, along with other sharp writers of the period, relished using hornbooks as figures for satire and insult. Dekker's underappreciated mock-conduct manual, *The guls horne-booke* (1609), takes the hornbook itself as a conceit for offering advice on such matters as "How a young Gallant shall not onely keepe his clothes (which many of them can hardly doe for Brokers) but also saue the charges of taking physicke [i.e., medicine]."[131] In another book titled *Nevves from hell brought by the Diuells carrier* (1606), Dekker notes that the Devil has "no skill but in his own Horne-booke."[132] Decades earlier, in his anti-Martinist *Pappe with an hatchet* (1589) John Lyly claims that "such vnmannerlie knaues as Martin, must bee set againe to their A. B. C and learne to spell Our Father in a Horne booke," while three years later Thomas Nashe would likewise appeal to the hornbook as a figure against Lyly's books:

> Because your books do call for a litle more drinke and a fewe more clothes when they are gone to bed, that is, when they lie dead, you thinke ours should do so too. No, no, we doe not vse to clappe a coat ouer a ierkin, or thrust any of the children of our braine into their mothers wombe againe, & beget them a new after they are once borne. If it bee a horne booke at his

---

[128] John Trapp, *A Commentary or Exposition upon the Four Evangelists, and the Acts of the Apostles* (London, 1647), sig. Y3v. Wing T2042; Francis Beaumont and John Fletcher, *Fifty Comedies and Tragedies* (London, 1679), sig. Q4v. Wing B1582.

[129] Shakespeare, *A Pleasant Conceited Comedie Called, Loues Labors Lost*, sig, F3r. STC 22294.

[130] Thomas Dekker, *The Vvonderfull Yeare* (London, 1603), sig. A3r. STC 6535.5.

[131] Thomas Dekker, *The Guls Horne-Booke: By T. Deckar* (London, 1609), sig. Cr. STC 6500.

[132] Thomas Dekker, *Nevves from Hell Brought by the Diuells Carrier* (London, 1606), sig. B2r. STC 6514. The passage goes on to describe how the Devil cannot find a scrivener to write for him because he has employed them elsewhere throughout London in nefarious activities.

first conception, let it be a horne booke still, and turne not cat in the panne, conuert the Pater noster to a Primer, when it hath begd it selfe out at the elbowes vp and downe the cuntrey.[133]

In short, Nashe tells Lyly to stop trying to make his books more than they are. To "turne … cat in the panne" means "to reverse the order of things so dexterously as to make them appear the very opposite of what they really are," a sense that conforms to Nashe's exhortation that Lyly let hornbooks be hornbooks and no more.[134] In a defense of women's inconstancy, Donne observes that "The greatest Scholler, if hee once take a Wife, is found so unlearned, that he must begin his Horne-booke."[135] Donne wrote this before he married.

Examples proliferate, but the point is simply that hornbooks, like other material features of books, acquired associations and affordances that writers turned into figures. Whether it is John Taylor's poem claiming that "Some Thieues are like a Horne-booke" or Thomas Overbury calling a hypocrite "a Horne-booke without a Christ-crosse afore it," or William Hornby's show-stopping *Hornbyes hornbook* (1622), which consists of a long poem in praise of hornbooks featuring plenty of hornbook metaphors, writers extended this child's tool as a descriptive register of the world.[136]

While hornbooks and the alphabet they feature carry one set of affordances generating figures of sequence and basic knowledge, rubrication or red letters in texts carry a different set that writers nevertheless extended as a mode of descriptive figuration. Rubrication, which comes from the Latin "ruber" or red, is the practice of introducing red ink to a manuscript or printed book, often for the purpose of emphasis. In manuscripts, the task of rubrication was often assigned to a separate scribe and process, and many later medieval scriptoria featured designated rubricators. In the earliest days of the printing press, rubrication functioned as a way for printers to maintain continuity with the manuscript form despite the additional work and expense involved. The 42-line Gutenberg Bible, to pick a well-known instance, was printed with spaces and printed directions for rubricated initials and other forms of emphasis (see Figure 3.6 and Plate I).

---

[133] John Lyly, *Pappe with an Hatchet* (London, 1589), sig. C2v-3r. STC 17463; Thomas Nash, *The Apologie of Pierce Pennilesse* (London, 1592), sig. Mv. STC 18378.
[134] *OED* s.v. "cat n.1 III.12.a."
[135] John Donne, *Iuuenilia or Certaine Paradoxes and Problemes* (London, 1633), sig. A4v. STC 7044.
[136] John Taylor, *An Arrant Thiefe, Vvhom Euery Man May Trust in Vvord and Deed, Exceeding True and Iust. With a Comparison Betweene a Thiefe and a Booke* (London, 1622), sig. C6r. STC 23728; Overbury, *Sir Thomas Ouerburie His Wife with New Elegies Vpon His (Now Knowne) Vntimely Death*, sig. K2r-v. STC 18909; William Hornby, *Hornbyes Hornbook Iudge Not Too Rashly, till through All You Looke; If Nothing Then Doth Please You, Burne the Booke* (s.l., 1622). STC 13814. On Hornby, see also Masten, *Queer Philologies*, 27–31.

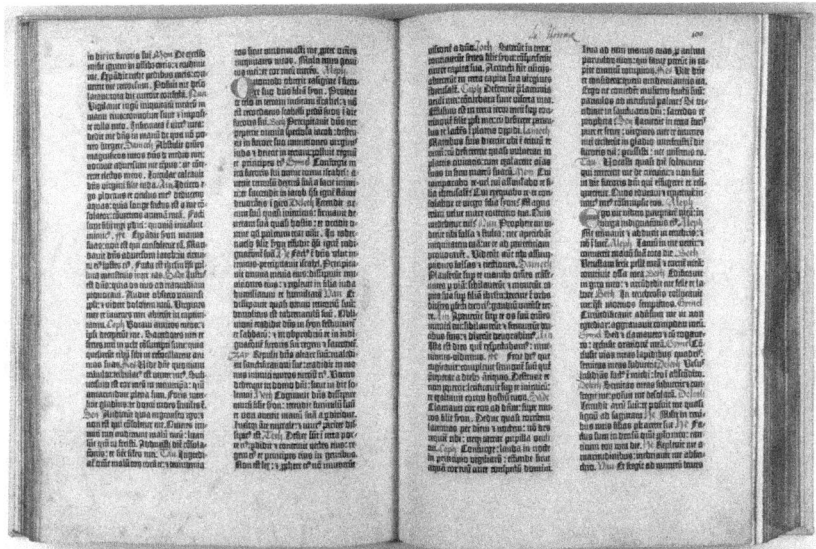

Figure 3.6   Rubricated opening in the "Gutenberg Bible," Bridwell Library Special Collections, SMU. A black and white version of this figure will appear in some formats. For the colour version, refer to the plate section.

One common medieval use of rubrication that persisted into printing was the implementation of red letters in almanacs and calendars (see Figure 3.7 and Plate II). Feast days, saints' days, and other holy days were set apart by means of red letters. This practice became a special mark of printed almanacs, calendars, and the *Book of Common Prayer*. Figure 3.8 and Plate III show the month of May in a 1565 almanac. This practice would continue through the eighteenth and nineteenth centuries and is still used today, though the tradition of rubricating the words of Jesus in Bibles has somewhat displaced this practice, particularly in the United States.[137]

In the broad context of these uses, a rhetoric of rubrication developed in sixteenth- and seventeenth-century England. Writers used the familiar red letters for dramatic or polemic punch. One well-known instance occurs in the rebellion of Shakespeare's *Henry VI* Part 2, written sometime in the early 1590s. Just after the famous call to kill all the lawyers, one of the rebels brings in a clerk and says "he can write and reade & cast account, I tooke him setting of boies copies, and he has a book in his pocket with

[137]   See Philip Sellew, "Red Letter Bible," in *The Oxford Companion to the Bible*, ed. Bruce M. Metzger and Michael D. Coogan (Oxford: Oxford University Press, 1993), www.oxfordreference.com/display/10.1093/acref/9780195046458.001.0001/acref-9780195046458-e-0589.

Figure 3.7   English folding almanac in Latin. Public Domain Mark. Source: Wellcome Collection. A black and white version of this figure will appear in some formats. For the colour version, refer to the plate section.

red letters." The leader of the rebels, Jack Cade, replies, "Sounes, hees a coniurer."[138] Later, Cade accuses one of the aristocracy:

> thou hast most traiterously erected a grammer school, to infect the youth of the realm, & against the kings Crowne and dignitie, thou hast built vp a paper-mil, nay it wil be said to thy face, that thou keepst men in thy house that daily reades of bookes with red letters, and talkes of a Nowne and a Verb, and such abominable words, as no christian care is able to indure it[.][139]

---

[138]   William Shakespeare, *The First Part of the Contention Betwixt the Two Famous Houses of Yorke and Lancaster* (London, 1600), sig. F3v. STC 26100.

[139]   Shakespeare, sig. G2r. STC 26100.

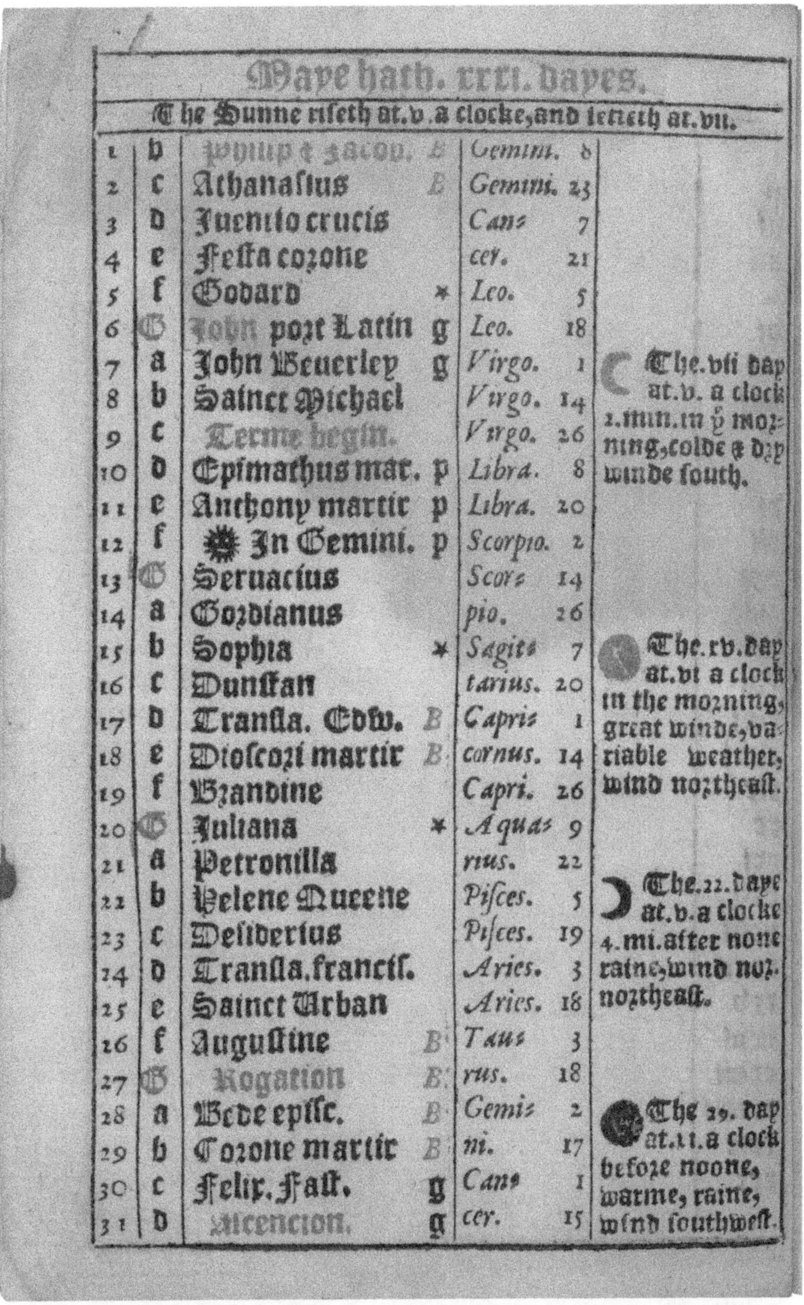

☞ The Sunne riseth at.v. a clocke, and setteth at.vii.

1	b	Pyllip & Iacob.	E	Gemini.	♉
2	c	Athanasius	E	Gemini.	23
3	d	Iuentio crucis		Cans	7
4	e	Festa corone		cer.	21
5	f	Godard	*	Leo.	5
6	G	Iohn port Latin	g	Leo.	18
7	a	Iohn Beuerley	g	Virgo.	1
8	b	Sainct Michael		Virgo.	14
9	c	Terme begin.		Virgo.	26
10	d	Epimachus mar.	p	Libra.	8
11	e	Anthony martir	p	Libra.	20
12	f	☀ In Gemini.	p	Scorpio.	2
13	G	Seruacius		Scor	14
14	a	Gordianus		pio.	26
15	b	Sophia	*	Sagit	7
16	c	Dunstan		tarius.	20
17	d	Transla. Edw.	B	Capris	1
18	e	Dioscori martir	B	cornus.	14
19	f	Brandine		Capri.	26
20	G	Iuliana	*	Aquas	9
21	a	Petronilla		rius.	22
22	b	Helene Queene		Pisces.	5
23	c	Desiderius		Pisces.	19
24	d	Transla. francis.		Aries.	3
25	e	Sainct Urban		Aries.	18
26	f	Augustine	B	Taus	3
27	G	Rogation	E	rus.	18
28	a	Bede epise.	B	Gemis	2
29	b	Corone martir	B	ni.	17
30	c	Felir. Fast.	g	Cans	1
31	d	Ascencion.	g	cer.	15

☾ The.vii. day at.v. a clock i.min. in ý morning, colde & dry winde south.

☽ The.rv. day at.vi a clock in the morning, great winde, variable weather, wind northeast.

☽ The.22. daye at.v. a clocke 4.mi. after none raine, wind nor. northeast.

☾ The 29. day at.ii. a clock before noone, warme, raine, wind southwest.

Figure 3.8 *An almanacke, and prognostication, for the yeare of our Lorde God* (1565), sig. A7v, STC 462.2, image 51623, Folger Shakespeare Library. A black and white version of this figure will appear in some formats. For the colour version, refer to the plate section.

The offense here is that the clerk and the schoolmasters in question are reading books that look mysterious. Cade first implies that red letters have some arcane, magical quality that makes the clerk a conjurer. The joke in the later speech is likewise that red letters are inherently suspicious, just like people who care about grammar. Shakespeare clearly draws on a rhetoric of red letters for these lines and expects his audience to get the joke without assistance. Behind and around Cade's mistrust of red letters is a whole process by which rubrication acquires particular, sometimes opposing associations in early modern England. These associations tend to fall into a four-part taxonomy, even though such a separation effaces the significant overlap and interaction among the categories.

The first association arising from the material affordances of rubrication is the use of "red letter" to refer to Roman Catholicism and its adherents. In 1534, shortly after the Reformation began in England, a book appeared that offered prayers and meditations for people who "vnderstonde not the Latyne tongue." In the preface epistle, the anonymous author complains about Catholic "bokes" that "haue sore deceiued the vnlearned multitude" because "thei were garnished with gloryous tytles and with redde letters promysyng moch grace and pardon (though it were but vanite)."[140] Like Shakespeare's Cade, the author uses red letters as part of a Protestant emphasis on vernacularity and suspicion of books that made what he regards as empty promises and "infynyte errours." Another writer complains that Roman Catholics "[have] no shame to enclose the bodie of Iesus in their wafer cake: also (brainles heretikes as thei be) thei haue had no shame to saie, that if the Rattes, Spiders, or any other vermine, as it is written of redde letters in their Missaulles," eat the body of Jesus, then those too must be burned and included as holy relics.[141] Like the previous writer, this one accuses Roman Catholics of giving too great authority to texts in red letters.

Later writers would get much more creative in slamming Catholicism. Henri Estienne jokes about "A poore Priest [... who found] in an olde Almanack, Sol in Cancro, written with red letters, [and] supposed it had bene the name of some solemne Saint[.]"[142] This imaginary priest mistakenly assumes that "Sol in Cancro" (i.e., the sun in Cancer) refers to a saint because it is written in red. Gregory Martin tells a similar story about "searchers in

---

[140] Anonymous, *A Prymer in Englyshe with Certeyn Prayers [et] Godly Meditations* (London, 1534), sig. Br. STC 15986.

[141] Anonymous, *Against the Detestable Masse, and More Then Abhominable Popishe Heresie* (London, 1566), sig. a8r. STC 17625.5.

[142] Henri Estienne, *The Stage of Popish Toyes Conteining Both Tragicall and Comicall Partes* (London, 1581), sig. Hv. STC 10552.

Oxford (as it is said) maisters of art, vvho hauing to seeke for Papistical bookes in a lavvyers studie, and seing there bookes vvith redde letters, cried out, Masse bookes, Masse bookes: vvhereas it vvas the Code or some other booke of the Ciuil or Canon Lavv."[143] A later writer tells almost the same story about the dissolution of the monasteries under Henry VIII: "many manuscripts, guilty of no other superstition then Red letters in the Front, were condemned to the Fire." This response was so extreme that "where a Red letter or a Mathematicall Diagram appeared, they were sufficient to intitle the Booke to be Popish or Diabolicall."[144] All these zealous searchers make a reflexive identification of red letters with "masse" or "Popish" books.

This identification underlies most references to red letters in the period. John Bridges writes that Catholic "Primers and prayer bookes […] are solemnly set out in redde letters, to egge the people to pray vnto your Images," while another writer claims the Pope "challenges [i.e., claims] from Peter that which Peter himselfe neuer had; power to forgeue sinnes of his owne absolute aucthority, to canonize & make saintes, and set their names in red letters, which power none euer had or hath but God" and yet another, writing the wake of the Gunpowder Plot, notes that "If any zealous Catholike Romane can performe any on [i.e., one] of those [assassinations], for expiation of his fault he shall bee canonized as a Martyr [….] a day shalbe consecrated to his execrable fact, & his name marked with red letters in their bloudy Callender."[145] This last example is just one of many wherein "red letters" crop up around major events, including the Gunpowder Plot, the Popish Plot, the execution of Charles I, the execution of William Laud, and more. In one such instance, a writer describes how the 1678 Popish Plot was committed by those who could not restrain "the killing Red Letter within" – meaning, a hidden Catholicism.[146]

By the seventeenth century, as the Reformation became more distinct in retrospect, writers frequently made the connection explicit.[147] William

---

[143] Gregory Martin, *A Discouerie of the Manifold Corruptions of the Holy Scriptures by the Heretikes of Our Daies* (Reims, 1582), sig. A8r. STC 17503.

[144] Anonymous, *Theatrum Chemicum Britannicum·Containing Severall Poeticall Pieces of Our Famous English Philosophers, Who Have Written the Hermetique Mysteries in Their Owne Ancient Language* (London, 1652), sig. A2v. Wing A3987.

[145] John Bridges, *The Supremacie of Christian Princes Ouer All Persons throughout Theor Dominions* (London, 1573), sig. Rrriiir. STC 3737; Thomas Carew, *Foure Godlie and Profitable Sermons* (London, 1605), sig. C6r-v. STC 4617; James Cleland, *Hērō-Paideia, or The Institution of a Young Noble Man* (Oxford, 1607), sig. P2v. STC 5393.

[146] Thomas Jones, *Elymas the Sorcerer, or, A Memorial towards the Discovery of the Bottom of This Popish-Plot and How Far His R. Highness's Directors Have Been Faithful to His Honour and Interest, or the Peace of the Nation* (London, 1682), sig. Br. Wing J992.

[147] See Benjamin Guyer, *How the English Reformation Was Named: The Politics of History, 1400–1700* (Oxford: Oxford University Press, 2022).

Attersoll refuses to define saints as those who "are inrolled in the Popes Register, and stand in redde Letters in the Popish Kalender[.]"[148] A 1662 Italian-English dictionary spells it out:

> the English have a way of alluding [...] when they will signifie a Roman Catholick, they will say he is a Red letter man, because the Roman Calendar is full of Rubricks, and red letters, and when contrary wise, they will signifie a drunkard, they say he is a Red lettice man, viz. a hanter of Ale-houses, which usually are with red lettices.[149]

This definition makes in short what this chapter has been arguing: that the material affordances of things (in this case, letters and lattices) entail figurative language.

Space prohibits more examples, but the idea is clear: premodern English writers used red letters as a handle for Roman Catholics and Roman Catholicism. They seem to have done so based on the association of Catholicism with almanacs containing rubricated holy days – though, as we have already seen, Protestant Christians used red letters too. The *OED* catches the association with Catholicism as well, citing as its first instance Thomas Middleton's play *The Family of Love*, in which a character named Dry claims, "I keepe no holy daies, nor fasts, but eate most flesh o'frydayes of all dayes i'the week: J do vse to say inspir'd graces able to starue a wicked man with length, I haue *Aminadabs* and *Abrams* to my godsonnes, and I chide them when they aske me blessing: and I doe hate the red letter[.]"[150] Dry eschews any liturgy that bears even a remote attachment to the Roman church, including fasts, fish on Fridays, scripted prayers, blessings, and above all red letters.

The second major category of the rhetoric of rubrication appeals to the resemblance between red ink and human blood, though the association with Catholicism often remains. Writing in the so-called Book of Martyrs, John Foxe combines the first category and the second when he argues that the Pope:

> maketh mo martyrs & Saints of these foresayd poore laymen, & laywomen, then euer he did of any other. For he burneth them, he hangeth them, hee drowneth them, imprisoneth & famisheth them, & so maketh truer

---

[148] William Attersoll, *A Commentarie Vpon the Epistle of Saint Paule to Philemon* (London, 1612), sig. Liv. STC 890.

[149] Giovanni Torriano, *The Second Alphabet Consisting of Proverbial Phrases Interpreted and Illustrated Where Most Necessary* (London, 1662), sig. Rr. Wing T1930.

[150] *OED*, s.v. "red letter n. 1b." Thomas Middleton, *The Famelie of Loue* (London, 1608), sig. Er. STC 17879.

martyrs of Christ, then any other of his new shrined saints, whom he hath so dignified in his Calendar. For the one he doth rubricate, only wt [with] his red letters, the other he doth rubricate wt [with] their owne bloud.[151]

Foxe plays upon the way saints' days were rubricated in church calendars well before the Reformation, and he does so by comparing that ink to the blood of the martyrs (which, in his mind, is an authentic sign of a saint).

Notwithstanding the durable and common identification of red letters with Catholicism, however, some writers referred to red letters in a positive way. One writer commenting on the St. Bartholomew's Day massacre, in which numerous Huguenot Protestants were killed, asserts that while some people mark the day "wyth blackt letters, in token of heauynesse, sorow, and blot euerlasting[,] me thinkes it rather deserued to haue dwelte in red letters, in remembrance, that the same day all Fraunce was dyed red, wyth the bloude of hir children[n]."[152] Moreover, Edward Elton strains to explain how husbands should love their wives as much as they love themselves: "let him but looke into his owne heart, and there hee shall find loue to himselfe drawne out in liuely red letters, euen in his owne blood[.]"[153] George Swinnock uses an elaborate bookish metaphor to talk about Jesus: "his death wrot his love in the greatest Print, in the largest Character, though all in red letters, for his whole body was the book, his precious blood was the ink, the nails were the pens, the contents of it from the beginning to the end are Love, Love."[154] Likewise, the poet Richard Crashaw writes of Christ's wounds:

> Every red letter
> A wound of thine,
> Now, (what is better)
> Balsome for mine.[155]

These examples demonstrate that red letters are not exclusively affiliated with Roman Catholicism. Red letters remain available for all sorts of imaginative use, as the next categories will illustrate. These writers use a recognizable and distinct feature of books as a way of talking about religious and temporal difference. They presume an attachment, with some degree

---

[151] John Foxe, *Actes and Monuments* (London, 1583), sig. FFiiiv. STC 11225.

[152] Innocent Gentillet, *A Declaration Concerning the Needfulnesse of Peace to Be Made in Fraunce and the Means for the Making of the Same* (London, 1575), sig. Gr. STC 11266.

[153] Edward Elton, *An Exposition of the Epistle of St Paule to the Colossians Deliuered in Sundry Sermons* (London, 1615), sig. Bbbb7v-8r. STC 7612.

[154] George Swinnock, *The Christian-Man's Calling: Or, A Treatise of Making Religion Ones Business* (London, 1662), sig. Pp4v. Wing S6266A.

[155] Richard Crashaw, *Steps to the Temple Sacred Poems, with Other Delights of the Muses* (London, 1646), sig. B5r. Wing C6836.

of durability, of red letters to the traditions of the past, but they do so in ways that remain reflexively rhetorical.

A third category of red letters features the phrase referring to something other than Catholicism, blood, or almanacs. At the risk of overreduction, these are *literary* or *poetic* red letters, not least in the sense that nearly all of these examples come from fictional or imaginative writings. The princess Philoclea in Philip Sidney's epic romance *Arcadia* says to the man she loves, "O most happy were we, if we did set our loues one vpon another" and then the narrator adds, "(And as she spake that worde, her cheekes in red letters writ more, then her tongue did speake.)"[156] In Ben Jonson's play *The Alchemist*, one con-man named Face says to the other con-man Subtle that he will:

> Write thee vp Baud, in Paules; haue all thy trickes
> Of cosning with a hollow cole, dust, scrapings,
> Searching for things lost, with a siue, and sheeres,
> Erecting figures, in your rowes of Houses,
> And taking in of shadowes, with a glasse,
> Told in red letters[.][157]

Face is saying he will put up a broadside accusing Subtle of being a fake alchemist (which of course he is) in the courtyard of St. Paul's Cathedral. He claims he will tell of his "tricks / of cosning" in red letters, which will make them more visible. In another play, James Shirley's tragedy *The Traytor*, one character tries to talk another out of killing his sister: "make not thy selfe, by murthering of thy sister, / All a red letter." That is, do not mark yourself out as a murderer as red letters mark out text. The would-be killer's reply, "You shall be the martir," twists the association of rubrication with martyrs into a threat.[158] Finally, in a book of elegies for the executed King Charles I, one writer dramatically asks the regicides:

> Thinke yee the extirpation of a Race
> Divinely Royall, can establish Peace?
> Or seat rude Traytors in our Princes place?
> Or blood can fill our garners with increase?
> No, no, VENGEANCE but writes in these red letters
> How much to Hell, and torment ye are debters.[159]

[156] Sir Philip Sidney, *The Countesse of Pembrokes Arcadia* (London, 1590), sig. Y2v. STC 22539. See Jonathan P. Lamb, "Parentheses and Privacy in Philip Sidney's *Arcadia*," *Studies in Philology* 107, no. 3 (2010): 310–35.

[157] Ben Jonson, *The Alchemist* (London, 1612), sig. B2r-v. STC 14755.

[158] James Shirley, *The Traytor A Tragedie* (London, 1635), sig. I4v. STC 22458.

[159] F. H., *An Elogie, and Epitaph, Consecrated to the Ever Sacred Memory of That Most Illustrious, and Incomparable Monarch, Charles, by the Grace of God, of England, Scotland, France, and Ireland, Late King, &c.* (London, 1649), sig. A2v-3r. Wing H25.

In these imaginative and poetic texts, red letters stand for emphasis; they appear on the body; they convey blood-thirstiness or victimhood; and they often maintain implicit connections with the first two categories.

In the fourth and final category, red letters carry their relationship with almanacs (and secondarily with blood) into figurative uses, many of which use the affordances of rubrication as a way to talk about the passage and measurement of time. In Thomas Randolph's play *Hey for honesty, down with knavery*, a character named Anus says what she wishes she could do to another character:

> these nailes that by a good token have not been pared since eighty eight, should have scratcht your face till it had been a dominical one, and as full of red letters as any Ponds Almanack in Christendome, 'twere suitable to your prognosticating Nose.[160]

Anus's long fingernails will leave red marks on this man's face, so that he looks like an almanac filled with red letter days – hence, "dominical" and thus "prognosticating."[161] The reference to 1588 ("eighty eight"), the year of the defeat of the Spanish Armada, hints at a connection with Spanish Catholicism. In a tragedy called *King John and Matilda*, the character Young Bruce stabs a man named Brand who has killed the titular Matilda, unspooling a series of almanac references too dense not to be a little funny:

> Y[oung]. Bru[ce]. [...] Slave! i'le stick thy Trunck
> So thick with wounds, it shall appear a Book
> Full of red Letters,
> Characters of thy cruelty
> [stabs him.]
> Bra[nd]. This is no bleeding moneth sir.
> Y[oung]. Bru[ce]. Thou lyest, look yonder;
> There lyes mine Almanack, a celestiall body,
> [Points to Matilda's Course. Stabs.]
> Whose revolution, period, pale aspect,
> All tell me 'tis high time that thou shouldst bleed.[162]

Like Anus, Young Bruce says he will make Brand's body look like an almanac "Full of red Letters." With remarkable pluck for someone in such trouble, Brand pulls on the almanac metaphor and asserts that it is not

---

[160] Thomas Randolph, *A Pleasant Comedie, Entituled Hey for Honesty, down with Knavery* (London, 1651), sig. F3v. Wing A3685.

[161] *OED* s.v. "dominical adj. A1.b."

[162] Robert Davenport, *King Iohn and Matilda a Tragedy* (London, 1655), sig. I1v. Wing D370. Brackets in original.

> ⟨ Alas! howfaith-les and how modeſt-les
> ⟨ Are you,that(in your *Ephemerides*)
> Mark th'yeer,the month and day,which euermore
> Gainſt yeers,months,dayes,ſhal dám-vp *Saturnes* dore!
> (At thought whereof (euen now) my heart doth ake,
> My fleſh doth faint,my very foule doth ſhake)
> You haue miſ-caſt in your *Arithmetike,*
> Miſ-laid your Counters,groapingly ye feek
> In Nights black darknes forthe fecret things
> Seal'd in the Casket of the King of Kings.
> 'Tis hee,that keeps th'eternall Clocke of Time,
> And holds the waights of that appointed Chime:
> Hee in his hand the *facred* book doth bear
> Of that cloſe-claſped finall *Calendar,*
> Where,in *Redletters* (not with vs frequented)
> The certaine Date of that *Great Day* is printed;
> That dreadfull Day,which doth fo fwiftly poſt,
> That 'twill be feen,beforefore-feene of moſt.

Figure 3.9   Detail of Guillaume Du Bartas, *Du Bartas His Deuine Weekes and Workes*
(London, 1613), sig. C6v, B1957, Kenneth Spencer Research Library, University
of Kansas, Lawrence, Kansas.

a "bleeding moneth." But Bruce turns the metaphor back, gesturing at
Matilda's already-bleeding body as itself an almanac. Real almanacs, of
course, contained information on the sun, moon, and stars ("celestiall
bod[ies]"), on the turning of the earth ("revolution"), and on the phases of
the moon and planets ("aspect"). Bruce buries Brand in metaphors before
he buries him in the dirt.

   This fourth category persisted over the course of the 1600s, with writers
appealing to rubrication's association with the marking and measurement
of time. For instance, the French poet Du Bartas, translated by Joshua
Sylvester, expresses his annoyance at people who try to predict the return
of Jesus and the end of the world (see Figure 3.9).[163] Du Bartas imagines
Jesus ("King of Kings") holding a clasped book containing a rubricated

[163] Guillaume Du Bartas, *Du Bartas His Deuine Weekes and Workes* (London, 1613), sig. C6v. STC 21652.

calendar, adjacent to the eternal clock of time that Jesus also keeps. The image contrasts with the attempts by prognosticators to "Mark th' yeer, the month and day" of Christ's return. Sylvester's parentheses helpfully annotate the contrast, with his nested "euen now" calling attention to the mistaken temporality of the empty predictions and his "not with vs frequented" to the lack of access anyone has to the great red letters. Du Bartas's is just one of many appeals to red letters as markers of time, which space prevents me from quoting here.[164]

The poet Robert Hayman combines the figurative affordances of alphabet and rubrication, and thus helps bring this chapter to a close. He describes the devastation of war:

> Warre begets Famine, famine, Plague, plague Death,
> War breathes forth woes, but Death stops all woes breath,
> Warre is great A of ills, and Death is Z.
> In warres red Letters, Deaths feast-dayes are read.[165]

In a terrible twist of the almanac figure, the bloody "red Letters" of war mediate the awful particularity of death. Hayman's internal rhyme of "red" with "read," which in turn rhymes with "Z" ("zed"), reinforces this mortal mediation in which death ends ("Z") and makes legible what war initiates ("A"). The personification of Death hints at a play on "feast-days," which Death celebrates by feasting on the dead.

The overwhelming abundance of bookish metaphors from early modern England shows the impressive creativity by which writers like Hayman wrote *with* the affordances of books. These figurations behave not as dead or calcified metaphors but living ones; every writer cited here *intended* to make figurations using bookish features in rhetorically specific ways.[166] The language of books thus functions as a technology just as books do. Everywhere present in the many, many examples cited here is a kind of recursion process, in which one technology (books) gives rise to another technology (figurative language) that extends media to frame the world as a book. But metaphor remains only one available vector for studying the bookish lexicon philologically. The next two chapters follow premoderns writing with the book as something other than metaphor.

---

[164] For example, see John Wing, *Abels Offering. Or The Earely, and Most Accepted Sacrifice of a Christian* (Vlissingen, 1621), sig. E3r. STC 25842 and Sampson Price, *Londons Remembrancer: For the Staying of the Contagious Sicknes of the Plague by Dauids Memoriall* (London, 1626), sig. D2v. STC 20332.

[165] Robert Hayman, *Quodlibets Lately Come Ouer from New Britaniola, Old Newfound-Land Epigrams and Other Small Parcels, Both Morall and Diuine* (London, 1628), sig. C2r-v. STC 12974.

[166] See David Schalkwyk, "Giving Intention Its Due?," *Style* 44, no. 3 (2010): 311–27.

CHAPTER 4

Book Size and Information Management

In *Loues labors lost* (1598), Shakespeare's Don Armado declares that he is in love: "Adue Valoure, rust Rapier, be still Drum, for your manager is in loue; yea he loueth. Assist me some extemporall God of Rime, for I am sure I shall turne Sonnet. Deuise Wit, write Pen, for I am for whole volumes in folio."[1] The joke comes at the expense of Armado's literary ambitions. He seems to think that his folio volumes will carry the reputational value normally attached to large, folio format books. He thinks that his "turning sonnet" will launch him to a certain status – that of an author of books in folio. The joke is not simply that Armado is full of himself, too proud and pompous, but rather that his wordy, elaborate speech has just demonstrated that he can indeed fill folio volumes. Armado thinks the big books he writes will signify one thing (value, prestige, or what Pierre Bourdieu calls "consecration"), when we all know his big books will signify another (they will be too long for their own good).[2]

The capacity of book size to signify makes up the primary concern of this chapter. Armado was hardly alone in assigning value to the size of books, which is, after all, one of the most obvious material features of books. When Geoffrey Chaucer ends *Troilus and Criseyde* with the envoi "Go litel boke," he invokes a long tradition of literary diminution, one that would expand as books proliferated in the sixteenth and seventeenth centuries.[3] Writers and printers remained deeply self-aware about the size of their books. "One thing me thinkes my father should like in me," writes the literary persona Martin Marprelate in 1589, "and that is, my modestie, for I haue not presumed, to publishe mine [i.e., my writings] in as large a print or volume as my father doth his." Characteristically, Martin takes the statement one gratuitous step further: "Nay, I thinke it well, if I can

---

[1] Shakespeare, *A Pleasant Conceited Comedie Called, Loues Labors Lost*, sig. B4r. STC 22294.
[2] Pierre Bourdieu, *The Field of Cultural Production: Essays on Art and Literature*, trans. Randal Johnson (New York: Columbia University Press, 1993).
[3] John S. P. Tatlock, "The Epilog of Chaucer's 'Troilus,'" *Modern Philology* 18, no. 12 (1921): 625–59.

drible out a Pistle in octaue [i.e., an epistle in octavo format] nowe and then."[4] At the other end of the size spectrum, Armado's boast is just one of thousands of references to the folio format as a mark of prestige as well as the ability to contain a lot of text.

Book size is no new topic to scholarship. Scholars have often appealed to format (folio, quarto, etc.), material cost (mainly paper), and durability ("cheap" quartos versus "durable" folios) as major factors in the history of the production and circulation of books in early modern Europe. A longstanding orthodoxy has associated big books, folios in particular, with symbolic, cultural, and economic value. David Greetham, for instance, asserts grandly that "Folio volumes were large, cumbersome books reserved for only the most monumental works" while "the more common format was quarto ... a smaller, more easily handled book."[5] This claim echoes Fredson Bowers' earlier one: "in general the Elizabethans printed works in folio that they considered to be of a superior merit or of some permanent value."[6] In this account, the size of a book is commensurate with (and perhaps the cause of) the value and cost of the book.

Recent scholarship has called these associations into question. Deconstructing the "myth of the cheap quarto," Alexandra Gillespie and Joseph Dane demonstrate the great variety of factors that determined the cost of a book: "not only format, but also – or perhaps rather – size of type, paper size, amount of white space, presence or absence of commentary and type of commentary."[7] Like much textual scholarship of the last decade, Dane and Gillespie emphasize a more complex view of early modern books, in particular that book format and size did not carry a reflexive set of signifying qualities (e.g., "cheap quarto"). Rather, book size is a major factor in and an important product of a set of mechanical, economic, cultural, and literary categories. As Dane writes elsewhere:

> size is a factor in all aspects of book production and reception: it indicates the cost of producing and distributing a title; it affects the way books are and can be read; and it also affects the way books are collected. The size of books in some cases defines for us the material basis of what we consider book history to be.[8]

---

[4] Martin Marprelate, *Theses Martinianae* (Wolston, 1589), sig D4v. STC 17457.

[5] D. C. Greetham, *Textual Scholarship: An Introduction* (New York: Garland, 1994), 123–24.

[6] Fredson Bowers, *Bibliography and Textual Criticism*, 1959 (Oxford: Clarendon Press, 1964), 76.

[7] Joseph A. Dane and Alexandra Gillespie, "The Myth of the Cheap Quarto," in *Tudor Books and Readers: Materiality and the Construction of Meaning*, ed. John N. King (Cambridge: Cambridge University Press, 2010), 37.

[8] Joseph A. Dane, *What Is a Book?: The Study of Early Printed Books* (Notre Dame: University of Notre Dame Press, 2012), 38.

The size of books functions as one of the chief ways they signify in culture, but that signification (as in Armado's "whole volumes in folio") involves the coordination of variable factors.

How, then, did book size signify in early modern England? What account can encompass the 1545 John Skelton title page, *Here after foloweth a lytell booke, whiche hath to name, Why come ye nat to courte*, and John Dunton's 1700 exclamation, "what abundance of sweetness is bound up in the small Volume of a Flower? I read no less then a Deity in the Few Folios of a Damask Rose"?[9] If Dane and Gillespie are right to assert that "ideas about books may exist before or independently of facts about them," then how can we describe the relationship between the "facts" about book size (e.g., format and its affordances) and the ideas about them that circulate in culture (e.g., "Go litel boke" and "in folio")?[10]

This chapter explores how the discourse and rhetoric of book size offered premodern writers and readers a way to address the question of what books contain and how they can be said to contain it.[11] I argue that book size offered a language for coordinating the *informational content* of books with their *material capacities* without necessarily collapsing one into the other. Armado's ambition to be an author of "whole volumes in folio" nicely exemplifies this coordination: the joke is premised on our awareness (and Armado's ignorance) that a big book's bigness can contain not just a lot of words but a lot of needless words. A version of the form/content trope that structures much of Western thought, the pervasive notion of books as containers is in many ways the product of the language of book size. This language helped writers describe what books, as media, mediate.

More Information on Information

In most cases, the bigger the container, the more it can include. Seemingly obvious, this statement implies a simple, reflexive relationship between size and contents. If I want to carry a lot of water, I need a big bottle. If I want

---

[9] John Skelton, *Here after Foloweth a Lytell Boke, Whiche Hath to Name, Why Come Ye Nat to Courte* (London, 1545), sig. A1r. STC 22615; John Dunton, *The Art of Living Incognito Being a Thousand Letters on as Many Uncommon Subjects* (London, 1700), sig M3v. Wing D2620.

[10] Cf. Dane and Gillespie, "The Myth of the Cheap Quarto," 43. "Ideas about books may exist before or independently of facts about them." See also Roger Chartier, *The Order of Books: Readers, Authors and Libraries in Europe Between the Fourteenth and Eighteenth Centuries* (Stanford: Stanford University Press, 1994); Stephen K. Galbraith, "English Literary Folios 1593–1623: Studying Shifts in Format," in *Tudor Books and Readers: Materiality and the Construction of Meaning*, ed. John N. King (Cambridge: Cambridge University Press, 2010), 46–67.

[11] On books as containers, see Lucy Razzall, *Boxes and Books in Early Modern England: Materiality, Metaphor, Containment* (Cambridge: Cambridge University Press, 2021).

to store jellybeans, I need a big suitcase. Unlike water or jellybeans, however, words are not identical to informational content, and this difference is essential for exploring book size in early modern England because it implies that the relationship between words and content is always *rhetorically* as well as mechanically situated. Importantly, the term "informational content" requires a gloss, for it gestures at a relevant genealogy of the concept of information. In an important article about the effects of digital technologies on a bookish world, Geoffrey Nunberg makes a crucial distinction between different kinds of "information." First, there is the technical sense of the term, formulated in the twentieth century to refer to the relationship between signal and noise.[12] Most people who use the word "information" are not using it in this influential technical sense, however, and many remain altogether unaware of its existence. Second, there is the "particularistic" usage, such as when we seek "information" about train times or the exact height of a chair. Nunberg works hard to show the difference between this second sense and a third, "abstract" sense: not "knowledge ... concerning some particular fact, subject or event" but rather "a kind of intentional substance that is present in the world."[13] Phrases such as "information explosion" and "information age" feature the term in this abstract sense. Nunberg persuasively argues that this abstract "information" underlies the widespread modern assumption "that content is a noble substance that is indifferent to the transformations of its vehicles."[14] For Nunberg, this assumption is deeply mistaken. Indeed, the whole field of textual scholarship takes precisely the opposite assumption as its founding premise: content is *never* indifferent to the transformations of its vehicles.[15] (If you disagree, ask yourself why you found the thought of jellybeans in a suitcase odd.)

These distinctions are relevant here because of the historical dimension of Nunberg's claims, which assert that abstract "information" is a coordinate of modernity: this sense of the word "did not appear in English (or in any other language) until the mid-nineteenth century." Jonathan Swift, for

---

[12] An indispensable resource on information theory is Eric Hayot, Anatoly Detwyler, and Lea Pao, eds., *Information: A Reader* (New York: Columbia University Press, 2021). See also N. Katherine Hayles, *How We Became Posthuman: Virtual Bodies in Cybernetics, Literature, and Informatics* (Chicago: University of Chicago Press, 1999); Ronald E. Day, *The Modern Invention of Information: Discourse, History, and Power* (Carbondale: Southern Illinois University Press, 2001); Alan Galey, *The Shakespearean Archive: Experiments in New Media from the Renaissance to Postmodernity* (Cambridge: Cambridge University Press, 2014). On early modern concepts of information, see Paul M. Dover, *The Information Revolution in Early Modern Europe* (Cambridge: Cambridge University Press, 2021); Razzall, *Boxes and Books in Early Modern England*.

[13] Geoffrey Nunberg, "Farewell to the Information Age," in *The Future of the Book*, ed. Geoffrey Nunberg (Berkeley: University of California Press, 1996), 110.

[14] Nunberg, 107.

[15] See McLeod, "Information on Information."

instance, "had no way ... to speak of information as a kind of abstract stuff present in the world, disconnected from the situations that it is *about*."[16] Nunberg cites the oft-repeated claim that the daily paper *New York Times* contains more "information" than the average seventeenth-century person encountered in their lifetime, but he notes that this abstract use of the term is historically inappropriate:

> When people refer to the amount of information that the average seventeenth-century Englishman came across in a lifetime ... they are talking about the information in published documents, in the broad sense of the term.... [T]his way of talking rests on two assumptions. First, they assume a correlation between the size of a text (as measured in characters, bytes, column inches, or whatever) and the amount of content it conveys .... And at the same time they privilege this content communicated in this way at the expense of content communicated privately or irreproducibly.[17]

The crucial shift occurred in the nineteenth century, when "'information' was taken to denote not the instruction derived from books [as had previously been the case], but the content of books from which instruction derived."[18] Like the transformation of "literary" from a property of readers to a property of texts, "information" ceased referring to "the moral education instilled by reading" and began to refer to disembodied content, detachable from its containers.[19] As Nunberg describes it elsewhere, from then on, "information" described "a self-sufficient substance detached from its source and independent of any individual consciousness."[20]

Along with a parallel account by John Durham Peters, Nunberg's genealogy traces the contours of a premodern concept of information, which this chapter fills in and explores. Early modern readers and writers did not share the assumptions that size equals content and that content is isomorphic with words in printed documents, nor did they regard information, in Peters' words, as merely "knowledge with the human body taken out of it."[21]

---

[16] Nunberg, "Farewell to the Information Age," 111.
[17] Nunberg, 112.
[18] Nunberg, 113.
[19] Geoffrey Nunberg, "Information, Disinformation, Misinformation," in *Information: A Historical Companion*, ed. Ann Blair et al. (Princeton: Princeton University Press, 2021), 496. On the transformation of "literature," see Raymond Williams, *Keywords: A Vocabulary of Culture and Society* (New York: Oxford University Press, 1985), 185ff.
[20] Nunberg, "Information, Disinformation, Misinformation," 497.
[21] John Durham Peters, "Information: Notes Toward a Critical History," *Journal of Communication Inquiry* 12, no. 2 (1988): 15, https://doi.org/10.1177/019685998801200202. In Peters' account, two crucial transitions occurred when empiricism relocated information to the knowing consciousness of the person in-formed, then when the functional needs of the state required a disembodied notion of information.

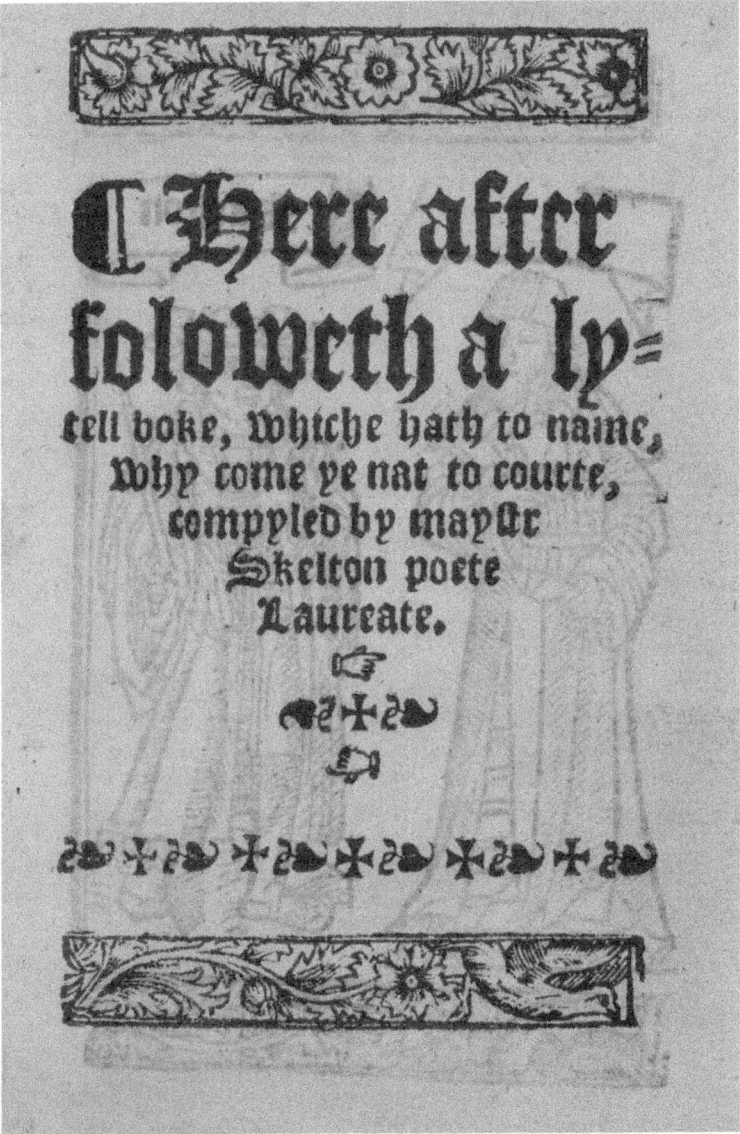

Figure 4.1   John Skelton, *Here after Foloweth a Lytell Boke, Whiche Hath to Name, Why Come Ye Nat to Courte* (London, 1545), sig. A1r, RB 69485, The Huntington Library, San Marino, California.

As we will see, for early modern English readers and writers, information always has a body: content is not fully detachable from its human knowers or textual containers, even if the size of a book and its content remain separate and separable qualities. When writers addressed the content of books, they rarely, if ever, treated it as a "self-sufficient substance detached from its source," but they did show an impressive array of rhetorical strategies for talking about the relationship between that content and the size of books – between, that is, books' informational content and their material capacities. In this way, the discourse of book size expanded the premodern concept of information and potentially, though not inevitably, opened the door for the later, disembodied and abstract concept of information.

We will proceed in four further sections. First, I survey the language of book size across the late fifteenth, sixteenth, and seventeenth centuries. From Chaucer's "Go litel boke" to Armado's "volumes in folio" to later invocations of oversized books, this discourse offered writers a rich resource for talking about what books contain. Second, I turn to the category of big books to show the flexible and fruitful relationship writers imagined between book size and book content. Third, I turn to the many instances of writers comparing book formats to each other as a way of organizing and differentiating types and amounts. Fourth, I focus on the term "in folio," which functioned across the period as a marker of capacity. Books in folio could contain a lot of information, but that information was never "detachable from its containers." The conceptual flexibility of "in folio" offered writers a way to speak of form and content as inextricably linked, necessarily vexed, but never fixed.

Premodern Book Size

When addressing book size, early modern writers and publishers maintain the strong current of self-awareness we have already seen in previous chapters. Often, this reflexivity occurs front and center, as in the Skelton title page quoted above and pictured in Figure 4.1.[22] Another Skelton book published in the same year (1545) features the same phrase: "here after foloweth a litel boke called Colyn Cloute."[23] This formula appears on the first page of many of the earliest English printed books, where William Caxton and his successor Wynkyn de Worde worked to link the products of the press to the familiar

[22] Skelton, *Here after Foloweth a Lytell Boke, Whiche Hath to Name, Why Come Ye Nat to Courte.* STC 22615.
[23] John Skelton, *Here after Foloweth a Litel Boke Called Colyn Cloute* (London, 1545). STC 22601.

modes of self-reference in manuscript culture. Translating the conventional manuscript "incipit," books proclaimed, for instance, "Here begynneth a litil boke the whiche traytied and reherced many gode thinges necessaries for the infirmite & grete sekenesse called pestilence."[24] Another book reads, "Here begynneth a lytyll treatyse schortely compyled and called ars moriendi that is to saye the craft for to deye for the helthe of mannes sowle."[25] De Worde's 1495 edition of a John Lydgate poem reads, "Here begynneth a lytell treatyse of the horse, the sheep, and the ghoos," while other books are announced as "a lytell treatyse for to lerne Englysshe and Frensshe," "a lytell boke called good maners," and "a lytyll treatyse whiche is called the.xii. profytes of trybulacyon."[26]

The phrases "little book" and "little treatise" emerge from an earlier tradition, but their rhetorical function shifts as title pages acquire new importance in printed books.[27] These phrases reach back to the "fanciful, confidential, and quaint" address to the "litel book" invoked by Chaucer. in *Troilus and Criseyde*.[28] Chaucer was hardly alone in using "little" to signal both "short [or] brief" and "affectionate disparagement."[29] Poets writing in Chaucer's wake, including Langland and John Gower, referred to their own "little books" as a tip of the hat to their fellow poet's charming false modesty. A size term ("little") was thus already working to bridge physical, material size with the conceptual stuff of books – poetry, medical advice, preparation for death, and so on. The apparent interchangeability of "book" and "treatise" (like the conceptual ambiguity of the word "book" itself) supports this bridging work by affirming the correspondence between a genre (a treatise) and a physical object (the book). By the mid-sixteenth century, however, as the title page emerged as an important component of the market for printed

[24] Joannes Jacobi, *Here Begynneth a Litil Boke the Whiche Traytied and Reherced Many Gode Thinges Necessaries for the Infirmite & Grete Sekenesse Called Pestilence the Whiche Often Times Enfecteth Vs* (London, 1485). STC 4589.

[25] Anonymous, *Here Begynneth a Lytyll Treatyse Schortely Compyled and Called Ars Moriendi* (London, 1491). STC 786.

[26] John Lydgate, *Here Begynneth a Lytell Treatyse of the Horse, the Sheep, and the Ghoos* (London, 1495); Anonymous, *Here Begynneth a Lytell Treatyse for to Lerne Englysshe and Frensshe* (London, 1497); Jacques Legrand, *Here Begynneth a Lytell Boke Called Good Maners* (London, 1498); Peter Du Bois, *Here Begynnethe a Lytyll Treatyse Whiche Is Called the.Xii. Profytes of Trybulacyon* (London, 1499). STC 17020, 24866, 15397, and 20412.

[27] Much scholarship on title pages focuses on playbooks. See Corns, "The Early Modern Search Engine"; Tiffany Stern, "'On Each Wall and Corner Poast': Playbills, Title-pages, and Advertising in Early Modern London," *English Literary Renaissance* 36, no. 1 (2006): 57–89, https://doi .org/10.1111/j.1475-6757.2006.00072.x; Gabriel Egan, "'As It Was, Is, or Will Be Played': Title-Pages and the Theatre Industry to 1610," in *From Performance to Print in Shakespeare's England* (Basingstoke, England: Palgrave Macmillan, 2006), 92–110.

[28] Tatlock, "The Epilog of Chaucer's 'Troilus,'" 628.

[29] *MED* s.v. "little" 3a.

books, that bridge became much more apparent, as in the Skelton book in Figure 4.1. A reader holding Skelton's slim octavo does not need reminding that it is in fact a "lytell booke," but the type and syntax of the title emphasize the book's diminutive physical size over title or author. Size has eclipsed false modesty – or real modesty, for that matter.

The rhetoric of small books is hardly the only size language that matters, but its Chaucerian, Caxtonian associations of modesty and economy gave writers a wagon to which to hitch their little books. Often the stakes are low. William Hayward's translation (1569) of a grammatical "war" between the noun and verb claims that "learnyng" and "martial prowesse" are "are in this present small volume comprised."[30] Dudley Fenner asks why the "infinite and contradictory" canon law must so outnumber "God his worde in a small volume."[31] Richard Jones explains how he "reduced" a longer work "into this small volume," while John Dove expresses trust that "this small volume shall not seem tedious."[32] Sometimes the stakes are higher, however. In her epistle "to the vertvovs Reader" preceding her poem *Salue deus rex iudæorum*, Aemilia Lanyer asserts her intention to correct apparent misperceptions about women:

> often haue I heard, that it is the property of some women, not only to emulate the virtues and perfections of the rest, but also by all their powers of ill speaking, to ecclipse the brightnes of their deserued fame: now contrary to this custome, which men I hope vniustly lay to their charge, I haue written this small volume, or little booke, for the generall vse of all virtuous Ladies and Gentlewomen of this kingdome; and in commendation of some particular persons of our owne sexe, such as for the most part, are so well knowne to my selfe, and others, that I dare vndertake Fame dares not to call any better.[33]

This ingenious framing defies easy paraphrase. Lanyer avoids confirming or denying women's reputation for emulation and overreach, even as she strongly implies the injustice of that reputation. Lanyer promises to give "Ladies and Gentlewomen" examples to displace that supposed reputation,

[30] Andrea Guarna, *Bellum Grammaticale a Discourse of Great War and Dissention Betwene Two Worthy Princes, the Noune and the Uerbe, Contending for the Chefe Place or Dignitie in Oration* (London, 1569), sig. A8v. STC 12419.
[31] Anonymous, *A Counter-Poyson Modestly Written for the Time, to Make Aunswere to the Obiections and Reproches, Wherewith the Aunswerer to the Abstract, Would Disgrace the Holy Discipline of Christ* (London, 1584), sig. H1r. STC 10770.
[32] Richard Jones, *The Booke of Honor and Armes* (London, 1590), sig. A2v; John Dove, *An Aduertisement to the English Seminaries, Amd Iesuites Shewing Their Loose Kind of Writing, and Negligent Handling the Cause of Religion, in the Whole Course of Their Workes* (London, 1610), sig. A3v. STC 22163 and STC 7077.
[33] Aemilia Lanyer, *Salue Deus Rex Iudæorum* (London, 1611), sig. F3r. STC 15227.

then implies that women (but perhaps not men) already know these examples. Lanyer's savvy rhetoric, which addresses women one way and men another, may cause us to ignore the strategic redundancy at the heart of the sentence: "this small volume, or little booke." It is probably fair to call this 110-page quarto a "small volume," but Lanyer's unnecessary gloss links her "little book" directly with the Chaucerian modesty topos. The wink to convention takes advantage of a situation in which modesty itself is in question, opening the door for her insistence, later in the letter, that the poem will cause "honourable minded men to speak reuerently of our sexe." To recuperate the false reputation for female immodesty, Lanyer appeals to the male reputation for false modesty.

Across instances, a salient pattern emerges among references to little books: a great many writers assert the value and, paradoxically, the *quantity* of what fits in their small volumes. One writer defends abridgements because they:

> comprise in one small volume, the marrow, quintessence, and most remarkable usefull materials comprised in many large Records, and Voluminous Tomes; as one precious Jewel or small peece of Gold contains within it the value of many peeces and pounds of Iron, Brass, Tinn, Silver; and one sheet in a small Pica letter, the substance of many sheets set in Capitals.[34]

This writer, none other than long-winded polemicist William Prynne, knew a thing or two about "Voluminous Tomes." He begins with a claim about books (abridgements give us the "marrow" of many records), then introduces a comparison with coins (a gold coin is worth as much as many iron ones), and then swerves back to a book metaphor, noting that the smaller Pica typeface allows printers to cram a lot of words on a sheet. Books stand for money, which in turn stands for books. Other writers were hardly so elaborate. Johannes Sturm declares his intention "to conteyne in one small volume … large theames," and John Sanford acknowledges his book "is but a smal volume, but in deed a golden booke, both for the stuffe and the matter thereof, as containing in it the true and vndoubted word of God."[35] Jos Prat assures readers that his "litle Book … though it contain much in effect, yet I haue contriued into this small Octauo" in order that it "might become a sociable companion for euery mans pocket."[36] Likewise,

---

[34] Anonymous, *An Exact Abridgement of the Records in the Tower of London from the Reign of King Edward the Second, unto King Richard the Third* (London, 1657), sig. A2v. Wing C6489.

[35] Johannes Sturm, *A Ritch Storehouse or Treasurie for Nobilitye and Gentlemen* (London, 1570), sig. B1r; John Sanford, *Gods Arrowe of the Pestilence* (Oxford, 1604), sig. A5r. STC 23408 and STC 21734.

[36] Jos Prat, *The Order of Orthographie: Or, Sixty Six Rules Shortly Directing to the True Writing, Speaking, and Pronouncing the English Tongue* (London, 1622), sig. A2r-v. STC 20186.7.

Thomas Powell notes that he has condensed a law book into "such a small Volume, as may be portable in euery pocket."[37]

Writers grew quite inventive. The author of *The golden meane* (1613) claims to "cast into a small Volumne a large summe of Loue," and Barnabe Rich to "cast into a small volume, a large discourse of sin and wickednes."[38] Robert Basset compares small books to small people:

> by the reason that the productive force, or generative vertue being enclosed, and as it were crammed or erouded into a small volume, (as I may say) is so much the more vigorous, and forcible: as generally is observed in little persons, who are great in a little volume, but for the most part full of spirit and vigour[.][39]

Another preface epistle, decrying the supposedly depraved state of Germany, promises the "tender hearted reader" that "in this small volume is briefly disected (or anatomized) the largest subject of misery that the lanthorne of time ever shewed to the world."[40] Thomas White says he is doing his readers a favor: "these endeavours I have crowded into this small Volume, for the benefit and conveniencies of such as take delight in Dissertations of this nature."[41] Elkanah Settle's 1667 "Elegie on the late Fire on London" conventionally grapples with whether poetry can "intomb" the scope of the tragedy:

> all
> That we may height, or worth, or greatness call,
> Like Troy intomb'd in Iliads, story showes
> The compass of a Nutshel may inclose
> Or like deceased Potentates of old
> The narrow volume of a Sheet may hold.[42]

Glancing ahead to the nut metaphor we will crack open in the next chapter, Settle decides that "narrow volume" can in fact "inclose" or "hold"

---

[37] Thomas Powell, *The Attourneys Academy, or, The Manner and Forme of Proceeding Practically Vpon Any Suite, Plaint or Action Whatsoever, in Any Court of Record Whatsoever, within This Kingdome* (London, 1623), sig. M3v. STC 20163.5.

[38] Anonymous, *The Golden Meane Lately Written, as Occasion Serued, to a Great Lord* (London, 1613), sig. A4v; Barnabe Rich, *My Ladies Looking Glasse* (London, 1616), sig. I3r. STC 17757 and STC 20991.7.

[39] Robert Basset, *Curiosities: Or the Cabinet of Nature* (London, 1637), sig. H2r. STC 1557.

[40] M. P., *A Briefe Dissection of Germaines Affliction with Warre, Pestilence, and Famine* (London, 1638), sig. A2r. STC 19222.

[41] Thomas White, *The Middle State of Souls from the Hour of Death to the Day of Judgment* (London, 1659), sig. M1or. Wing W1836.

[42] Elkanah Settle, *An Elegie on the Late Fire and Ruines of London* (London, 1667), sig. A2r. Wing S2677A.

(i.e., *contain*) such a huge event. Bafflingly, John Mennes includes an epigram "On a young Gentlewoman" in his book of jests:

> Nature in this small volume was about
> To perfect what in woman was left out:
> Yet carefull least a piece so well begun,
> Should want preservatives when she had done:
> Ere she could finish what she undertook,
> Threw dust upon it, and shut up the Book.[43]

Consider the great distance between Lanyer's use of "small volume" as part of a project to disabuse men of harmful, sexist assumptions and Mennes's use of the same term to elaborate those assumptions. However this joke is supposed to work, it does so at the expense of women. Nature, figured as the author of the "piece" – composition, but also a sexualized term applied to women – fears that too perfect a woman/book will lack "preservatives."[44] With a hint at sexual violence, Mennes manages to insult all women as imperfect and this particular gentlewoman as unattractive. In the terms of this chapter's argument, Mennes's sexist joke nevertheless depends on the same flexible relationship between size and content that others do, including Lanyer.

The rhetoric of small books was hardly the only one writers used to coordinate the content of books with their material size. The extensible rhetoric of book size allowed the development of a complex literary repertoire with which writers could use book size to make claims about what they called the content, substance, or matter of books. Many instances are not particularly exciting, as when the author of *A myrroure for magistrates* (1559) notes that he has rehearsed some details of a story in prose "for the better ope[n]ing of the story, which if it should have bene spoken in his tragedy would rather have made a volume than a Pamphlete."[45] The recusant author of *The Conuerted Iew* (1630) says that George Abbot, Archbishop of Canterbury, "most impertinently dilateth and spreadeth hymselfe, in long and tedious discourses ... thereby to spine out his booke to some resonable lenght [sic] or quantity."[46] Francis Quarrels writes that his search of the scriptures led him to "as many places to that purpose, as

---

[43] John Mennes, *Recreation for Ingenious Head-Peeces* (London, 1654), sig. M8r. Wing M1714.

[44] *OED*, s.v. "piece," 9b.

[45] Anonymous, *A Myrroure for Magistrates* (London, 1559), sig. C3r. STC 1247.

[46] John Clare, *The Conuerted Iew or Certaine Dialogues Betweene Micheas a Learned Iew and Others, Touching Diuers Points of Religion, Controuerted Betweene the Catholicks and Protestants*, 1630, sig. V1v. STC 5351.

would swell this Sheet into a Volume."[47] William Lacey makes the size/
content slippage explicit when he opines that "a large volume in folio may
be a Pamphlet in substance, and a Manuall booke of a very few sheets may
contain the waight & worth of an ample volume."[48]

Other writers manage more flare. In an odd pamphlet, John Taylor
describes a "monstrous bigge huge Quarrel" full of nonsense words that
"fill up a sheet in print," and he later complains that "the pestilent penns
of pestiferous Pragmaticall, Aquaticall poetasters hath sweat out whole
Reames [of paper] to small purpose."[49] Like Don Armado, with whom this
chapter began, Taylor apparently ignores his own propensity to verbosity.
Thomas Bastard, in his epigram "Ad Lectorem" (to the reader), takes the
idea in another direction:

> AN heauie book reader my weary pen,
> Doth here present to thee, which doth containe
> The faultes and euils of so many men,
> With which my paper doth euen sinke againe.
> They haue confest their sinnes into my booke,
> Which here vnloaded, all they haue forsaken.[50]

Bastard uses the term for the very concept in question here: "containe."
This book, which takes aim at a variety of social types and specific people, *contains* the confessed "sinnes" of many men. Yet even so stark a
reference to the containment work of books is undermined by Bastard's
elaboration of the conceit. Writing as if the paper itself has soaked up the
"faultes and euils" that this octavo book of epigrams describes, Bastard
gives the ideas of the book a greater figurative weight than the book itself
can contain. Far less facetious, William Goodwin later used a similar
conceit: "that sinfull eating of Adam in Paradise may seem but a small
matter in the judgement of man, but in the eye of God a whole volume
of iniquity was in it."[51]

One final example will wrap up this section. Praising the fishing village
of Yarmouth in *Lenten stuffe* (1599), Thomas Nashe runs out of space, or so
he claims: "I am posting to my proposed scope, or else I could runne tenne
quier of paper out of breath, in further trauersing her [Yarmouth's] rightes

---

[47] Francis Quarles, *The Loyall Convert* (Oxford, 1644), sig. B2r. Wing Q107.
[48] William Lacey, *The Iudgment of an Vniuersity-Man Concerning M. VVilliam Chillingvvorth His Late Pamphlet, in Ansvvere to Charity Maintayned* (Saint-Omer, 1639), sig. B2r. STC 15117.
[49] John Taylor, *Mercurius Nonsencicus* (London, 1648), sig. A2r-3v. Wing T482A.
[50] Thomas Bastard, *Chrestoleros Seuen Bookes of Epigrames* (London, 1598), sig. H5v. STC 1559.
[51] Philip Goodwin, *The Evangelicall Communicant in the Eucharisticall Sacrament* (London, 1649), sig. Aa5r. Wing G1215.

and dignities."[52] Like all the writers cited in this section, Nashe builds a rhetorical bridge between the material capacity of books – in this case, the imagined additional ten quires of paper – and the content – the village's "rightes and dignities" – without presuming an equivalence between the two. Indeed, like Shakespeare's joke about Armado's folios, Nashe's joke about running ten quires out of breath depends upon our recognition that so much praise would be indecorous, though not impossible given that *Lenten stuffe* is a book written in mock praise of the red herring.

The bodily vector of Nashe's joke returns us, *mutatis mutandis*, to Nunberg's genealogy of the modern idea of information, in which information is "indifferent to the transformations of its vehicles."[53] The discourse of book size surveyed here shows that premodern writers worked upon the opposite assumption. They remain alive to the relationship between books and what those books contain, even as they persistently keep the two separate. Such a view of informational content presents a clear contrast to modern information, which Eric Hayot glosses as "a morselized, contextless piece of … something" and as "that which has no fixed form, but can be passed on from one person to another, or one medium to another, without either being significantly altered in itself, or altering that which it touches."[54] Nashe's whole point is that his "information" about Yarmouth necessarily alters and is altered by what it touches. To praise the red herring and the village known for it, Nashe definitely does not need a bigger book.

Big Books and Their Readers

The previous section showed how the rhetoric of book size stages a flexible, productive relationship between form and content. With that rhetoric, premodern writers crafted jokes, insults, literary self-positioning, and conceits for political, social, and theological claims. Book size thus invokes a premodern idea of information as always contextualized and situated – information with a body. This does not mean, however, that premodern English writers did not clearly apprehend the capacity of books to store and make accessible. Such an apprehension underlies most of the examples above. However they understood the stuff books contain (as content, subject matter, information, text, language, knowledge, or some combination of these), they remained mindful that books are material objects devised

---

[52] Thomas Nash, *Nashes Lenten Stuffe* (London, 1599), sig. D2r. STC 18370.
[53] Nunberg, "Farewell to the Information Age," 107.
[54] Hayot, Detwyler, and Pao, *Information*, 7. Ellipsis in original.

primarily to support a set of marks. These marks are often but hardly always graphical representations of language, and because bigger books can sustain more of these marks, they received widespread attention. In particular, the prevalence of big books in the English cultural imagination introduced both an opportunity – big books hold more words! – and a set of liabilities: who will read them? What if books are too long for their own good? What do big books afford that small books do not? The discourse of big books gives us a sense of the scope and direction of the information concept in premodern England.

Adjectives tell the story. The three most common adjectives for describing a big-sized book were *large, great,* and *big.* Each term had a particular convention of use (overlapping with others, of course), and thus gave writers a particular way to talk about what those big books contain. *Large* most often referred to the size of a book in a more or less neutral way. John Stow, for instance, in the *Abridgement of the English Chronicle,* notes several times that the reader should "read my larger booke," while the *Abridgement of the booke of acts and monuments* similarly points readers to "much more in the large volume, where all such matters lie open at the full."[55] The poet John Davies writes of "Memories large volume," the poet William Habington of the "Large volume write[n] by Time" and the "large volumes of the skies," and George Wither of the "large Volume of History."[56] Presbyterian John Howe appeals to multiple figures to convey how humans grasp God's glory: "the Notion therefore we can hence form of this glory, is only such as we may have of a large volume by a brief Synopsis or Table; of a magnificent fabrick, by a small Module or Platform, a spacious Countrey by a little Landskip."[57] Sometimes, the neutrality of "large" provides a contrast, as when Thomas Wilson writes that "The holy Byble, which, though a large booke considered by it selfe, yet if it bee compared with the huge volumes of Popish ordinances and decrees, it is but little."[58]

Even these somewhat neutral instances suggest the capacity of large books, but other writers appeal to "large" books as holding a lot of stuff.

[55] John Stow, *The Abridgement of the English Chronicle* (London, 1618), sig. D4v; John Foxe, *An Abridgement of the Booke of Acts and Monumentes of the Church* (London, 1589), sig. [3r]. STC 23332 and STC 11229.
[56] John Davies, *Nosce Teipsum This Oracle Expounded in Two Elegies, 1. Of Humane Knowledge, 2. Of the Soule of Man, and the Immortalitie Thereof* (London, 1599), sig. G4r; William Habington, *Castara* (London, 1640), sig. C8v-9r; George Wither, *The Modern States-Man* (London, 1653), sig. K6r. STC 6355.54, STC 12585, and Wing W3172.
[57] John Howe, *The Blessednesse of the Righteous Discoursed from Psal. 17, 15* (London, 1668), sig. D6r. Wing H3015.
[58] Thomas Wilson, *A Christian Dictionarie* (London, 1612), sig. F5r. STC 25786.

John Alday, translating Pierre Boaistuau, writes of an herb, "if we should rehearse and declare all the singularities and excellencies that are manifested and shewed [...] I should occupy a large volume."[59] Thomas Tymme translates a historical commentary whose authors acknowledge, late in the book, that it has grown "vnto a great and large volume."[60] A translator of the cartographer Abraham Ortelius notes that praise of Italy "would rather requyre a large volume then so brief a description as a page of paper wil admit."[61] And Godfrey Goodman complains that the "large volumes of Galen" are not sufficient, and doctors keep making new medical discoveries:

> is it possible that all these huge and large volumes, farre exceeding mans body in largenesse and weight, should not bee able sufficiently to describe it, but that euery yeere should finde out some place & part of mans body for a new incroaching disease, vnknowne to the Ancients, and wondred at by the professors?[62]

Importantly, these examples come from fields of knowledge that were expanding in the early modern period, including botany, history, cartography, and medicine. The writers' sense that there is *so much stuff* leads them to the same bookish language, sometimes literal and sometimes figurative. The language allows writers to express this sense of overload, but it also shapes their conception of what exactly has become so abundant. Goodman's mistrust of new medical knowledge, for instance, locates itself in large books, which in turn conceptualize that knowledge as contained in books, even if inflated.

Along these lines, one pattern of "large volume" deserves mention here, though Chapter 6 will address it more extensively. Many writers appealed to a large book to refer to knowledge concerning the natural world – the so-called great book of nature. The idea, once again, is that the world contains such a diversity and abundance of creatures that the book containing them must be a large one. Gabriel Powel, for instance, promises to "produce against [atheists] sundrie witnesses out of the large volume of Gods creatures, which manifestly testifie that there is a God."[63] James Cleland

[59] Pierre Boaistuau, *Theatrum Mundi the Theatre or Rule of the World* (London, 1566), sig. D7v. STC 3168.
[60] Jean de Serres, *The Three Partes of Commentaries Containing the Whole and Perfect Discourse of the Ciuill Warres of Fraunce* (London, 1574), sig. Ggg1r. STC 22241.5.
[61] Abraham Ortelius, *An Epitome of Ortelius His Theater of the Vuorld, Vuherein the Principal Regions of the Earth Are Descriued in Smalle Mappes* (Antwerp, 1601), sig. I4v. STC 18857.
[62] Godfrey Goodman, *The Fall of Man, or the Corruption of Nature, Proued by the Light of Our Naturall Reason* (London, 1616), sig. G8v. STC 12023.
[63] Gabriel Powel, *The Resolued Christian, Exhorting to Resolution Written, to Recall the Worldling, to Comfort the Faint-Harted, to Strengthen the Faithfull, and to Perswade All Men, so to Runne, That They May Obtaine* (London, 1600), sig. M1r. STC 20150.

likewise writes that God "hath laid open vnto vs, [...] the large volume of this world, wherein wee may see his Image painted more liuely vpon it all."[64] Ephraim Huit appeals to the common "two books" metaphor that "any thing worth obseruance is learned, either out of the large volume of creatures or the written will of the Lord."[65] And Thomas Fuller, writing about polygamy, figures God as a stationer-author:

> when God first made the large volume of the world, and all creatures therein, and set it forth, *Cum regali privilegio, Behold all things therein were very good*, hee made one *Eve* for one *Adam*. *Poligamy* is an *Erratum*, and needs an *Index expurgatorius*, being crept in, being more than what was in the maiden coppy.[66]

Fuller's thick and apparently joyous use of book trade language unfolds from the large book of nature to another imagined book, which erroneously includes polygamy and thus deserves to be banned (and thus placed on the famous *Index* of banned books). This imagined book contains something like what we would call misinformation, which Nunberg notes is different from a lie or falsehood.[67] Fuller and others reach instinctively for "large" when they want to describe quantity.

Great books, meanwhile, boasted a huge semantic range in keeping with the usage of "great" in this period.[68] Pierre de la Primaudaye, for instance, in the *French Academy*, writes that "the holy Ghost doth often propound vnto vs in holy scriptures this whole visible world, as a great booke of nature."[69] Likewise John Boys, concerning the relationship between humans and the world, writes that man is the "compendious Index of Gods great booke in folio."[70] In a similar vein, Nicholas Byfield instructed that if Christians want to learn to meditate, "let them lay before them either of these bookes of God, either the great Booke of the creatures, or little booke of the Scriptures; and so praying God to direct them, take those things that easily offer themselves from thence."[71] John Calvin

---

[64] Cleland, *Hērō-Paideia, or The Institution of a Young Noble Man*, sig. N2v. STC 5393.
[65] Ephraim Huit, *The Anatomy of Conscience, or, The Summe of Pauls Regeneracy* (London, 1626), sig. G2v. STC 13928.
[66] Thomas Fuller, *Ioseph's Partie-Colored Coat* (London, 1640), sig. P4v. STC 11466.3, emphasis in original.
[67] Nunberg, "Information, Disinformation, Misinformation," 499.
[68] *OED*, s.v., "great."
[69] Pierre de La Primaudaye, *The Second Part of the French Academie* (London, 1594), sig. A2v. STC 15238.
[70] John Boys, *An Exposition of the Festiuall Epistles and Gospels Vsed in Our English Liturgie Together with a Reason Why the Church Did Chuse the Same* (London, 1615), sig. K7r. STC 3462.3.
[71] Nicholas Byfield, *A Commentary upon the Three First Chapters of the First Epistle Generall of St. Peter* (London, 1637), sig. Oor. STC 4212.

(in Arthur Golding's translation) said of his critics, "Let me haue a strong partie to put in accusation against mee, yea and let him make a great booke of it: it shall not greeue me to carry it vpon my shoulder."[72] Bartolomé de las Casas claimed that "Certaynely if I shoulde stande to tell the particularities of these cruelties: I shoulde make a great booke thereof, whiche shoulde astonishe the worlde."[73] *Great*'s range allows writers to combine reference to size with claims about quality (las Casas), intensity (Calvin), or comprehensiveness (Boys).

Great books may not always be good for you, at least proverbially speaking. William Barlow quotes what he calls a "heathen proverbial sentence" that "a great booke was a great Mischiefe."[74] Martin Fotherby names the source of this proverb in his attempt to defend his inclusion of copious and even unnecessary detail. He writes, "though it hath made the Booke some what bigger: yet hath it also (I hope) made it better. So that I am the lesse fearefull of *Callimachus* his censure, that, Magnus Liber, est magno malo par. A great Booke is little better then a great euill."[75] Many writers riffed on this proverb, including Richard Baxter, who complains that students learn words but not knowledge, and "so their saying is too often true, that a great Book is a great Evil, while it containeth so great a number of uncertain words, which become the matter of great contentions."[76]

Let us pause here before moving to the third adjective to consider what these examples show us. The fact that Barlow, Fotherby, and Baxter are just three of the many writers who quote or paraphrase Callimachus's proverb suggests that a whole variety of people were deeply conscious – we might even say self-conscious – of how the size of big books signified, whether "size" means format or simply overall girth. This awareness underlies an implicit truism with which modern scholars tend to operate when they talk about early modern books. Roger Chartier, for example, has described how book size intersected with social class distinctions in the period: large, deluxe books "provided food for thought for the wealthiest or the best-educated members of society," while smaller, shorter, and more ephemeral books "fed the curiosities of the common people." Perhaps that is true.

---

[72] Jean Calvin, *Sermons of Master Iohn Caluin, Vpon the Booke of Iob* (London, 1574), sig. Pp7r. STC 4445.

[73] Bartolomé de las Casas, *The Spanish Colonie, or Briefe Chronicle of the Acts and Gestes of the Spaniardes in the West Indies* (London, 1583), sig. C4v. STC 4739.

[74] William Barlow, *An Answer to a Catholike English-Man* (London, 1609), sig. Br. STC 1446.5.

[75] Martin Fotherby, *Atheomastix Clearing Foure Truthes, against Atheists and Infidels* (London, 1622), sig. B5v. STC 11205.

[76] Richard Baxter, *Richard Baxter's Dying Thoughts upon Phil. I, 23 Written for His Own Life and the Latter Times of His Corporal Pains and Weakness* (London, 1683), sig. H2v. Wing B1256.

Perhaps Chartier is right to claim that publishers' "contrasting intentions" for their books along social lines "can be read in the material aspect of the book."[77] But it is also the case that readers across social lines could see and play upon those intentions, as the examples presented here do. What makes book size significant is not merely that it points to prior, stable values, but that it entails an array of value-laden responses, as writers thought about how the "stuff" of books made its way to readers.

The question of readers takes us to *big*, the flashpoint adjective for the cultural, and specifically literary (i.e., readerly), significance of big books. *Large* and *great* often took a positive spin, but *big* went the opposite way. In 1547, the physician Christopher Langton published *A very brief treatise, orderly declaring the principal parts of physick*, to which was attached a commendatory poem by William Baldwin. The book, it reads,

> Whiche smal though it seme contayneth as much
> Of arte to be knowen of them that are wyse,
> As byg myghty bokes agastfull to tuche,
> As well for the wayght, as for the heauy pryce.
> Reade it therfore all ye that loue your healthe,
> Learne here in an houre, elles where in a yere
> Scarce red, the which Langton willing our welth
> Hath englyshed brefe, as it doth appere.[78]

This wonderful little poem has it all: it stands in for much of the early modern discourse about book size. First, it plays on the belief, suggested too in the Callimachus proverb, that big books are artificially and unnecessarily inflated, that their size indicates not their value but their vacuity and even their potential to cause harm. Peter Heylyn, for instance, accuses another writer of artificial inflation:

> to make his Book look big upon us, hee left out nothing that hee met with in his own collections; or had beene sent in to him by his friends to set out the worke: and that it might appear a most learned piece, hee hath dressed up his margin with quotations of all sorts, and uses.[79]

Likewise, John Hall writes to William Prynne that:

> your Books themselves ... though they appear'd big and tall were extreame feeble and ill complexion'd.... For (Sir) 'Tis the generall opinion of all

---

[77] Roger Chartier, *The Cultural Uses of Print in Early Modern France*, trans. Lydia G. Cochrane (Princeton: Princeton University Press, 1987), 181.

[78] Christopher Langton, *A Uery Brefe Treatise, Ordrely Declaring the Pri[n]Cipal Partes of Phisick* (London, 1547). STC 15205. The poem appears on the unsigned verso side of the title page.

[79] Peter Heylyn, *Antidotum Lincolniense* (London, 1637), sig. Aaar. STC 13267.

> Learned men ... that books large and empty are the greatest enemies to
> that perpetuity and largenesse of fame, that every diligent Writer ought to
> aime at.[80]

Little books make people famous; big books make people infamous.

Baldwin's commendatory poem also highlights the disjunction between
the use value and exchange value of a big book. "Big myghty bokes" are
"agastfull to tuche" because they are physically heavy and expensive,
whereas Langton's *very brief treatise* is lighter, cheaper, and contains the
same information. Indeed, many writers who instrumentalize the bigness
of books do so with an eye toward the market. Richard Mulcaster, for
instance, in the *Elementarie*, writes that he covers so much ground in the
first part that "the book thereby growing to som bulk, I thought it good
to deuide it into parts, vpon sundrie causes, but chefelie for the printer,
whose sale will be quik if the book be not big."[81] A small book is a better
commodity, for Mulcaster as for many university presses today. Similarly,
Anthony Munday in a preface explains that "a Booke growing too bigge in
quantitie, is profitable neither to the minde nor the pursse: for that men
are now so wise, and the world so hard, as they looue not to buie pleasure
at vnreasonable price."[82] Bigger in this case is not merely not better but in
fact lowers the profitability of the commodity.

Many writers show self-consciousness about their books' growing so
big that they become worthless. Johann Rivius notes defensively that "it
is not our minde in this place to alleadge all, least our booke doo growe
ouer-big."[83] Thomas Morton admits that "this booke groweth bigge and
corpulent,"[84] while Thomas Gainsford confronts the problem of too
much material by claiming that "a whole history might fill your eares
with pleasure and instances of worthy prosecution, which I desist from,
for swelling the booke too bigg with so poore a breath of common and
knowne relations, and will only goe forward with some slender descriptions."[85] These writers anticipate the very market conditions that Munday
describes.

---

[80] John Hall, *A Serious Epistle to Mr. William Prynne* (London, 1649), sig. A2r. Wing H359A.

[81] Mulcaster, *The First Part of the Elementarie*, sig. *[iv]v. STC 18250.

[82] Anonymous, *Palmerin D'Oliua The Mirrour of Nobilitie, Mappe of Honor, Anatomie of Rare Fortunes, Heroycall President of Loue* (London, 1588), sig. *[iii]. STC 19157.

[83] Johann Rivius, *Of the Foolishnes of Men in Putting-off the Amendement of Their Liues from Daie to Daie a Godlie and Profitable Treatise for the Present Time* (London, 1582), sig. H7v. STC 21066.

[84] Thomas Morton, *The Encounter against M. Parsons, by a Revievv of His Last Sober Reckoning, and His Exceptions Vrged in the Treatise of His Mitigation* (London, 1610), sig. V3r. STC 18183.

[85] Thomas Gainsford, *The Glory of England, or A True Description of Many Excellent Prerogatiues and Remarkeable Blessings* (London, 1618), sig. E2r. STC 11517.

As we might expect, writers weaponized book size, as in the case of William Jenkin, one of the many controversialists of the Civil War to attack the size of the books of his opponents:

> the bulk of his booke, being a heap of *defamations and scurrilities*, fitter for a sinke than a study, concerning which, I say, 'twere easie to returne him *reviling for* [*reviling;*] but this were to lay aside the Minister, the Christian, nay the man; and as ridiculous as for a man whom an asse hath kickt, to kick the asse again.[86]

In these cases, a bigger book guarantees lower value. The size dilates what a shorter book could contain. Alternatively, a big book masks the lack of any valuable contribution. Or, a big book is not worth the price and heft it takes to own it. Or, finally, responding to a valueless big book with another big book is unnecessary and useless. These and others make up the tropes of book size in the emerging public sphere of the premodern period.

The third thing Baldwin's poem calls attention to is the activity of reading. Baldwin exhorts readers, "Read it therfore all ye that loue your healthe, / Learn here in an hour elsewhcre in a yere scarce red." A shorter, smaller book affords reading much more effectively and directly than a big book. Many writers addressed this very question as they considered the relationship between big books and readers. William Slatyer, for instance, noting that his "whole book, though indifferent big, and seeming sufficient large, for the subject is but a Compendium," goes on to list the ways in which his book is accommodating to its readers with a table of contents, marginal notes, commonplace markers, and so on.[87] In a slightly different act of accommodation, James Hart announces in his *Anatomy of Urines* that:

> I could make this small Tractate swell vp into a big and voluminous booke, if I should instance in a many [sic] of these casuall cures ... which for feare of tediousnesse and prolixitie I am loth to go about: yet before I make an end, I will offer to the Readers view, two or three Stories.[88]

Hart suggests that two or three stories will prove more effective than a tedious, prolix, swollen tractate. (The word "swell" is used frequently in the context of book size, and in Hart's case, the good doctor is making a bladder joke.) Last and best, the Catholic writer John Floyd, attacking the writings of the Protestant William Chillingworth, claims that "His Booke

---

[86] William Jenkyn, *The Blind Guide, or, The Doting Doctor Composed by Way of Reply to a Late Tediously Trifling Pamphlet* (London, 1648), sig. R2r. Wing J645.

[87] William Slatyer, *The Compleat Christian, and Compleat Armour and Armoury of a Christian, Fitting Him with All Necessary Furniture for That His Holy Profession* (London, 1643), sig. A7v. Wing S3983.

[88] James Hart, *The Anatomie of Vrines* (London, 1625), sig. S2v. STC 12887a.

indeed is a vast bulke made big, not with variety of matters and proofes, but by … repetition." Floyd goes on, "These Arguments for multitude innumerable, and diffused by large extent ouer all the leaues, pages, and numbers of his booke, make it vnworthy to be read."[89]

Floyd's assertion that a long, repetitive book ("a vast bulke") is unworthy to be read points to the key conjunction across these many examples of big book language. He takes the relationship between form (format, size, bulk, "leaves, pages, and numbers") and content (number of words, "matters and proofes," "repetition," "arguments for multitude innumerable") as an object of analysis and critique instead of a stable correlation. Likewise, for the writers sampled here, the symbolic status of big books (or books of any size) does not function as a shared assumption but rather a shared *trope* available for use and abuse. For these writers, a book's "information" still literally referred to the instruction derived from it, not the content it contains. As Nunberg notes, "information" would not refer to content until the nineteenth century, when the size of a book became closely identified with its content capacity even as that content was understood as detachable from its carrier (and thus became "information" in the modern sense). By contrast, these premodern writers refuse to identify size with content capacity while also retaining the ability to play upon the resemblance of size and content. They also maintain a constitutional rhetorical insistence on the attachment of content to carrier. For them, content is always, somehow attached to form; big books make this attachment readily apparent.

Comparative Format and Storage Space

This notion of a book as a container that is attached but not identical to what it contains provides a prompt for the imagination. Many of the examples already cited do not refer to actual books but rather use book size, along with its potent tension of form and content, as a conceit or figure. The "large volume" of creatures is one prominent example of this imaginative work; a big book signifies and expresses the vastness of the world because a big book has a lot of big pages and thus includes a lot of words. Especially in the seventeenth century, one particular set of terms gave book size a local habitation and a name: the language of format. Just as casual references to "DVD" or "VHS" carry durable associations of

[89] John Floyd, *The Church Conquerant Ouer Humane Wit* (Saint-Omer, 1638), sig. Aa4v. STC 11110.

interface and storage for someone born in the late twentieth century, so too did the terms "folio," "quarto," "octavo," "duodecimo," and "decimo-sexto" come loaded with a specific set of values for early modern writers and readers. Importantly, as we will see, these values were relational, emerging from the status of the various formats as categories of the book trade and enabling comparisons across formats. In these comparative references to folio, quarto, and so on, a lively picture comes into view: books as storage spaces and, in turn, format language as a figure of capacity.

Technically, of course, book format refers not to the size of books but to how they are constructed.[90] Bibliographers often identify formats by how sheets of paper were imprinted (or "imposed") and folded to make a book (see Figure 4.2): a folio book consists of sheets folded once, while a quarto consists of sheets folded twice, thus requiring printers to print what would become four (hence, *quarto*) pages of printed text on each side of a sheet of paper. Three folds create an octavo (thus, eight pages of printed text on each side of a sheet) and four folds a decimo-sexto (sixteen pages), while a duodecimo book requires printing twelve (hence, "duo + dec" or two-and-ten) leaves on every sheet of paper. As illustrated in Figure 4.2, folio books were usually the largest format, while quartos were smaller, octavos smaller still, and so on. G. Thomas Tanselle has persuasively demonstrated that the concept of format, along with the term itself, has a complex history, and that the general descriptive rules I just relayed have limitations.[91]

For early modern English writers and readers, however, format was not just a tool of bibliographical description but also a phenomenon of the book trade, a category of book use, and a general marker of book size. Imposition schemes and paper direction mattered much less than the uses format made possible. For instance, the last page of Thomas Churchyard's quarto *Churchyardes chance* promises more poems "in a large volume" but notes that "a booke of Meta incognita, and some other small volumes, [...] can not be bound in quarto."[92] Similarly, Thomas Blundeville explains

[90] Helpful guides include Gaskell, *A New Introduction to Bibliography*; Sarah Werner, *Studying Early Printed Books, 1450–1800: A Practical Guide* (Hoboken, NJ: Wiley Blackwell, 2019).

[91] Tanselle proposes a more precise definition: "format is a designation of the number of page-units (whether of printing surface handwritten text, or blank space) that the producers of a printed or manuscript item decided upon to fill each side of a sheet of paper or vellum of the selected size(s); if paper came to a printing press in rolls rather than sheets, format can only refer to the number of page-units placed on the press at one time for the purpose of printing one side of the paper." See G. Thomas Tanselle, "The Concept of Format," *Studies in Bibliography* 53 (2000): 112–13.

[92] Thomas Churchyard, *A Pleasaunte Laborinth Called Churchyardes Chance Framed on Fancies, Vttered with Verses, and Writte[n] to Giue Solace to Euery Well Disposed Mynde* (London, 1580), sig. K4v. STC 5250.

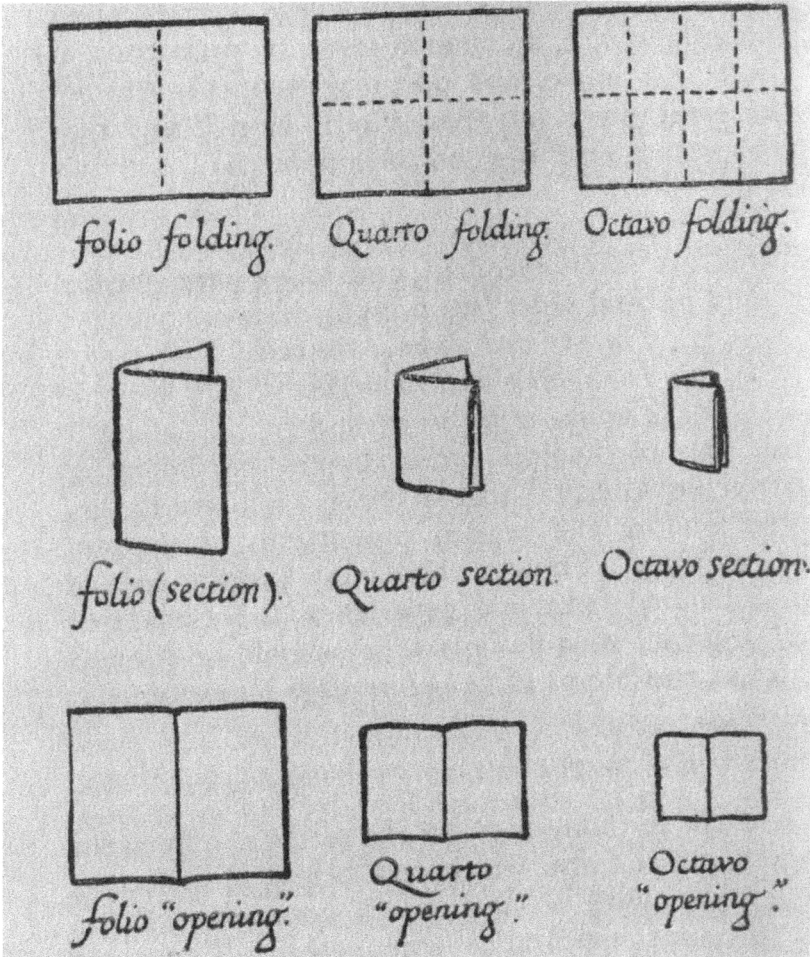

Figure 4.2   Detail of Edward Johnston, *Writing & Illuminating & Lettering* (London: Pitman & Sons, 1906), 102.

that printing trigonometry tables "in quarto and not in folio" works better because quartos "are the more portable, and the more commodious, as well for that they are more truely Printed, as also for that the complement of euery Arke is set downe in euery Page at the foote of euery collum."[93] Here as elsewhere, the references to format concern the capacity of the

[93] Thomas Blundeville, *M. Blundevile His Exercises Containing Sixe Treatises* (London, 1594), sig. H2r. STC 3146.

book, the use to which it will be put, the relationship of one format to others, and the market value the book will carry. This range of concerns underpins what we might call, with only minimal exaggeration, a format imaginary, by which the storage capacity of book formats is mapped figuratively across premodern English culture.

A crucial point about this imaginary is that calling it *figurative* is not the same as calling it *metaphorical*. Unlike the examples in Chapter 3, many uses of format language as a conceit for storage space refer to actual books. This habit, in turn, guarantees the cultural legibility of more metaphorical uses of that language. Thomas Fuller cites the many editions of William Camden's *Brittania* as evidence of how books grow as they pass through editions: "his first Edition was a Babe in a little; the second, a Childe in a bigger Octavo; the third, a Youth in a Quarto (but Map-less;) the last, a Man in a fair Folio."[94] Whereas most writers compare humankind to books, Fuller compares books to the body. Andrew Marvell writes, about one of his opponents, that "it is scarce credible how vuluminous and pithy he is in extravagance: and one of his sides in Quarto, for Falshood, Insolence, and Absurdity contains a Book in Folio."[95] The apparent contradiction of "voluminous" with "pithy" only computes when we grasp that there can be a folio's worth of absurdity contained in a quarto leaf of paper ("side").[96] Richard Eedes's prefatory poem to his long, octavo format book on Christian salvation, addresses the size problem:

> Though in Octavo written, you must know
> The Subjects are the largest Folio:
> Though Book and Price be small (excuse that wrong),
> The names are short, but yet the Things are long.
> Salvation, and Damnation![97]

While Marvell insults with format, Eedes asserts his book's value with it. He maps format onto the content of the book, so that "long ... Things" are themselves said to be folio sized. Similarly, the preacher Richard Vines contents himself "to speak in decimo sexto, what might be spoken in

---

[94] Thomas Fuller, *The Appeal of Iniured Innocence, unto the Religious Learned and Ingenuous Reader in a Controversie Betwixt the Animadvertor, Dr. Peter Heylyn, and the Author, Thomas Fuller* (London, 1659), sig. B3r. Wing F2410.

[95] Andrew Marvell, *Mr. Smirke; or, The Divine in Mode* (London, 1676), sig. C3v. Wing M873.

[96] *OED*, s.v., "side," n.1, 15a, citing this instance.

[97] Richard Eedes, *Great Salvation by Jesus Christ Tenderd to the Greatest of Sinners and in Particular to Such as Have Been Refusers of It, If God Shall Now at Last Make Them Willing to Receive It* (London, 1659), sig. B3r. Wing E243.

folio," excusing himself from "the labour of so large a volume."[98] More colorfully, in a preface epistle to a long book about church history, Daniel Featley asks, "is it not a shame to see in many mens studies idle Poems, Astreas, Guzmans, and play-books in folio, but divinity books in decimo sexto, or slender pamphlets, stitcht up in blew coats?"[99] Featley is not (or not merely) being puritanical; his objection only partly concerns the value attributed to poems, romances (Honoré d'Urfé's *Astrea*), picaresque novels (Mateo Alemán's *Guzman de Alfrache*), and plays. His principal "shame" is that, in his opinion, the world needs longer divinity books: "what though the worke be of some bulke and waight? who ever found fault with gold for that it was too massie and heavy? When *Tully* [i.e., Cicero] was asked which Oration of *Demosthenes* he liked best, hee answered, the longest."[100] For Featley, the difference in format stands for a whole knot of associations, foremost of which is the tension between the forms books take and what they contain.

Format makes possible a huge range of expressions premised on the differential storage capacity of the various formats. Thomas Adams, whom we will meet several times in the next few pages, argues that a hypocrite's "profession is in Folio, but his sincerity is so abridged, that it is contained in Decimo-sexto; nothing in the world to speake of."[101] Another writer notes that wicked and foolish men "promise in folio, though they can not perform in decimo sexto."[102] Thomas Culpepper claims that Fame "registers [virtues] indeed in Quarto, but splendid crimes are recorded in Folio."[103] And Nehemiah Rogers explains that "actuall sins committed by us are of a thousand kinds, and every vice hath its latitude and degree; some are bound up in Folio, other some in Quarto, others in Octavo, and the sins of some other in a Decimo sexto." The fact that Rogers's metaphor is not especially interesting is one reason it is so significant. By the mid-seventeenth century, format terms had become so commonplace that writers like Rogers could make somewhat unimaginative use of them and expect readers to

---

[98] Richard Vines, *Sermons Preached upon Several Publike and Eminent Occasions* (London, 1656), sig. G4r. Wing V569.

[99] Richard Crakanthorpe, *Vigilius Dormitans Romes Seer Overseene* (London, 1631), sig. A5v. STC 5983.

[100] Crakanthorpe, sig. A5v.

[101] Adams, *A Commentary or, Exposition Vpon the Diuine Second Epistle Generall, Written by the Blessed Apostle St. Peter*, sig. P5r. STC 108.

[102] John Ferret, *Didascaliæ Discourses on Severall Places of the Holy Scriptures* (Amsterdam, 1643), sig. E3v. Wing F817.

[103] Thomas Culpeper, *Morall Discourses and Essayes, upon Severall Select Subjects* (London, 1655), sig. B9r. Wing C7559.

grasp the difference in size and storage capacity. A decimo sexto sin is no great harm, but sin in folio must be a bad one, like talking in the theater. Likewise, when the author of *The Decoy Duck* writes that "some tooke [the duck] to bee a Buzzard in Quarto, others a Peacock in Folio," he is counting on his readers grasping the size comparisons at work.[104] Finally, Thorowgood, a character in Henry Glapthorne's play *Wit in a Constable*, complains that other characters "were made / But fooles in Quarto, but I find my selfe / An asse in Folio."[105] The difference between being made a fool and being made an ass is the same as the difference between the size of a quarto and a folio.

Format often describes bodies, for better and worse. In John Lyly's play *Mother Bombie*, the page Dromio remarks on the page Halfpenny's entrance: "looke where Halfepenie [...] commeth, though bound vp in decimo sexto for carriage, yet a wit in folio for coosnage."[106] Halfpenny, small in stature and bearing in keeping with his name, has a capacious wit. Richard West makes the opposite move, noting those "whose heads indeed are of a block in Folio, but their witte is in the least decimo sexto."[107] The poet John Taylor complains about the Lenten fast, in which "a mans stomacke is in Folio, and knowes not where to haue a dinner in decimo sexto."[108] Predictably and often unfortunately, writers use the body/format conjunction to address gender. A woman named Sister in *The Country Captaine* declares to a male character: "I'le fight with thee my selfe in this smale volume against your bulke in folio."[109] More disturbingly, Thomas Middleton's pawnshop owner Frip asks the "Bawde-Gallant" (i.e., pimp) Primero what size of clothes a woman wears: "of what volume is this booke, that I may fit a couer too't?" Primero responds, "Faith neither in folio, nor in Decimo sexto, but in Octauo between both, a prety middle sizde trug" (i.e., prostitute).[110]

Format as a trope for life and personhood also developed over the course of the seventeenth century. Although it remains unclear who

[104] Anonymous, *The Decoy Duck: Together with the Discovery of the Knot in the Dragons Tayle Called &c.* (London, 1642), sig. A2r. Wing D804.

[105] Henry Glapthorne, *Wit in a Constable A Comedy* (London, 1640), sig. A2r. STC 11914.

[106] John Lyly, *Mother Bombie* (London, 1594), sig. C1v. STC 17084.

[107] Anonymous, *VVits A.B.C. or A Centurie of Epigrams* (London, 1608), sig. A2v. STC 25262.

[108] John Taylor, *Iack a Lent His Beginning and Entertainment with the Many Pranks of His Gentleman-Vsher Shroue Tuesday That Goes before Him, and His Foot-Man Hunger Attending* (London, 1620), sig. B1v. STC 23765.5.

[109] William Cavendish, *The Country Captaine and the Varietie* (London, 1649), sig. D4r-v. Wing N877.

[110] Thomas Middleton, *Your Fiue Gallants* (London, 1608), sig. A4r. STC 17907.

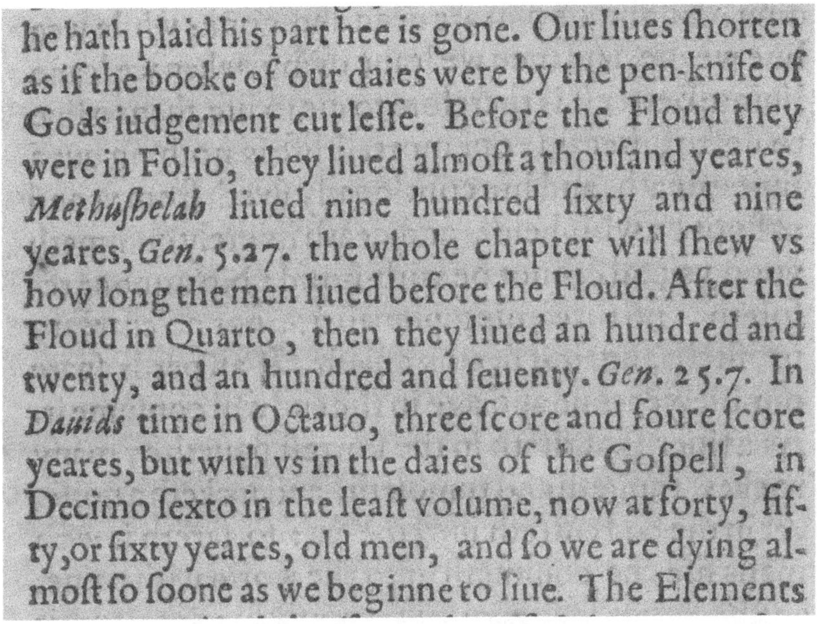

> he hath plaid his part hee is gone. Our liues ſhorten as if the booke of our daies were by the pen-knife of Gods iudgement cut leſſe. Before the Floud they were in Folio, they liued almoſt a thouſand yeares, *Methuſhelah* liued nine hundred ſixty and nine yeares, *Gen.* 5.27. the whole chapter will ſhew vs how long the men liued before the Floud. After the Floud in Quarto, then they liued an hundred and twenty, and an hundred and ſeuenty. *Gen.* 25.7. In *Dauids* time in Octauo, three ſcore and foure ſcore yeares, but with vs in the daies of the Goſpell, in Decimo ſexto in the leaſt volume, now at forty, fifty, or ſixty yeares, old men, and ſo we are dying almoſt ſo ſoone as we beginne to liue. The Elements

Figure 4.3 Detail of John Preston, *A Sermon Preached at the Funerall of Mr. Iosiah Reynel Esquire, the 13. of August 1614* (London, 1615), sig. B4v, 235130, The Huntington Library, San Marino, California.

originated it, multiple writers used format to consider the term of human life, as John Preston did in a 1615 funeral sermon (see Figure 4.3).[111] Just a year earlier, similar albeit less elaborate language appeared in another sermon.[112] Other preachers would adapt this trope liberally, as Nathaniel Hardy did decades later: "the life of man before the flood, was as a large Volume bound up in folio, but since it is contracted to a far lesser volume, and is (as it were) bound up in decimo sexto."[113] With something like pleasure, these writers appeal to the differential capacities of books to talk about the brevity of life.

Thomas Adams made extensive use of format language as a metaphor for personhood and its limits. "Whom did GOD thus love," he asks his reader.

[111] John Preston, *A Sermon Preached at the Funerall of Mr. Iosiah Reynel Esquire, the 13. of August 1614* (London, 1615), sig. B4v. STC 20282.5.
[112] Thomas Adams, *The Deuills Banket Described in Foure Sermons* (London, 1614), sig. Dd2v. STC 110.5.
[113] Nathaniel Hardy, *A Looking-Glasse of Hvmane Frailty Set before Us in a Sermon* (London, 1654), sig. D3v. Wing H729.

the World: not the frame of heaven and earth, but the little world, Man: the compendium and abridgement of all creatures. That whatsoever is imprinted with capitall letters in that large volume, as in Folio, is sweetly and harmoniously contracted in Decimo sexto, in the briefe Text of Man, who includes all.[114]

Adams wryly compares humanity's compact diversity to the storage capacity of the tiny decimo-sexto format. Elsewhere, and more profoundly, Adams claims that "Mans selfe is a good booke to study." He admonishes his readers to read themselves: "Reade this booke in Folio, in thy prosperity: reade it in Quarto, abridged by calamitie: reade it in Octavo, made lesse by penury: reade it in Decimo-sexto, made contemptible by ignominie: reade it in Nihilo, made nothing of this world by death."[115] The metaphor has much to commend it. Adams compares the capacity of different formats to degrees of well-being, ending with the clever wordplay on "Nihilo" (nothing) as if it too were a format one might read. For Edward Buckler, like Adams, format makes death comprehensible:

> One man (a book in folio) lives till age
> Hath made him crooked and put out his eyes:
> His beard doth penance. And death in a rage
> Mows down another whilst the infant cries
> In 's midwives lap: (that's an Epitome)
> Both wear deaths liverie.[116]

The folio format contains, in this figure, the years of an old man's life, while a smaller book (the "Epitome") stands for the short life of an infant.

Format even helps writers grapple with drastic changes in the City of London. James Howell remarks on the rapid expansion of the city, remarking that London, "being compared to what she was then, may be said, in point of magnitude, to be as large a Volume in Folio, to a Book in Decimo Sexto."[117] More hauntingly, writers attempting to describe the destruction of the fire of 1666 also appealed to format. Nathaniel Hardy laments how:

> this City was called (when in her Glory) by Ammianus, Macellinus, Augusta [Latin for "majestic"], the stately magnificent City; but how is she

[114] Adams, *A Commentary or, Exposition Vpon the Diuine Second Epistle Generall, Written by the Blessed Apostle St. Peter*, sig. Mm3r. STC 108.

[115] Adams, sig. K3r. STC 108.

[116] Edward Buckler, *Midnights Meditations of Death: With Pious and Profitable Observations, and Consolations* (London, 1646), sig. Bv. Wing B5350.

[117] James Howell, *Londinopolis an Historicall Discourse or Perlustration of the City of London, the Imperial Chamber, and Chief Emporium of Great Britain* (London, 1657), sig a2r. Wing H3091.

now become angusta [Latin for "low, poor"]? this large Volume in Folio abridged almost to an Octavo, there being, as is probably computed, scarce a sixth part remaining within the Walls.[118]

Samuel Rolle writes even more dramatically about the devastation:

> so might we call a sometimes great and famous Inne, the Crown or Miter, as it was formerly called, though burnt down to the proportion of a Cottage, because the sign and sign post are still to be seen, and there is yet some small part of the old Building. Is it not rather the Epitome of London, which we now have than London it self, as if the abridgement of a Book in Folio (be it Aquinas his Summes or any other such) should go by the name of Aquinas his Sums (or what other name it bore in Folio) when contracted into a smal Manual or Pocket-Book. It is London in short hand, such as might contain the Decalogue within the compasse of a single penny, rather than so at length if yet we may call it London.[119]

Hardy and Rolle, like the other writers cited here, turn to format when they need to describe differences in capacity and containment as well as size. The burned city, like an abridgement of Aquinas's *Summa* (a long book), is much smaller than it once was. It bears noting, however, that there is a slight tension between Rolle's figures and the city he is using them to describe. He introduces a bookish metaphor because he wants to express how small the fire has made the city, but the comparison leaves him making statements about the relationship between containers and what they "contain." The abridgement of Aquinas and the compressed Ten Commandments (the "Decalogue") into "the compasse of a single penny" are not the same thing as the longer versions, just as London is no longer "London it selfe," even though there is still a relationship between them. Rolle intuits, like the other writers here, that transforming the container necessarily transforms the thing contained in it. Form (and here, *format*) shapes the concept of information storage.

Capacity "in Folio"

Book size helps writers imagine and express what books contain, and the language of book size, in turn, operates as a figure to describe other kinds of size, containment, quality, and capacity. It is possible to discern, among

---

[118] Nathaniel Hardy, *Lamentation, Mourning, and Woe Sighed Forth in a Sermon* (London, 1666), sig. D3r. Wing H728.

[119] Samuel Rolle, *Shlohavot, or, The Burning of London in the Year 1666* (London, 1667), sig. B3r. Wing R1877.

these many examples of such language, the emergence of an idea of information similar to the one Nunberg and Peters, in their genealogies of the term, detect in premodern England. Here is Peters' characterization of the shift, which he attributes to the advent of empiricism in the seventeenth century:

> at first *informed* meant *shaped by*; later it came to mean *received reports from*.... [T]he term's sense shifted from unities (Aristotle's forms) to units (of sensation). *Information* came less and less to refer to internal ordering or formation, since empiricism allowed for no preexisting intellectual forms outside of sensation itself. Instead, *information* came to refer to the fragmentary, fluctuating, haphazard stuff of sense.... Under the tutelage of empiricism, *information* gradually moved from structure to stuff, from form to substance, from intellectual order to sensory impulses.[120]

To be clear, this shift "from structure to stuff" preceded the more familiar shift, which Nunberg locates in the nineteenth century and others to the twentieth, to information as "a self-sufficient substance detached from its source."[121] Premodern information is no superhighway. Rather, as books became widely and durably imagined as embodied storage space, they further elaborated the idea of information as the "stuff" books store.

One prepositional phrase became a handle for storage capacity in premodern England, and it is the one with which this chapter began: "in folio." When Don Armado boasts that he is "for whole volumes in folio," he has literary fame in mind, but the audience would have thought about size as much as value and form as much as content. To refer to "in folio" is to invoke the bookish form that achieves storage capacity and signifies it too. Over the course of the sixteenth and seventeenth centuries, writers used "in folio" – one is tempted to say they overused it – to refer to a big thing that holds a lot of stuff. The format imaginary I sketched in the previous section finally yields a premodern idea of information in the many references to the biggest, most capacious format of all.

"In folio" began, predictably enough, as a reference to actual folio format books. Even these mundane uses, including Shakespeare's, depend upon associations with storage space. Thomas Harding, defending his writings against John Jewel's attacks, speculates that they have been received as "trifles ... bicause I printe not my Bookes in Folio, as [Jewel] dooth."[122]

---

[120] Peters, "Information," 13. Emphasis in original.
[121] Nunberg, "Information, Disinformation, Misinformation," 497.
[122] Thomas Harding, *A Detection of Sundrie Foule Errours, Lies, Sclaunders, Corruptions, and Other False Dealinges, Touching Doctrine, and Other Matters Vttered and Practized by M.Iewel, in a Booke Lately by Him Set Foorth Entituled, a Defence of the Apologie* (Leuven, 1568), sig. *****iv-iir. STC 12763.

Plate I. Rubricated opening in the "Gutenberg Bible," Bridwell Library Special Collections, SMU.

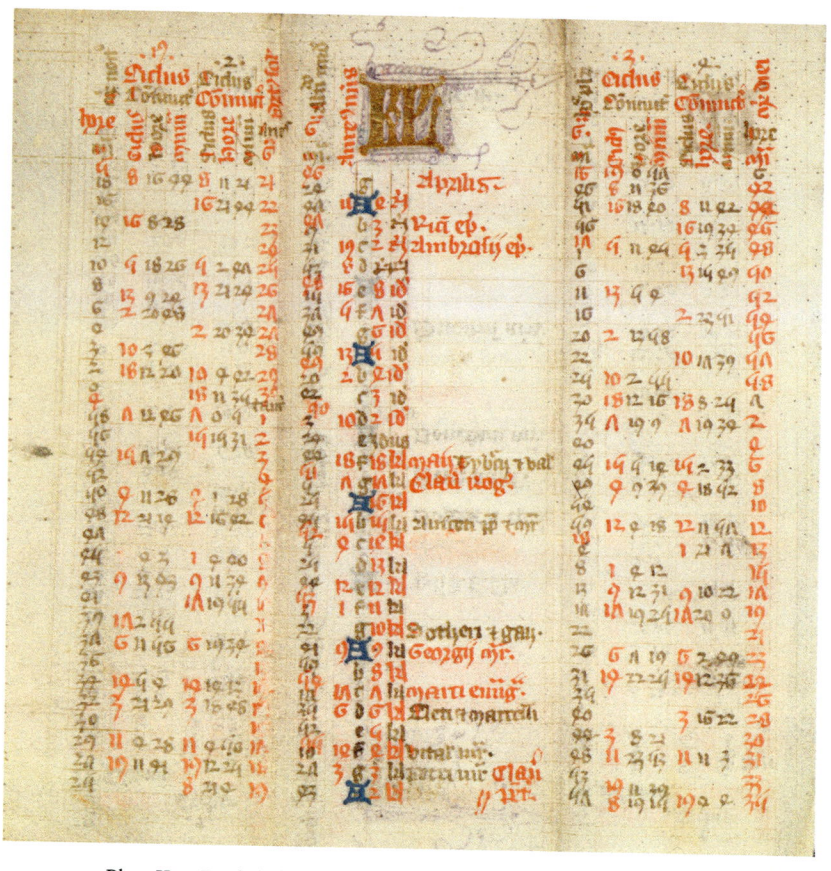

Plate II. English folding almanac in Latin. Public Domain Mark.
Source: Wellcome Collection.

The Sunne riseth at.v. a clocke, and setteth at.vii.

1	b	Phillip & Iacob.	B	Gemini.	8	
2	c	Athanasius	B	Gemini.	23	
3	d	Iuentio crucis		Cans	7	
4	e	Festa corone		cer.	21	
5	f	Godard	*	Leo.	5	
6	G	John port Latin	g	Leo.	18	
7	a	John Beuerley	g	Virgo.	1	☽ The.vii day at.v. a clock 2.min.in y̆ morning,colde & dry winde south.
8	b	Sainct Michael		Virgo.	14	
9	c	Terme begin.		Virgo.	26	
10	d	Epimachus mar.	p	Libra.	8	
11	e	Anthony martir	p	Libra.	20	
12	f	☀ In Gemini.	p	Scorpio.	2	
13	G	Seruacius		Scor-	14	
14	a	Gordianus		pio.	26	
15	b	Sophia	*	Sagit-	7	⬤ The.xv.day at.vi a clock in the morning, great winde,variable weather, wind northeast.
16	c	Dunstan		tarius.	20	
17	d	Transla. Edw.	B	Capri-	1	
18	e	Dioscori martir	B	cornus.	14	
19	f	Brandine		Capri.	26	
20	G	Iuliana	*	Aqua-	9	
21	a	Petronilla		rius.	22	☽ The.22.daye at.v.a clocke 4.mi.after none raine,wind nor. northeast.
22	b	Helene Queene		Pisces.	5	
23	c	Desiderius		Pisces.	19	
24	d	Transla.francis.		Aries.	3	
25	e	Sainct Urban		Aries.	18	
26	f	Augustine	B	Tau-	3	
27	G	Rogation	E	rus.	18	
28	a	Bede episc.	B	Gemi-	2	⬤ The 29. day at.11.a clock before noone, warme, raine, wind southwest.
29	b	Corone martir	B	ni.	17	
30	c	Felix. Fast.	g	Cans	1	
31	d	Ascencion.	g	cer.	15	

Plate III.   *An almanacke, and prognostication, for the yeare of our Lorde God* (1565), sig. A7v, STC 462.2, image 51623, Folger Shakespeare Library.

A Marprelate-adjacent pamphlet (likely by Job Throckmorton) asks why his adversary, Robert Some, "cannot [...] see into these words [...] vnlesse they be written in great text letters or printed in Folio?"[123] More floridly, the pseudonymous poet T. Cutwode begins one lyric declaring, "My Herball booke in Folio I vnfold, / I pipe of Plants, I sing of somer flowers."[124] The idea seems to be that Cutwode will sing about many plants, and indeed he does. George Chapman's Monsieur d'Olive expresses his desire to have pages attend on him (i.e., to be "mand"), but finds none: "the world's now growne thrifitie: he that fils a whole Page in folio, with his Stile; thinkes it veriest Noble, to be mand with one bare Page and a *Pandare*."[125] Perhaps with Armado in the rearview mirror, Chapman's D'Olive complains that even those of the highest style (figured by the ability to fill a folio page) no longer keep appropriate retinues. Far less tongue-in-cheek, Alexander Spicer's elegy for Sir Arthur Chichester deploys a similar figure:

> With armes of valour, the report of them
> May be a Chronicle: for so large a theame
> Requires a booke in Folio, not one leafe,
> To shew the homage due to Iosephs Sheafe,
> All bow'd to his, and no worth finds extent
> Beyond the bounds of his, whom I lament.

This is not a good poem, but that is part of my point. Spicer strains to convey the greatness of Chichester's honor and the poet's own lament, and of all possible figures for storage, he reaches for "in folio."

As we saw in the earlier section on big books, the language of bigness is always rhetorically situated and motivated. "In folio" is no exception. Barnabe Rich explains his brevity by saying he has "but glanced at things [...] which if I shoulde inlarge but as they deserue, I might write a whole volume in folio."[126] John Boys alters a claim by the biblical writer John, asserting that "if all the things which Iesus did should bee written euery one, the number of the bookes in folio would be without number."[127] Biblical John does not specify the format or size of Jesus's innumerable books, but English John does. "In folio" could refer to reading as well as writing, as when the lawyer Throat in Lording Barry's *Ram Alley* boasts of

[123] Job Throckmorton, *M. Some Laid Open in His Coulers* (La Rochelle, 1589), sig. Q2r. STC 12342.
[124] Anonymous, *Caltha Poetarum: Or The Bumble Bee* (London, 1599), sig. Br. STC 6151.
[125] George Chapman, *Monsieur D'Oliue A Comedie* (London, 1606), sig. E2r. STC 4983.
[126] Barnabe Rich, *A Nevv Description of Ireland Vvherein Is Described the Disposition of the Irish Whereunto They Are Inclined* (London, 1610), sig. Rr. STC 20992.
[127] Boys, *An Exposition of the Festiuall Epistles and Gospels Vsed in Our English Liturgie Together with a Reason Why the Church Did Chuse the Same*, sig. H7r. STC 3462.3.

his large reading: "faith some hundred bookes in folio I haue / Turnd ouer to better my owne knowledge."[128]

These instances of "in folio," which refer to more or less real books, show the basic utility of the phrase as a reference to size and capacity. The phrase quickly traveled into metaphor, of course. A character in Henry Porter's *The Two Angry Women of Abington* responds in frustration to another character's overuse of proverbs: "why ye whoreson prouerb booke bound vp in folio, / Haue yee no other sence to answer me, / But euery worde a prouerbe, no other English?"[129] He has so many proverbs memorized that he cannot possibly be a book in quarto. Peter Barker argues that images, regarded with suspicion following the Reformation, may yet have value for those who cannot read:

> Oh but they [images] bee lay mens books, and where as the Bible to them that cannot reade is as a sealed letter, images be letters patents, they lie open to euery one, are written in folio, that standing a farre off they may reade, they are great capitall letters that running men may reade God, and the very sight of them doth stirre vp a maruailous deuotion in men, women, and children.[130]

Even "running men" can "reade God" in these large letters patent.[131] Along similar lines, Thomas Adams paraphrases Saint Paul, writing how "the Heathen, by this great Booke in Folio, the Heavens layd open, did reade there was a God."[132] As we have already seen, the world-as-folio was highly conventional, often entailing the use of "in folio" and always carrying the capacity of the format with it: "the world is Gods great booke in Folio" (L. Brinkmair); "The heavens [...] are a booke in folio, there God is layd open in his creatures" (Richard Sibbes); "The world's a booke in Folio printed all / With God's great works in Letters capital" (Du Bartas, translated by Joshua Sylvester, here quoted by Edward Browne); "A Learned man is the best chararacter [sic] in the world, Gods great book in Folio" (H. Browne).[133] If the world is a book, its diversity requires a format with a lot of storage.

---

[128] Lording Barry, *Ram-Alley: Or Merrie-Trickes* (London, 1611), sig. B4v. STC 1502.
[129] Henry Porter, *The Pleasant History of the Two Angry Women of Abington* (London, 1599), sig. D1r. STC 20122.
[130] Barker, *A Iudicious and Painefull Exposition Vpon the Ten Commandements*, sig. N1v. STC 1425.
[131] Barker is riffing on Habakkuk 2:2: "and the LORD answered me, and said, Write the vision, and make it plain upon tables, that he may run that readeth it."
[132] Adams, *A Commentary or, Exposition Vpon the Diuine Second Epistle Generall, Written by the Blessed Apostle St. Peter*, sig. Lllll1v. STC 108.
[133] L. Brinckmair, *The Vvarnings of Germany By Wonderfull Signes, and Strange Prodigies Seene in Divers Parts of That Countrey of Germany, Betweene the Yeare 1618. and 1638* (London, 1638), sig.

These examples merely hint at the expansive use of "in folio." The little-known and, I think, underappreciated polemic writer Thomas Hall makes a meaningful leap in his 1657 *Chiliasto-mastix redivivus*, a book attempting to confute millenarianism. Explaining his own brevity and his opponent's prolixity, Hall opens up an attack worthy of Martin Marprelate, worth quoting in full and retaining the typeface to show his emphasis:

> *herein I shall be directly opposite to the Doctor* [Nathanael Homes], *for I have used all means to contract my self, and have compacted as much matter in as little a compass as possibly I could;* whereas he *doth* de Industria *use all meanes to swel his book into a Folio, and therefore he hath put a great part of it into Latin and English, for the credit of the Cause,* that all the world may see he Lyes in Folio: *in the mean time forgetting the Proverb* [...] *that a great book (especially when stuft with such a cramb* [...] *as the Doctor hath stuft his book withall, is a great burden, especially to an Ingenious Reader, who delights in Laconick brevity, and must have much in a little.*[134]

Hall's move will not surprise readers of this chapter: as with so many others, book size helps him situate his own text rhetorically. His short book offers "much in a little," again invoking the flexible relation of form and content made possible by book size. Hall's first use of "in folio," which refers to an actual book, brilliantly sets up his second, emphasized by the Roman typeface: "that all the world may see he Lyes in Folio." This switch may indicate the proverbial quality of the line; even so, it alerts Hall's readers to the very different use of "in folio" to describe the opponent's capacious lies. A few pages later, Hall uses the figure again: "whereas others lye in Quarto, his in Folio."[135]

These "Lyes in Folio" bring us, at last, to the one of the most widespread (not to mention entertaining) bookish terms in premodern England: the template "X in folio," of which there are many hundreds of instances. Edward Hoby, in a book with the unforgettable title *A curry-combe for a coxe-combe*, declares of his opponent that "if this bee not a Lye in Folio, wee must confesse, there can nothing but trueth droppe from a Shauelings penne."[136] "Shaveling" here is a term of derision for a tonsured churchman,

*2v; Richard Sibbes, *The Excellencie of the Gospell above the Law* (London, 1639), sig. O5r; Edward Browne, *A Description of an Annuall Vvorld* (London, 1641), sig. C6v; H. Browne, *A Map of the Microcosme, or, A Morall Description of Man Newly Compiled into Essayes* (London, 1642), sig. A11r. STC 3758, STC 22492, Wing B5102A, and Wing B5115.

134 Thomas Hall, *Chiliasto-Mastix Redivivus, Sive Homesus Enervatus. A Confutation of the Millenarian Opinion* (London, 1657), sig. *5v. Wing H428.

135 Hall, sig. A2r.

136 Hoby, *A Curry-Combe for a Coxe-Combe*, sig. I2v. STC 13540.

so the lie in folio must be truly capacious. Commonly, as with Hoby's lies, writers used "in folio" to aggrandize their moral claims. John Vicars writes of one "Who shall in's hand a Booke in folio beare,/ Wherein mans faults and follies written were," and William Hall expands the same metaphor in verse:

> If these vngodly sinnes wee follow still,
> And the inticers of them doe obay;
> And follow it: in Folio wee shall fill
> A Volume great compil'd against that day,
> In which one good deed done will profit more
> Then thousands of Gold hoorded vp in store.[137]

Edmund Calamy accuses Civil-War-era covenant breakers of committing "a sin in Folio, a sin of a high nature"; multiple writers would later quote this line in the years following the Restoration.[138] John Paradise vividly describes the sin of regicide:

> it was a voluminous, and bigbellied sin; a sin in folio, which containeth a great litter of other sins, in the belly of it. Ingratitude envy, malice, covetousnesse, ambition, rebellion, perjury, Treason, blasphemy were the bitter ingredients, whereof this confection of poyson was compounded.[139]

More redemptively, a later writer claims that the "Summ of the Gospel" is preached even "to Sinners in Folio."[140] Good things, too, can be big. Silver-tongued preacher Henry Smith praises the marks of a true Protestant Englishman: "he which can sweare that the Pope is Antichrist, and that flesh is good on Fridaies, is a protestant at least, a Christian euerie inche: hee hath zeale, knowledge and religion in Folio."[141] Richard Brathwaite refers to sycamore trees as "our large professing friends in Folio," while Thomas Jordan twice invokes the phrase in short poems: in an elegy for Mrs. Margaret Jessop, he writes that "All the small vertues God did e're bestow / On Woman-kind, lyes here in Folio," and in another poem to

[137] John Vicars, *A Prospectiue Glasse to Looke into Heauen* (London, 1618), sig. B2v; William Hall, *Mortalities Meditation: Or, A Description of Sinne* (London, 1624), sig. D3v. STC 24698 and STC 12720.

[138] Edmund Calamy, *The Great Danger of Covenant-Refusing, and Covenant-Breaking* (London, 1646), sig. E4v. Wing C254. See Robert Douglas, *A Phenix, or, The Solemn League and Covenant* (Edinburgh, 1662), sig. G7v-r; Roger L'Estrange, *Considerations and Proposals in Order to the Regulation of the Press* (London, 1663), sig. D3v-D4r. Wing D2034 and Wing L1229.

[139] John Paradise, *Hadadrimmon, Sive, Threnodia Anglicana Ob Regicidium a Sermon on Davids Humiliation for Cutting off the Royal Robe, and Detestation of Cutting off the Royal Head of the Lords Anointed* (London, 1661), sig. Cr. Wing P327.

[140] R. Mayhew, *Sichah: Or, A Continued Tract of Meditation* (London, 1683), sig. M6r. Wing M1442.

[141] Henry Smith, *The Sermons of Maister Henrie Smith* (London, 1593), sig. Hhh5r. STC 22719.

a woman, he writes how "Such looks as yours would make a Poet grow Fluent and chast but love in Folio."[142] For better and worse applications, "in folio" conveys volume, intensity, gravity, greatness, and, above and in all these, capacity.

An even more vivid use of "X in folio" involves labeling and sometimes insulting others. In one of his most inspired moments of literary criticism, Gabriel Harvey emphasizes the importance of writing credible fictions:

> Euen Lucians true Tales are spiced with conceite: and neither his, nor Apuleius Asse, is altogether an Asse. It is a piece of cunning in the most fabulous Legends, to interlace some credible narratio[n]s, & verie probable occurrences, to countenance and authorize the excessiue licentiousnesse of the rest. Vnreasonable fictions palpably bewray their odious grosnesse: and hee that will be a famous deuiser in folio, must be content with the rewarde of a notable Lier, not to be credited, when he auoweth a trueth.[143]

Like the fabled boy who cried "wolf," a great deviser of unreasonable fictions – a deviser in folio – must be prepared to be disbelieved when he tells the truth. (In this scheme, Philip Sidney's maker-poet must be a deviser in quarto.) A character in John Mason's play *The Turke* exclaims, "Why her's a slaue in folio will seeme to slight the loue of a Princesse, when he would willingly spend his talent on an oyster wife."[144] It is not entirely clear how pursuing an oyster wife makes this person a "slaue in folio," but the idea is that it makes him a big one. Far more common is the accusation that others are "fools in folio." Richard Brathwaite claims that "Prodigals" who "make a losse / Of credit, bodie, state, to yield delight / For one poor moment" will eventually "style themselues [...] Fooles in folio."[145] Likewise, Samuel Otes argues that "they that sport and laugh at sinne, are fooles, and damned fooles, reprobate fooles, fooles in folio, fooles in print," and later Richard Younge would more seriously write that "all impenitent persons, all unbelievers [...] are arrant fools; yea, fools in folio."[146] The phrase was so common that at least one book appeared (unsurprisingly, in the late 1640s

---

[142] Richard Brathwaite, *History Surveyed in a Brief Epitomy* (London, 1651), sig. Ee2r; Thomas Jordan, *Divinity and Morality in Robes of Poetry* (London, 1660), sig. S8v; Thomas Jordan, *Jevvels of Ingenuity* (London, 1660), sig. *3r. Wing B4265, Wing J1030, and Wing J1033A.

[143] Gabriel Harvey, *Foure Letters, and Certaine Sonnets* (London, 1592), sig. E2r. STC 12900.5.

[144] John Mason, *The Turke A Worthie Tragedie* (London, 1610), sig. C3r. STC 17617.

[145] Richard Brathwaite, *The Good Vvife: Or, A Rare One amongst Women* (London, 1618), sig. B2r. STC 3568.5.

[146] Samuel Otes, *An Explanation of the Generall Epistle of Saint Iude* (London, 1633), sig. Ss5v; Richard Younge, *A Christian Library, or, A Pleasant and Plentiful Paradise of Practical Divinity* (London, 1660), sig. B3v. STC 18896 and Wing Y145.

pamphlet frenzy) with the title *Knaves and Fooles in Folio*.[147] A "fool in folio" is not merely foolish, but foolish to the same order of distinction that a folio book is bigger than a quarto. Again, the apparently offhanded manner of these insults makes them more culturally resonant. The same is true for other appellations, including "Coxcombes in folio," Charles I as a "Tyrant in folio," Absalom as a "traitor in Folio to his own Father," a character in a play as "Gentleman in Folio," a royalist as "Cuckold in Folio," and Mountebanks as "Asses in Folio."[148] What these writers lack in imagination they make up for in exuberant use of a readily available linguistic form.

Many things can be "in folio": ideas, things, food. Smirke the clown in the comedy *The Two Merry Milke-maids* wishes aloud that he "had bin so happy to haue liu'd and cleft wood i'the countrey, preacht at the Buttery barre vnto the Ploughmen, and there haue vsde my authoritie in Folio, when all the seruants of the house shud be drunke at midnight, Cum Priuilegio."[149] Although his imagined country life would have been smaller, his authority would have been bigger with respect to his situation. Caranto, a character in the play *Lady Alimony*, laughs in an aside to the audience: "so, good Sir Iasper, you've your Doom in Folio."[150] More earnestly, Samuel Annesley worries about the Christian whose prayers are "haunt[ed]" by "vain thoughts": "the heart is set open to Gods adversary in Gods presence, and the World and Satan are suffered to interpose, in the very time of the reign of grace, then when it should be in folio, in its royalty, commanding all our faculties to serve it."[151] The "it" that should be in folio could be "grace," so that Annesley is saying that God's grace should be so capacious as to command all of one's faculties. Alternatively, "it"

---

[147] S. H., *Knaves and Fooles in Folio* (London, 1648). Wing H121. Other examples of "fools in folio" include Wing T233, sig. Bv; Wing B4962A, sig. H2v-3r; Wing L795, sig. E3v; and Wing W1538, sig. D7r-v.

[148] Anonymous, *Eikōn Alēthinē. The Pourtraiture of Truths Most Sacred Majesty Truly Suffering, Though Not Solely* (London, 1649), sig. Av; T. L. W., *Refractoria Disputatio* (London, 1654), sig. I6v-7r; S. L., *Three Sermons Viz. Davids Tears for His Rebellious Son Absalom, Israels Tears for Abners Fall by Bloudy Joab, Infants Tears for Athaliahs Treason* (London, 1660), sig. H5v; James Shirley, *Love Tricks, or, The School of Complements* (London, 1667), sig. D3v; Thomas D'Urfey, *The Royalist a Comedy* (London, 1682), sig. I3r; Adrian von Mynsicht, *Thesaurus & Armamentarium Medico-Chymicum, or, A Treasury of Physick with the Most Secret Way of Preparing Remedies against All Diseases* (London, 1682), sig. Bb7v. Wing E267, Wing W136, Wing L66, Wing S3477, Wing D2770, and Wing M3177.

[149] J. C., *A Pleasant Comedie, Called the Tvvo Merry Milke-Maids. Or, the Best Words Weare the Garland* (London, 1620), sig. H4r. STC 4281.

[150] Anonymous, *Lady Alimony, or, The Alimony Lady an Excellent, Pleasant, New Comedy, Duly Authorized, Daily Acted and Frequently Followed* (London, 1659), sig. E4v. Wing L162A.

[151] Anonymous, *The Morning Exercise [at] Cri[Ppleg]Ate, or, Several Cases of Conscience Practically Resolved by Sundry Ministers* (London, 1661), sig. Sss4r. Wing A3232.

could be the heart, which "in its royalty" should be "set open" to God's grace. Either way, the folio as a container supplies the figure. Words without a big book never to heaven go. Perhaps frivolously, Richard Lassels describes Italian men's hairstyles by saying, "They haue short hair on their heads, but beards in folio," while a later writer describes someone's doublet as "but one great Patch in Folio."[152] Not even fashion is safe from format.

Two particularly instructive instances of "in folio" come from the plays of John Fletcher and his collaborators. First, in a comic scene in *The Elder Brother*, three servants are debating whether Charles, the scholarly titular brother, studies "conjuring" or magic. Charles's servant Andrew defends his master, asking, "Have you / Lost any plate, Butler?" Plates being an expensive commodity, Andrew asks if any have been magicked away; he then expresses ambitions much bigger than stealing:

> We meddle
> With no spirits oth'Buttry, they taste too small for us;
> Keepe me a pye in folio, I beseech thee,
> And thou shalt see how learnedly Ile translate him[.][153]

Glancing ahead to the question of eating books in the next chapter, Andrew uses mediation as a figure for digestion. He also leaves no question that he wants a very big pie that contains a lot of filling. The second instance appears in *Loves Cure, or The Martiall Maid*. Lucio, a boy who was raised as a girl and is now being asked to dress as a man, complains to the family servant Bobadilla about his attire, only to be mocked in reply (see Figure 4.4).[154] We do not have to condone Bobadilla's essentialist mockery to commend the "folio" wordplay here. Lucio lists the "uneasie" components of masculine attire, which leave him "bound up" tight, setting up the bookish conceit of binding "in folio." Woman's attire is figured here as capacious enough to permit freer movement of the body; men's pants come only in decimosexto. Bobadilla adds an "o" to make "foolio" and turns it against Lucio, unbooking the conceit.

These two instances of "in folio," both likely the work of John Fletcher, suggest the extent of the format imaginary in the seventeenth century, and more broadly the significance of book size as storage space. "Folio" works as a figure for class and gender and provides material for gendered insults in turn. For better and worse, book size functions as a reflex of the imagination,

---

[152] Richard Lassels, *The Voyage of Italy, or, A Compleat Journey through Italy in Two Parts* (Paris, 1670), sig. C11v; W. R., *Wallography, or, The Britton Describ'd* (London, 1682), sig. C7v. Wing L465 and Wing R101.

[153] Fletcher, *The Elder Brother a Comedie*, sig. D2v-3r. STC 11066.

[154] Beaumont and Fletcher, *Fifty Comedies and Tragedies*, sig. Y2r. Wing B1582, emphasis in original.

> *Luc.* What would you have me do? this scurvy sword
> So galls my thigh: I would 't were burnt: pish, look,
> This Cloak will ne'r keep on: these Boots too hide-bound,
> Make me walk stiff, as if my legs were frozen,
> And my Spurs gingle like a Morris-dancer:
> Lord, how my head akes with this roguish Hat;
> This masculine attire is most uneasie,
> I am bound up in it: I had rather walk
> In *folio*, again, loose like a woman.
> *Bob.* In *Foolio*, had you not?
> Thou mock to heav'n, and nature, and thy Parents,
> Thou tender Leg of Lamb; oh, how he walks
> As if he had bepifs'd himself, and fleers!
> Is this a gate for the young Cavalier,
> Don *Lucio*, Son and Heir to *Alvarez*?
> Has it a corn? or do's it walk on conscience,
> It treads so gingerly? Come on your ways,
> Suppose me now your Fathers foe, *Vitelli*,
> And spying you i' th' street, thus I advance
> I twist my Beard, and then I draw my sword.

Figure 4.4   Detail of Francis Beaumont and John Fletcher, *Fifty Comedies and Tragedies* (London, 1679), sig. Y2r, G578, Kenneth Spencer Research Library, University of Kansas, Lawrence, Kansas.

conjuring and giving expression to a premodern information concept. Even at its most offensive, as in the example of Thomas Jeamson's *Artificiall embellishments, or Arts best directions how to preserve beauty or procure it*, book size maintains the connection of material capacities and informational content:

> IT can be no pleasing sight, to see a soul prest under a mountaine of flesh, and the body stretcht to such dimensions that make it represent a walking barrell. [...] For when ere the carcase swels it self into a bulk too *voluminous*, idlenesse is there describ'd in *folio*. Have a care Ladies then to keep your bodies in a mean proportion, and if ever they enlarge themselves to extravagant limits, use these directions to reduce them to their former bounds, so you may regaine your credit and your beautie too.[155]

---

[155] Thomas Jeamson, *Artificiall Embellishments, or Arts Best Directions How to Preserve Beauty or Procure It* (Oxford, 1665), sig. E8r-v. Wing J503, emphasis in original.

Jeamson goes on to prescribe exercise and bleeding to lose weight. The bookish metaphor here, by which the body is said to make letters "too legible" and to describe idleness as a folio, works as a body-shaming device because big books carry lots of words.

For Jeamson and the many other writers we have explored here, information always has a body. No firewall separates information and vessel, and no isomorphism inevitably ties form with content. Premodern writers use this flexible relation for their rhetorical and imaginative benefit when they appeal to book size. If it seems difficult or even impossible to abstract a consistent, coherent information concept from the multifarious language of book size sampled in this chapter, then that is all for the better, since the very absence of a single orthodoxy on that question makes possible these rich appropriations of book size. In Chapter 5, we will take up the adjacent question of mediation. The language of book size helps writers articulate *what* books mediate, but the language of sensation helps articulate *how*.

The Bookish Sensorium

In *Actes and Monuments* (1583), often known as the "Book of Martyrs," John Foxe portrays the invention of the printing press as "the fountain of reformation."[1] Foxe's influential and still oft-cited account attributes to printing a massive set of changes: "tongues are knowne, knowledge groweth, iudgment increaseth, books are dispersed, the Scripture is seene, the Doctours be read[,] stories be opened, times compared, truth decerned, falshod detected, and with finger poynted, and all (as I sayd) thorough the benefite of printing."[2] As we will see in greater detail in Chapter 7, for Foxe the "art of printing" constructs and authenticates European Protestant identity by way of an appeal to bookishness. Foxe's account of printing as divinely sanctioned technological determinism, moreover, accords generally with grand narratives of totality and modernity that the present book aims to decompose. God, by means of the press, "disperse[s]" revelation to humankind.

Foxe's language deserves a second glance, however. He appeals to printed books not merely as containers of truth, knowledge, or information but as mediators to the senses. Scripture, he writes, "is seene" and stories are "opened" and accessible. Falsehood is detected not by some disembodied intellect, but "with finger poynted" so that all may see it. Later, Foxe writes that "God hath opened the presse to preach, whose voyce the Pope is neuer able to stop." Even a writer like Foxe, who anticipates (and provides evidence for) the Eisensteinian narrative that a "communications revolution" made possible the Protestant Reformation, appeals to the language of sensation to describe how books and readers relate. Readers do not simply know the scripture; they *see* it. The press does not merely transmit but *preaches* with a *voice*. What we might initially take to be a theory

---

[1] Foxe, *Actes and Monuments*, sig. DD6r-v. STC 11225. "Fountain of reformation" appears in a marginal note, referring the reader to Foxe's lengthy statement on the invention of printing.
[2] Foxe, sig. Pp6r.

of disembodied reading suggests the opposite: a theory of reading with the skin, eyes, ears, mouth, and nose.

This chapter argues that, like Foxe, when early modern writers came to describe books and reading, they used a repertoire of sensory language. They often refer to seeing or smelling something in a book, tasting an author's point, or touching on a subject. Although some writers use this language to describe actual sensory encounters with books, it remains mostly figurative. I say "mostly" because even though much language coordinating senses and books qualifies as metaphorical, it never strays far from the sensations of touching, seeing, and listening to books. This proximity makes such language really exciting: just as the senses make the world available to human experience, interaction, and thought, so too did the language of the bookish sensorium give writers a way to describe how we come to know what we find in books. It gave them, in short, a way to model mediation.

This chapter extends and elaborates a bodily turn in recent scholarship. Across the discipline of English studies, an emphasis on bodily experience as both the subject and ground of analysis has taken hold, opening up new avenues of inquiry and insight.[3] In scholarship on books and other text technologies, this turn has reconfigured the study of how texts and readers affect each other. Claire Bourne, for instance, has shown how the typography of early modern printed plays models performance for readers to embody.[4] Katherine Tycz has explored how women in early modern Italy folded and sealed printed images of the Virgin Mary as devotional objects.[5] Whitney Sperrazza has examined the way white space in Mary Wroth's manuscript directs the reader's eyes.[6] And Joshua Cahoun has called for a new "ecology of the book" that attends to the interaction of poetic material and material material.[7] More broadly, the fieldwide shift of attention to marginalia and other forms of book use leaves many longstanding historicist commitments by the wayside.[8] This scholarship exemplifies a new

---

[3] See, for instance, Elizabeth D. Harvey, ed., *Sensible Flesh: On Touch in Early Modern Culture* (Philadelphia: University of Pennsylvania Press, 2003); Valerie Traub, ed., *The Oxford Handbook of Shakespeare and Embodiment: Gender, Sexuality, and Race* (Oxford: Oxford University Press, 2016).

[4] Bourne, *Typographies of Performance in Early Modern England*.

[5] Katherine M. Tycz, "Material Prayers and Maternity in Early Modern Italy: Signed, Sealed, Delivered," in *Domestic Devotions in Early Modern Italy*, ed. Maya Corry, Marco Faini, and Alessia Meneghin (Leiden: Brill, 2019), 244–71.

[6] Whitney Sperrazza, "Knowing Mary Wroth's Pamphilia," *Journal for Early Modern Cultural Studies* 19, no. 3 (2019): 1–35, https://doi.org/10.1353/jem.2019.0027.12/13/22 2:45:00 PM.

[7] Calhoun, *The Nature of the Page*.

[8] See, for instance, William H. Sherman, *Used Books: Marking Readers in Renaissance England* (Philadelphia: University of Pennsylvania Press, 2008); Knight, *Bound to Read*; Smyth, *Material Texts in Early Modern England*; Price, *What We Talk About When We Talk About Books*.

phenomenology of the book, in which books and other text objects are studied as interfaces for bodily expression and action.[9]

This chapter has little to say about how people physically experienced books, but it will contribute to the new phenomenology. Bookish words cannot tell us how premodern books felt: not a lot of writers attempted to describe, in language, their sensory experience of books. There are some such descriptions, to be sure. In marginalia and in written accounts, books are described as heavy or light, their pages dusty and worn or brand new, their smell rotten, their appearance pleasing or displeasing. These infrequent accounts often occur in interstitial and paratextual parts of texts where readers' and writers' bodies are more readily acknowledged; they provide an invaluable record of readers' (and in some cases nonreaders') encounters with manuscript and printed books.[10] But they remain a rarity. Instead, in this chapter I will explore how language coordinating books with sensation offers a theory of mediation developing over the sixteenth and seventeenth centuries. Tracing how the body supplies a terminology for how books function as media will give us a new sense (as it were) of the body's crucial importance for reading in a premodern world.

What does it mean to say that this language offers a theory (or theories) of mediation? Put simply, it shows that people thought about and found rhetorical mechanisms to address the problem of books as expressive media much earlier than most accounts suggest. John Guillory, for instance, has claimed broadly that "the concept of a medium of communication was absent but *wanted* for the several centuries prior to its appearance [in the nineteenth century], a lacuna in the philosophical tradition that exerted a distinctive pressure, as if from the future, on early efforts to theorize communication."[11] For Guillory, the emergence of the modern concept of communication – the transmission of ideas from one mind to another – and media – the instrument by which that transmission occurs – required the displacement of the art of rhetoric and a general disembodiment in theories of language. This account conforms (with some differences) to John Durham Peters' history of communication, in which John Locke and others "nudg[ed] the term's orbit from matter to mind."[12] In these narratives, it is not that premodern cultures did not include mediation (that would be

---

[9] On interface, see Johanna Drucker, *Graphesis: Visual Forms of Knowledge Production*, MetaLABprojects (Cambridge: Harvard University Press, 2014).

[10] Sherman, *Used Books: Marking Readers in Renaissance England*, 2008.

[11] Guillory, "Genesis of the Media Concept," 321. Emphasis in original.

[12] John Durham Peters, *Speaking into the Air: A History of the Idea of Communication* (Chicago: University of Chicago Press, 1999), 80.

impossible), but that few writers labeled it as such. Such narratives often inadvertently tend to assume that "media consciousness" – awareness of a medium as such – is a distinctly modern idea commensurate with Enlightenment philosophies of language and communication.

The evidence presented in this chapter shows how pervasively the concepts and questions, if not always the precise terms, of mediation functioned in premodern England as available categories of thought. The many writers quoted here were deeply aware of media as "socially realized structures of communication," in Lisa Gitelman's influential phrasing.[13] To describe these structures, premoderns often reached for the language of the body. The choice of that language afforded them a way of addressing both the possibility and impossibility of what we now call communication, and the inevitability of mediation. Insofar as it is appropriate to speak of books transmitting ideas, the bookish sensorium helped writers describe how that transmission happens. That transmitted set of ideas – sometimes but not always identified with the actual words in a book – is modeled on sensation. We *see* a moral point in a book, *taste* the value of a book, and *smell* a book's author: readers apprehend something in books that books somehow convey. The bookish sensorium, however, also helped writers articulate the implausibility of books as pure idea transmitters. Here, the disciplinary expertise of bibliography and textual studies proves indispensable, because for decades this scholarship has advanced our awareness that any content a book can be said to include is made knowable and distinct only in its textual formations. There is no naïve, neutral, disembodied, nonmaterial transmission of ideas (see "Ecologies" in Chapter 1). The writings I explore here demonstrate a deep familiarity with this proposition, suggesting that the concept of mediation was very much present in premodern England. In the following sections, we will touch on touching books, look at seeing books, and get a taste of tasting books.

Haptic Gestures

Modern booklovers know how profoundly the feel of a book affects the act of reading. On the one hand, if the spine is inflexible or the paper badly cut, the whole experience suffers. On the other hand, Garamond letters raised, ever-so-slightly, over a crisp page, sharpened pencil in hand and a cup of tea nearby – now that's reading. You can and will pick your own scenario, but the point is that touch inevitably accompanies not just

---

[13] Gitelman, *Always Already New*, 7.

reading but a range human–book relations.[14] It is easy to understand why design teams creating digital devices put so much emphasis on the "feel" and "haptic" qualities of the user's experience: they know that *touch* is the key to a whole range of reading practices. If it does not feel right, then it does not work well (or sell well, come to that).

Precisely because touch has long been viewed as indispensable to personal and social acts such as reading, it has also functioned as a potent symbol. Elizabeth Harvey writes of how readily touch "becomes a metaphor for conveyance into the interior of the subject." Touch, she writes, "evokes at once agency and receptivity, authority and reciprocity, pleasure and pain, sensual indulgence and epistemological certainty."[15] We call songs, paintings, and stories "touching" when they stir our emotions and intellect. In some contexts (e.g., preschool) to touch is to know, while in others (art museums) we prevent touch in order to preserve. And when we want to explain what we are talking about, we say we will "touch on" this or that subject.

These dual functions – the actual touching of books and the figurative use of books touching – circulated widely in early modern England. Indeed, readers and writers made frequent use of the language of touch to talk about how books function both as material objects capable of acquiring social and cultural value and as objects responsible for the transmission of language and ideas in the form of texts. To reframe a well-known phrase from Natalie Zemon Davis, touch language allowed writers to talk about books at once as "source[s] for ideas and images" *and* as "carrier[s] of relationships."[16] In particular, this extensive language of touch and books helped early modern writers develop a robust and comprehensive theory of mediation: touch addresses the question of how books relate to the ideas they supposedly contain.

First, how did premoderns address the actual touching of physical books? To answer this question is to establish, as we will see later, the parameters by which we can address book touch as a symbol of mediation. A little over a hundred pages before it expounds on the divine gift of printing, Foxe's *Actes and Monuments* prints the story of William Thorpe,

---

[14] On book touch as a challenge to literary criticism's addiction to meaning, see Gillian Silverman, "Neurodiversity and the Revision of Book History," *PMLA: Publications of the Modern Language Association of America* 131, no. 2 (2016): 307–23.

[15] Harvey, *Sensible Flesh*, 2. See also Andrew Piper, *Book Was There: Reading in Electronic Times* (Chicago: University of Chicago Press, 2012).

[16] Natalie Zemon Davis, *Society and Culture in Early Modern France: Eight Essays* (Stanford: Stanford University Press, 1975), 192.

a fourteenth-century Lollard. Or rather, Foxe reprints the story: Thorpe's apparently autobiographical account of his interrogation by Archbishop Thomas Arundel first appeared in print in a 1530 text likely printed in Antwerp.[17] Foxe simply incorporated that earlier text into the massive "book of martyrs" (a decision to which we will return). The charges brought against Thorpe concerned the question of oaths, particularly whether it is lawful to put one's hand on a book to swear an oath. This narrow set of concerns gives Thorpe's story its wider purchase about premodern England's reflexive association of books with touch. Although somewhat obscure and confusing, Thorpe's story became a point of reference in its own right, reappearing at key moments in the following centuries when the question of touching books became pertinent. More broadly, Thorpe's story helps articulate the stakes of mediation in early modern England.

Hauled before the Archbishop for questioning, Thorpe maintains that he will not put his hand on a book and swear. To explain why, he tells a story:

> I was once in a gentlema[n]s house, and there were then two Clarkes there, [...] And among other things, these men s[p]oake of othes, & the man of law sayd: at the bidding of his soueraigne, which had power to charge him to sweare, he would lay his hand vpon a booke, and heare hys charge: and if his charge to his vnderstanding were vnlefull [i.e., unlawful], he would hastely withdraw his hand vpo[n] the booke, taking there onely God to witnes, that he would fulfil that lefull [i.e., lawful] charge, after his power. And the maister of diuinitie sayde then to him thus. Certaine, he that layeth his hand vpo[n] a booke in this wise, and maketh there a promise to do that thing that he is commaunded: is obliged therby by boke othe, then to fulfil his charge.[18]

This get-together may never have happened, but it lends institutional and intellectual capital to Thorpe's position against swearing on a book. Both of the learned men in Thorpe's story express reservations about swearing with a hand touching a book, not because such an oath is meaningless but rather the opposite. The first man claims he will remove his hand if he perceives that he is swearing to do something "vnlefull," and the other attests that such a "boke othe" obligates the swearer, apparently even if the act one swears to do is unlawful.

It is remarkable how seriously Thorpe's clerks (and thus Thorpe himself) take books, but it is not yet clear why. Although a modern perspective

---

[17] William Thorpe, *The Examinacion of Master William Thorpe Preste* (Antwerp, 1530). STC 24045.
[18] Here quoting from Foxe, *Actes and Monuments*, sig. Yy6r. Foxe adds predictably slanted marginal commentary.

may not mind the difference between swearing with a hand on a book and swearing with "onely God to witnes," the difference mattered to the clerks, to Thorpe, and to the Archbishop. Why? Because, Thorpe explains by way of his story about the two clerks, books matter:

> [H]ee that chargeth him to lay his hand thus vpon a booke (*touching* the booke, & swearing by it, and *kissing* it, promisinge in this forme to do this thing or that) wil say and witnes, that he that *toucheth* thus a booke, and *kisseth* it, hath sworne vpon that booke. [...] *for euery booke is nothing els, but diuers creatures, of which it is made of.* Therefore to sweare vpon a booke, is to sweare by creatures, and this swearinge is euer vnlefull.[19]

Consider the extent of Thorpe's language of embodiment. He repeats the key terms "touch" and "kiss," emphasizing that a "boke othe" makes for a sensuous affair with something nonhuman, especially since the book in this case would have been made of animal skins. For Thorpe, touching and kissing a book in the act of swearing means something very specific. Touch wrongly confers on the object an allegiance due, not to that object, but to another entity (e.g., God, another person, an institution). And such an obligation to a creature is, in Thorpe's words, "vnlefull."

The surprisingly relevant question seems to be, to whom is one's obligation sworn when sworn with hand on book? Is it to the book? To the person or institution to whom the oath is made? Or to God? The question is relevant because it formulates the parameters of books' capacity to mediate. In Thorpe's account of the interrogation, a debate ensues over this question, culminating in the Archbishop's insistence that Thorpe swear and Thorpe's equally insistent refusal, claiming that "it is al one to touch a booke and to swear by a booke." This admittedly confusing statement – by which Thorpe means that if one touches a book to swear an oath, then one is swearing by the book, no matter to whom the oath is sworn – seems at once a repudiation of the material of books and a frank assertion of their materiality. This is not quite dualism, by which a book's creatureliness would cheapen its value. It is, rather, a clumsy attempt to affirm the high stakes of the bookish medium.

As the debate continues, Thorpe wades into the very question of mediation – that is, of how books relate to the ideas they are said to convey, contain, or stand for. One of the Archbishop's clerks demands that Thorpe swear by laying his "hand vpon the booke, touching the holy Gospell of God," but Thorpe again refuses, now arguing the "holy

---

[19] Foxe, sig. Yy6v. Emphasis mine.

Gospell of God may not be touched with mans hand." He elaborates the point, arguing that:

> the gospel is not the gospel for reading of the letter, but for the belief that men haue in the word of God. That it is the gospel that we beleve, and not the letter that we read: for because the letter that is touched with mans hand, is not the Gospel, but [the] sentence that is verily beleved in ma[n]s hart, is the Gospel.

It bears repeating what Thorpe is not saying. He is not arguing that one should not touch a Bible to swear because it is unworthy of touch or unable to function as a book. He affirms that we can and should "read" and even "touch" the letter, but that the letter should not be confused with the "sentence that is verily beleved." The Bible, as a made material thing, is not identical to the message it is tasked with conveying. In other words, Thorpe does not disregard the materiality of books, even if he does not also treat them as sacramental. There is no straightforward form/content or container/idea notion of mediation at work here, and this is why, for Thorpe, touching a book comes with such high stakes. A touchable book can never simply convey information.

Protestant and nonconformist writers for the next 150 years appealed to Thorpe as a point of reference for questions about oath-making and about the difference between "the gospel that we beleve" and the "letter that we read." Concerns with oath-making were often linked with Wycliff and his followers. The 1530 text of Thorpe's account also features an account of Sir John Oldcastle, another proto-Protestant figure. Foxe and his collaborators feature Thorpe's account as a proto-Protestant refusal of the Roman Catholic church's authority. The exciting consequence of these associations is that, from this moment on, debates about oath-taking carry with them the question of book-touch. Robert Parker, for instance, supports his argument that Roman Catholics value the cross over Jesus himself by appealing to "the followers of Wiclife," who were ordered to "touch the booke of the Gospell and the Image of the crucifixe." For Parker, this means that "the Crosse then was honoured in an oath aswell as the Gospels booke, which thar it was matcht with Christ."[20] William Ames refers to Thorpe in his discussion of oaths, though Ames ultimately concludes that "it is all one vvhether we shew our assent one way [touch] or another [lifting a hand], so it be shewen in a decent manner."[21] Likewise, Robert Sanderson argues

[20] Robert Parker, *A Scholasticall Discourse against Symbolizing with Antichrist in Ceremonies: Especially in the Signe of the Crosse* (Middelburg, 1607), sig. A3v. STC 19294.
[21] William Ames, *A Reply to Dr. Mortons Generall Defence of Three Nocent Ceremonies* (Amsterdam, 1622), sig. I1v-I2r. STC 559.

that touch is *not* required to swear an oath in front of a book – a departure from Thorpe that looks ahead to a later notion of oaths, perhaps.[22]

References to Thorpe increase in the Civil War and Interregnum, as the question of oaths became more vexed. John Stalham, in an anti-Quaker pamphlet, suggests that other anti-Quakers who had made a controversy out of swearing on books should imitate Thorpe and "deny the Superstition, and minde the Institution; refuse not the oath, but the oath by, or upon a Book."[23] Quaker Ellis Hookes, meanwhile, appeals to Thorpe to support his case against swearing oaths at all.[24] Similarly, George Whitehead defends the Quakers' refusal to swear against their consciences. Rehearsing and then extending Thorpe's story, Whitehead historicizes the act of touching a book to swear an oath: in the Hebrew scriptures, swearing was allowed "lest men should worship idols," "but now after so many Arguments of Power" *any* swearing must not be insisted upon.[25]

These echoes of Thorpe suggest how seriously premoderns took the act of touching a book, even when they argued that one need not touch a book to swear an oath. Thorpe's insistence on the creaturely materiality of books reappears in subsequent references to his story, and the writers here seem to register a set of norms against which one must situate any claim about book touch. To be clear, Thorpe and those who refer to him are not dualistically disregarding materiality. What these writers find so alarming is that touching books comes with consequences and obligations. Erasmus, without citing Thorpe, emphasizes the same point from a different angle. The great humanist argues that Christians:

> with cleane handes and verye reuerentlye [...] touche the holy boke of the gospell, and with filthy myndes doe we despise the preceptes of the gospel: why doe we not rather lay them to our hert? why doe we not kisse them with mind and pure affeccion? why do we not here boewe down our neckes; Certain there be that hath hanging about their necke, and cariethe about with them a part of S. Iohns gospell, as a remedie againste diseases, and suche other heuy misfortunes. Why doe not we rather beare aboute with vs the doctrine of the gospell in our mynde, the whiche maye remedy al disease of synne and vice?

---

[22] Robert Sanderson, *De Juramento Seven Lectures Concerning the Obligation of Promissory Oathes* (London, 1655), sig. N6r. Wing S589.

[23] Stalham, *The Reviler Rebuked: Or, A Re-Inforcement of the Charge against the Quakers*, sig. Gg4v. Wing S5186.

[24] Anonymous, *The Spirit of Christ, and the Spirit of the Apostles and the Spirit of the Martyrs Is Arisen, Which Beareth Testimony against Swearing and Oaths* (London, 1661), sig. Dr. Wing H2662.

[25] George Whitehead, *The Case of the Quakers Concerning Oaths Defended as Evangelical* (London, 1674), sig. E3v. Wing W1899.

Erasmus contrasts the devotional touch of the Bible with hands to the "filthy myndes" that despise the Bible's "preceptes," and he compares those who think to ward off sickness by wearing the book of John around their necks to those who carry the book's message in their minds. Why, he asks, driving the language of the senses into the figurative mode, "do we not kisse [the precepts] with mind and pure affeccion?" As with Thorpe, the sensual availability of the book invites Erasmus to address the question of mediation, and like Thorpe, Erasmus does not diminish the value of the bookish sensorium so much as he attempts to clarify the connection between the material object and its message. He goes on to claim, "I doe not discommend any ceremonies, I doe not raile vpon the deuocion of the simple people" – that is, he will not begrudge people for book touch – but rather asserts that those devotions "profit vs, if we put in practyse that thynge whiche the visible signes putteth vs in remembraunce of."

In considering the question of touching books, Thorpe, Erasmus, and others almost unavoidably confront the question of how books mediate. That is, they confront the question of how a book's material features, accessible to the senses, relate to what we might call its communicative function: how does a book's textual form relate to its conceptual content? Addressing this question requires them to formulate a set of parameters, which in turn provoke our attention to the far more common use of touch language as a *figure* for mediation. When writers refer to books "touching on" certain subjects or to "touching on" another book in theirs, they address the very same questions Thorpe raised. Let me emphasize in passing that textual theory and scholarship of the last fifty years has addressed itself to these same questions, often with the implication that an earlier "print culture" lacked a capacity for self-critique.[26] Premodern writers, however, used different terms to talk about mediation, touch prominent among them. Indeed, the notion that a book has a "communicative function" (a phrase I used earlier in this paragraph) is in many ways a back-formation, applied clumsily at best by a post-Enlightenment view of textuality, across what Bruno Latour calls the "modern parenthesis," onto a pre-Enlightenment one.[27]

---

[26] See, for instance, McLeod, "Information on Information"; Greetham, *Textual Scholarship*; D. C. Greetham, "Textual Forensics," *PMLA* 111, no. 1 (1996): 32–51, https://doi.org/10.2307/463132; McKenzie, *Bibliography and the Sociology of Texts*; Neil Fraistat and Julia Flanders, eds., *The Cambridge Companion to Textual Scholarship* (Cambridge: Cambridge University Press, 2013).

[27] Latour, *We Have Never Been Modern*.

Most broadly, writers used "touch" as a figure to describe how books relate to ideas. The point seems almost too obvious, but that is exactly what makes it meaningful. Although "touched on this book" or "this book touches on" are more lexically specific than grammatical constructions, they were common enough to work as parts of a shared linguistic repertoire.[28] Sometimes touch language referred to mediation itself, the bookish function of books. An early translation of Cicero concludes, "Thus endeth the remembraunce of thistoryes comprysed and towchid in this lytil book."[29] In *The Scholemaster*, Roger Ascham refers to another Cicero text: "there is a waie, touched in the first booke of Cicero De Oratore, which [...] would [...] worke a true choice and placing of wordes, a right ordering of sentences, an easie vnderstandyng of the tonge, a readines to speake, a facilitie to write, a true iudgement, both of his owne, and other mens doinges, what tonge so euer he doth vse."[30] Books themselves "touch" certain ideas, making them available to readers.

In other cases, to touch is to read, as in a translation of Juan Luis Vives criticizing bawdy books: "I neuer harde [i.e., heard] man say that he lyked these bokes: but those that neuer touched good bokes. And I my selfe some tyme haue redde in them but I neuer founde in them one steppe either of goodnes or wit."[31] Sometimes the book touches the reader – as when John Davies prays that God would "giue power to the perswasions in this booke contained, to touch the heart but euen of any one whose conuersion might bee wished, and whose amendment might ensue"[32] – and sometimes the author is the one touched, as when Stephen Gardiner writes, "I am by name touched in the sayde boke."[33] This range of possibilities shows how versatile "touch" could be in describing how books do what books do.

By far the most common use of the figure of book touch is when a writer or book *touches (on)* another, in the sense of "discuss" or "refer

[28] On constructions and construction grammar, see Adele E. Goldberg, *Constructions at Work: The Nature of Generalization in Language* (Oxford: Oxford University Press, 2006); Shore, *Cyberformalism*.

[29] Marcus Tullius Cicero, *hEre Begynneth the Prohemye Vpon the Reducynge, Both out of Latyn as of Frensshe in to Our Englyssh Tongue, of the Polytyque Book Named Tullius de Senectute* (London, 1481), sig. a5v. STC 5293.

[30] Roger Ascham, *The Scholemaster or Plaine and Perfite Way of Teachyng Children, to Vnderstand, Write, and Speake, the Latin Tong* (London, 1570), sig. Cj4-v. STC 832.

[31] Juan Luis Vives, *A Very Frutefull and Pleasant Boke Called the Instructio[n] of a Christen Woma[n]* (London, 1529), sig. E4v. STC 24856.5.

[32] John Davies, *[O Vtinam 1 For Queene Elizabeths Securitie, 2 for Hir Subiects Prosperitie]* (London, 1591), sig. E2v-E3r. STC 6328.

[33] Stephen Gardiner, *An Explicatio[n] and Assertion of the True Catholique Fayth* (Rouen, 1551), sig. [A2]v. STC 11592.

to." In his *Apologye* (1533), Thomas More mixes the language of touch and sight: "I Sayed before, that I wolde towche of thys boke, and so haue I towched, hys fyrste chapyter hole, by cause it hath for the fyrste settyng forth the chyefe countenaunce of myldenes and charyte. And yet what charyte there is therin, whan it is considered I suppose you se."[34] More offers a basic formula, in which he touches on another writer's book (indeed the whole first chapter) and thus makes available (or in his terms, *visible*) something about that book to the reader. William Turner refers to things he did not discuss: "ordinances did not i ones touch in my booke / let them be iudges which haue red the book."[35] In the same text mentioned above, Gardiner declares his intention "to touch the further matter of the booke with the maner of the handelyng of it, and where an euident vntruth is."[36] A translation of Euclid uses "touch" to effect transitions, saying how "IN THIS NINTH BOOKE Euclide continueth his purpose touching numbers: partly prosecuting thynges more fully, which were before somewhat spoken of."[37] "Touching" here makes rhetorically possible a connection of the earlier partial treatment of numbers with the more complete discussion to follow. The Catholic writer William Rainolds refers to a book "touching the sacrament of Confirmation" and a translation of John Calvin refers to the "booke of numbers, as shalbe touched againe anon."[38] William Garrard may be guilty of overusing the figure: "but touching these respects, looke in my fourth booke, where I haue particularly touched this matter."[39] Hugh Broughton says he "will briefly touch the sum of this booke," while Thomas Brightman asks "Why, o ye Iesuites doe ye touch this booke?"[40]

These examples offer just a taste of the range of possible configurations of book-touch language from premodern England. It is not sufficient,

[34] Thomas More, *The Apologye of Syr Thomas More Knyght* (London, 1533), sig. Jjiiiv. STC 18078.

[35] William Turner, *The Rescuynge of the Romishe Fox* (Bonn, 1545), sig. Bijv. STC 24355.

[36] Gardiner, *An Explicatio[n] and Assertion of the True Catholique Fayth*, sig. Fvjv. STC 11592.

[37] Euclid, *The Elements of Geometrie of the Most Auncient Philosopher Euclide of Megara* (London, 1570), sig. Yyvjr. STC 10560.

[38] William Rainolds, *A Refutation of Sundry Reprehensions, Cauils, and False Sleightes, by Which M. Whitaker Laboureth to Deface the Late English Translation, and Catholike Annotations of the New Testament, and the Booke of Discouery of Heretical Corruptions* (Paris, 1583), sig. a7r; Calvin, *The Sermons of M. Iohn Caluin Vpon the Fifth Booke of Moses Called Deuteronomie*, sig. D5v. STC 20632 and STC 4442.

[39] William Garrard, *The Arte of Vvarre* (London, 1591), sig. Xx4r. STC 11625.

[40] Hugh Broughton, *A Require of Agreement to the Groundes of Divinitie Studie Wherin Great Scholers Falling, & Being Caught of Iewes Disgrace the Gospel: & Trap Them to Destruction* (Middelburg, 1611), sig. Bv; Thomas Brightman, *A Revelation of the Apocalyps* (Amsterdam, 1611), sig. C2r. STC 3882 and STC 3754.

however, simply to assert that "touch" functions as a synonym for "mediate," in the sense of "convey a message."[41] Like Thorpe, whose attempts to articulate the consequences and commitments of actual book touch led him to question the ordinary form/content distinction of text technologies, this book-touch language confounds any expectation that books simply function as conveyors. Rather, this language shows premodern writers' widespread media consciousness, not only of the *fact of* bookish mediation but also of the *complexity and inescapability of* that mediation.[42] Touch is richer and more capacious than mere mediation: it is access, summary, interaction, comment, and intimacy – and *never signals immediacy*. Garrard's line above, for instance, invites readers to "looke" (yet another sensory term) to the book (in this case meaning "section") where he has already made his discussion available. Instead of a naïve sense of books conveying the "matter," Garrard's touch language emphasizes an awareness that (1) readers need to be told where to "looke" for "matter," (2) the prior, "fourth" book does not simply contain the "matter" but actively mediates it ("particularly touched"), and (3) that the rhetorical task of the current text (the one quoted) is to connect, by way of touch language ("touching these respects"), the mediation of the prior book to the present moment of the reader. The figural use of book-touch, like discussions of actual book touch, offered premodern English writers a rhetorical template for speaking about the interaction of writers, readers, and books.

Here, our story takes an odd but not entirely unexpected turn. The book-touch language I have sampled here appeared in a great variety of early modern English texts, but in the sixteenth century, it was especially concentrated in prominent Protestant texts. The phrase appeared many times, for example, in the so-called "*Admonition* controversy" between puritans and bishops over church government. The 1574 *Defense of the aunsvvere to the Admonition*, which lists John Whitgift as its author, actually contains language from several books. It includes text from the *Admonition to the Parliament* (1572), the book whose criticism of the Elizabethan settlement sparked the controversy, from subsequent texts by Whitgift's great opponent Thomas Cartwright, and finally text by Whitgift himself. A dramatist of sorts, the printer of the *Defense*

41 *OED* s.v., "mediate" 3a.
42 See John Guillory, "The Memo and Modernity," *Critical Inquiry* 31, no. 1 (2004): 108–32, https://doi.org/10.1086/427304; John Guillory, "Mercury's Words: The End of Rhetoric and the Beginning of Prose," *Representations* 138, no. 1 (May 1, 2017): 59–86, https://doi.org/10.1525/rep.2017.138.1.59.

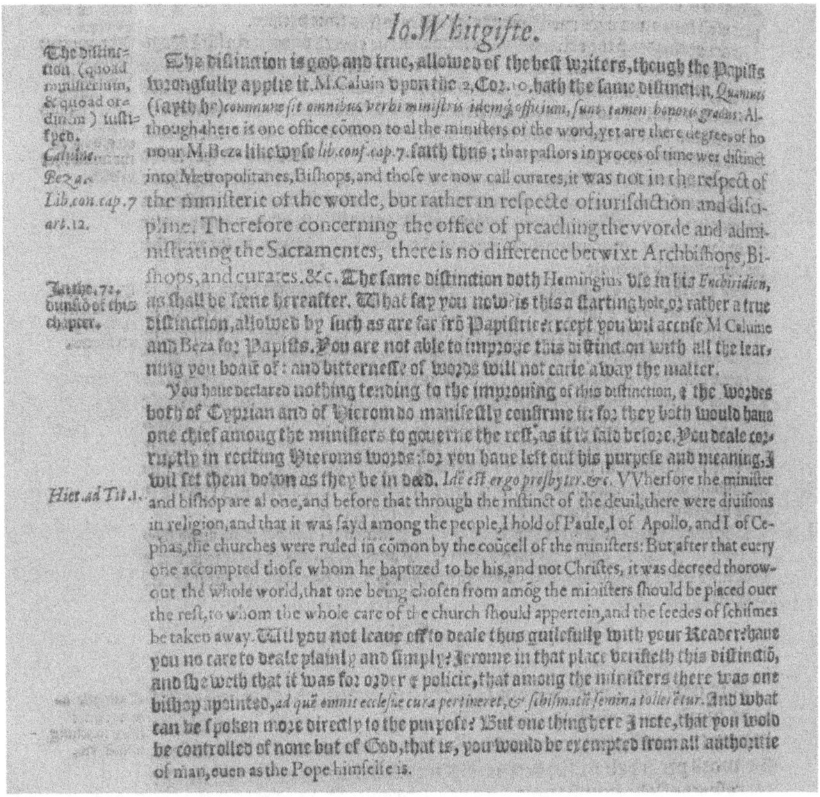

Figure 5.1   Detail of John Whitgift, *Defense of the aunsvvere to the Admonition* (1574), sig. Kkiiiv, 18380, The Huntington Library, San Marino, California.

distinguishes these various voices by means of sections breaks, prefixes, and different sizes of black letter typeface (see Figure 5.1). This format allows Whitgift to respond to Cartwright and the original *Admonition* point by point, and it calls attention to the way all voices use touch language to coordinate the books and writers in the controversy. Cartwright, for instance, writes that "in sundry other places repeated in this booke, I will touch that which is not repeated, and that is, that M. Doctor [Whitgift] maketh it a[n] indifferent thing for men and women to receiue the supper of the Lord, clothed or naked."[43] Whitgift

[43] John Whitgift, *The Defense of the Aunsvvere to the Admonition against the Replie of T.C.* (London, 1574), sig. Bviv. STC 25430.

responds to one of Cartwright's points, arguing "Your answere is there very confused, and vncertaine: but for the proofe of this article, I referre the reader to certaine notes which I haue collected out of your booke touching this matter in this my defense" and elsewhere that "this nothing toucheth the order or substance of the booke, and therefore no sufficient reason agaynst it, if it were true."[44] Still later, he attempts to link his and Cartwright's books with John Calvin's more famous one:

> touching this booke of institutions of M. Caluines, which I now follow, I haue spoken before, and declared why I do vse it rather than any other: I haue laboured it, noted it, I am acquainted with it, and belike, I red it, before you knew whether there was any such booke or no[.][45]

The "you" here is Cartwright, and Whitgift's use of "touching" sets off a miniature self-defense of his reading and accusation of Cartwright. Perhaps more than his opponents, Whitgift uses "touch" in this way so often that it functions as his standby rhetorical maneuver for calling attention to how his book relates to other books or ideas.

Other prominent Protestant texts of the century feature similarly zealous use of "touch" as a metaphor for mediation. In a book that, like Whitgift's, excerpts his opponent's writings in order to dispute them, Thomas Cranmer quotes Stephen Gardiner at length and then argues strenuously against him. Each writer's book "touches" the other's.[46] In English translation, the Italian Protestant theologian Peter Martyr Vermigli uses the phrase to move from one point to the next, referring (for instance) to "a litle booke as touching the personall vnion of the two natures in Christ."[47] Foxe's *Actes and Monuments*, a compendium of Protestantism as well as the main showcase for Thorpe's story of actual book touch, features enthusiastic use of the term. The book speaks of "[John] Bales booke touching the death of Luther," and "touching Iohn Wickleffes bookes, and that whole secte," and dozens more such phrases.[48] Importantly, many uses of "touch" to describe how writers and writings relate to other writers or books are not knowingly and specifically bookish. That is, "to touch (on)" was used generally to mean "discuss," and "touching" to mean "concerning,"

---

[44] Whitgift, sigs. Eiiiv, Ssiiir.

[45] Whitgift, sig. Vvjv.

[46] Thomas Cranmer, *An Aunsvvere by the Reuerend Father in God Thomas Archbyshop of Canterbury, Primate of All England and Metropolitane, Vnto a Craftie and Sophisticall Cauillation, Deuised by Stephen Gardiner Doctour of Law, Late Byshop of Winchester Agaynst the True and Godly Doctrine of the Most Holy Sacrament, of the Body and Bloud of Our Sauiour Iesu Christ* (London, 1580). STC 5992.

[47] Pietro Martire Vermigli, *The Common Places of the Most Famous and Renowmed Diuine Doctor Peter Martyr* (London, 1583), sig. Rrr. STC 24669.

[48] Foxe, *Actes and Monuments*, sigs. EEEeiiiv and Ppiiv.

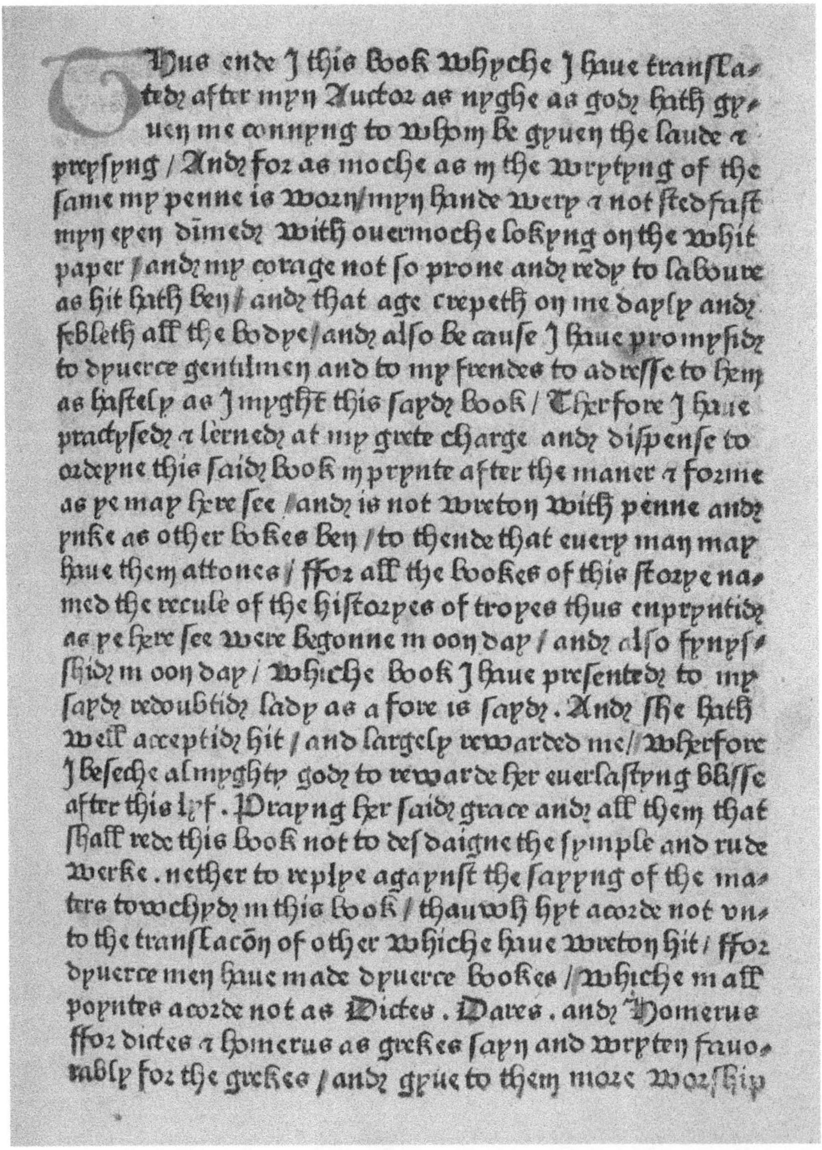

Thus ende I this book whyche I haue translated after myn Auctor as nyghe as god hath gyuen me connyng to whom be gyuen the laude &
preysyng / And for as moche as in the wrytyng of the
same my penne is worn/myn hande wery & not stedfast
myn eyen dimed with ouermoche lokyng on the whit
paper / and my corage not so prone and redy to laboure
as hit hath ben / and that age crepeth on me dayly and
febleth all the bodye / and also be cause I haue promysed
to dyuerce gentilmen and to my frendes to adresse to hem
as hastely as I myght this sayd book / Therfore I haue
practysed & lerned at my grete charge and dispense to
ordeyne this said book in prynte after the maner & forme
as ye may here see / and is not wreton with penne and
ynke as other bokes ben / to thende that euery man may
haue them attones / ffor all the bookes of this storye named the recule of the historyes of troyes thus enprynted
as ye here see were begonne in oon day / and also fynys-
shid in oon day / whiche book I haue presented to my
sayd redoubtid lady as afore is sayd. And she hath
well acceptid hit / and largely rewarded me / wherfore
I beseche almyghty god to rewarde her euerlastyng blysse
after this lyf. Prayng her sayd grace and all them that
shall rede this book not to desdaigne the symple and rude
werke . nether to replye agaynst the sayyng of the maters towchyd in this book / thauwgh hyt accorde not vnto the translacon of other whiche haue wreton hit / ffor
dyuerce men haue made dyuerce bookes / whiche in all
poyntes acorde not as Dictes . Dares . and Homerus
ffor dictes & homerus as grekes sayn and wryten fauo-
rably for the grekes / and gyue to them more worship

Figure 5.2   Detail of Raoul Lefèvre, *hEre Begynneth the Volume Intituled and Named the Recuyell of the Historyes of Troye* (Bruges, 1473), 62222, The Huntington Library, San Marino, California.

even when writers did not have books in mind. Like Thorpe's account of touching real books, touch language cuts across a straightforward form/content distinction. To touch is to access another book by forging a connection modeled on bodily contact; as such it functions as a signifier of mediation.

In the seventeenth century, writers would expand upon what had been a mainly Protestant rhetorical habit, and "touch" grew still more common.[49] Although touch's attachment to bookish mediation existed long before and long after the early modern period, that attachment (like the press's relationship with Protestantism) reached a new intensity during these centuries. Even at the inaugural moment of English printing, William Caxton's 1473 translation of *Recuyell of the historyes of Troye*, touch intrudes. In his much-cited epilogue to the book, Caxton situates the text as a printed book as opposed to manuscript (see Figure 5.2).[50] Caxton cites the speed ("oon day") and scale ("attonce") of printing, and also the cost of the endeavor ("grete charge and dispense") – he cites, in an almost prophetic manner, the very economics that would determine and define the development of the book trade and the establishment of a culture of printing.[51] Then, Caxton goes on to request "all them that shall rede this book not to desdaigne [i.e., disdain] the simple and rude werke. nether to replye against the sayyng of the maters towchyd in this book, thauwh hyt acorde not vnto the translac[i]on of other whiche haue wreton hit[.]" Having asserted the features of the book's printedness, Caxton defends his translation and thus confronts the book's status as a mediator of the Troy story to English readers. Fittingly, he uses "touch" to describe how readers access the book's "sayyng of the maters." Like his predecessor Thorpe, who was also his successor in print, for Caxton a book's touch is a very serious matter indeed.

Looks Like Printing

If "touch" provides an apt figure for how books connect readers to writers, what happens when we *see* a book?[52] In the preface "Too the Reader" of his translation of Ovid's *Metamorphosis*, Arthur Golding grafts Roman mythology into Christian history, asserting that in the

---

[49] The examples in *OED*, s.v., "touch" bear out this point.
[50] Raoul Lefèvre, *hEre Begynneth the Volume Intituled and Named the Recuyell of the Historyes of Troye* (Bruges, 1473). STC 15375. The epilogue appears on the unsigned penultimate leaf.
[51] See N. F. Blake, *William Caxton and English Literary Culture* (London: Hambledon Press, 1991); William Kuskin, *Symbolic Caxton: Literary Culture and Print Capitalism* (Notre Dame: University of Notre Dame Press, 2008); Lotte Hellinga, *William Caxton and Early Printing in England* (London: British Library, 2010); A. E. B. Coldiron, *Printers without Borders: Translation and Textuality in the Renaissance* (Cambridge: Cambridge University Press, 2015).
[52] On visual perception in book history, see Reid, *Reading by Design*.

absence of knowledge of "the trewe and euerliuing God," Romans assigned divinity to all sorts of things. But, in Golding's telling, this did not turn out very well:

> For God perceyuing mannes peruers and wicked will too sinne
> Did giue him ouer too his lust too sinke or swim therin.
> By meanes wherof it came too passe (as in this booke yée sée)
> That all theyr Goddes with whoordome, theft, or murder blotted bée.[53]

Consider the rhetorical savvy of Golding's parenthesis. Faced with the combined task of asserting the literary value of Ovid's poem and defending it against accusations of blasphemy and obscenity, Golding first situates the poem in a larger divine pattern (God "did giue him ouer" – alluding to Romans 1:24) and then explains the poem's events in terms of that pattern. This move – common in Renaissance defenses of classical learning – thus enables Golding to separate himself and his readers from the not-exactly-decent events of the poem: "as in this booke yée sée." Sight functions as a kind of remote access.

As with touch, premodern texts abound with language of sight. Often inconspicuous like Golding's parenthesis, this language affords writers a way to prescribe what a book makes available to a reader's attention. Sebastian Munster writes that his reader "may in this smal as in a little glasse, see some cleare light...."[54] The preface epistle to John Bradford's *Complaynt of veritie* (1559) claims that in a commonplace book "a man might see in that booke, the signes of his smitten heart."[55] Another preface asserts that "we may all see in this booke the liuely paterne of a trewe remorse, here may we see how Saul doeth become Paul."[56] Other writers exhort their readers to look on or in a book. Joseph Hall claims that some "men yet haue Holinesse written vpon them, and are like [...] to a faire gilt bossed booke: looke within, there is the Tragedie of Thyestes, or perhaps Arrius his Thalia; the name of a Muse, the matter heresie."[57] When we "looke within," we find (or rather, *see*) that the "matter" of the "text" does not conform to the cover's promise. Sight, for better and worse, identifies what the book is supposed to represent to its readers.

[53] Thomas Lever, *A Treatise of the Right Way Fro[m] Danger of Sinne & Vengeance in This Wicked World, Vnto Godly Wealth and Saluation in Christe* (London, 1575), sig. A1r. STC 15552.
[54] Sebastian Münster, *A Treatyse of the Newe India* (London, 1553), sig. aaiiiv. STC 18244.
[55] John Bradford, *The Complaynt of Veritie* (London, 1559), sig. A5r-v. STC 3479.
[56] Hugues Sureau Du Rosier, *A lamentable discourse of the fall of Hughe Sureau (commonly called Du Rosier) from the truth* (London, 1573), sig. Aiiiv-Aiiiir. STC 7369.
[57] Hall, *The Vvorks of Ioseph Hall Doctor in Diuinitie, and Deane of Worcester*, sig. Qq2v. STC 12635b.

Here again, the story takes an odd turn, this one back to William Caxton, who took pains from the very introduction of the printing press to England to call attention to what made printed texts special.[58] As Seth Lerer writes, Caxton's prologues and epilogues "relocate their literary texts within new narratives of the texts' technological production and social reception."[59] As we have already seen, Caxton emphasized his hard work and great investment in printing his translation of Lefevre's Trojan history. But he also gestures, apparently nonchalantly, at sight. Here again is his claim (see also Figure 5.2):

> I haue practysed & lerned at my grete charge and dispense to ordeyne this said book in prynte after the maner & forme *as ye may here see*, and is not wreton with penne and ynke as other bokes ben, to thende that euery man may haue them attonce, ffor all the bookes of this storye [...] thus enpryntid *as ye here see were* bygonne in oon day, and also fynysshed in oon day.[60]

Twice Caxton refers to the reader seeing something, first the "maner & forme" of the printed book and second the number of "bookes of this storye" that took just one day to print. He does so by way of a direct address, both times referring to "ye" and "here," directing our attention to the very book we are presumably reading. The offhandedness and conventionality of the statement makes it even more suggestive in this context. One is almost tempted to suspect a sort of anxiety at work, in which Caxton's effort to advertise the value of this printed book entails his insistence that we "see" it for what it is. If this were just one instance, we may be able to overlook (overlook!) it. But Caxton repeatedly asks his readers to "see" his books, promises they will "see" something "in" his books, and even publishes books in which other writers refer to "seeing" in books. To my knowledge never noticed by scholars, this habit shows us Caxton's attempts to rationalize and market the new medium of print using the conventional Western priority of sight.

For example, Caxton dedicates his translation of Jacobus de Cessolis's morality book on chess to George, Duke of Clarence, using sight language. Having relayed that the "lityll book" came "in to myn handes" (note again the haptic language), Caxton claims that he finds in it "thauctorites. Dictees [i.e., sayings]. and stories of auncient Doctours philosophes poetes and of other wyse men whiche been recounted & applied vnto the

---

[58] See note 50.
[59] Seth Lerer, "Medieval English Literature and the Idea of the Anthology," *PMLA* 118, no. 5 (October 2003): 1261, https://doi.org/10.1632/003081203X68018.
[60] Lefèvre, *The Recuyell of the Historyes of Troye*. Emphasis mine.

moralite of the publique wele as well of the nobles as of the comyn peple after the game and playe of the chesse."[61] In other words, the book applies chess scenarios to political and moral topics, not just for the Duke but for anyone who reads it: "but to thentent that other [i.e., other people] of what estate or degre he or they stande in may see in this sayd lityll book yf they gouerned them self as they ought to doo [...]." Anyone "may see" whether they have governed themselves in a manner appropriate to their situation. Sight thus signifies the allegorical, moral purpose of the bookish medium: readers see, in the book and by way of chess, their own identities with respect to their "estate or degre." Caxton then declares the purpose of the table of contents that follows the dedication: "for more clerely to procede in this sayd book I haue ordeyned that the chapitres ben sette in the begynnynge to thende *that ye may see more playnly the mater wherof the book treteth*" (emphasis mine). We access the book's discursive "mater," like its allegorical message, on the model of sight. In the space of a few lines, Caxton offers a multiform theory of how the book coordinates a moral-philosophical content, the language of the text, and the reader's perceiving faculties, here figured as eyes.

However easily overlooked, this language forms the basis of Caxton's rhetoric concerning books. Sometimes he refers to seeing books as a way of explaining how he came by them, as in the preface to his *Dictes and sayings of the philosophers* (1477), when he explains how a gentleman introduced him to "a book that he trusted I shuld lyke it right wele and brought it to me whyche book I had neuer seen before. and is called the saynges or dictis of the Philosophers."[62] More often, Caxton speaks of seeing and reading as conjoined but separable actions. In the preface to *Eracles, and also of Godefrey of Boloyne* (1481), he "exhorte[s] alle noble riten of hye courage to see this booke and here it redde," and his later preface to *Somme des vices et vertus* (1485), he similarly "exhorte[s] & desire[s] euery ma[n] that entendeth to the prouffyt & seluacyon of his soule to ouer see this sayd book in whiche he shal fynde good & prouffytable doctryne."[63] Reading, thus figured, is not a direct access to the book's contents (its "mater") but one embodied in and mediated by the faculty of sight. That this seeing is partly

[61] de Cessolis Jacobus, *[De Ludo Scachorum]* (Bruges, 1474). STC 4920. The preface appears on the first, unsigned leaves of the book.

[62] *[Dictes or Sayengis of the Philosophhres]* (London, 1477). STC 6826.

[63] *Here Begynneth the Boke Intituled Eracles, and Also of Godefrey of Boloyne* (London, 1481), sig. A3v-A4r; Dominican Laurent, *This Book Was Compyled [and] Made Atte Requeste of Kyng Phelyp of Fraunce ... Whyche Book Is Callyd in Frensshe. Le Liure Royal That Is to Say the Ryal Book. or a Book for a Kyng* (London, 1485), sig. aiiv. STC 13175 and STC 21429.

figurative does not make it less significant as an apparently indispensable way for Caxton to describe the bookishness of books.

The most frequent use of this sight language occurs when Caxton or a writer Caxton publishes refers to seeing something in a book, as in the first example from the chess book above. Many such instances occur at points where the stakes of bookishness are high. In the epistle attached to Chaucer's translation of Boethius, Caxton famously describes how Chaucer, "the worshipful fader & first fou[n]deur & enbelissher of ornate eloquence in our english," followed "the latyn as neygh [i.e., nigh, closely] as is possible to be vnderstande."[64] This work deserves our thanks, Caxton writes, especially "them that shall rede & vnderstande it. For in the sayd boke they may see what this transitorie & mutable world is And wherto euery man[n] liuyng in hit ought to entende." This is no modest effect: to see what the world is and how to "entende" in it. But Caxton goes on to link this "understanding" to the printing press, noting that "this sayd boke so translated is ra[r]e & not spred ne knowen as it is digne and worthy." Too few people have *seen* the book, and thus what the book allows them to see. Thus, Caxton took pains "tenprynte it [...] In hopyng that it shal proufite much people." The grand promise of the book and its author is linked to the scale of the printing press by way of the language of sight.

As scholars have long observed, Caxton faced a double challenge as both printer and translator; in both cases, mediation sits front and center.[65] Given what we have already seen about Caxton's media self-consciousness, it is hardly surprising to find that he invokes sight to coordinate translation with books and readers. For instance, in his translation of a biography-romance of Charlemagne, Caxton explains his motives:

> for to satysfye the desyre & requeste of my good synguler lordes & specyal maysters and frendes I haue enprysed and concluded in my self to reduce this sayd book in to our englysshe as all alonge and playnely ye may rede here and see in thys book here folowyng [...].[66]

In this case, what readers "see" (as well as hear and read) is Caxton's translation, but elsewhere in the preface Caxton writes that the purpose of the translation is "for prouffyte of euery man." Similarly, in his edition of Geoffroy de la Tour Landry's behavior manual for girls at court, known as "The Book of the Knight of the Tower," Caxton similarly expresses his

---

[64] Boethius, *Boecius de Consolacione Philosophie* (London, 1478). STC 3199.
[65] See Coldiron, *Printers without Borders*.
[66] Anonymous, *[Thystorye and Lyf of the Noble and Crysten Prynce Charles the Grete Kynge of Frauuce]* (London, 1485), sig. aiiv. STC 5013.

desire that "all them that shall lerne or see ony thynge in this sayd book by whiche they shal ben the wyser & better that they gyue laude & tha[n]kyng to the sayd ladyes good grace and also to praye for her."[67] Importantly, the "lady" in question here is the woman who encouraged Caxton to translate this text into English, so once again Caxton forges a rhetorical connection between seeing, reading, and the book's content ("ony thynge"), which has been mediated once by translation and again by printing.

Other Caxton books feature similar moves. His insistent sight language functions not simply as a metaphor for mediation but as a conceptual and rhetorical linchpin holding the whole process together. With "see," he addresses questions that twenty-first-century textual scholarship continues to discuss, in particular, the relationship between symbols rendered graphically on a substrate (e.g., letters) and the concepts sometimes labeled "content," "message," or "subject matter." In *the myrrour of the worlde* (1481), he writes that:

> emonge alle other this [present] booke whiche is called the ymage or myr-rour of the world ought to be visyted redde & knowen by cause it treateth of the world and of the wondreful dyuision therof in whiche book a man resonable may see and vnderstande more clerer by the visytyng and seeyng of it and the figures therin the situac[i]on and moeuyng of the firmament.[68]

Even though "seeyng" occurs toward the end of this quotation, the larger context shows how, once again, Caxton connects the dots between the actual book in the reader's hands, the activity of reading ("visyted redde & knowen"), the conceptual content of the book ("the world and of the wondreful dyuision therof"), the textual content of the book ("it and the figures therin"), and the faculty by which all these things cohere ("visytyng and seeyng"). He makes a similar case in his preface to Mallory's *Morte d'Arthur* (1485), also worth quoting at length. This time, Mallory is the translator (or "reducer"):

> whyche copye Syr Thomas Malorye dyd take oute of certeyn bookes of frensshe and reduced it in to Englysshe And I accordyng to my copye haue doon sette it in enprynte to the entente that noble men may *see and lerne* the noble actes of chyualrye the Ientyl and vertuous dedes that somme knyghtes vsed in tho dayes by whyche they came to honour and how they that were vycious were punysshed and ofte put to shame and rebuke

---

[67] Geoffroy de La Tour Landry, *[Here Begynneth the Booke Which the Knyght of the Toure Made and Speketh of Many Fayre Ensamples and Thensygnementys and Techyng of His Doughters]* (London, 1484), sig. ir-v. STC 15296.

[68] *Hier Begynneth the Book Callid the Myrrour of the Worlde* (London, 1481), sig. a4r-v. STC 24762.

humbly bysechyng al noble lordes and ladyes wyth al other estates of what estate or degree they been of that shal *see and rede* in this sayd book and werke that they take the good and honest actes in their remembraunce and to folowe the same wherin they shalle fynde many Ioyous and playsaunt hystoryes and noble & renomed actes of humanyte gentylnesse and chyualryes.[69]

Caxton says readers "see" the deeds of honor and the punishment of vice narrated in Mallory's writing, but in fact, like other symbolic instances of "see" above, readers do not see those things at all. Rather, as still other instances above indicate, readers actually see the book itself and then "rede" it. Caxton's "see and rede" bridges the gap of bookish mediation: books mediate by enabling readers to access the abstract "content" or "message" of a book by way of marks on the page we know as letters. The distinct processes of seeing and reading, moreover, lead to "remembraunce" and finally moral imitation ("folowe the same"). The language of sight provides Caxton an effective way to describe what readers "get" (or "take") from his books.

Tastes Like Book Spirit

This final section turns to the sense of taste to add a red-letter date to the history of the book: 1597. The 1590s already represent a crucial turning point in what some call print culture. In this decade, the Marprelate controversy (at least the tail end), the 1599 Bishops' Ban, the explosion of prose romances and sermon collections, and other key events and changes in the book trade confirmed the place of printed books at the center of English culture – particularly in London. As Georgia Brown has so energetically demonstrated, the 1590s "were characterized [...] by the expansion of literary activity" but also a revolution in which "writers and readers started to express a changing sense of the forms and functions of literature."[70] Extending Brown's analysis, Samuel Fallon explores the way in which literary personae of the 1590s function as "products of ... the reflexive consciousness of a hybrid media culture" (hybrid in the sense of manuscript and print).[71] Clearly, the 1590s were a key moment in the relationship between the print medium and imaginative literature.

---

[69] Thomas Malory, *[Le Morte Darthur]* (London, 1485), sig. iiir. STC 801, my emphasis.
[70] Georgia Brown, *Redefining Elizabethan Literature* (Cambridge: Cambridge University Press, 2004), 4.
[71] Samuel Fallon, *Paper Monsters: Persona and Literary Culture in Elizabethan England*, Material Texts (Philadelphia: University of Pennsylvania Press, 2019), 16.

These accounts point us to an even bigger history of mediation. At stake in scholarship on the 1590s is the question of how a culture becomes book-ish – that is, how a culture becomes not just *literary* in the familiar modern sense but in the premodern sense, "of or belonging to books."[72] If there was a *print culture* before 1700, then it existed in the sense that books signified. Rather than a *print* culture, which has an uneasy metonymical relationship with the press, we might speak of a *bookish* culture, in which books acquired a set of durable associations. And that is why 1597 is such an important date: in that year, Francis Bacon's *Essayes* were first pub-lished, featuring this crispy nugget of Baconian brevity: "some bookes are to bee tasted, others to bee swallowed, and some few to bee chewed and digested: that is, some bookes are to be read only in partes; others to be read, but cursorily, and some few to be read wholly and with diligence and attention."[73] Having shown how writers appealed to touch and sight to describe how books mediate, in this section, I will explore the relationship of premodern books with taste.[74] My main claim is that Bacon's statement forms a hinge in the story, in which books acquire a new set of signifying capacities and the story of mediation takes a drastic turn.

Bacon's axiom does not make gastrointestinal sense. The relationship between tasting a book metaphorically and reading seems relatively clear. To taste a book is to take in parts of it, in Bacon's words. It is not entirely clear, however, what mode of reading Bacon has in mind here. If he is thinking about instrumental reading, such as consulting a dictionary or perhaps the practice of commonplacing, then the taste readers get is the point of the book. But he does not say that, and the fact that this is ini-tially a statement about *books*, as distinct from reading, suggests a value-laden judgment. Some books, he implies but does not state, are worth just a sample. But the metaphor gets still more complicated as it elaborates. The difference between swallowing a book and chewing and digesting a book is a bit fuzzier. Surely Bacon knew that to swallow something is part of digesting it. Swallowing and digesting do not seem distinct enough to measure the difference between cursory and diligent reading – unless, of course, we change our focus from the eaten to the eater. The fuzziness of

---

[72] *OED* s.v., "bookish adj. 2."

[73] Francis Bacon, *Essayes Religious meditations. Places of perswasion and disswasion. Seene and allowed* (London, 1597), sig. B1v. STC 1137.

[74] My claims supplement the incredibly rich and far broader discussion of taste and knowledge in Elizabeth L. Swann, *Taste and Knowledge in Early Modern England* (Cambridge: Cambridge University Press, 2020). My argument here aligns with Swann's that "literary taste, usually dated to the eighteenth century, emerges much earlier" (35).

the differences notwithstanding, readers know the difference Bacon is try-ing to describe. It is one thing to swallow a book, but to *chew* on it, to read it with *attention* – now that's digestion. Incidentally, this presents an exem-plary case of Stanley Fish's reading of Bacon's *Essays* as self-consuming arti-facts: to fully understand this metaphor, we have to digest it ourselves.[75] In a flash, what begins as a statement about books, the grammatical subject of the sentence, becomes a statement about readers, the agents who effect the distinction between tasting, swallowing, and chewing.

The metaphor of tasting books did not come from nowhere. One might begin with the early hermeneutic notion of the *integumentum* or covering of a text, which often conceptualized reading as the removal of a shell or husk to eat the nut or juice beneath. The metaphor evolved with the sixteenth-century print market. The 1519 translation of Raymond of Capua's *Life of Saint Catherine of Siena* criticizes wrongful interpretations of the Bible: "they vnderstonde rather holy wrytte after the letter or after theyr owne felynge than after the very vnderstondynge & so by tastynge onely of the lettre they make many bokes but they taste not the pythe [...]."[76] The tasting of *letters* is distinct from tasting the *pith* of the Bible – an assertion that seems less like a form/content claim than one about mediation. Letters, instead of conveying the "very" or true "understand-ing," stimulate the production of misreading – and more books. Merely tasting letters leads to failed comprehension. Thomas More uses a similar metaphor to describe successful comprehension. More declares that when the person who has argued against him can "proue his worde [against More] wysely spoken," then that man should "kepe one copye therof wyth hym selfe for lesynge, & sende an other to me and than that copye that I receyue, I wyll be bounden to eate it though the booke be bounden in bordes."[77] Here, eating the book means not just grasping the writer's point (in the sense of comprehension) but acknowledging the successful proof of that point. More's little joke on the word "bounden" suggests his skepticism that the writer can prove his objection. It also highlights the deliberate bookishness of this particular moment, as we imagine the great More shrugging his shoulders with resignation as he begins to eat a bound book.

[75] Stanley Fish, *Self-Consuming Artifacts; the Experience of Seventeenth-Century Literature* (Berkeley: University of California Press, 1972).
[76] Raymond of Capua, *Here Begynneth the Orcharde of Syon in the Whiche Is Conteyned the Reuelacyons of Seynt Katheryne of Sene, with Ghostly Fruytes [and] Precyous Plantes for the Helthe of Mannes Soule.* (London, 1519), sig. miiiiv. STC 4815.
[77] More, *The Apologye of Syr Thomas More Knyght*, sig. F2v. STC 18078.

This notion of tasting or eating books was fairly common throughout the sixteenth and seventeenth centuries, with writers using the metaphor as a model for understanding. Pierre Viret complains about people who cannot "applye themselues to reade those good bookes, and can take no taste of them, bicause that their mouthe is not fitte for such meate, and that they are to precious for them."[78] These readers cannot apprehend good books. As we saw with Thorpe and Erasmus earlier, Viret appeals to a bodily metaphor for a process he does not think involves the body. Somewhat differently, Foxe's *Actes and Monuments* notes that the people of Bohemia came "to the knowledge of Wickliffes bookes here in England," and therefore "began first to taste and sauor Christes gospell."[79] By way of books, the Bohemians taste something else. (I mention, parenthetically, that later writers would grab this particular phrase – "taste and savor" – in reference to evangelism.[80]) In a book on the history of the Netherlands, Jean Francois Le Petit's translator refers readers to "the books themselues," where they "shall haue better tast and information."[81] Shakespeare's sonnet 77 assures us that "of this booke, this learning maist thou taste."[82] You get the idea: taste and eating easily fill at least one of the variables in descriptions of understanding.

We might benefit from a taxonomy of this language. Most references to *eating* books imply comprehension, while references to *tasting* books usually imply sampling. The nearly archetypal instance of the first category is Revelation 10:9, here in the Coverdale translation: "take the boke, and eate it vp, and it shall make thy belly to become bytter, but in thy mouth it shalbe swete as hony: and I toke the boke of the angels hande, and I dyd eate it vp, and it was swete in my mouth as hony."[83] This verse served all sorts of writers as a metaphorical prompt. The preacher Henry Smith, for instance, wrote that:

> as the Angel taught Iohn to reade the booke when hee bad him eate it: so we must put on Christ, as if wee did eate him, not as the Papists doe in their Masse, but as the meate is turned into the substance of the body, and goeth through euery part of man: so Christ & his worde should goe from

[78] Pierre Viret, *The Christian Disputations* (London, 1579), sig. B7v. STC 24776.
[79] Foxe, *Actes and Monuments*, sig. EE6v.
[80] See, for instance, William Symonds, *Pisgah Euangelica* (London, 1605), sig. Ee4r. STC 23592.
[81] Jean François Le Petit, *A Generall Historie of the Netherlands* (London, 1608), fol 1608. STC 12374. [n.b.: the EEBO images for this book are not indexed properly, so the page number cited may not be correct.]
[82] William Shakespeare, *Shake-Speares Sonnets* (London, 1609), sig. E4v-Fr. STC 22353.
[83] *The newe testamente both Latine and Englyshe ech correspondent to the other after the vulgare texte, communely called S. Ieroms* (London, 1538). STC 2816.

part to part, from eare to heart, from heart to mouth, from mouth to hand, till wee be of one nature with them, that they bee the very substance of our thoughts & speeches, and actions, as the meate is of our bodies. This is to eate Christ and his word, or els wee doe not eate them, but chew them, and when our tast is satisfied, spue them out againe.[84]

Smith's appeal to eating-as-comprehension leads him to taste-as-sample. Likewise, Samuel Ward complains about those who "reade the Bible by fits vpon rainy dayes, not eating the booke with Iohn, but tasting onely with the tippe of the tongue." These rainy-day readers, he says, "meditate by snatches, neuer chewing the cud and digesting their meat, they may happely get a smackering for discourse and table-talke; but not enough to keepe soule & life together, much lesse for strength and vigour."[85] Ward's reference to the Revelation verse slingshots him into the second category of taste-as-sample.

This second category was everywhere, as writers used the metaphor of taste to stand in for the idea of sampling a book. Martin Luther, in translation, reports that "Surely a very small tast of this booke [Ecclesiastes] was to me a great pleasure."[86] John Bale, in his *Pageant of Popes*, offers "in this booke a little taste of theyr [that is, the popes'] vnsauorye liues."[87] Thomas Cartwright writes to his opponent that, "not to waste paper in rehersall of all: I will onely giue a tast of your later book."[88] The preface to John Calvin's enormous book of sermons on Deuteronomy offers "to giue the readers some tast of the whole booke of the said sermo[n]s."[89] In these and dozens of other cases of this language from the period, the metaphor offers a thorny theory of mediation. In most instances, a taste of a book (that is, a sample) cannot and must not stand in for knowledge of the whole book. These examples here tend to work upon the assumption that a taste does not confer or convey sufficient knowledge of the book to the extent that a taste can be equivalent to the whole thing. A taste of Calvin's sermons is supposed to offer us some idea of what those sermons consist of,

---

[84] Henry Smith, *The Vvedding Garment* (London, 1590), sig. C3r-C4v. STC 22713.

[85] Samuel Ward, *A Coal from the Altar, to Kindle the Holy Fire of Zeale* (London, 1615), sig. E5r-v. STC 25039.

[86] Martin Luther, *An Exposition of Salomons Booke Called Ecclesiastes or the Preacher* (London, 1573), sig. A5v. STC 16979.

[87] John Bale, *The Pageant of Popes Contayninge the Lyues of All the Bishops of Rome, from the Beginninge of Them to the Yeare of Grace 1555* (London, 1574), sig. *a8v. STC 1304.

[88] Thomas Cartwright, *The Second Replie of Thomas Cartwright: Agaynst Maister Doctor Whitgiftes Second Answer, Touching the Churche Discipline* (Heidelberg, 1575), sig.)()(4r. STC 4714.

[89] Calvin, *The Sermons of M. Iohn Caluin Vpon the Fifth Booke of Moses Called Deuteronomie*, [Pilcrow]3v. STC 4442.

but the taste cannot and is not supposed to replace the actual reading of the sermons. If a taste, in this line of thinking, can mediate, it does so by approximation, which is after all the whole point of the metaphor. Peter Vermigli (or Peter Martyr) helpfully traces out this theory of mediation by criticizing partial reading:

> mans wisedome as it hath bin accustomed, began to loath and contemne the holy scriptures, as though the same were now wearie of Manna, and of the bread giuen from heauen, and it iudged the holy scripture to be so vile and simple, as though it could straightwaie attaine to the whole vnderstanding thereof euen with one twinke of eye, and with one breath. It supposed it to be ynough to reade ouer the same once, and by a taste of one or two Bookes it iudged of the whole woorthinesse thereof, it laide it aside and determined to séeke wisedome elsewhere also.[90]

Vermigli critiques those who think, wrongly in his mind, that a taste of the Bible can adequately replace knowledge of the whole. This is not, of course, an either–or situation, in which a taste either replaces or does not replace the whole book. Rather, the notion of mediation in view in these many examples is distinctly premodern, modeled as an intimate and embodied interaction that, when imagined as a taste, does not satisfy.

This returns us to Bacon, who makes a subtle but important reconfiguration of the metaphor. Whereas in most cases (like all the ones above), the emphasis of the metaphor falls on the *insufficiency* of a taste to mediate (a taste is not enough to know), Bacon's line suggests that it is sufficient. Some books are just to be tasted, and a taste is, specifically, all you need. In the calculus of Bacon's metaphor, a reader does not need to ingest fully the whole book but only read it "in parts," and those parts stand in for and can effectively replace the whole. The emphasis, as I argued earlier, falls rather on the reader's capacity to distinguish between books worth tasting and books worth swallowing or digesting.

Bacon's reconfiguration of an extremely common metaphor is special, though not unique. Other writers referred to tasting books as a sufficient replacement for the whole. What makes Bacon's version special is, first, that he crosses the idea of tasting as sample with the idea of eating as comprehension, and, second, that dozens of writers repeated his line and used it as a prompt, just as writers used Revelation 10:9. By rerouting the notion of taste from a quality of books to a faculty of readers, even as his line suggests that a taste is all you need, Bacon opens the door for

---

[90] Vermigli, *The Common Places of the Most Famous and Renowmed Diuine Doctor Peter Martyr*, sig. Cc5r. STC 24669.

the modern notion of taste as aesthetic discrimination. The *OED* calls this kind of taste "a sense of what is appropriate, harmonious, or beautiful," specifically "the faculty of perceiving and enjoying what is excellent in art, literature, and the like."[91] *OED* dates this notion of taste to 1671, in Milton's *Paradise Regained*, which refers to "Sion's songs, to all true tasts excelling, Where God is prais'd aright." The *OED* then cites William Congreve's 1694 *Double-dealer* – "No, no hang him, he has no tast" – followed by Joseph Addison in the *Spectator*: "Rules.how we may acquire that fine Taste of Writing, which is so much talked of among the Polite World." In the space of three quotations, we arrive at the modern notion of taste as an assertion of cultural distinction and superiority, which Pierre Bourdieu and others have described.[92] The key assumptions in the development of this notion of taste are that the person in possession of it can discern the value of things, and that this discernment is implicitly marked by *dis*embodiment. The elite, tasteful reader has everything but a body.

To put too fine a point on it, this is the very assumption that Bacon formulates in his statement about tasting, swallowing, and eating books. Underwriting the modern notion of taste – this idea of aesthetic judgment that informs the best and worst of modernity – is a twist in the theory of mediation in which a taste of a book goes from being not enough to being more than enough. What was, for most writers, a mark of deficiency becomes, in Bacon's aphorism, a ranked sufficiency (we taste James Patterson, swallow the *New Yorker*, and chew and digest Toni Morrison). This move seems to invert Jacques Derrida's notion of the trace, which Juliet Fleming glosses as the term used "to suggest that what a signifier marks is not only 'not there' but, more importantly, 'not that'; the trace is not the remainder of something gone but the mark of what was never fully there."[93] Bacon's line works in the opposite direction: whereas for many writers, perhaps channeling Derrida *avant la lettre*, a taste marks insufficient mediation, for Bacon a taste can and does constitute presence. Indeed, that he then elaborates the metaphor in terms of swallowing, chewing, and digesting as more intensive forms of making books present to oneself suggests precisely this vector of thinking. If Derrida's notion of the trace aims to dismantle a modern notion of mediation rooted in a metaphysics of presence, then in Bacon's aphorism we see the very formulation

[91] *OED*, s.v., "taste, n.1" 8a.
[92] Pierre Bourdieu, *Distinction: A Social Critique of the Judgement of Taste* (Cambridge: Harvard University Press, 1984); John Guillory, *Cultural Capital: The Problem of Literary Canon Formation* (Chicago: University of Chicago Press, 1993).
[93] Fleming, *Cultural Graphology*, 7.

of that modern idea – formulated, it is worth repeating, in language concerning books. For Bacon, a taste of a book is a trace that can make that book present to the taster.

Later writers adapted Bacon's line with great relish. Most use his threefold division as a way of distinguishing which books are worth tasting, swallowing, or chewing and digesting. Richard Braithwaite, for instance, explains that books worth tasting include "Stories of modest accomplement, superficiall flourishes" and so on, whereas the "Amorous, and fruitlesse labours of braine-sicke Authors" are for swallowing, and "discourse tending both to instruction and delight" is worth chewing and digesting.[94] Other writers pick up on the implicit theory of mediation. Edward Leigh, for instance, in a 1646 preface to the reader, writes that:

> the number of bookes is without number, the Presses are daily oppressed with them. Yet (though the world abound with unprofitable, nay pernicious Pamphlets) there are many excellent subjects which are either not handled, or not sufficiently. There is a great variety in mens fancies as well as in their faces; and bookes (the fruit of mens brains) are as various as men themselves. Some books are to be tasted onely, some chewed, and some swallowed.[95]

The aphorism punctuates Leigh's attempt to articulate what to do with all the books coming off the press. This is not a Lockean theory of communication, by which ideas are transmitted from one brain to another by way of the medium of words. But it's close. Leigh presents the variety of books as a reflection of the variety of human consciousness, with the faint suggestion (by way of the fruit metaphor) that access to and distinction among books entails access to and distinction among people. For Leigh, as for Bacon, as for Bourdieu, to have a taste is not merely to sample but to judge.

Most of the examples in this chapter were found by means of a proximity search. The command "touch NEAR/5 book" returns any instance of "touch" within five words of "book," for example. Such a search expression seeks texts bringing the body literally close to the book. Proximity also makes for an evocative metaphor for what these instances of book touch, sight, and taste describe: the senses bring books near. For William Thorpe and others, the touch of books became a high-stakes affair. For others, touch figures access. For William Caxton, writing at the advent of printing

---

[94] Brathwaite, *History Surveyed in a Brief Epitomy*, sig. Ss2r-v. Wing B4265.
[95] Edward Leigh, *A Treatise of Divinity Consisting of Three Bookes* (London, 1646), sig. ***3r. Wing L1011.

in England, and Francis Bacon, sight and taste bring the subjects of books into proximity with readers' bodies in a variety of ways. The language of touching, seeing, and tasting books thus shows us not an emerging *print* culture but an established and continually unfolding *bookish* one. The difference between these two cultural models cannot be overstated. In one, books ground and produce cultural change. In the other, books have signifying functions related to their status as text carriers – that is, as media. With this complex array of figurations, the senses help convey how we come to know what books offer. In Chapter 6, we will consider how books figure knowledge itself.

The World Is a Book

The Book of Nature has a Wikipedia page. Likely the best-known bookish metaphor, the world as a book has certainly attracted significant attention from scholars for reasons apparent even on Wikipedia: the book of nature implies that the whole natural world may be "read for knowledge and understanding."[1] The image of a person reading all of nature as one reads a book has done powerful imaginative work across time and cultures. The "book of nature" metaphor appears abundantly in ancient and medieval texts, and in the seventeenth century it flared up again in ways this chapter will explore. Ernst Robert Curtius, whom we met in Chapter 1, summarizes how "the concept of the world or nature as a 'book' originated in pulpit eloquence, was then adopted by medieval mystico-philosophical speculation, and finally passed into common usage."[2] Subsequent accounts have added to this one, emphasizing the broader classical origins and modern familiarity with what Hans Blumenberg calls the "readability of the world."[3]

The book of nature's prominent place in the cultural imagination arises from ambiguities built into the figure itself. It implies that knowledge of the world can be easily apprehended, and it requires us to consider who can read the "book" and what exactly such reading entails. When Robert Boyle, for instance, writes that "each Page in the great Volume of Nature is full of real Hieroglyphicks," does he suggest that one need simply to look at those glyphs but not interpret them, or does he mean that one must learn to interpret them?[4] Moreover, can everyone or only certain

---

[1] "Book of Nature," in *Wikipedia*, February 4, 2024, https://en.wikipedia.org/wiki/Book_of_Nature. Henceforth, I will not capitalize the phrase "book of nature," though many writers I cite do so.
[2] Curtius, *European Literature and the Latin Middle Ages*, 321.
[3] Hans Blumenberg, *The Readability of the World*, trans. Robert Savage and David Roberts, Signale/ Transfer: German Thought in Translation (Ithaca: Cornell University Press, 2022).
[4] Robert Boyle, *Some Considerations Touching the Vsefulnesse of Experimental Naturall Philosophy* (Oxford, 1663), sig. Hr.

people (say, gentlemen of the Royal Society of London, the scientific society Boyle helped found in 1660) acquire the knowledge the hieroglyphs make available?[5] Does conveying knowledge of the book of nature require us to abandon the art of rhetoric in favor of a plain style of writing?[6] Can an illiterate person read and understand the book of nature's message? Can a heretic? A woman? An African? By giving expression to these questions and to possible answers, the book of nature mediates the complexity of the physical world, but it also gives that complexity a sheen of straightforwardness as media often do.

Importantly, the book of nature metaphor does this work because a book is itself a hybrid: natural materials make it up, but it is a thing that must be made (an artifice).[7] It is inescapably material, yet its affordances make conceptual work possible.[8] It is a hybrid of form and content, as we saw in Chapter 4. It is one thing (a bound and coherent whole) and many things (a configuration of quires, pages, letters, and words).[9] A book can signify totality but also fragmentation, impersonal and public knowledge but also personal and private knowledge. The book of nature provides a way to talk about knowledge precisely because of this combination of form and content, material and conceptual, medium and message, totality and fragmentation. It can simplify and systematize knowledge by anthropocentrically putting Nature in its place.[10] And yet, as we will see in this chapter, by carrying the hybridity of books into widespread figurative use, the book of nature confounds the totalizing modern epistemology for which it has been seen to stand.

This chapter argues that the book of nature gave premodern English writers a way to talk about knowledge in shifting epistemic circumstances.[11] As

---

[5] As Latour, Shapin and Simon Schaffer, and other scholars have demonstrated, Boyle's infamous air pump experiments depend upon interpretation while pretending interpretation is not necessary. See Shapin, *Leviathan and the Air-Pump*; Latour, *We Have Never Been Modern*.

[6] See Guillory, "Mercury's Words."

[7] On books as habitats, see Calhoun, *The Nature of the Page*. See also Kiefer, *Writing on the Renaissance Stage*, 163–218.

[8] See Maguire, *The Rhetoric of the Page*.

[9] On books as wholes and compilations, see Knight, *Bound to Read*.

[10] See Carolyn Merchant, *The Death of Nature: Women, Ecology, and the Scientific Revolution: A Feminist Reappraisal of the Scientific Revolution*, 1st ed. (San Francisco: Harper & Row, 1980); Lorne Leslie Neil Evernden, *The Social Creation of Nature* (Baltimore: Johns Hopkins University Press, 1992); Carolyn Merchant, *Reinventing Eden: The Fate of Nature in Western Culture*, 2nd ed. (New York: Routledge, 2013); Latour, *An Inquiry into Modes of Existence*.

[11] On the sense among premoderns of a "rupture," see Mary Thomas Crane, *Losing Touch with Nature: Literature and the New Science in Sixteenth-Century England* (Baltimore: Johns Hopkins University Press, 2014); Steven Shapin, *The Scientific Revolution*, 2nd ed. (Chicago: University of Chicago Press, 2018).

we have seen throughout this book, the ecological emphasis of recent book history scholarship has undermined longstanding orthodoxies about books in premodern England (see Chapter 1). Books were read to pulp, cut up and scribbled on, bound and rebound, read aloud and in private. If a book could stand for the summation of all knowledge (as it does in modernity), it could also stand for the decomposition, contingency, and even failure of knowledge. Just as cultural and social historians have focused on the entanglements of established and emerging ideas in the period (including the idea of "nature" itself), therefore, I aim to demonstrate the *rhetorical* and *imaginative* entanglements of the book of nature metaphor.[12] Extending an ecology of books to this most important bookish metaphor, we will look anew at canonical instances of the book of nature while introducing less familiar examples to show that, broadly speaking, it gave people a way to situate knowledge rhetorically in a variety of situations. After a detailed discussion of the book of nature's place in histories of science and theories of modernity (the first section), this chapter will highlight how English writers used the book of nature metaphor with impressive flexibility: to relate sources of knowledge to each other (the second section), to convey the immense complexity, beauty, and comprehensibility of the world (the third section), and to model acts and methods of knowledge-making as forms of reading (the fourth).

The Book of Nature, Science, and Modernity

Scholars writing about the book of nature have emphasized the high stakes of the symbol's use in English and European cultures. For Michel Foucault, the world-as-readable-text bespeaks an entire epistemic foundation, while Curtius argues that the book of nature frames the "world as a hermeneutic problem" – a thing we must interpret.[13] For Blumenberg, a German philosopher whose book about the book of nature reaches biblical length, the very premise of the world's "readability" arises from a desire to understand and communicate experience of the world. Blumenberg argues that the "alliance" between nature and the book is the result of human beings' "fascination with the power wielded by the book through its production of totality."[14] In this account, the world is figured as a book

---

[12] Merchant, *Reinventing Eden*; Kellie Robertson, *Nature Speaks: Medieval Literature and Aristotelian Philosophy*, The Middle Ages Series (Philadelphia: University of Pennsylvania Press, 2017).
[13] Curtius, *European Literature and the Latin Middle Ages*; Foucault, *The Order of Things; an Archaeology of the Human Sciences*.
[14] Blumenberg, *The Readability of the World*, 9.

because the book stands in for and brings everything we experience into a unified, coherent whole.

While various cultures have featured the conceit of the world as a text, social and cultural factors made premodern England especially hospitable to the book of nature. The Protestant emphasis on Biblical interpretation, the relatively late arrival of the Renaissance in England, and the so-called counter-Renaissance of skepticism toward traditional authorities required English writers to position themselves within shifting parameters for what counts as knowledge.[15] Peter Harrison helpfully articulates how this positioning played out with respect to the Bible, the other of "God's two books":

> the image of the "book of nature" went considerably further than alternative metaphors which expressed the unity of the cosmos, for it implied firstly, that nature was to be read, expounded, investigated; that those meticulous labours which had hitherto been expended on the methodical investigation of that other book [the Bible] could now be directed toward the natural world[...]. Equally importantly, this metaphor implied that the world, like scripture, was a locus of divine revelation, and potentially both a source of knowledge of God and a means by which mankind might be reconciled to him. Nature was a new authority, an alternative text, a doorway to the divine which could stand alongside the sacred page[...]. Study of the world took on a religious significance, and the exegesis of the book of nature became a vital concern.[16]

This description of the cultural stakes of the book of nature metaphor gestures at what we have explored in each chapter of *How the World Became a Book*: the language of books gives writers a way to address urgent questions in their world. In this case, writers appeal to the book of nature to consider how to know the physical world itself and how that knowledge relates to received knowledge.

As Harrison implies, the book of nature has been linked specifically with the "rise" of modern science in seventeenth-century England, a rise linked in turn with the onset of modernity in the eighteenth century. The

[15] See Hiram Collins Haydn, *The Counter-Renaissance* (New York: Scribner, 1950); Neil Rhodes, *Common: The Development of Literary Culture in Sixteenth-Century England*, 1st ed. (Oxford: Oxford University Press, 2018); Thomas Fulton, *The Book of Books: Biblical Interpretation, Literary Culture, and the Political Imagination from Erasmus to Milton* (Philadelphia: University of Pennsylvania Press, 2021). Simultaneously, the Reformation also layered new meanings into the natural world itself. See Alexandra Walsham, *The Reformation of the Landscape: Religion, Identity, and Memory in Early Modern Britain and Ireland* (Oxford: Oxford University Press, 2011).

[16] Peter Harrison, *The Bible, Protestantism, and the Rise of Natural Science* (Cambridge: Cambridge University Press, 1998), 45. See also the conclusion to Eisenstein, *The Printing Press as an Agent of Change*, 683–708.

most cartoonish version of this "rise," to which the "Book of Nature" Wikipedia page explicitly appeals, tells how in the sixteenth and seventeenth centuries, forward-thinking natural philosophers such as Galileo and Francis Bacon rejected the traditional authority of Aristotle and the Bible and instead studied the natural world, the "book of nature" itself. These thinkers laid a foundation of rationalist skepticism on which later Enlightenment thinkers would build the modern world.[17]

In recent decades, history of science scholars have drastically revised the narrative of science and modernity, emphasizing entanglement over revolution and continuity over change. As Ann Blair and Nicholas Popper describe the change, whereas once we had "Whiggish visions" that the period 1450–1800 "was the seedbed of modernity," in recent scholarship "the elements of emergent modernity detectable in [the sixteenth and seventeenth centuries] now seem contingent and precarious rather than inexorable, universal, and irreversible."[18] Just as book history scholars have learned to resist media determinisms about the printing press, so history of science scholars have, as Popper writes elsewhere, "confirmed that the intellectual culture pulsating through and beyond early modern Europe was characterized by vitality, precisely because of the fluidity and permeability between different types of inquiry in an ecosystem that promoted cross-pollination."[19] Rather than a narrow history of science, scholars now emphasize a broader history of knowledge.[20] Scholars have explored, to offer just one example, the entanglement of alchemy with the development of experimental method.[21]

Even though scholars have discarded this "Whig history" of inevitable revolutionary progress, the book of nature retains a prominent place in the

---

[17] On this narrative, see Stephen Gaukroger, *The Emergence of a Scientific Culture: Science and the Shaping of Modernity, 1210–1685* (Oxford: Oxford University Press, 2006); Craig Martin, *Subverting Aristotle: Religion, History, and Philosophy in Early Modern Science* (Baltimore: Johns Hopkins University Press, 2014); David Wootton, *The Invention of Science: A New History of the Scientific Revolution*, First U.S. edition (New York: Harper, an imprint of HarperCollinsPublishers, 2015); Shapin, *The Scientific Revolution*.

[18] Blair and Popper, *New Horizons in Early Modern Scholarship*, 4. See also H. Floris Cohen, *The Rise of Modern Science Explained: A Comparative History* (Cambridge: Cambridge University Press, 2015); Peter Remien, *The Concept of Nature in Early Modern English Literature* (Cambridge: Cambridge University Press, 2019), https://doi.org/10.1017/9781108654906.

[19] Nicholas Popper, "The Knowledge of Early Modernity: New Histories of Sciences and the Humanities," in *New Horizons in Early Modern Scholarship*, ed. Ann Blair and Nicholas Popper (Baltimore: Johns Hopkins University Press, 2021), 135.

[20] See Blair and Popper, *New Horizons in Early Modern Scholarship*.

[21] See Margaret Healy, *Shakespeare, Alchemy and the Creative Imagination: The Sonnets and A Lover's Complaint* (Cambridge: Cambridge University Press, 2011); Katherine Eggert, *Disknowledge: Literature, Alchemy, and the End of Humanism in Renaissance England* (Philadelphia: University of Pennsylvania Press, 2015).

language of the history of modern science and modernity. Steven Shapin's justly celebrated *The Scientific Revolution*, for instance, features an entire section on "Reading Nature's Book."[22] Shapin cites a "who's who" of writers with reputations as proto-modern thinkers: Descartes claiming he will "seek no other knowledge than that which I might find within myself, or perhaps in the great book of nature," William Harvey (credited for first describing the circulation of blood) arguing that "the book of Nature lies so open and is so easy of consultation," Galileo famously claiming that "Philosophy is written in this grand book, the universe, which stands continually open to our gaze," and Boyle writing, as we have already seen, that "each page in the great volume of nature is full of real hieroglyphs."[23] Stacked up this way, these quotations give the impression that the seventeenth-century book of nature was, in Blair and Popper's words, "inexorabl[y], universal[ly], and irreversibl[y]" modern.

The book of nature thus finds itself in an awkward position. Scholars have rightly disposed of narratives of outright secularization, revolution, inevitability, and uncomplicated modernization, but the book of nature still stands for and fits into those narratives. For Shapin, despite his avowedly "uneasy" relationship with the term "scientific revolution" that gives his book its title, the claims of Descartes, Harvey, Galileo, and Boyle cited above are "recommending [the book of nature's] direct inspection over the texts of human authorities, however ancient and however highly valued they had been."[24] Likewise, Harrison claims that unlike medieval uses of the metaphor, "in the early modern period [...], the general tendency now is to elevate nature over some alternative authority – such as scripture or the writings of Aristotle – or to contrast nature with written authorities by arguing that it has a different purpose, that it is to be interpreted by a different strategy, that it enjoys particular advantages over written texts."[25] Blumenberg cites writers who attempt to assert the epistemic agreement of the book of nature and other authorities, but he ultimately commits to the modern assumption that the two are incompatible.[26] Even so circumspect a scholar as Curtius writes that "the 'book

[22] Shapin, *The Scientific Revolution*, 65–80.
[23] Cited in Shapin, 68–69.
[24] Shapin, 69.
[25] Harrison, *The Bible, Protestantism, and the Rise of Natural Science*, 194.
[26] See Blumenberg, *The Readability of the World*, 63–65: "the new discoveries in the book of nature forced the admission that something could happen in one of the books that was completely ruled out for the other: the right to expand the text indefinitely before human eyes and for their sake" (65).

of the world' was frequently secularized, i.e., was alienated from its theological origin."[27]

The basic structure of the metaphor itself cuts against these accounts of the book of nature. Because the book of nature metaphor can permit the neat compartmentalization of nature as a separate object of knowledge and experience, scholars continue to recruit the figure in the service of scientific naturalism. It continues to function as an index of the inevitability of modern scientific rationality. In the terms of metaphor theory, these accounts assume that the "vehicle" or "source" of the metaphor (the book) makes the "tenor" or "target" of the metaphor (the natural world) simpler and more concrete, as is the case with most metaphors. For instance, in the sentence "he burned with love," the source/vehicle (fire) makes something so complex and inexpressible as the tenor/target (love) easier to understand. The many examples in this chapter, however, show that the book of nature does not work like most metaphors. As a complex vehicle/source mapped onto a complex natural world, the book maintains the complexity of the natural world but nevertheless renders it comprehensible. The book of nature is far too messy to stand in simply for scientific rationality.

In sum, scholars have revised and updated their account of science and the modernity to which it supposedly leads, but we lack an updated understanding of the book of nature figure's place in this account. A brief return to Bruno Latour's influential account of modernity will clarify the point I am making. Latour argues that "we have never been modern" because modernity enforces a paradoxical and ultimately unsustainable division between Nature and Society, all the while encouraging the proliferation of hybrids. What Latour calls the "modern Constitution" involves constant purification against these hybrids, so that, for instance, in modernity disabled bodies are both systematically produced and willfully ignored.[28] To emphasize the book of nature's totalizing elevation at the exclusion of other forms and sources of knowledge imposes a modernizing template on premodern England and Europe more broadly. This view assumes that for those who used the metaphor, nature was an objective, disentangled, and unified thing opposed to culture or society and that the metaphor expressed and reinforced this opposition. In such an account, thinkers like Bacon or Boyle were simply waiting around to study the book of nature exclusively and thus to separate a natural world from a cultural one, a

---

[27] Curtius, *European Literature and the Latin Middle Ages*, 321.
[28] See the chart in Latour, *We Have Never Been Modern*, 58.

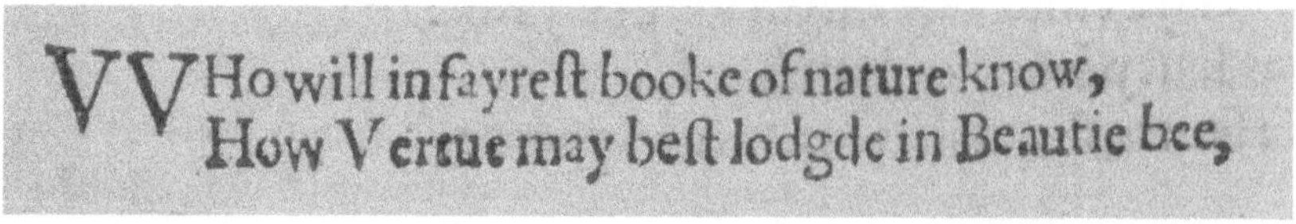

VVHo will in fayreſt booke of nature know,
How Vertue may beſt lodgde in Beautie bee,

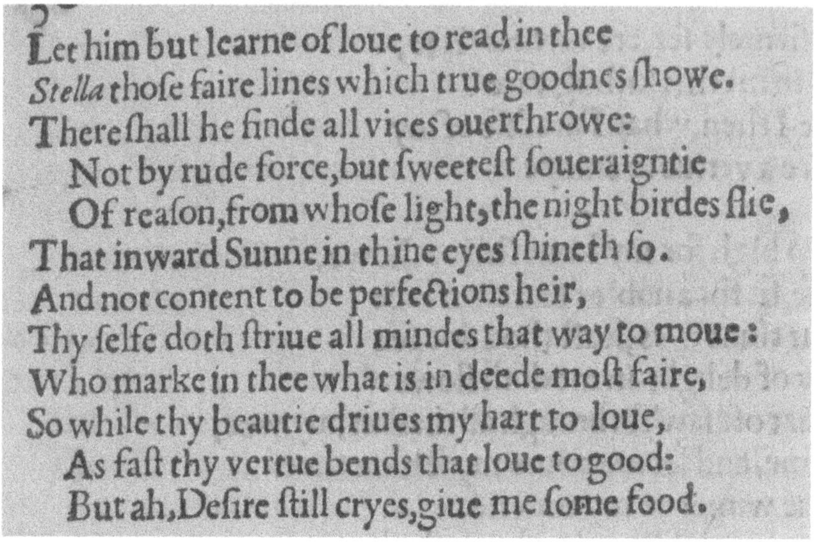

Let him but learne of loue to read in thee
Stella thoſe faire lines which true goodnes ſhowe.
Thereſhall he finde all vices ouerthrowe:
  Not by rude force,but ſweeteſt foueraigntie
  Of reaſon,from whoſe light,the night birdes flie,
That inward Sunne in thine eyes ſhineth ſo.
And not content to be perfections heir,
Thy ſelfe doth ſtriue all mindes that way to moue :
Who marke in thee what is in deede moſt faire,
So while thy beautie driues my hart to loue,
  As faſt thy vertue bends that loue to good:
  But ah,Deſire ſtill cryes,giue me ſome food.

Figures 6.1 and 6.2   Detail from Sir Philip Sidney, *Sir P.S. His Astrophel and Stella*
(London, 1591), sigs. E3r-v, 69457, The Huntington Library, San Marino, California.

description at odds with what these writers themselves wrote. But the book
of nature, like books themselves, hardly ever behaves as an objective, disentangled, unified thing.

How Many Books Are There?

In Sonnet 71 of *Astrophil and Stella* (1591), Philip Sidney's besotted Astrophil
has to come to terms with the material world (see Figures 6.1 and 6.2).[29] If
you want to know how virtue can best be "lodgde in Beautie," Astrophil
writes, look at Stella, where you will find vices flying away from "reason"
as nocturnal birds flee the sunlight. Wannabe Neoplatonist Astrophil goes
a step further as the concluding sextet opens: Stella does not sit "content"
in her perfection, but "moue[s]" other "mindes" (not bodies) to become

[29] Philip Sidney Sir, *Sir P.S. His Astrophel and Stella* (London, 1591), sig. E3r-v. STC 22537.

more perfect. But this material girl is living in a material world, and hungry desire undercuts Astrophil's attempt to abstract Stella's beauty to the moral realm. However high-minded he may try to be, Astrophil cannot escape his embodiment (nor Stella's), and he does not seem to want to. We might have seen the poem's final rug-pull coming in the first line, where Astrophil invokes the grandest and best-known piece of bookish language: the "booke of nature."[30] What I initially glossed as "if you want to know" might better be paraphrased as "whoever wants to learn from the natural world...." This more accurate phrasing shows how the first line of the poem anticipates the last, for Astrophil begins just as he ends, not with abstract, disembodied knowledge but with knowledge located in the physical world.

In staging Astrophil's departure from and return to materiality, Sidney counted on his readers' reflexive familiarity with "the book of nature." His use of the figure evokes some of its key features in premodern English culture: the physical world compared to a book, of course, but also the implication that we can "knowe" something from this book, the mandate to acquire such knowledge by "learn[ing]," the portrayal of that learning as "read[ing]," and above all the suggestion that there are multiple sources of knowledge. Crucially for this poem, there are two metaphorical books in play, the book of nature and Stella herself. In line 3, Astrophil dismisses the former in the interest of the latter ("Let him but learne ... to read in thee"), a decision that ultimately, perhaps inevitably, leads him back to the embodied world of "Desire" and "food." Though elaborately described, the basic conflict animating the sonnet pits the "booke of nature" as an established authority against the "lines" one is supposed to "read" in the book of Stella's face. Sidney appeals to the distinction between two sources of knowledge as the premise of the sonnet; even if Astrophil thinks he can jettison one in favor of the other, the poem undercuts the attempt to keep the books separate.

Like Sidney, many English writers worked to situate knowledge of or derived from the natural world with respect to other sources and kinds of knowledge. Unsurprisingly, these comparisons took a theological turn, often invoking the "two books" of nature and the Bible and referring to the book of nature as God's expressive mechanism. Surveying this history, Harrison argues that by the end of the seventeenth century, "the book of nature ... came to represent a source of theological knowledge

---

[30] The language of "fair" was already racialized at this time. See Hall, *Things of Darkness*; Smith, *Black Shakespeare*, 82ff.

independent, to a degree, of the book of scripture. The investigation of the world was commended as a theological activity."[31] More aggressively, Blumenberg asserts that by the eighteenth century, "the parity of the 'two books' was destroyed once and for all."[32] To be sure, the "two books" metaphor is bound up with a longer history of theology – in which "natural" theology derived from general reason, common sense, and scientific experiment came to rival dogmatic or biblical theology for preeminence; this is, as I have already discussed, the wonky history of modernity.[33] But the vast majority of premodern writers who appealed to the book of nature as a metaphor for knowledge of the divine were not trying to separate the two (or three, or four) books *tout court*. As Carolyn Merchant and many others have demonstrated, the modern concept of "nature" was barely taking shape in the seventeenth century. The book metaphor affords a relationality between this emergent nature and other knowledge forms, and that is exactly what we will see in the evidence: writers putting the "books" and the epistemes for which they stand into a variety of relations.

The "two books" figure offers plenty of opportunities for such expression. Pierre de La Primaudaye's grand use of the metaphor manages to implement much of the bookish language we have already explored:

> [W]e must lay before our eyes two bookes which God hath giuen vnto vs to instruct vs by, and to lead vs to the knowledge of himselfe, namely the booke of nature, and the booke of his word, which we must ioyne both together, as also that doctrine, which is set forth vnto vs in them concerning the knowledge of our selues, especially of the soule, which is the true man. For the first booke would stand vs in small stead without the second, as we see it dayly by experience, yea euery one of vs hath trial thereof in himselfe. Therefore God of his great mercy hath added the second booke vnto the first, to supply the want that is in our nature through sinne. For if man had not sinned, this booke of nature would haue sufficed to haue kept him alwayes in the knowledge, contemplation; and obedience of God his creator. For then he should himselfe haue caried the booke whole and perfect imprinted in his heart and mind[.][34]

Even this conventional use of the "two books" rewards attention. Primaudaye and his translator appeal to the language of sight to refer to mediation ("lay before our eyes"), "set forth" to bookish publication, and

---

[31] Harrison, *The Bible, Protestantism, and the Rise of Natural Science*, 199.
[32] Blumenberg, *The Readability of the World*, 65.
[33] See Alister E. McGrath, *Historical Theology: An Introduction to the History of Christian Thought* (London: Wiley-Blackwell, 2012), 182–94.
[34] La Primaudaye, *The Second Part of the French Academie*, sig. A7r. STC 15328.

the language of printing to the formation of the self. He imagines two physical books, one supplementing the other because of humankind's inability to read the first perfectly, that must be "ioyne[d] both together" as a kind of divine *sammelband*. Even if, like so many of the writers we will meet here, Primaudaye's Christian commitments encourage him to view the "booke of [God's] word" as authenticating the "booke of nature," the metaphor does not mandate an explanation of how we know that "the first booke would stand vs in small stead without the second." Indeed, the second book functions as a Derridean *supplement*, "supply[ing] the want" or lack while also framing the very existence of the book of nature.[35] By contrast to Primaudaye's muted approach, the preacher John Dove uses the metaphor to address head on the question of how we know which book is which: "we are taught by the Scriptures, that God hath two bookes, and both of them are written for vs to read[.]"[36] For Dove, the very existence of the two books is "taught by the Scriptures." Bishop Joseph Hall remains more equivocal in a section titled "How to know God": "GOd doth reueale, and as it were make himselfe visible vnto vs after two manner of waies: first, in the booke of his word, by the mouthes of his holy prophets, Apostles, and Patriarches: and secondly, by the book of nature, in the whole frame of heauen and earth[.]"[37] La Primaudaye lists the book of nature first and then the Bible, but Hall switches the order. The difference is not insignificant, because La Primaudaye intends to emphasize the knowledge of "our selues" while Hall's addresses knowledge of "God."

Predictably but intriguingly, many writers appeal to the "two books" figure to address the insufficiency or inadequacy of knowledge derived from the natural world compared to that derived from the Bible. These uses of the figure are predictable because they indicate what we would expect a Protestant Christian view of the natural world to consist of.[38] From this perspective, the natural world sits at a peculiar, almost paradoxical intersection of revelation and impoverishment. On the one hand, the natural world can tell us something about something beyond it – God, the immaterial world, the soul, the self, and so on. Many writers cite Romans

---

[35] Juliet Fleming glosses Derrida's *supplement* as that which "completes an entity and thereby shows it never was or could be entire in and of itself." See *Cultural Graphology*, 7–8.

[36] John Dove, *A Sermon Preached at Pauls Crosse, the 3 of Nouember 1594* (London, 1594), sig. B4v. STC 7086.5.

[37] Anonymous, *Two Guides to a Good Life The Genealogy of Vertue and the Nathomy of Sinne* (London, 1604), sig. B5r. STC 12466.

[38] Harrison also gathers many examples of this use of the book of nature figure. See *The Bible, Protestantism, and the Rise of Natural Science*.

1:20 ("the invisible things of him from the creation of the world are clearly
seen, being understood by the things that are made, even his eternal power
and Godhead") as part of an appeal to the book of nature metaphor,
emphasizing that there are certain things we can know about God through
the natural world.

On the other hand, however, that incomplete knowledge requires a supplement, as we saw in La Primaudaye above. Many writers also cite Genesis
3:17 ("cursed is the ground for thy sake; in sorrow shalt thou eat of it all
the days of thy life") to emphasize that nature does not adequately convey
knowledge of the divine creator. In a sermon, for instance, Samuel Hieron
opines, "So weake an instrument is the Booke of nature to beget Truth in
our heartes. There is then another Truth, which hath beene framed by God
himselfe."[39] John Hayward writes of the "the holy scriptures; deliuered
vnto vs by himselfe, as liuely registers of that eternall law, which before
he had more obscurely written, only in the book of nature."[40] Richard
Baxter fervently describes God's intention to "Write a Book in which his
will should be more plainly read, than in the blotted Book of Nature:
Yea in which he that in the Creature appeared most eminently in Power,
might now appear most eminently in LOVE, even redeeming, reconciling,
adopting, justifying and saving Love."[41] Thomas Vincent admits that "You
may arrive to some knowledge of God by reading the Book of Nature;
the whole world is full of God, and every Creature doth represent him."
But in the "Book of the Scriptures you have the most glorious discoveries
of God, in his greatness, majesty, power, holiness, love, mercy, and the
like[.]"[42] The point in rehearsing these common metaphors is to emphasize that writers found a surprising variety of ways to address the relationship between the books of nature and scripture. Importantly, however,
even these apparently similar examples demonstrate great variety. There is
a significant difference, for instance, between Hayward calling the book of
nature "obscurely written" and Baxter vividly calling it "blotted."

To put the point another way, appeals to the "two books" do not
come from nowhere; they are always rhetorically motivated and situated.

---

[39] Samuel Hieron, *Truths Purchase: Or A Commoditie, Which No Man May Either Neglect to Buie, or Dare to Sell* (Cambridge, 1606), sig. B2r. STC 13429.

[40] John Hayward Sir, *The Second Part of the Sanctuary of a Troubled Soule* (London, 1607), sig. R10v-11r. STC 13005a.

[41] Richard Baxter, *The Divine Appointment of the Lords Day Proved as a Separated Day for Holy Worship, Especially in the Church Assemblies, and Consequently the Cessation of the Seventh Day Sabbath* (London, 1671), sig. N5r-v. Wing B1253.

[42] Thomas Vincent, *The Wells of Salvation Opened* (London, 1668), sig. M7r. Wing V451.

Thomas Wright, a Roman Catholic writer defending transubstantiation (the belief that the bread and wine of the sacrament actually transform into Jesus's body and blood), argues that God first "presented his diuinitie vnto vs by his creatures, that whilst wee reade in the booke of nature the admirable wisedome, power and goodnes of GOD (all which wee may manifestly discouer in euery creature) wee might loue, worship, and adore him."[43] But "this meat seemed too grosse for corrupted appetites," so God "opened the booke of faith, there vnder veiles, and shadowes, tropes and figures, discribing himselfe, the Trinitie, and other wonderfull attributes of his deitie[.]" But this too "was somthing obscure, therfore he clothed himselfe with flesh and bloud" in the Incarnation, and subsequently "cloathed himselfe with the huskes of bread & wine" in the sacrament. Wright's appeal to the books of nature and "faith" work to support his argument that transubstantiation is a reasonable point on the spectrum of divine revelation. More starkly, in a 1644 sermon, Edmund Calamy politicizes the two books to decry the civil war:

> my purpose is to handle these words [i.e., 'every kingdome divided against it selfe, is brought to desolation'], only as they are an intire proposition in themselves; as they are a generall Maxime, written in great Characters, not only in the Booke of God, but in the Booke of Nature: and as they are a cleare Looking-glasse, in which with sad countenances we may behold the woefull condition that England is in at this present.[44]

For Calamy, the two books span all possible knowledge and thus convey the universality of the claim that a divided kingdom will fall. In both cases, as in many others, these writers bend the two books to their rhetorical purposes with impressive flair.

Peculiarly, one of the "two books" refers to an actual book (the Bible) while the other is a metaphorical book. Even when the Bible in question is an abstraction – in the same way that we can refer to an edition of a book as an abstraction of a set of single copies printed from the same typesetting – it nevertheless points to a material book. By contrast, the book of nature is a metaphor, yet it behaves unlike many other metaphors, retaining the complexity of what it translates. The world does not necessarily become simpler when figured as a book. This tension between actual book and symbolic book gives the "two books" figure an imaginative

---

[43] Wright, *A Treatise, Shewing the Possibilitie, and Conueniencie of the Reall Presence of Our Sauiour in the Blessed Sacrament*, sig. G7r. STC 26043.5.
[44] Edmund Calamy, *An Indictment against England Because of Her Selfe-Murdering Divisions* (London, 1645), sig. Bv. Wing C256.

charge that writers found productive. Writing in a vague political allegory in the plague year of 1604, James Godskall notes that "there haue
bene diuers opinions concerning the cause of the corporall Plague: some
attributing it to the infection of the ayre, and inwarde corruption of the
humours (out of the booke of Nature:) others, to the slaying Angell, out of
the booke of God."[45] Later, Godskall makes a similar move, writing that
"As the Physitions make the euill and corrupt humour ingendred in the
body, the inward cause of the pestilence, out of the booke of Nature: so
wee may make the inwarde corruptions in the soule, the inward cause of
the bodily infection, out of the booke of God."[46] Godskall's figure effects
a figurative chiasmus, by which the metaphorical book of nature refers to
physical causes and the physical "booke of God" refers to spiritual ones.
Similarly, Theodore Herring explains why the Bible contains such a mixture of styles and modes:

> yet as in the large *folio* of the booke of *Nature*, though euery Creature carry
> in it the sparkles of the power, goodnesse, and prouidence of the Creator;
> those *rayes* shine out more brightly in some, more dimmely in others; so
> in the lesser *Epitome* of the Scripture, albeit all the parcels of sacred Writ,
> breath forth one and the selfe-same diuine truth in a most sweete and
> heauenly harmony; yet in some passages the Spirit of God takes to himselfe
> (as it were) the winges of an *Eagle*, soaring aloft aboue the capacity of the
> highest: in others he creepes (as it were) on the ground, stooping to the
> shallow conceit of the meanest.[47]

Perhaps more inventively than Godskall, Herring's use of the "two books"
describes symbols in the material artifact (the Bible) while materializing
the symbolic one (the book of nature). While the Bible "breath[es] forth"
a "diuine truth" (a metaphor) in a mixture of low and high signified by an
eagle and a creepy crawler (and Herring tips his hand by including the parenthetical "(as it were)"), the metaphorical book of the natural world contains actual "Creature[s]" that, in their materiality, tell something about
the "Creator."

A figure as familiar as the "two books" metaphor nevertheless opens
pathways to rich, extensive expression of what one knows and how they
know it. Indeed, what we might call the figure's epistemic function makes
up its primary use among English writers, but there is no clear trend

---

[45] James Godskall, *The Kings Medicine for This Present Yeere* (London, 1604), sig. C3v. STC 11936.
[46] Godskall, sig. E3r. STC 11936.
[47] Theodore Herring, *Panacea Christiana, or, A Christians Soueraigne Salue for Euery Soare Deliuered in Two Seuerall Sermons, and Now Digested into One Treatise* (London, 1624), sig. Bv. STC 13203.5.

toward a modern, secular use of the figure. Even writers eager to distinguish the authority of the "two books" use the metaphor to define their relationship to each other. Writing about Psalm 19:2 ("One day telleth another, and one night certifieth another"), Edward Evans spiritualizes the book of nature's metaphorical features:

> these words of my Text are some part of *The Booke of the World*, where *Nights* are as it were the *Blacke Inkie Lines* of learning, *Dayes* the *White Lightsome Spaces* betweene the *Lines*: where GOD hath Imprinted a very legible Delineation of his *Glory*. And whereby GOD teacheth ma[n] knowledge [...]. Yea even very now doth GOD teach man knowledge by the *Booke of the World*, when as the *Booke of his Word* lyeth before vs. This booke directing vs vnto that booke, and that booke leading vs vnto to this: and all to make *Good Schollers* of vs, if such rare and excellent Bookes may beget any learning in vs. It is written then in the booke of GOD, & wrought by GOD in the booke of the world, *One Day Telleth another*. So that whether we wil learne it by wrote [i.e., rote], or else by the Booke; the booke of GOD, or the booke of the world: we haue our choice.[48]

Evans correlates day and night respectively to the white and black of a printed page, in which divine glory is "Imprinted." The double metaphor allows him to compare the book of nature favorably to the Bible or, in a pun no less enjoyable than obvious, the "Booke of the Word." For Evans, the two books remain mutually illuminating, one book "directing vs" to the other and both capable of "teach[ing] man knowledge." John Bunyan likewise appeals to the "two books" to talk about Judgment Day:

> he who could overthrow the Land of Egypt, with frogs, lice, flies, Locusts, &c. will overthrow the World, at the last day, by the Book of the Creatures; and that by the least, and most inconsiderable of them, as well as by the rest. This Book of the Creatures, it is so excellent, and so full, so easie, and so suiting the capacity of all, that there is not one man in the World, but is catched, convicted, and cast by it. This is the Book, that he who knows no letters, may read in: yea, and that he who neither saw New Testament, nor Old, may know both much of God, and himself, by. 'Tis this Book, out of which generally, both Job and his friends did so profoundly discourse of the Judgements of God, and that out of which God himself did so convincingly answer Job. Job was as perfect in this Book, as we are, many of us in the Scriptures, yea, and could see further by it, then many now a dayes do see by the new Testament and old. This is the Book out of which, both Christ, the Prophets, and Apostles, do so frequently discourse by their Similitudes,

---

[48] Edward Evans, *Verba Dierum, or, The Dayes Report of Gods Glory* (Oxford, 1615), sig. A1r-A2v. STC 10583. Evans quotes from the Tyndale/Coverdale Psalms.

> Proverbs, and Parables: as being the most easie way to convince the World, though by reason of their ignorance, nothing will work with them, but what is set on their heart by the holy Ghost.[49]

In this long passage, Bunyan adumbrates the hermeneutic circle implicit in all appeals to epistemic authority. He supports his main point that a Judgment Day will come by appealing to the universal design of the "Book of the Creatures": it suits "the capacity of all" and thus all are "convicted" by it. Even someone who has not read the Bible ("neither saw New Testament, nor Old") may "know both much of God, and himself" by way of the book of nature. But the authenticity of the knowledge derived from the natural world depends upon the testimony of Job, Christ, the prophets, and apostle and finally upon the supernatural instruction of the "holy Ghost." The point here is not that Bunyan articulates a fully developed theory of knowledge (he does not) but rather that in making a larger point about Judgment Day, he appeals to the bookish metaphor to support his conviction that god "will overthrow the World, at the last day, by the Book of the Creatures."

Writers paired the book of nature and the Bible with understandable frequency, but there were plenty of other bookish metaphors for knowledge. There could, for instance, be more than two books. In a sermon, John King claims that "we maie read ple[n]tifully [...] in the book of nature, more happily in the bookes of grace [i.e., the Bible], but hereafter most blessedlie & contentedlie in the lardge volumes of glorie."[50] Henry Carpenter asserts that three "Books [will] be opened at the last day": the "Book of the Creatures, The Book of the Sciptures, The Book of the Conscience" in which a record of one's deeds is kept. Likewise, Thomas Barnes relates the "booke of nature" to that of the conscience, claiming that "in this volume of mans conscience, whatsoeuer the Lord of the conscience sets downe, be it good or euill, it is most infallibly and vndoubtedly true."[51] Richard Bernard grows downright drastic when he claims that "They that grow cunning in the Booke of Conscience by reading Gods and good Mens Books, are vndoubtedly the best Christians, the best Lawyers to pleade their owne Cause, and the best Iudges to Iudge of themselues aright. This book is of Gods own hand writing; it is also

---

John Bunyan, *The Resurrection of the Dead and Eternall Judgement* (London, 1665), sig. I3r.
John King, *A Sermon Preached in Oxon: The 5. of November. 1607* (Oxford, 1607), sig. B2v. STC 14985.
Thomas Barnes, *The Court of Conscience: Or, Iosephs Brethrens Iudgement Barre* (London, 1623), sig. H6v. STC 1475, sig. H6v.

very legible to any that will giue themselues to reade it."[52] John Jackson offers a scheme by which "there are foure Bookes written by God, for the sons of men": the "Bookes of Grace," which include the Bible and the "inward Book of [...] the holy Spirit," and the books of "nature," the natural world and the "inward Booke of [...] Conscience."[53] And with characteristic verve, John Donne offers a series of books in his *Devotions* written when he was sick: the books of life, nature, the Bible, laws, conscience, and finally the book from Revelation, "which only *the Lamb which was slaine, was found worthy to ope[n]*." Having summarized these books, Donne writes to God, "if thou refer me to these *Bookes* to a new reading, a new trial by these *bookes*, this *feuer* may be but a burning in the hand."[54] Donne's metaphorical books comfort him by resituating the contextual knowledge of his sickness.

As these examples demonstrate, writers used the book of nature metaphor to situate sources and forms of knowledge with respect to each other. In just the last two examples, the accumulation of books gives Donne comfort while King's four books provide a neat taxonomy by which one can classify knowledge in the world. But do these examples suggest an alternative to the standing narrative in which the book of nature figure effects or expresses a modern separation of nature and culture or society? If we wanted to answer "no" to this question, we could argue that the metaphor objectifies nature and sets the imaginative conditions for its exploitation. We may even call these metaphors *anthropocentric* because they sometimes situate humankind at the center of the knowledge-making process. Bunyan's "book of the creatures," for instance, might be said to figure nature as that which humankind apprehends, separating human observers from the natural world as readers are separated from a book.

But my answer is "yes" for several related reasons. First, the range of book metaphors cited above are metaphors not strictly speaking for the world but for knowledge of the world. They do not, in Shapin's words, "recommend" the book of nature's "direct inspection over the texts of human authorities, however ancient and however highly valued they had been," but precisely the opposite.[55] With exceptions, these metaphors help writers make sense of their experience of the world by collating sources of

[52] Richard Bernard, *Christian See to Thy Conscience or a Treatise of the Nature, the Kinds and Manifold Differences of Conscience* (London, 1631), sig. Av. STC 1928.
[53] John Jackson, *The Booke of Conscience Opened and Read in a Sermon Preached at the Spittle on Easter-Tuesday, Being April 12, 1642 / by John Jackson* (London, 1642), sig. A3v-4r. Wing J76.
[54] John Donne, *Devotions Vpon Emergent Occasions* (London, 1624), sig. Lr-L2v. STC 7033a.
[55] Shapin, *The Scientific Revolution*, 69.

knowledge. The second reason is that, as I touched on earlier, the book metaphor is itself a hybrid of nature and culture, an enchanted object that resists objectification and instrumentalization. When writers compare their world to a book, they are comparing one complex, mysterious thing with another as they try to articulate how knowledge of the world comes to exist and be recognized as knowledge. The knowledge that comes from books is not – and has never been, as we saw in Chapters 4 and 5 – the mere reception of content by way of a conduit. Likewise, as Latour's early work on scientific laboratories vividly demonstrates, knowledge of the natural world is made, not merely discovered. In this light, Bunyan's "book of the creatures" and the other examples offer much more than a mere subject–object relationship: they implicate humankind in the natural world as readers are (and always have been) implicated in their books.[56]

If there were a genuinely modern use of the "two books" metaphor from premodern England, we might expect to find it in these two final examples, which are the best-known of the bunch. But the accumulated rhetorical usage of the figure that we have explored puts these canonical examples in a new light. The first is Thomas Browne's characteristically baroque and counterintuitive approach to the question of nature. Having declared himself more interested in "Bees, Aunts, and Spiders" than in "prodigious pieces of nature" such as elephants and camels, Browne explains that "in these narrow Engines [i.e., flies, etc.] there is more curious Mathematickes; and the civility of these little Citizens, more neatly sets forth the wisdome of their Maker."[57] The bookish term "sets forth" seems to catapult Browne, apparently inevitably, toward a more extended book metaphor (see Figures 6.3 and 6.4). It can be difficult to follow Browne through this famous passage. He begins by restating his preference for the ordinary and familiar over the exotic (e.g., the tides and floods of the Nile), but then he swerves to appeal to the "Cosmography of my selfe," which functions as a *"compendium"* or shorter version of the "endlesse volume" of nature. Then, having invoked one book, Browne loops in the other (the Bible) and launches into a discussion of how well "the Heathens" read the book of nature. Notwithstanding Browne's undeniably delicious language, however, it must be admitted that he is not saying anything new. Indeed, he brilliantly riffs on the familiar tropes of the book of nature: it is "exposed" to all, pairs with the Scripture, tells us something about God, and needs to

[56] See "ecologies" section of Chapter 1.
[57] Thomas Browne Sir, *Religio Medici* (London, 1642), sig. B5r. Wing B5166. This is the unauthorized first edition. The authorized edition is Wing B5169.

my felfe ; we carry with us the wonders, we feeke without us : There is all *Africa*, and all her prodigies within us ; we are that bold and adventurous piece of nature, which he that ftudies wifely, learnes in a *compendium*, what others labour at in a divided piece and endleffe volume. Thus there are two bookes from whence I collect my Divinity; befides that written one of God, another of his fervant Nature, that univerfall and publique Manufcript, that lies expofed to the eyes of all;thofe that never faw him in the one, have difcovered him in the other: This was theScripture and Theology of the Heathens ; the naturall motion of the Sunne made them more admire him, than his fupernaturall ftation did the Children of Ifrael ; the ordinary effect of nature wrought more admiration in them, than in the other all his miracles: furely the Heathens knew better how to joyne and reade thefe myfticall letters, than we Chriftians, who caft a

Figures 6.3 and 6.4   Detail from Sir Thomas Browne, *Religio Medici* (London, 1642), sigs. B5v-6r, 106445, The Huntington Library, San Marino, California.

> more common eye on thofe Hierogly-
> phicks, and difdaine to fuck Divinity from
> the flowers of nature; nor doe I forget
> God, as to adore the name of Nature,
> which I define not with the Schooles, the
> principles of motion and reft, but that
> ftreight and regular line, that fetled and
> conftant courfe the wifdome of God hath
> ordained to guide the actions of his crea-
> tures, according to their feverall kinds : to
> make a revolution every day is the nature
> of the Sun, becaufe that neceffary courfe
> which God hath ordained it, from which
> it cannot fwarve, by the faculty of the
> voyce which firft did give it motion. Now

Figures 6.3 and 6.4   (cont.)

be read well. However well-earned Browne's reputation as the *bête noir* of seventeenth-century English prose, here he is downright orthodox.

The second appears in a book that many view as a founding document of modernity, Thomas Sprat's *The history of the Royal-Society of London for the improving of natural knowledge* (1667). Sprat's polemic account of the 1660 founding of the Royal Society does at length what many of the metaphors we have explored do: he attempts to situate new "natural" knowledge alongside other sources and authorities of knowledge. One key moment occurs as Sprat responds to those who claim the Society will undermine the Protestant Church of England:

> I will farther urge, That the *Church of England* will not only be safe amidst the consequences of a *Rational Age*, but amidst all the improvements of *Knowledge*, and the subversion of old Opinions about *Nature*, and introduction of new ways of Reasoning thereon. This will be evident, when

we behold the agreement that is between the present *Design* of the *Royal Society*, and that of our *Church* in its beginning. They both may lay equal claim to the word *Reformation*; the one having compass'd it in *Religion*, the other purposing it in *Philosophy*. They both have taken a like cours to bring this about; each of them passing by the *corrupt Copies*, and referring themselves to the *perfect Originals* for their instruction; the one to the *Scripture*, the other to the large Volume of the *Creatures*. They are both unjustly accus'd by their enemies of the same crimes, of having forsaken the *Ancient Traditions*, and ventur'd on *Novelties*. They both suppose alike, that their *Ancestors* might err; and yet retain a sufficient reverence for them.[58]

Just as the church has enacted "reformation" by "referring" itself to the "*perfect Original*" of the Bible, Sprat contends, so too the Royal Society intends to reform philosophy by consulting nature itself rather than antiquated theories about it. As we might expect, the two books figure helps justify the ways of the Society to the public; Sprat recruits the deeply familiar image to assert that the church is "safe" from this second reformation, which he links with the first by way of the book metaphor of "*corrupt Copies*" and "*perfect* [i.e., complete and error-free] *Originals.*" He goes so far as to refer to a new "*Rational Age*," echoing the language opposing ancients and moderns that Francis Bacon and other writers invoked.[59] Even this appeal to rationality and its apparent demarcation of natural knowledge trips up on the book metaphor, however. Not only does he not argue for the superiority or even separation of the book of nature over "*Ancient Traditions*," but he is also unable to separate Nature fully from the knowledge-making processes of Culture. Though it seems to seal off nature from human contact, the hybrid "large Volume of the *Creatures*" instead serves as a reminder that human contact is indispensable to the knowledge-making process. Even if Sprat would like to maintain nature's objective status, the very hybridity of the book metaphor undermines that status. Sprat even indicates as much when he backtracks to assert that the Royal Society has "sufficient reverence" for "*Ancestors*" such as Aristotle and Galen. He hints at an awareness of what the Royal Society could never forget: that bookish knowledge – which is how the metaphor frames knowledge of nature – is made, just as all reformations and revolutions are made, not inevitable.[60]

---

[58] Thomas Sprat, *The History of the Royal-Society of London for the Improving of Natural Knowledge* (London, 1667), sig. Aaav-Aaa2r. Wing S5032.

[59] See Martin, *Subverting Aristotle*; Crane, *Losing Touch with Nature*.

[60] See Shapin, *A Social History of Truth*; David Carroll Simon, *Light without Heat: The Observational Mood from Bacon to Milton* (Ithaca: Cornell University Press, 2018).

What Kind of Book Is the World?

Sprat calls the "Volume of the *Creatures*" a "large" book. As we explored in Chapter 4, the size adjective marks a book as medium and mediator. Browne, moreover, calls the book of nature a "publique Manuscript," another acknowledgement of the medium's materiality. As these two canonical examples suggest, imagining the world as a book encouraged – perhaps required – writers to think about nature in terms of the material possibilities and protocols of books. Curtius hints at this process, noting offhand that "the simile of the book is not logically confined to a single function and a single significance but rather serves to illustrate very various facts," but he does not take the claim far enough.[61] In fact, premodern writers, for whom the book of nature functioned as a metaphor for knowledge, regularly carried the material features of books into their use of the metaphor.

The stakes of this pattern are higher than they may seem. Recall that, for Harrison, the book of nature "expresse[s] the unity of the cosmos," while for Blumenberg the metaphor offers a "production of totality" inevitably culminating in Diderot's *Encyclopédie*, another document of European modernity.[62] Unity and totality are modern – or at least modernizing – attributes when elevated above all others. But if the book of nature shaped the premodern English cultural imaginary as an actual material book – and this brief section will argue it did – then "unity" and "totality" are just two of the many divergent modes of expression made available in the metaphor. If the world is a book, it behaves like one.

Many writers compared the world to a book almost as if looking for an excuse to indulge in bookish materiality. William Cornwallis opens his *Essayes* (1601) with the flat assertion that "THe Worlde is a booke," then elaborates that "the words and actio[n]s of men [are] Co[m]mentaries vpon that volume: the former lyke manuscriptes priuate: the latter common; lyke things printed."[63] The metaphor establishes the distinction between private actions (manuscripts) and public witness (printed books) that animates many of Cornwallis's essays. Nicholas Byfield echoes much of the rhetoric we have already explored when he writes that the world:

> may be likened to a great Booke, in which God hath written glorious things that concerne the praise of his goodnesse, wisdome and power: Euery creature is, as it were, a distinct leafe of that Booke, and the properties and vses

---

[61] Curtius, *European Literature and the Latin Middle Ages*, 321.
[62] Harrison, *The Bible, Protestantism, and the Rise of Natural Science*, 45; Blumenberg, *The Readability of the World*, 9.
[63] Cornwallis, *Essayes*, sig. Br-v. STC 5775.

of these creatures are, as it were, the seuerall lines and letters of that leafe: and the more admirable, because it is a Booke; the writing whereof is indelible, and the vses whereof are vniuersall: the Booke so opened, that all men in all parts of the world may see and read.[64]

The emphasis on the book's size ("great"), constituent formal and material elements ("leafe," "lines," and "letters"), permanence ("indelible"), and physical position ("opened") lead Byfield to the language of sight we saw in Caxton in Chapter 5. This book is not a closed, impenetrable totality but a rustling, multifarious anthology of lines and letters. Other writers focus specifically on the leaves of the book. Lodowick Lloyd writes that "the vniuersall world is a Booke of three leaues, the Heauens, the Earth, and the Seas," while Richard Ward claims the world is a book with "three leaves, the Heaven, the Earth, the Sea, and there are as many letters and histories in those leaves, as there are stars in the heaven, creatures in the earth, & fishes in the sea [...] all which are [...] Schoolmasters which will teach us gratis, without any salarie."[65] Free instruction from the fish of the sea. John Melton modifies the figure, arguing that "The World it selfe is a Book consisting of foure leaues: Fire, Aire, Earth and Water; whose letters are Stars, Birds, Beasts and Fishes: and (Man that is the Epitome and Abstract of the World) is a Book consisting of two leaues; Soule and Body: whose Letters are his good and bad Affections."[66] These figures imagine slim tracts unlike Byfield's "great" book.

The material richness and complexity of books leads some writers to develop elaborate metaphors integrating various bookish material features. John Cragge casts his mind back before the creation of the physical world and finds books even there:

a time there was before all Times, when there was no Day, but the Antient of Dayes, no Good but God, no Light but the Father of Lights: arts were but Idea's; the World, a Map of Providence; Heavens, the Book in Folio; Earth, Water, Aire, and Fire, in Quarto; Hell, the Doomes-day pageant; Men and Angells but Capitall Letters, in the Margent of Gods Thoughts.[67]

---

[64] Nicholas Byfield, *The Rule of Faith, or, An Exposition of the Apostles Creed so Handled as It Affordeth Both Milke for Babes, and Strong Meat for Such as Are at Full Age* (London, 1626), sig. Mr. STC 4233.3.

[65] Lodowick Lloyd, *The Tragicocomedie of Serpents* (London, 1607), sig. E2v-3r. STC 16631; Richard Ward, *Theologicall Questions, Dogmaticall Observations, and Evangelicall Essays, Vpon the Gospel of Jesus Christ, According to St. Matthew* (London, 1640), sig. G4v. STC 25024. Both writers cite Clement of Alexandria.

[66] John Melton Sir, *Astrologaster, or, The Figure-Caster* (London, 1620), sig. A2r. STC 17804.

[67] John Cragge, *A Cabinet of Spirituall Iewells Wherein Man's Misery, God's Mercy, Christ's Treasury, Truth's Prevalency, Errour's Ignominy, Grace's Excellency, a Christian's Duty, the Saint's Glory, Is Set Forth in Eight Sermons* (London, 1657), sig. Br. Wing C6783.

Before the beginning, the vastness of the heavens was to the elements as folio is to quarto, and creaturely beings are merely marginalia. Similarly imaginative, Henry More imagines himself back in school:

> the whole world is a booke, the fayrest, the learnedost, the greatest that ever was made, Everie creature is a letter, Everie Accident a line, Everie motion a sentence, Everie disposition a lesson, the whole a most eloqvent Oration, a most ample Treatise, full of all Rhetoricall persuasions; pregnant in teaching, forcible in moving, pleasant in delighting, sounding out thy divine prayses, speaking thy wonders, inviting to thy service, withdrawing from thy offence, inflaming in thy love. O that my vnderstanding were so instructed, my will so inclined, as to apply themselves with profit to read of these lines, to learne by these lessons. There is nothing but may be vsed; nothing but is ordayned for my benefit.[68]

More mixes material forms of books (letters and lines) with more abstract ones such as sentences, lessons, treatises, and persuasions to imagine the world itself as an object of sacred knowledge. He figures the book as a thing to be read, an impulse to which we will return in the final section of this chapter.

The book of nature, figured as a real, material book, can figuratively be interacted with. One particularly vivid image of such interaction seized several writers' imaginations in the mid-seventeenth century. As if the story of the flood in Genesis 6–9 were not grievous enough – or precisely because of its grievousness – writers compared the deluge to a defaced and blotted book. In a 1640 funereal poem about Edward, Lord Stafford, Anthony Stafford writes:

> When the Deluge did deface
> The booke of nature, humane race
> Reprinted was, and found supply
> From the floating Library.[69]

Stafford goes on to claim that Lord Stafford's death has "bereft" us of "all," with no possibility of reprinting. The "floating Library" refers to Noah's ark, in which a remainder of human and animal life was preserved for its reprinting after the flood. Samuel Clarke repeats the metaphor in a book published two years later, describing how Noah, "when the deluge of waters had defaced the great booke of nature, had a coppy of every kind of creature in that famous Library of the Arke, out of which all were

---

[68] Henry More, *The Life and Doctrine of Ovr Savior Iesvs Christ* (Ghent, 1656), sig. L8v. Wing M2665.
[69] Anthony Stafford, *Honour and Vertue, Triumphing over the Grave* (London, 1640), sig. Q3r-v. STC 23125.

reprinted to the world."[70] Another writer borrows Clarke's very language to compare the Civil War to the flood:

> as Noah, when the deluge of waters had defaced the great Book of Nature, had a Copy of every kind of Creature in that famous Liberary of the Ark, out of which all were reprinted to the world; so we, that have God, have the Original Copy of all blessings, out of which, if by this generation of monsters, I mean those that have put the Army into this distemper, all were perished, all might easily be restored again[.][71]

Thomas Adams repeats the metaphor nearly word-for-word in a 1652 sermon, as does John Spencer in a 1658 book about the ruin of the Civil War.[72] The funeral and wartime context of these utterances may help explain their resonance for multiple writers. Both a family member's death and a brutal civil war evoke the wide-angle devastation of the Genesis flood, and the metaphor of a defaced book of nature secures the link by way of its more familiar imagery. It hardly seems unreasonable to suggest that if the Civil War felt like a flood, then the bookish imagery of reprinting makes available a redemptive interpretation of the devastation.[73]

Flood-book comparisons were hardly the only or most widely quoted book of nature metaphor that emphasizes its built-in materiality. These lines would ripple through the seventeenth century:

> The World's a Book in *Folio*, printed all
> With God's great Works in letters Capitall:
> Each Creature is a Page; and each Effect,
> A faire Character, void of all defect.

Written by the French poet Guillaume du Bartas and translated by Josuah Sylvester, these lines inspired dozens of writers to quote, rework, and expand them.[74] Du Bartas' long poem, which extensively narrates the days of creation,

---

[70] Samuel Clarke, *The Saints Nosegay, or, A Posie of 741 Spirituall Flowers Both Fragrant and Fruitfull, Pleasant and Profitable* (London, 1642), sig. E11v. Wing C4555.

[71] Anonymous, *A Vvord to Lieut. Gen. Cromwel and Two Vvords for the Setling of the King, Parliament and Kingdom* (London, 1647), sig. G4r. Wing W3565.

[72] Thomas Adams, *God's Anger; and, Man's Comfort Two Sermons* (London, 1652), sig. B4v. Wing A492; Anonymous, *Kaina Kai Palaia Things New and Old, or, A Store-House of Similies, Sentences, Allegories, Apophthegms, Adagies, Apologues, Divine, Morall, Politicall, &c* (London, 1658), fol. 47. Wing S4960.

[73] On Noah's ark, see Jeffrey J. Cohen and Julian Yates, *Noah's Arkive* (Minneapolis: University of Minnesota Press, 2023).

[74] Guillaume Du Bartas, *Du Bartas His Deuine Weekes and Workes* (London, 1611), sig. C3v. STC 21651.

> The World's a Book in *Folio*, printed all
> With God's great Works in letters Capitall:
> Each Creature is a Page; and each Effect,
> A faire Character, void of all defect.
>   But, as young Trewants, toying in the Schools,
> In steed of learning, learn to play the fools:
> We gaze but on the Babies and the Couer,
> The gawdy Flowrs, and Edges gilded-ouer;
> And neuer farther for our *Leſſon* look
> Within the Volume of this various Book;
> Where learned Nature rudeſt ones inſtructs,
> That, by His wiſedome, God the World conducts.
>   To read This Book, we need not vnderſtand
> Each ſtrangers gibbriſh; neither take in hand
> *Turks* Characters, nor *Hebrue* Points to ſeek,
> *Nyle's* Hieroglyphikes, nor the Notes of *Greek*.
> The wandring *Tartars*, the *Antartiks* wilde;
> Th' *Alarbies* fierce, the *Scythians* fel, the Childe
> Scarce ſeav'n year old, the bleared aged eye,
> Though void of Art, read heer indifferently.
> But he that wears the ſpectacles of *Faith*,
> Sees through the Sphears, aboue their higheſt heighth;
> He comprehends th' Arch-moouer of all Motions,
> And reads (though running) all theſe needfull Notions.
> Therefore, by *Faith's* pure rayes illumined,
> Theſe ſacred *Pandects* I deſire to read:
> And, God the better to beholde, beholde
> Th' Orb from his Birth, in's Ages manifolde.
>   Th' admired Author's Fancy fin.]

Figure 6.5   Guillaume Du Bartas, *Du Bartas His Deuine Weekes and Workes* (London, 1611), sig. C3v, 69238, The Huntington Library, San Marino, California.

had appeared in partial English translations prior to Sylvester's, but his complete English version was easily the most popular (reprinted multiple times in the seventeenth century). The quoted lines appear early in the poem's opening section about the "first Daie of the First VVeek."[75] Before them, Du Bartas offers a rapid series of statements about the world: "the World's a School, where (in a general Story) / God alwayes reads dumb lectures of his Glory"; "The World's a Cloud, through which there shineth cleer [...] the true *Phoebus*"; and "The World's a Stage, where Gods Omnipotence, / His Iustice, Knowledge, Loue, and Prouidence, / Do act their Parts[.]."[76] This series culminates in Du Bartas' extended comparison of the world to a book, itself culminating in the poet donning the "spectacles of *Faith*" to "read" the book of nature rightly (see Figure 6.5). Even the first four lines of the metaphor appeal both to physical affordances of books – format, printing, letters, and pages – and to categories of the book trade – *Works*, characters, and defects. Subsequent lines apply familiar aspects of books and reading to the conceit, including Du Bartas's accusation that most of us "gaze but on" the cover's decorations but never read "the Volume of this various Book[.]" Even as it appeals to the unifying image of a single folio book, the metaphor also underscores the book's disunified, "various" features.

Although Du Bartas carries the metaphor well beyond the first four lines, as Figure 6.5 illustrates, that quatrain would become a cultural sensation. Short enough to be punchy and long enough to create a complex image, these lines offer a portable, flexible expression of a belief about the world anchored in the materiality of the codex form.[77] Thomas Nash (not *the* Thomas Nash) quotes the lines in a marginal note on God's creative power.[78] Edward Browne inserts them in a patchwork of borrowed lines and marks each line with an inverted comma to acknowledge its status as a commonplace.[79] Richard Gove quotes them in a section headed with the description, "*That he that cannot* read, *may yet* spell *so much of the* God-head *in the* Book *of* Nature, that it will leave him without excuse."[80] Francis Raworth quotes them to support the claim that the clergy are "Readers of God to the World."[81] And Robert Dingley quotes them in a book on thunder.[82] Others likely exist.[83]

---

[75] Du Bartas, sig. C3r. STC 21651.

[76] Du Bartas, sig. C3r-v. STC 21651.

[77] On such extracted circulations, see Laura Estill, *Dramatic Extracts in Seventeenth-Century English Manuscripts: Watching, Reading, Changing Plays* (Newark: University of Delaware Press, 2015).

[78] Thomas Nash, *Quaternio or A Fourefold Vvay to a Happie Life* (London, 1633), sig. N3r. STC 18382.

[79] Browne, *A Description of an Annuall Vvorld*, sig. E6v. Wing B5102A. Browne prints the same poem in Wing B5106.

[80] Richard Gove, *The Saints Hony-Comb, Full of Divine Truths* (London, 1652), sig. H7v. Wing G1454.

[81] Francis Raworth, *Jacobs Ladder, or The Protectorship of Sion, Laid on the Shoulders of the Almighty* (London, 1655), sig. C2r. Wing R373.

[82] Robert Dingley, *Vox Cæli; or, Philosophical, Historicall, and Theological Observations, of Thunder* (London, 1658), sig. E4r. Wing D1502.

[83] Curtius incorrectly claims, without reference to Du Bartas, that Frances Quarles wrote the lines and that they appear his 1635 *Emblems*.

Beyond exact quotation, many writers adapted the lines as they appear in Sylvester's translation. Samuel Hinde cites Du Bartas in the margin next to his claim that "This world is a booke in Folio wherein are written the workes and wonders of Gods omnipotent hand, the acts and monuments of our maker and preserver in his owne proper characters."[84] A book about Germany offers that "The world is Gods great booke in Folio. Every creature is a severall page, in which we may reade some instruction to further us in heavenly wisedome."[85] The figure grew so common that it is difficult to tell whether writers knew they were echoing Du Bartas or else merely using a familiar trope. William Bloys, for instance, may simply be using a general figure when he writes that "The great volume of nature, the book of the creatures is laid open before us; and in every leafe, and page, and line of it, God hath imprinted such evident characters of his divine properties [...]."[86] Charles Anthony hits most of the same notes as Du Bartas when he writes that the world is "a book in folio, every page whereof is written full of his excellent works, and those in capitall letters, insomuch that hee that runneth may reade."[87] The same goes for Lewis Griffin – "This visible world is a great Book written by the hand of God for his own glory and mans use; Every Creature is a leaf or page of this Volume"[88] – and an anonymous writer – "the whole World being nothing else but Gods Book in Folio, and every Creature and providence as a several page, in which we may plainly read his eternal Power and God-head"[89] – and Richard Steele – "Gods creatures are a book in Folio, each creature is a word, and each part of it a letter[.]"[90] The unknowing rehearsal of Du Bartas is precisely the point, of course, because these writers' appeals to the world as a book in folio replete with pages and letters demonstrate just how pervasive this materially driven metaphor had become throughout the seventeenth century. The most vivid evidence of this point takes the form of Nicholas Billingsley's epigram "On Abridgment":

[84] Samuel Hinde, *A Free-Vvill Offering, or, a Pillar of Praise with a Thankfull Remembrance for the Receit of Mercies* (London, 1634), sig. F4v. STC 13511.
[85] Brinckmair, *The Vvarnings of Germany By Wonderfull Signes, and Strange Prodigies Seene in Divers Parts of That Countrey of Germany, Betweene the Yeare 1618. and 1638*, sig. *2v. STC 3758.
[86] William Bloys, *Adam in His Innocencie* (London, 1638), sig. A5v-A6r. STC 3139.
[87] Charles Anthony, *Gods Presence Mans Comfort: Or, Gods Invisibilitie Manifested unto Mans Capacitie* (London, 1646), sig. Fv. Wing A3477.
[88] Lewis Griffin, *Essayes and Characters* (London, 1661), sig. B1r. Wing G1982A.
[89] Anonymous, *Eniaytos Terastios Mirabilis Annus, or, The Year of Prodigies and Wonders Being a Faithful and Impartial Collection of Severall Signs That Have Been Seen in the Heavens, in the Earth, and in the Waters* (London, 1661), sig. A2r. Wing E3127.
[90] Richard Steele, *The Husbandmans Calling Shewing the Excellencies, Temptations, Graces, Duties &c. of the Christian Husbandman* (London, 1668), sig. Dr. Wing S5387.

THe World's a Book in Folio, fairly writ
With Gods own hand, the creatures found in it
Are Letters, spelling out the Authors Glory,
And man's th' Abridgment of that ample story.[91]

Unlike Du Bartas's printed book of nature, Billingsley's is a manuscript, but we still have letters and, more important, identical opening words. If Billingsley knew Du Bartas' lines and is willfully riffing on them, then that is a powerful statement of the poem's influence. If, however, he did not know Du Bartas and is merely using a familiar conceit, then that is an even more powerful statement of influence.

Unlike a mere totality, a book in folio with creatures for pages and works for letters creates a composite image. It may be unified, perhaps at some level of abstraction, but it is made up of discrete and distinct parts. Adam Smyth summarizes recent book history scholarship's analysis of the book "as a collection of pieces in motion: less a stable whole than a collection of parts that might be crumbled and reorganized into new forms."[92] Recall from Chapter 4, for instance, that the relevance of the folio format is not just that it usually makes a big book but that it refers to how the type was imposed to create sheets and how those sheets were folded into page gatherings. A book "in folio" is not a totality but a mode of composition, just as the divine creative act to which so many of these metaphors refer happened by parts rather than all at once.[93] Indeed, that segmented and partialized creation is the very subject of Du Bartas's poem. Partly because it precedes the modern Nature/Culture separation, the conceit permits a toggling between parts (days of creation, kinds of knowledge, sizes of animals) and whole, much like the persistent attempt among ecocritics to find a way to toggle between local and global imaginings of nature as part of an ecologically regenerative culture.[94]

How Should We Read the Book of Nature?

Attentive readers may have noticed something missing in this chapter's examples: gender. In Latin, "nature" is *natura*, a feminine noun; in French

[91] Nicholas Billingsley, *A Treasury of Divine Raptures* (London, 1667), sig. B2v. Wing B2913.

[92] Smyth, *Material Texts in Early Modern England*, 176. As a prime example of this work, Smyth cites Tiffany Stern, *Documents of Performance in Early Modern England* (Cambridge: Cambridge University Press, 2009).

[93] Composition is itself an ecologically entangled act. See Frances E. Dolan, *Digging the Past: How and Why to Imagine Seventeenth-Century Agriculture* (Philadelphia: University of Pennsylvania Press, 2020).

[94] See Ursula K. Heise, *Sense of Place and Sense of Planet: The Environmental Imagination of the Global* (Oxford: Oxford University Press, 2008); Ursula K. Heise, *Imagining Extinction: The Cultural Meanings of Endangered Species* (Chicago: The University of Chicago Press, 2016).

it is *la nature*; in Spanish and Italian, *la natura*. For many centuries prior to the seventeenth, nature was figured as a woman, sometimes a queen, often a mother. The imagery surrounding nature – or Nature, to give the word its typographical due – was deeply feminized and maternalized in Western and non-Western cultures.[95] Shakespeare's Sonnet 20, for instance, dramatizes the stakes of nature's gender. The poet writes that the beloved young man has "A Womans face with natures owne hand painted." He elaborates that the young man was "first created" as a woman, but something happened:

> [...] nature as she wrought thee fell a dotinge,
> And by addition me of thee defeated,
> By adding one thing to my purpose nothing.
> But since she prickt thee out for womens pleasure,
> Mine be thy loue and thy loues vse their treasure.[96]

Nature herself doted on the woman she had created, so she added a male reproductive organ, "defeat[ing]" the poet's purpose by making the woman a man. Shakespeare's riff about nature depends on a reflexive familiarity with nature as a woman, just as Sidney's above depends on a knowledge of the book of nature.

The *book* of nature is neither gendered nor personated, however. If nature-as-woman offers a way to explain things in the world (e.g., why the young man is a man), then nature-as-book offers a way to describe how we come to know things (e.g., that there is a God or how birds can fly). None of the male, Protestant writers cited here actually thinks nature is a woman or a book, but for that reason it is easy to see why writers increasingly seized on the latter image when faced with what Mary Thomas Crane has described as "an unprecedented epistemological rupture," in which "the settled Aristotelian, Galenic, and Ptolemaic accounts of how the universe worked began to fall apart."[97] This is not to say that the world suddenly swerved and became fully modern, of course, but to argue that the exuberant use of the book of nature metaphor attempts to reckon with this "rupture." Just as the Bohr model of the atom, for all its physical inaccuracy, provides a way to conceptualize and express atomic structure, the book of nature offers a way to conceptualize how one comes to know anything at all.[98] Given

---

[95] Carolyn Merchant, *Autonomous Nature: Problems of Prediction and Control from Ancient Times to the Scientific Revolution* (New York: Routledge, 2016).
[96] Shakespeare, *Shake-Speares Sonnets*, sig. Cr. STC 22353.
[97] Crane, *Losing Touch with Nature*, 2.
[98] See the *Nature* special issue: "Quantum Physics: The Quantum Atom," *Nature* 498, no. 7452 (June 1, 2013), https://doi.org/10.1038/498021a.

what we have seen of writers situating knowledge of the natural world alongside other forms of knowledge, the next question to ask is, what does it mean to read the book of nature?

The fact that it can be read at all is a primary consideration. Decades ago, in an important book that remains highly influential, Carolyn Merchant argued that the "rise of modern science" was coextensive with the moment when "our cosmos ceased to be viewed as an organism and became instead a machine."[99] Merchant argues that modernity requires "the death of nature as a living being [specifically, a woman] and the accelerating exploitation of both human and natural resources in the name of culture and progress."[100] Merchant sought to complicate the narrative of an easy transition to a benevolent modernity, emphasizing instead that modernity framed women and nature as exploitable, but her account lacks something important:

> by examining the transition from the organism to the machine as the dominant metaphor binding together the cosmos, society, and the self into a single cultural reality—a world view—I place less emphasis on the development of the internal content of science than on the social and intellectual factors involved in the transformation.

Merchant's brilliant counternarrative paved the way for the next forty years of scholarship studying the "social and intellectual factors" of science, which we explored above. But it omits the book of nature. After nature was a female "organism" to be feared and before it became a "machine" to be exploited, it was a book to be read. And unlike an organism or a machine, a book carries its own protocols for knowledge-production. We call these protocols *reading*.

In the same way that book history scholarship has critiqued the totality and coherence of books, scholarship on readers and reading has undermined assumptions about book use and affirmed the messy materiality of reading in premodern England. The notion of passive, silent, sophisticated, "literary" reading, commensurate with Enlightenment rationality and the brain-on-a-stick Cartesian selfhood, has gone. A vision of reading as embodied, interactive, mercenary, moralistic, and politically self-aware has taken its place.[101] The widespread practice of commonplacing, for

---

[99] Merchant, *The Death of Nature*, xvi.
[100] Merchant, xviii. Achille Mbembe makes a similar argument in terms of blackness. See *Critique of Black Reason*.
[101] See, among many others, Stephen B. Dobranski, *Readers and Authorship in Early Modern England* (Cambridge: Cambridge University Press, 2005); Price, "From The History of a Book to a 'History

instance, suggests that readers read with pen in hand (sometimes scissors), ready to extract whatever proverbial or eloquent lines they encounter. Likewise, readers wrote copiously in books, often making marks totally unrelated to the books themselves.[102] At the same time, makers of books (in print and manuscript) encouraged just such use and designed books with this kind of reading in mind.[103] In sum, for premodern readers, the materiality of reading remains persistently at the forefront amid an astonishing diversity of reading practices.

A variety of writers appealed to the book of nature metaphor to figure knowledge as reading, bringing the features of a distinctly premodern culture of reading into their use of the metaphor. La Primaudaye, whose long comment on the two books we already encountered, concludes that "euen now we haue an other good occasion to read in this great booke of nature."[104] In a treatise on eyesight, Andre Du Laurens is one of a few writers to mix the image of "Mother Nature" with the book of nature: "let vs reade in the booke of nature, and see how carefull she hath been to preserue the eyes, as her most deare and trustie messengers." Later, Du Laurens mentions that he has "with all carefulnes perused the leaues of this booke of nature."[105] John Boys calls the "great booke of the Creatures" a "Common-place booke" for all humanity to read in, while one character

---

of the Book'"; John N. King, ed., *Tudor Books and Readers: Materiality and the Construction of Meaning* (Cambridge: Cambridge University Press, 2010); Gill Partington and Adam Smyth, eds., *Book Destruction from the Medieval to the Contemporary*, New Directions in Book History (New York: Palgrave Macmillan, 2014); Jonathan P. Lamb, "Ben Jonson's Dead Body: Henry, Prince of Wales, and the 1616 Folio," *Huntington Library Quarterly* 79, no. 1 (March 24, 2016): 63–92, https://doi.org/10.1353/hlq.2016.0001; Christina Lupton, *Reading and the Making of Time in the Eighteenth Century* (Baltimore: Johns Hopkins University Press, 2018); Price, *What We Talk About When We Talk About Books*; Acheson, *Early Modern English Marginalia*; Smyth, *Material Texts in Early Modern England*; Megan L. Cook, *The Poet and the Antiquaries: Chaucerian Scholarship and the Rise of Literary History, 1532–1635* (Philadelphia: University of Pennsylvania Press, 2019); Calhoun, *The Nature of the Page*; Emma Smith, *Portable Magic: A History of Books and Their Readers*, First American edition (New York: Alfred A. Knopf, 2022).

[102] See Sherman, *Used Books: Marking Readers in Renaissance England*, 2008; Zachary Lesser and Peter Stallybrass, "The First Literary *Hamlet* and the Commonplacing of Professional Plays," *Shakespeare Quarterly* 59, no. 4 (2008): 371–420; Victoria E. Burke, "Recent Studies in Commonplace Books," *English Literary Renaissance* 43, no. 1 (2013): 153–77, https://doi.org/10.1111/1475-6757.12005; Lamb, *Shakespeare in the Marketplace of Words*; Acheson, *Early Modern English Marginalia*; Meghan C. Andrews, "The Commonplacing of Professional Plays Revisited: Print, Theater, and Early Modern Institutional Exchange," *Shakespeare Quarterly* 73, no. 3 (2022): 199–223.

[103] See Katherine O. Acheson, *Visual Rhetoric and Early Modern English Literature* (London: Routledge, 2013); Bourne, *Typographies of Performance in Early Modern England*; Heffernan, *Making the Miscellany*.

[104] La Primaudaye, *The Second Part of the French Academie*, sig. A3r. STC 15328.

[105] André Du Laurens, *A Discourse of the Preseruation of the Sight: Of Melancholike Diseases; of Rheumes, and of Old Age* (London, 1599), sigs. E3r and F3r. STC 7304.

in James Shirley's *The Traytor* (1635) attempts to woo another by citing the constant change in nature: "let us examine all the creatures, reade / The booke of Nature through, and we shall finde / Nothing doth still the same[.]"[106] A 1654 book on medicine grandly claims that "if God inlighten your eys, the best Book of Physick is the Book of nature and there you may read it, and search for it, by Chyromancie and Physiognomie" (i.e., palm and face reading).[107] Ralph Austen cites the people in the Bible who "read many things in the Book of the Creatures," and Oswald Croll asserts that "Physick [i.e., medical knowledge] is written in the book of Nature in Heaven and Earth."[108]

The material features of book reading carry into the figurative readings imagined here. "[T]hankes be to God," writes Edward Chaloner, for God has "spread this booke of Nature open to euery mans view"; in this book, "we must thinke no page vnwritten on."[109] To read it is to consult the open pages as one would a book on display. William Hodson makes a similar move more starkly, noting that "There is no book of nature unwritten on: and that which may not be a teacher to inform us, will be a witnesse to condemn us."[110] The preacher George Jay tells us to "Turne over the whole booke of nature, and you shall read mortality in every page."[111] Writing about effusions (escapes of bodily fluids), Thomas Browne suggests solving their mystery "will I feare prove the last leafe to be turned over in the booke of Nature."[112] Writing about Job, Joseph Caryl says the "Ancients were very frequent in this kinde of study, perusing the book of nature, and taking helps to better the understanding by every object of the eye."[113] Much later, Richard Preston marvels at how the "English Literati" have expanded knowledge of the natural world with experimental methods: "they have dis-

---

[106] John Boys, *An Exposition of the Proper Psalmes Vsed in Our English Liturgie Together with a Reason Why the Church Did Chuse the Same* (London, 1616), sig. Br. STC 3466a; Shirley, *The Traytor A Tragedie*, sig. D4v. STC 22458.

[107] Simeon Partlicius, *A New Method of Physick: Or, A Short View of Paracelsus and Galen's Practice* (London, 1654), sig. E7r. Wing P612.

[108] Ralph Austen, *The Spirituall Use of an Orchard, or Garden of Fruit-Trees* (Oxford, 1657), sig. [cross] 4r-v. Wing A4236; Oswald Croll, *Philosophy Reformed & Improved in Four Profound Tractates* (London, 1657), sig. C4r. Wing C7023.

[109] Edward Chaloner, *Sixe Sermons* (London, 1623), sig. Rr. STC 4936.

[110] William Hodson, *The Divine Cosmographer; or, A Brief Survey of the Whole World Delineated in a Tractate on the VIII Psalme* (Cambridge, 1640), sigs. G6v-G7r. STC 13554.

[111] George Jay, *A Sermon Preacht at the Funerall of the Lady Mary Villiers* (London, 1626), sig. Drv. STC 14479.

[112] Thomas Browne Sir, *Pseudodoxia Epidemica, or, Enquiries into Very Many Received Tenents and Commonly Presumed Truths* (London, 1646), sig. Hrv. Wing B5159.

[113] Joseph Caryl, *An Exposition with Practicall Observations Continued upon the Eighth, Ninth and Tenth Chapters of the Book of Job* (London, 1647), sig. L2r. Wing C761.

plaied a new Page of the Book of Nature."[114] In each case, however various the kind of knowledge being figured, the familiar act of reading expresses the production of knowledge. For some, the reading is public and social, with the book displayed for all; for others, it is private and intimate, with readers turning the pages themselves.

Many writers go still further, emphasizing that one must do something with the book of nature as one does with an actual book. Edward Philips describes children who die prematurely as "those to whom the Lord hath denied the verie contemplation of the booke of nature," while Matthew Stoneham says atheists should "a little more strictly, draw home the loose reines of their inconsiderate Sensuality, and meditate some-what more seriouslye on the bookes of Nature."[115] Both appeal to the figure to articulate what someone ought to do but does not or cannot. Our friend Du Bartas bookishly describes King Solomon's famous judgment between two women who claim to be the mother of a child (see 1 Kings 3:16–28):

> Then, thus He waighs (but as in dreaming wise);
> Th' industrious Iudge, when all proofs fail him, flies
> Vnto Coniectures, drawn (the probablest)
> Out of the book of Natures learned brest;
> Or to the Rack: Now, Mothers loue (thinks he)
> Is Natures owne vnchangeable Decree:
> And there's no Torture that exceeds the pains
> Which a kinde Mother in her Childe sustains.[116]

Bereft of "proofs" to help him decide what to do, Solomon resorts to "Coniectures" drawn from study of the book of nature. Like an experimental scientist using the hypothetico-deductive method, Solomon applies a test, calling for a sword to cut the child's body in half to find the true mother.[117] In addition to contemplating, meditating, and conjecturing from the book of nature, writers also thought to translate it. John Rawlinson asks "what instruction can we receiue from [the creatures], if wee onely plod and pore vpon this great booke of nature, and neuer translate it into the booke of grace?"[118] Thomas Adams likewise asks, "shall we

[114] Richard Graham Preston Viscount, *Angliae Speculum Morale The Moral State of England, with the Several Aspects It Beareth to Virtue and Vice* (London, 1670), sig. C8r. Wing P3310.
[115] Edward Philips, *Certain Godly and Learned Sermons* (London, 1607), sig. Z8v. STC 19854; Mathew Stoneham, *A Treatise on the First Psalme. By Mathew Stonham. Minister and Preacher in the Cittie of Norwich* (London, 1610), sig. I3v. STC 23289.
[116] Du Bartas, *Du Bartas His Deuine Weekes and Workes*, sig. Pp3v. STC 21651.
[117] See Larry Laudan, *Science and Hypothesis: Historical Essays on Scientific Methodology* (Dordrecht, Holland: D. Reidel, 1981).
[118] John Rawlinson, *Fishermen Fishers of Men* (London, 1609), sig. B3v. STC 20772.

be euer reading the great Booke of Nature, and neuer translate it to the Booke of Grace?"[119] Still more firmly, Nehemiah Rogers insists that we should "make euery thing we see a good instruction, and euery action a stirrop to heauenly meditation; translating the booke of nature into the vse of grace."[120] An extension of the conceit of reading-as-knowing binds such utterances together. These writers stretch what book reading entails to describe acts of knowing (or not knowing) and instruction.

To read the book of nature is one thing; to *study* it is another. Study implies not merely the concentration of reading but the subsequent production of knowledge. Andreas Hyperius addresses the benefits of natural philosophy, claiming that:

> who so euer shall haue studiouslye ensearched the natures and propertyes of thynges, hée vndoubtedlye may bée estéemed to haue (and that not a little) profited in the Booke of Nature, and to haue well deserued the prayse and worthye commendation of a diligente Scholler.[121]

Philippe Mornay invites his readers to "studie further in the booke of nature" for knowledge of God.[122] John Webster (not the playwright) complains that "we all study, and read too much upon the dead paper idolls of creaturely-invented letters, but do not, nor cannot read the legible characters that are onely written and impressed by the finger of the Almighty" upon the book of nature.[123] Nathanael Culverwel argues that Adam, unlike fallen human beings, knew how to study:

> he could read the smallest print, the least jot and tittle in the book of nature. See how quickly he tumbles o're the vast volume, and in a name gives a brief glosse upon every creature, a concise epitome of their naturall histories.[124]

But Adam was not the only Biblical character who could learn from the book of nature. Samuel Rutherford vividly claims that:

> the acquired knowledge of the Devill is great, hee being an advancing Student, and still learning now above five thousand yeares; and hee that teacheth others, becometh more learned himselfe: he is the great

[119] Adams, *The Deuills Banket Described in Foure Sermons*, sig. Ff2v. STC 110.5.
[120] Nehemiah Rogers, *A Strange Vineyard in Palaestina in an Exposition of Isaiahs Parabolical Song of the Beloued, Discouered* (London, 1623), sig. G4v. STC 21199.
[121] Andreas Hyperius, *The Course of Christianitie* (London, 1579), sig. Er. STC 11755.
[122] Philippe de Mornay seigneur du Plessis-Marly, *A Vvoorke Concerning the Trewnesse of the Christian Religion* (London, 1587), sig. A8r. STC 18149.
[123] John Webster, *Academiarum Examen, or, The Examination of Academies* (London, 1654), sig. F2r. Wing W1209.
[124] Culverwel, *Spiritual Opticks, or, A Glasse Discovering the Weaknesse and Imperfection of a Christians Knowledge in This Life*, sig. Dr. Wing C7573.

> Mint-master and Coyner of knowledge, in Magicians, Wise-men, Soothsayers, Sorcerers, is a carefull Reader in turning over the pages of the book of Nature, and the whole works of Creation.[125]

The devil is both scholar and teacher, acquiring knowledge of the book of nature and then dispensing it to magicians like currency. Finally, in his characteristically orthogonal way, John Donne appeals to knowledge derived from the book of nature to make an entirely different point about how knowledge in eternity differs from knowledge in the present:

> that great Library, those infinite Volumes of the Books of Creatures, shall be taken away, quite away, no more Nature; those reverend Manuscripts, written with Gods own hand, the Scriptures themselves, shall be taken away, quite away; no more preaching, no more reading of Scriptures, and that great School-Mistress, Experience, and Observation shall be remov'd, no new thing to be done, and in an instant, I shall know more, then they all could reveal unto me.[126]

Donne goes on much longer, of course, but the point is clear that, on the last day, knowledge acquired from the study of nature, as from the study of the Bible, will suddenly lose all its value. The accumulated knowledge derived from theology and natural philosophy will "in an instant" be quite unnecessary.

It should be obvious by now that most writers in English who appealed to the book of nature metaphor were Protestant Christians, usually using the metaphor to contextualize knowledge of the natural world within a religious framework. Given what we have seen of the figure's history, this is hardly surprising, but it is not inevitable. John Davies writes that reason, conventionally gendered female, can read the natural world. She:

> plainly can discerne,
> The Sence-transcending Heau'ns plurality,
> And in the booke of Nature she doth learne,
> VVhats taught in this Worldes Vniuersitie.[127]

Davies sets the metaphorical book in a metaphorical academy through which knowledge is dispensed. The poet John Taylor, who did not complete formal education or attend university, self-deprecates in order to accuse those who debase poetry and poets of scholar murder:

---

[125] Rutherford, *Christ Dying and Drawing Sinners to Himself*, sig. Dd2r-v. Wing R2373.
[126] John Donne, *XXVI Sermons* (London, 1661), sig. D5v. Wing D1873.
[127] John Davies, *Mirum in Modum A Glimpse of Gods Glorie and the Soules Shape.* (London, 1602), sig. Cv-C2r. STC 6336.

> Tis you dambde curres haue murderd liberall minds,
> And made best Poets worse esteem'd then hindes.
> But wherefore doe I take a Schollers part,
> That haue no grounds or Axioms of Art:
> That am in Poesie an artlesse creature,
> That haue no learning but the booke of Nature:
> No Academicall Poetike straines,
> But homespunne medley of my mottley braines.[128]

The "artless" natural knowledge Taylor claims for himself gives him the ability to speak as an outsider in a conflict between those who attack poetry and the "liberall minds" who possess "Academicall Poetike straines." Taylor's lines oddly resonate with Davies's, which similarly concern the instruction of the "Worldes Vniuersitie." In his *historie of foure-footed beastes* (1607), Edward Topsell uses the same move but takes it in a different direction. Having "left off" the study of medicine (or "phsyicke") for a time, Topsell later returned to it with a new appreciation:

> but when I considered the greate affinity of this Science [i.e., "physicke"] with naturall Phylosophy, and that not any one can be accounted an excellent or learned Physitian, which hath not drawne (as it were from a Fountaine) his first instruction from bookes of nature; I diligently began to peruse the writings of Philosophers, which haue disputed or debated of things pertaining to nature[.][129]

Topsell offers this account to explain his motives in studying four-footed beasts, a feat that fittingly combines natural philosophy with physic. These "bookes," however, which are also fountains, seem to be real, physical books of natural philosophy even as they "pertain" to the book of nature. Like Topsell's own book, they are books of nature about the book of nature. In *Micrographia* (1665), an important book for the history of science, Robert Hooke comments on greatly magnified images of poppy seeds:

> we might then, instead of studying Herbals (where so little is deliver'd of the virtues of a Plant, and less of truth) have recourse to the Book of Nature it self, and there find the most natural, usefull, and most effectual and specifick Medicines[.][130]

Just as Bacon and others had questioned the books of Aristotle and Galen, Hooke proposes to set aside "Herbals" or books about plants in favor of

---

[128] John Taylor, *The Nipping and Snipping of Abuses* (London, 1614), sig. B4v. STC 23779.
[129] Edward Topsell, *The Historie of Foure-Footed Beastes* (London, 1607). sig. ¶r. STC 24123.
[130] Robert Hooke, *Micrographia, or, Some Physiological Descriptions of Minute Bodies Made by Magnifying Glasses* (London, 1665), sig. Y2r. Wing H2620.

knowledge acquired directly from the figurative book, which ironically stands in for empirical details.

Hooke's poppy seeds hook us, as it were, back to natural philosophy and the experimental scientific methods in which it would culminate in the seventeenth century. One writer above all makes frequent and strategic appeals to the book of nature and to the act of reading it: Robert Boyle. Already quoted here and widely known for his attempts to situate the Royal Society's "new science" in traditionalist frameworks, Boyle combines the various rhetorical features of the book of nature metaphor this chapter has traced. Far from a metaphor of pure machinery, the book of nature gives Boyle a way to talk about knowledge without sundering nature from culture or society. Boyle features the book of nature in two important writings. The first, *Some considerations touching the vsefulnesse of experimental naturall philosophy* (1663), takes the form of a series of discourses to a friend named Pyrophilus. Early in the book, Boyle frames all of experimental science in terms of reading the book to seek "choice and acceptable Truths":

> to manifest these truths more distinctly, Pyrophilus, and yet without exceeding that Brevity my Avocations and the bounds of an Essay exact of me, I shall, among the numerous advantages accruing to Men from the Study of the Book of Nature, content my selfe to instance only in a Couple, that relate more properly to the Improving of Mens Understandings, and to mention a few of those many, by which it encreases their Power. The two chiefe advantages which a reall acquaintance with Nature brings to our Minds, are, First, by instructing our Understandings and gratifying our Curiosities; and next, by exciting and cherishing our Devotion.[131]

Undermining his promised "Brevity" better than Shakespeare's Polonius, Boyle goes on to detail the "advantages" of studying the book of nature. His appeals to instruction and devotion echo many of the writers we have already heard from, many of whom regard natural philosophy as a form of Christian worship. Later, Boyle contrasts a "bare beholding" of the natural world to one who studies it as "an Intelligent Spectator." He appeals once again to the familiar image to make his point:

> the Book of Nature is to an ordinary Gazer, and a Naturalist, like a rare Book of Hieroglyphicks to a Child, and a Philosopher: the one is sufficiently pleas'd with the Odnesse and Variety of the Curious Pictures that adorn it; whereas the other is not only delighted with those outward objects that

---

[131] Boyle, *Some Considerations Touching the Vsefulnesse of Experimental Naturall Philosophy*, sig. B1v. Wing B4029.

gratifie his sense, but receives a much higher satisfaction in admiring the knowledg of the Author, and in finding out and inriching himselfe with those abstruse and vailed Truths dexterously hinted in them.[132]

The comparison hinges on the difference between an illiterate child and a learned adult.

Importantly for Boyle, both these readers admire the figurative book; he does not disparage one while praising the other. More earnestly than other writers we have encountered, Boyle seeks to sanctify the knowledge derived from the book of nature even as he further consolidates the institutional legitimacy of experimental science. Boyle eventually builds to an argument that God wants people to "Prye into his Works." He premises this argument on a general appeal not to reason but to the other book, the Bible:

> for first he [God] begins the Book of Scripture with the Description of the Book of Nature; of which he not only gives us a general account, to informe us that he made the World; since for that end the very first Verse in the Bible might have suffic'd: but he vouchsafes us by retaile the Narrative of each Day's Proceedings, and in the two first Chapters of Genesis, is pleas'd to give nobler hints of Natural Philosophy, then men are yet perhaps aware of.[133]

The "very first Verse" is, of course, Genesis 1:1, which says God created the heavens and the earth. In a clever stroke, Boyle suggests that theologians, not natural philosophers, need to read more carefully to perceive the "hints" of natural philosophy. This image of the book of nature set forth, as it were, in the Bible harnesses the figurative power of the two books metaphor to identify knowledge derived from one book with knowledge derived from the other. If we follow the customary impulse to associate the book of nature with an inevitable and inexorable modernity, then we might interpret Boyle's figures here as the dawning of a new era of scientific rationality. And there is a sense in which that is true, for Boyle understood himself to be proposing a *new* science defined over and against an old one. But this novelty remained, to return to a word with which we began, rhetorically and conceptually entangled, just as the book of nature metaphor was always entangled with theological, material, and social forms of knowing. Boyle addresses these entanglements head on in a second book that features the book of nature, *The excellency of theology compar'd with natural philosophy (as both are objects of men's study)* (1674). Even the titular parenthesis hints that matters are going to get complicated. Like so many

---

[132] Boyle, sig. B2r-v. Wing B4029.
[133] Boyle, sig. E3v. Wing B4029.

other writers we have encountered, Boyle takes pains to situate knowledge derived from nature alongside established authorities, and he does so by recourse to the book of nature:

> I shall not scruple to say, That you should as little think, that there are no more Mysteries in the Books of Scripture, besides those that the School-Divines and Vulgar Commentators have taken notice of, and unfolded; as that there are no other Mysteries in the Book of Nature, than those which the same School-men (who have taken upon them to interpret Aristotle and Nature too) have observ'd and explain'd.[134]

Even though he says he will not "scruple," Boyle manages enough scruple to repeat the suggestion that just as established knowledge of the Bible can be surpassed (even "unfolded"), so too can reading nature's book discover more "Mysteries" than classical authorities have observed. This identification of the two forms of knowledge culminates in Boyle's grandly

But this is not all. For when you have brought an Experiment to an Iſſue, though the Event may often prove ſuch as you will be pleas'd with; yet it will ſeldome prove ſuch as you can acqviefce in. For it fares not with an Inquiſitive mind in ſtudying the Book of Nature, as in reading of Æſop's Fables, or ſome other collecti-on of Apologues of differing ſorts, and

Figures 6.6–6.8   Detail from Robert Boyle, *The Excellency of Theology Compar'd with Natural Philosophy (as Both Are Objects of Men's Study)* (London, 1674), sigs. I6r-I7r, 279608, The Huntington Library, San Marino, California.

[134] Robert Boyle, *The Excellency of Theology Compar'd with Natural Philosophy (as Both Are Objects of Men's Study)* (London, 1674), sig. E3v. Wing B3955.

independant one upon another; where when you have read over as many at one time as you think fit, you may leave off when you pleafe, and go away with the pleafure of underftanding thofe you have perus'd, without being follicited by any troublefome Itch of Curiofity to look after the reft, as thofe which are needful to the better underftanding of thofe you have already gone over, or that will be explicated *by* them, and fcarce *without* them. But in the Book of Nature, as in a well contriv'd Romance, the parts have fuch a connection and relation to one another, and the things we would difcover are fo darkly or incompleatly knowable by thofe that precede them, that the mind is never fatisfied till it comes to the end of the Book; till when all that is difcover'd in the progrefs, is unable to keep the mind from being molefted with Impatience to find that yet conceal'd, which will not be known till one does at leaft make a further progrefs. And yet the full difcovery of Natures Myfteries, is fo unlikely to fall to any mans fhare in this Life, that the cafe of the Purfuers of them is at beft like

Figures 6.6–6.8 (cont.)

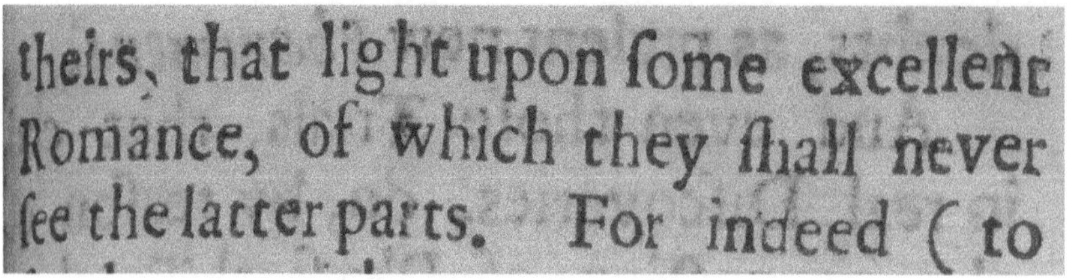

theirs, that light upon some excellent
Romance, of which they shall never
see the latter parts.   For indeed (to

Figures 6.6–6.8   (cont.)

straightforward claim that "as the two great Books, of Nature and of Scripture, have the same Authour; so the study of the latter does not at all hinder an Inquisitive man's delight in the study of the former."[135] This notion of the imperfect and constantly perfected study of the two books leads Boyle to offer a lengthy bookish figure worth quoting at length. Boyle describes how knowledge is acquired from experiments (see Figures 6.6–6.8).[136]

A lifelong reader of romances, Boyle compares the study of nature to familiar reading practices to emphasize the long, halting, digressive, darkly mysterious, and inherently social production of knowledge by experimental science.[137] An experiment is not like reading "Aesop's Fables," Boyle argues. One can "read over as many [fables] at one time" as seems fitting, then move on with no "Itch of Curiosity" because the moral knowledge fables produce is a function of their isolation. In the "well contriv'd Romance" that is the "Book of Nature," however, discrete parts "have such a connection and relation to one another [...] that the mind is never satisfied till it comes to the end of the Book." Knowledge is not complete until the "Itch" has been scratched. Moreover, in a nod at the romance genre's inescapability and incompleteness, Boyle underscores that the "full discovery" of knowledge of the natural world is necessarily partial but nevertheless grounded (as is romance) in readers' experience.[138] This hardly constitutes a mechanistic model of the natural world; figured as reading, Boyle's science proudly remains a nature-culture hybrid.

---

[135] Boyle, sig. I8r. Wing B3955.
[136] Boyle, sig. I6r-I7r. Wing B3955.
[137] Karl Popper, *The Logic of Scientific Discovery* (London: Routledge, 2002); Shapin, *A Social History of Truth*. On Boyle's affection for romance, see Lawrence M. Principe, "Virtuous Romance and Romantic Virtuoso: The Shaping of Robert Boyle's Literary Style," *Journal of the History of Ideas* 56, no. 3 (1995): 377–97, https://doi.org/10.2307/2710032.
[138] See Patricia A. Parker, *Inescapable Romance: Studies in the Poetics of a Mode* (Princeton: Princeton University Press, 1979); Lori Humphrey Newcomb, *Reading Popular Romance in Early Modern England* (New York: Columbia University Press, 2002).

Wading through many appeals to the book of nature, each of which deserves more attention than it has received, this chapter has argued that the figure of the world as a book gave writers a way to describe not only the natural world but also knowledge about it. I have extended book history scholarship's insights into how books were constructed and used to argue that the premodern book of nature hardly ever functioned as a symbol of totality, disembodiment, or purely modern rationality. Even where we might expect a disenchanted view of nature separated from society – in Browne, Sprat, Boyle, and puritan-leaning Protestants – we find instead a fecund hybridity. This is not to suggest that these writers bear no relation to modern scientific method or rationality, of course. The book of nature can and did stand for disembodied, totalizing knowledge, just as printing technology could and did function as a totem for certain aspects of modernity. In Chapter 7, we will study this signifying potential.

When Print Was White

Throughout its history, European thought has tended to conceive of identity less in terms of mutual belonging (cobelonging) to a common world than in terms of the relation between similar beings--of being itself emerging and manifesting itself in its own state, or its own mirror.

–Achille Mbembe[1]

This book has explored how books and book technologies shaped the English cultural imagination. Ranging from various metaphors to figures of book size and taste to the image of the world itself as a book, I have argued that the language of books gave premodern English writers a way to describe various facets of mediated human existence. As I promised in Chapter 2, most of the language we have explored is broader than printing technology, even if printed books occupied an increasingly important place in the imaginative world of English writers. We have, in other words, sought bookish language more broadly than printing even while acknowledging that the changing number and kind of books could affect such language.

This final chapter returns necessarily to printing. The close association of the printing press with modernity in cultural and scholarly narratives requires us to consider its place in a bookish premodern English culture. If I have been persistently emphasizing the *pre-* in *premodern* throughout much of this book, then we must confront the equally persistent habit among those writers of viewing the press as a historical disruption separating ancients from moderns. While many writers avoided commenting on the printing press, printed books, or the printed book trade, others went out of their way to talk about it. Even a writer like Shakespeare, who had

---

[1] Mbembe, *Critique of Black Reason*, 1.

very little to say explicitly about printing, shows signs of responding to its importance.[2]

One of the most infamous of all pronouncements about printing comes from Francis Bacon's *Novum Organon* (1620), printed here in the original Latin for reasons that will become clear:

> *Rursùs, vim & virtutem & consequentias Rerum inuentarum notare iuuat: quae non in alijs manifestiùs occurrunt, quàm in illis tribus, quae Antiquis incognitae; & quarum primordia, licèt recentia, obscura & ingloria sunt:* Artis nimirùm Imprimendi, Pulueris Tormentarij, & Acûs Nauticae. *Haec enim tria, rerum faciem & statum in Orbe terrarum mutauerunt: primum, in Re Literariâ; secundum, in Re Bellicâ: tertium, in Nauigationibus*[.][3]

> Again, it helps to notice the force, power and consequences of discoveries, which appear at their clearest in three things that were unknown to antiquity, and whose origins, though recent, are obscure and unsung: namely the art of printing, gunpowder and the nautical compass. In fact these three things have changed the face and condition of things all over the globe: the first in literature; the second in the art of war; the third in navigation[.][4]

This remark groups the printing press among the "Big Three" inventions changing the world and links printing directly with the moderns as opposed to "the ancients." Bacon's remark has been cited many times over the last four centuries as a bellwether of the modern era, both predicting and participating in a massive cultural shift.[5] Notably, it appears as an epigraph in Elizabeth Eisenstein's *The Printing Press as an Agent of Change*, a book that shares with Bacon the conviction that printing "changed the face and condition of things all over the globe."[6] Bacon's line

---

[2] On Shakespeare and printing, see David Scott Kastan, *Shakespeare and the Book* (Cambridge: Cambridge University Press, 2001); Hugh Craig, "Shakespeare and Print," *HEAT* 4 (2002): 49–63; Lukas Erne, *Shakespeare and the Book Trade* (Cambridge: Cambridge University Press, 2013); Adam G. Hooks, *Selling Shakespeare: Biography, Bibliography, and the Book Trade* (Cambridge: Cambridge University Press, 2016); Lamb, *Shakespeare in the Marketplace of Words*; Newman, *Impressive Shakespeare*.

[3] Francis Bacon, *Franciscy de Verulamio, summi Angliæ cancellarij instauratio magna* (London, 1620), sig. R4r-v. STC 1162.

[4] Francis Bacon, *Francis Bacon: The New Organon*, ed. Lisa Jardine and Michael Silverthorne, trans. Michael Silverthorne (Cambridge University Press, 2000), 100.

[5] See, for instance, Smith, *Modernity and Its Discontents*. Seventeenth-century writers relished quoting Bacon's line about the "Big Three" inventions: for instance, Cressy Dymock, *An Invention of Engines of Motion Lately Brought to Perfection* (London, 1651), sig. A2v. Wing D2971 and Francis Cradocke, *Wealth Discovered: Or, An Essay upon a Late Expedient for Taking Away All Impositions and Raising a Revenue without Taxes* (London, 1661), sig. B1r-v. Wing C6743.

[6] Eisenstein, *The Printing Press as an Agent of Change*, 43. Eisenstein first used the epigraph in an article that would grow into the book. See Elizabeth L. Eisenstein, "Some Conjectures about the Impact

is a motto, of sorts, for a certain approach to modernity and to the press's place in it.

As Joseph Rezek has observed, however, the context of Bacon's remark goes beyond a mere yoking of the press with other technologies, even those of maritime expansion and mass violence. Still more worrisome is the immediately preceding paragraph, where Bacon sets up his grandiose claim about "discoveries" and wades into developing discourses of race:

> [L]et anyone reflect how great is the difference between the life of men in any of the most civilised provinces of Europe and in the most savage and barbarous region of New India; and he will judge that they differ so much that deservedly it may be said that 'man is a God to man', not only for help and benefit, but also in the contrast between their conditions. And this is due not to soil, climate or bodily qualities, but to Arts [*Atque hoc, non Solum, non Caelum, non Corpora; sed Artes praestant*].[7]

For Bacon, the "Arts" distinguish life in Europe as "civilised" and therefore so superior to other cultures that Europeans are like gods to non-European others. Importantly, Bacon describes this distinction as specifically not "due" to "bodily qualities" ("*non Corpora*"); this is not quite modern biological racism. Rather, as Rezek argues, this comparison helps Bacon "to establish an ideological connection between European civilization and the technology of print," which "becomes European here through the geographical scale of [Bacon's] comparative method."[8] In Rezek's broad account, Bacon "lays the groundwork for print's racialization" by marking printed books as distinctly European, a distinction that would eventually amount to the racialized category "white."[9]

Rezek joins a chorus of scholars recently exploring racial formations in premodern Europe. This scholarship has demonstrated that race – including the discursive, material rendering of humans as both white and non-white – took up a far more prominent place in the sixteenth and seventeenth centuries than scholars had suspected or have been willing to acknowledge. The shift has been particularly dramatic for pre-1700

---

of Printing on Western Society and Thought: A Preliminary Report," *The Journal of Modern History* 40, no. 1 (1968): 1–56.

[7] Bacon, *Francis Bacon*, 100.

[8] Joseph Rezek, "The Racialization of Print," *American Literary History* 32, no. 3 (September 1, 2020): 424.

[9] On whiteness as a racialized category, see Nell Irvin Painter, *The History of White People* (New York: W. W. Norton & Company, 2011). On whiteness in early modern England, see Arthur L. Little, *White People in Shakespeare: Essays on Race, Culture and the Elite*, Shakespeare and Social Justice (London: The Arden Shakespeare, 2023). See also *OED*, s.v., "white adj. 1.5.a," which traces "white" as a racial distinction linked with European origin or descent to the fourteenth century.

England, whose relative isolation led many wrongly to presume the absence of race as a rhetorical or social construction despite ample evidence.[10] In many cases, as Joyce MacDonald writes, "race becomes more or less visible in early modern culture in the degree to which it is articulated through and articulates some other hegemonic category."[11] Ayanna Thompson gives this combinatory power of racial thinking the label "racework."[12] Even where the modern category of race is not made explicit as it would in subsequent centuries, racework is everywhere "visible" in premodern culture: in rhetoric, as Ian Smith has demonstrated; in conduct manuals, as Patricia Akhimie has shown; and in the language of service, as Urvashi Chakravarty has explored.[13] Along with scholars such as Brandi K. Adams and Miles Grier, Rezek adds figural and material printed books to this list, arguing for the "presumed whiteness of print" by the eighteenth century.[14]

Rezek, who has other fish to fry, skims over a crucial move in Bacon's language quoted above. Bacon twice makes this move, and in so doing links his claims with the broader, ongoing English discourse of print technology and identity, a discourse this chapter describes. Here, the Latin text guides us. In his Eurocentralizing assertion about discoveries, Bacon conspicuously names "Arts" ("*Artes*") as primary explanatory factors in Europe's superiority, then he names the "art of printing" ("Artis … Imprimendi"), set off in Roman typeface in the printed Latin text, as first among these arts. As with the varied "arts" of war, government, navigation, fiction, apothecary, and love, "art of printing" (along with the overlapping term "craft") suggests the application of knowledge and skill, often derived from the acquisition of a set of technical principles, to an activity,

---

[10] See Hall, *Things of Darkness*; Joyce Green MacDonald, ed., *Race, Ethnicity, and Power in the Renaissance* (Madison NJ: Fairleigh Dickinson University Press, 1997); Patricia Akhimie, *Shakespeare and the Cultivation of Difference: Race and Conduct in the Early Modern World*, Routledge Studies in Shakespeare 29 (New York: Routledge, 2018); Ayanna Thompson, *The Cambridge Companion to Shakespeare and Race* (Cambridge: Cambridge University Press, 2021); Smith, *Black Shakespeare*; Little, *White People in Shakespeare*.

[11] MacDonald, *Race, Ethnicity, and Power in the Renaissance*, 13.

[12] Thompson, *The Cambridge Companion to Shakespeare and Race*, 1–16.

[13] See Ian Smith, *Race and Rhetoric in the Renaissance: Barbarian Errors*, 1st ed., Early Modern Cultural Studies (New York: Palgrave Macmillan, 2009); Akhimie, *Shakespeare and the Cultivation of Difference*; Chakravarty, *Fictions of Consent*.

[14] Rezek, "The Racialization of Print," 422. See Brandi K. Adams, "'Inlaid with Inkie Spots of Jet': Early Modern Book History and Premodern Critical Race Studies," in *The Oxford Handbook of the History of the Book in Early Modern England*, ed. Adam Smyth (Oxford: Oxford University Press, 2023), 81–99; Miles P. Grier, *Inkface: Othello and White Authority in the Era of Atlantic Slavery*, Writing the Early Americas (Charlottesville: University of Virginia Press, 2023). Grier argues that white writers subjected black bodies to interpretive control by means of a process he calls "inkface," in which a person is transformed into a book to be read.

field, or situation.[15] The phrase thus refers to the press, its associated technologies and crafts, the book trade responsible for dissemination, and the printed texts themselves as artifacts (literally, the makings of an art) of printing knowledge.[16] Rezek nods at but does not explore the significance of the "art of printing," nor have other recent scholars yet connected the rhetorical and cultural work this phrase performs to the racialization of printing technology. Why would they? It seems so neutral.[17]

Bacon was not the only writer to elevate printing to the status of an art, nor was he the only one to fuse that art with cultural difference. Extending the insights of premodern critical race scholarship, this chapter shows how "the art of printing" came to function as a handle for English and European white identity. By way of this phrase, writers articulated temporal difference (ancient versus modern), political and religious difference (Protestant versus Roman Catholic, abundant in learning versus impoverished), and cultural difference (European or English versus others, civilized versus uncivilized) – all in ways that framed technological superiority as a distinction that was increasingly racialized. The "art of printing" did not presume but rather, over time and layered repetition, made possible printing technology's association with race.

This chapter proceeds through these layers even while acknowledging their interconnectedness as part of what Adams describes as the "structures of white racial formation that govern the act of printing ... in early modern texts."[18] The "art of printing" locates printing as a German or Dutch invention, reifying its Europeanness (section one). It interprets cultural distinctions and transformations as premised on printing technology (section two). And it explicitly distinguishes Europe from non-European others (section three). The climax of this layered exploration sets the stage for the conclusion of *How the World Became a Book* (section four), which returns to the animating questions of the entire project.

The stakes of this argument are high, and not only because scholars of later periods have laid democratic republicanism, Enlightenment, American national identity, the very notion of a public sphere, and much else at the foot of the printing press.[19] Still more existentially, as Achille Mbembe,

---

[15] *OED* s.v. "art n. 1."
[16] *OED* s.v. "artefact n."
[17] See especially Brandi K. Adams's critique of this neutrality with respect to the history of the book in Adams, "'Inlaid with Inkie Spots of Jet.'"
[18] Adams, "'Inlaid with Inkie Spots of Jet,'" 91.
[19] See also Benedict Anderson, *Imagined Communities: Reflections on the Origin and Spread of Nationalism*, Revised edition (London: Verso, 2016); Warner, *The Letters of the Republic*.

Denise Ferreira da Silva, and others have argued, European modernity is bound up with – there's that metaphor again – race and blackness in particular. Blackness, Mbembe memorably writes, "is in effect the ghost of modernity" and whiteness "the mark of a certain mode of Western presence in the world."[20] Race is thus the "nuclear power plant" of modernity.[21] Likewise, Da Silva has explored the mutually constitutive development of race with Enlightenment rationality.[22] Printing technology does not often appear in this scholarship connecting race with modernity, in part because the press predates the conventional "start" of modernity by over two centuries. Nevertheless, these accounts depend upon what Hartmut Rosa has called the "social acceleration" that conditions modern life, a compression of space and time that premodern English writers regularly attributed to the press.[23]

The chapters of this book have described *premodern* (and thus, to an extent, nonmodern) concepts that would later take more familiar forms: metaphor, information, mediation, knowledge. This chapter likewise argues that the discourse clustering around printing technology, however different from the externalized biological racism that would be more explicit in later centuries, set the imaginative conditions for European whiteness. Just as premodern England witnessed, as Chakravarty has argued, the "*collusion* of early modern fictions of consent [...] with the fictions of race" thus setting the conditions for chattel slavery, then this chapter shows the collusion of the fictions (or rather the *Arts*) of printing with the related racial fiction of whiteness expressed as civilization and technological superiority.[24] If the modern production of race was, as Mbembe puts it, "an act of imagination as much as an act of misunderstanding," then the printing press gave English writers a way to imagine their identity and misunderstand others in the same phrase: "the art of printing."

The European Origins of the Art of Printing

The origins of the printing press have received plenty of attention from scholars, who have surveyed the mythologies surrounding the introduction of

---

[20] Mbembe, *Critique of Black Reason*, 129 and 45–46.

[21] Mbembe, 2.

[22] Denise Ferreira da Silva, *Toward a Global Idea of Race*, Borderlines, v. 27 (Minneapolis: University of Minnesota Press, 2007); Denise Ferreira da Silva, *Unpayable Debt*, On the Antipolitical, v. 1 (London: Sternberg Press, 2022). See also Nicholas Hudson, ed., *A Cultural History of Race in the Reformation and Enlightenment* (London: Bloomsbury, 2023).

[23] Rosa, *Social Acceleration*.

[24] Chakravarty, *Fictions of Consent*, 7. Emphasis in original.

printing and movable type to Europe.[25] The story of Johannes Gutenberg's combination of metal-casting technology with pressing technology has been told (and retold) in books, magazines, YouTube series, and Broadway musicals, just as the more complicated stories about Gutenberg's business relationships have occupied scholars for many decades.[26] These mythologies are hardly new, however. As Rachel Stenner writes, "from the outset, the history of printing is laden with imaginative drama and symbolic potency."[27] Was Gutenberg a thief, theft victim, neither, or both? Did the printing press receive prompt, wide acclaim, or was the initial response more mixed? These worthwhile albeit worn questions do not answer the broader question about how printing technology itself became, in Jim Kearney's words about books, "an emblem, an idea, a thing good to think with?"[28] This section therefore explores how "the art of printing" acquired value as a durable handle for describing the distinctive qualities of printing. The phrase attaches to printing a mythology, a theology, and a sociology that would set the terms for identification of printing technology with Europe and England.

Deep in a list of events in the reign of Henry VI, John Rastell mentions that "the crafte of Printynge of bokes began in the citye of Almayne / named Magonce whiche is nowe meruaylously increasyd[.]"[29] Like Rastell, many writers referring to the myth of the press's invention assign as much importance to the question of *where* the invention occurred as they do to *who* invented it. This obsession with geographical origins and individual accomplishment is itself a Eurocentric and colonial habit that would become normative in the Enlightenment, but it germinates even here.[30] Rastell links the city ("Magonce" or Mayence or Maguntia,

[25] For just a sample, see Eisenstein, *Divine Art, Infernal Machine*; Keith Houston, *The Book: A Cover-to-Cover Exploration of the Most Powerful Object of Our Time*, First edition (New York: W.W. Norton & Company, 2016); Frédéric Barbier, *Gutenberg's Europe: The Book and the Invention of Western Modernity*, trans. Jean Birrell, English edition (Cambridge: Polity, 2017).

[26] For a helpful overview, see Chapter 1 of Eisenstein, *Divine Art, Infernal Machine*. See also Pierce Butler, *The Origin of Printing in Europe*, University of Chicago Studies in Library Science (Chicago: University of Chicago Press, 1940); Theo L. DeVinne, *The Invention of Printing: A Collection of Facts and Opinions Descriptive of Early Prints and Playing Cards, the Block Books of the Fifteenth Century, the Legend of Lourens Janszoon Coster, of Harlem, and the Work of John Gutenberg and His Associates* (Detroit: Gale Research Co., 1969); Paul Needham, "Haec Sancta Ars: Gutenberg's Invention as a Divine Gift," *Gazette of the Grolier Club* 42 (1990): 101–20; Smith, *Portable Magic*, 21–37.

[27] Stenner, *The Typographic Imaginary in Early Modern English Literature*, 33.

[28] Kearney, *The Incarnate Text*, 2.

[29] John Rastell, *The Pastyme of People* (London, 1530), sig. E6v. STC 20724.

[30] See Aníbal Quijano, "Coloniality and Modernity/Rationality," *Cultural Studies* 21, no. 2–3 (March 1, 2007): 168–78, https://doi.org/10.1080/09502380601164353. The classic discussion of this question is Frantz Fanon, *Black Skin, White Masks* (New York: Grove Press, 1968). See also Alia Al-Saji,

alternative names for Mainz) and country ("Almayne" or Germany) to the "great lernynge and knowelege" the press caused; knowledge and the city itself have grown proportionately. William Alley writes that the "noble arte of printyng" was "first inuented by one Iohannes Gutenbergius, a man of a rare and maruelous wit, in a certayne Citie of Germany called Maguntia[.]"³¹ In a list of cities in Germany, William Cunningham's entry for "MAguntia, Mentz" reads, "At this Citie was th'Art of Printing first fou[n]d (by Iohn Faustus) in [...] 1453."³² This "Faustus" is Johann Fust, who played a much-disputed role in the creation of the press, with some accounts attributing its invention to him rather than Gutenberg.³³ In a history of France, Jean de Serres (translated by Edward Grimeston) indicates that this dispute was fairly widespread:

> almost about the same time [as other events] the arte of Printing had his beginning. Some attribute it to the yeare 1440. to *Iohn Guttemberg* borne at *Strausbourg*, others to *Iohn Fauste* at *Mayence*, in the yeare 1452. Doubtlesse it is an excellent inuention to increase knowledge, although the vanity and malice of men makes it often times their baude, to the preuidice of the truth and all good manners.³⁴

Even as he notes the uncertainty surrounding the German origins of the press, Serres reflexively connects those origins with printing's capacity to "increase knowledge." Another French book, likewise translated by Grimeston, dives right into the controversy about the art of printing's origin, arguing that it was first invented by Laurens Koster in Haarlem, "to the which (and that iustly) wee may attribute the noble inuention of the Art of printing, although some (to selfe-willed) maintaine that it came from Mogunce ot Mentz, an imperiall and electorall towne of Germany."³⁵ The writer then narrates a lengthy account of a Haarlem burgher who invented printing but whose household servant stole the "art" away to Mainz. In *The treasurie of auncient and moderne times* (1613), an anthology of European writings translated by Thomas Miles, one writer swerves to mention "the famous Art of Printing," "whereby so many Bookes are

---

"Too Late: Fanon, the Dismembered Past, and a Phenomenology of Racialized Time," in *Fanon, Phenomenology, and Psychology*, ed. Derek Hook, Miraj Desai, and Leswin Laubscher (London: Routledge, 2022), 177–93, https://doi.org/10.4324/9781003037132-17.

³¹ William Alley, *Ptōchomuseion [Sic]. The Poore Mans Librarie* (London, 1565), sig. Hh5v. STC 374.

³² William Cuningham, *The Cosmographical Glasse Conteinyng the Pleasant Principles of Cosmographie, Geographie, Hydrographie, or Nauigation* (London, 1559), sig. Riv. STC 6119.

³³ See Eisenstein, *Divine Art, Infernal Machine*, 1–33.

³⁴ Jean de Serres, *A General Inuentorie of the History of France from the Beginning of That Monarchie, Vnto the Treatie of Veruins, in the Year 1598* (London, 1607), sig. Sss5r. STC 22244.

³⁵ Le Petit, *A Generall Historie of the Netherlands*, sig. E4r-v. STC 15485.

Imprinted, with no meane expedition, and which I doe ingeniously confesse, to be the best inuention in the world." This writer splits the difference in the narratives:

> by one Authour, the deuiser [of the art of printing] is said to be an *Allemaigne* or *Germaine*, of the Citty of *Mentz*, named *Iohn Faustus*, (although *Polidore Virgill* doe call him *Peter*) yet others tearme him *Iohn Cuthemberg*, confessing him also to be a *Germaine*, and a Knight, and that the first impression of any Booke, was in the yeare of our Lord, 1453.[36]

Twice this writer emphasizes that, whoever invented the art of printing, it was a "*Germaine.*"

The pattern in these examples deserves emphasis: many writers who retell the origin myth of printing technology appeal to its German or Dutch origins. Their attempts to articulate what the press does to cultures rests on an origin myth located in a particular time and slightly less particular place. This pattern would persist into the seventeenth century, when English writers developed an increasingly complex, if equally uncertain, account of printing's invention, using the "art of printing" as the key term by which to label the press and its products.[37] The term's association with the origins of printing would most clearly emerge in Joseph Moxon's *Mechanick Exercises* (1683), which we encountered in Chapter 2. The title page of the volume on printing features the phrase "the Art of Printing" itself, along with frontispiece portraits of Gutenberg and Koster. In the opening pages of the printing manual, Moxon wastes no time getting right to the controversy literally illustrated in the prefatory materials (see Figures 7.1 and 7.2).[38] He goes on to recite the claims for Koster and Gutenberg as the first to create the press, finally offering the summary statement that "About the year of our Lord 1460. The Art of *Printing* began to be invented and practiced in *Germany* [...]."[39] We will return to Moxon's invocation of Chinese printing shortly; for now, consider how Moxon avoids choosing a single inventor to mythologize (though he tips the scales slightly

---

[36] Anonymous, *The Treasurie of Auncient and Moderne Times* (London, 1613), sig. Vvv5v-6r. STC 17936.

[37] For instance, see Patrick Simson, *The Historie of the Church since the Dayes of Our Saviour Iesus Christ, Vntill This Present Age* (London, 1624), sig. Hh7r-v. STC 23598. Edward Leigh, *A Treatise of Religion & Learning and of Religious and Learned Men* (London, 1656), sig. H3r-v. Wing L1013. Samuel Clarke, *A Geographicall Description of All the Countries in the Known Vvorld as Also of the Greatest and Famousest Cities and Fabricks Which Have Been, or Are Now Remaining* (London, 1657), sig. Ffr-v. Wing C4516. Nathaniel Wanley, *The Wonders of the Little World, or, A General History of Man in Six Books* (London, 1673), sig. Ddv. Wing W709. Robert Young, *A Breviary of the Later Persecutions of the Professors of the Gospel of Christ Jesus* (Glasgow, 1674), sig. B8r. Wing Y74.

[38] Moxon, *Mechanick Exercises*, sig. Br-v.

[39] Moxon, sig. B2v. Moxon cites a "Dr Wallis of Oxford."

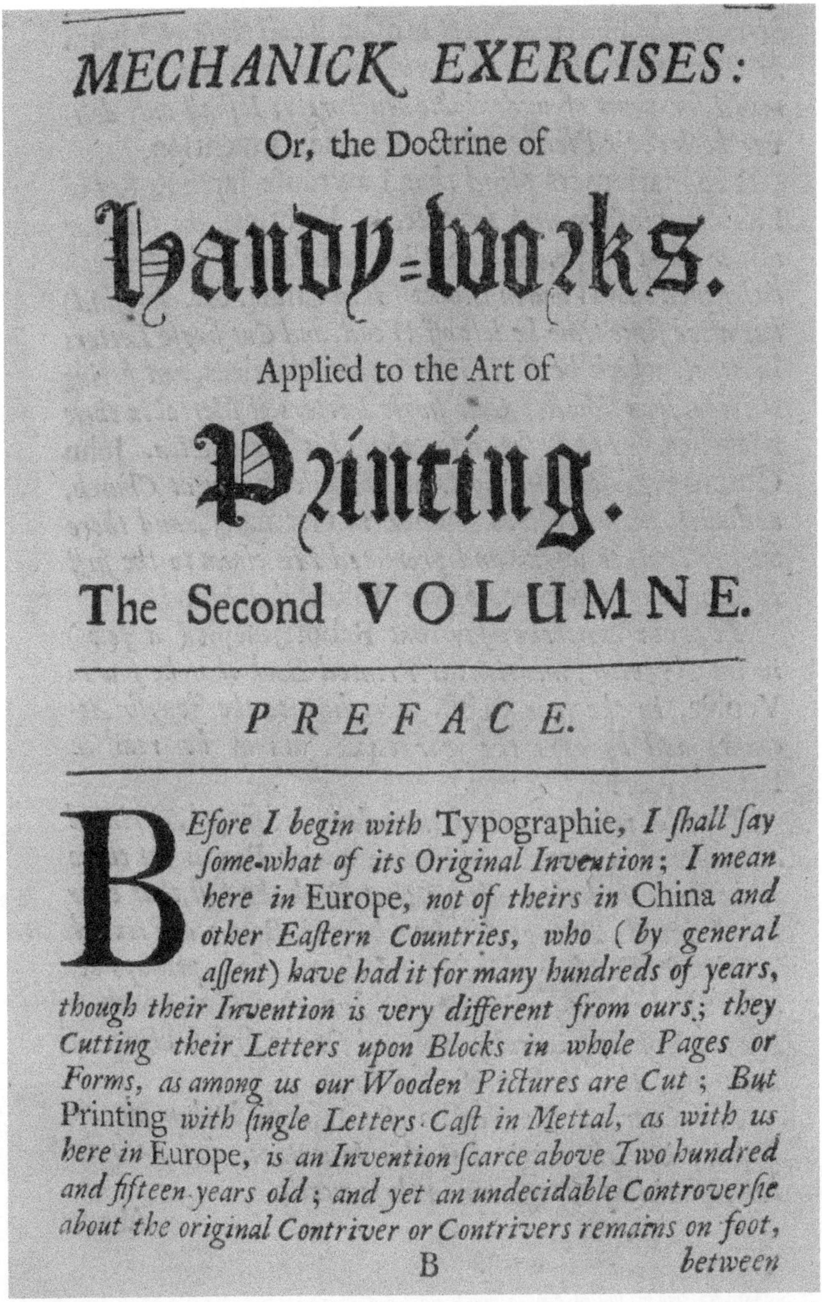

MECHANICK EXERCISES:

Or, the Doctrine of

ᕼandy-works.

Applied to the Art of

Pꞛinting.

The Second VOLUMNE.

PREFACE.

BEfore I begin with Typographie, I ſhall ſay ſome-what of its Original Invention; I mean here in Europe, not of theirs in China and other Eaſtern Countries, who (by general aſſent) have had it for many hundreds of years, though their Invention is very different from ours; they Cutting their Letters upon Blocks in whole Pages or Forms, as among us our Wooden Pictures are Cut ; But Printing with ſingle Letters Caſt in Mettal, as with us here in Europe, is an Invention ſcarce above Two hundred and fifteen years old ; and yet an undecidable Controverſie about the original Contriver or Contrivers remains on foot, between

B

Figures 7.1 and 7.2   Detail of Joseph Moxon, *Mechanick Exercises, or, The Doctrine of Handy-Works* (London, 1677), sigs. Br-v, 138367, The Huntington Library, San Marino, California.

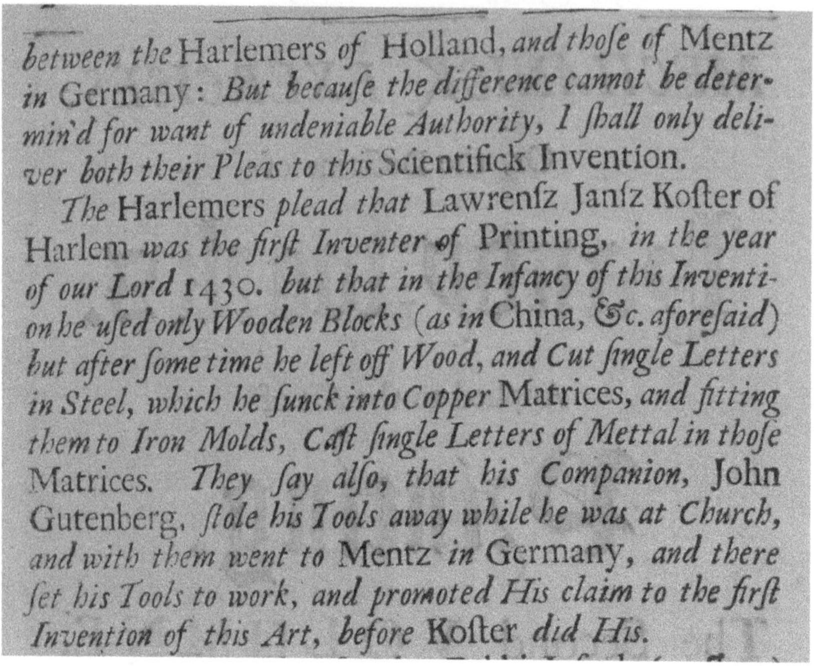

between the Harlemers *of* Holland, *and thofe of* Mentz *in* Germany: *But becaufe the difference cannot be deter-min'd for want of undeniable Authority, I fhall only deli-ver both their Pleas to this* Scientifick Invention.

The Harlemers *plead that* Lawrenfz Janfz Kofter of Harlem *was the firft Inventer of* Printing, *in the year of our Lord* 1430. *but that in the Infancy of this Inventi-on he ufed only Wooden Blocks (as in* China, *&c. aforefaid) but after fome time he left off Wood, and Cut fingle Letters in Steel, which he funck into Copper* Matrices, *and fitting them to Iron Molds, Caft fingle Letters of Mettal in thofe* Matrices. *They fay alfo, that his Companion,* John Gutenberg, *ftole his Tools away while he was at Church, and with them went to* Mentz *in* Germany, *and there fet his Tools to work, and promoted His claim to the firft Invention of this Art, before* Kofter *did His.*

Figures 7.1 and 7.2   (cont.)

toward Gutenberg) and instead emphasizes *where* the invention occurred. It may have been Haarlem or Mentz, but it was certainly "*here in* Europe." Adams notes that such a move makes the "Scientifick Invention" of print-ing "exceptional within a clear (presumably white) European lineage."[40]

This tight link between the German (or Dutch) origins of the press and the resonant phrase "the art of printing" developed still more asso-ciations over the course of the sixteenth and seventeenth centuries. The best-known of these is the impact of printing on the Reformation, much discussed in book history scholarship.[41] Previous scholars have used the term "impact" to attribute social and cultural changes unproblematically to printing, but I use it here to describe the rhetorically situated instances in which writers assess the difference the press makes.[42] Under the sign of the "art of printing," writers organized their claims about what printing technology has done. The most influential of these in England was John

[40] Adams, "Inlaid with Inkie Spots of Jet," 93.
[41] See Guyer, *How the English Reformation Was Named.*
[42] See Baron, Lindquist, and Shevlin, *Agent of Change.*

Foxe, who seized on the phrase as an operator for calculating the effect of God's gift of the press to Christendom at a particular time and place. Foxe begins his preface to a collection of the writings of William Tyndale and others by drawing a clear picture that he would recycle and elaborate elsewhere:

> AS we haue great cause to geeue thankes to the high prouidence of almighty God, for the excellent arte of Printing, most happely of late found out, and now commonly practised euery where, to the singular benefite of Christes Church, wherby great increase of learnyng and knowledge, with innumerable commodities els haue ensued, and dayly doe ensue to the lyfe of man, and especially to the fartheraunce of true Religion[.][43]

Despite his optimistic view of printing technology, Foxe was no media determinist. Indeed, he remains downright distressed that the benefits of printing can be deformed, insisting that those who trade in printed books must "not [...] abuse vnworthely that worthy facultie, eyther in thrusting into the worlde euery vnworthy trifle that commeth to hand, or hauing respecte more to their owne priuate gayne, then regarde to the publike edifyng of Christes Church[.]"[44] To punctuate his assertions of the impacts of printing, Foxe laments that many writings have not survived: "no doubt but many thinges had remayned in lyght, which now be lefte in obliuion. But by reason the Arte of Printing was not yet inuented, their worthy bookes were the sooner abolyshed."[45] For Foxe, to borrow terms from Adrian Johns, the properties and impacts of printing are not "inherent" but "transitive," the products of labor – or rather, of art.[46]

Foxe's more famous and lengthy statement on printing ties all these loops into a bow. In *Actes and monuments*, he sharpens his anti-Roman Catholic rhetoric to argue for the divine origins and purposes of "The arte of printing."[47] He argues the pope must recognize that "through the light of printing, the worlde beginneth nowe to haue eyes to see, and heades to iudge," then he proceeds grandly to conclude that:

> God of hys mercifull prouidence, seeing both what lacked in the church, and how also to remedy the same, for [the] aduauncement of his glory, gaue the vnderstanding of this excellent arte or science of printing, whereby three

---

[43] William Tyndale, *The Vvhole Workes of W. Tyndall, Iohn Frith, and Doct. Barnes, Three Worthy Martyrs, and Principall Teachers of This Churche of England* (London, 1573), sig. Aiir. STC 24436.
[44] Tyndale, sig. Aiir. STC 24436.
[45] Tyndale, sig. Aiir. STC 24436.
[46] Johns, *The Nature of the Book*, 19.
[47] Foxe, *Actes and Monuments*, sig. DD6v. STC 11225.

singular co[m]modities at one time came to the world. First, the price of all bookes diminished. Secondly [the] speedy helpe of reading, more furthered. And thirdly the plenty of all good authors enlarged[.][48]

Again, Foxe articulates a view of printing's impact as the product of material factors ("com[m]odities"), however providential. Crucially, moreover, Foxe begins his section on "The benefite and inuention of Printing" not with claims about God's gifts but instead with the same uncertain German origin story to which we have seen other writers appeal. In brief, Foxe relates how the "industrious" John Faustus (i.e., Fust) began printing on movable type, followed by Gutenberg and others, but even then, "The Arte beyng yet but rude, in processe of tyme, was set forward by inuentiue wittes."[49] For Foxe and many others, the "Arte" of printing was not begotten but made – and made in Europe.

The European Distinctions of the Art of Printing

A mixture of economic realism and theological polemic, Foxe's interpretation of the invention of printing proved highly influential from the sixteenth century into the present. Beyond the Dutch-German origins, furthermore, "art of printing" broadly signified a combination of European, English, and Protestant forms of distinction. In another book called *The Pope confuted* (1580), for instance, Foxe looks back on the pre-printing, pre-Reformation past to ask:

what maruel then, if, the pure and eloquent sciences, both sacred and prophane, being vtterly extinct, barbarous blindnesse had ouerwhelmed all things, with grosse ignoraunce, whereby no man coulde become either more expert in learning, or more virtuous in manners, when as neither bookes, nor authours were extant [...]?[50]

Without books and authors, "barbarous blindnesse" and "grosse ignoraunce" prevail because "as yet came not to light that most happie, and heauenly Jewel, to witte, the Arte of Printing bookes." As many scholars have noted, this discourse of barbarity as opposed to civilized learning provides a rhetorical template for racialized discourse, which categorizes uncivilized others as a lower order of being.[51] This language makes a

---

[48] Foxe, sig. DD6r. STC 11225.
[49] Foxe, sig. DD6r. STC 11225.
[50] John Foxe, *The Pope Confuted The Holy and Apostolique Church Confuting the Pope* (London, 1580), sig. B3v. STC 11241.
[51] See Smith, *Race and Rhetoric in the Renaissance*; Heng, *The Invention of Race in the European Middle Ages*.

distinction that would subsequently manufacture a difference. In premodern England broadly, this distinction became legible in the way writers employ the "art of printing" to describe how printing reforms a culture and sets it apart. While the previous section showed how the "art of printing" marks the press's origin story, this section shows how premodern writers use the phrase to talk about what makes their culture special, more civilized, and even superior. The "art of printing" forges a distinction that would become a difference.

As Foxe's multiple statements about printing make plain, it is hardly news to observe a tendency among Protestant writers to point to the printing press as either the spark or the fuel of the fire of reformation. Importantly, however, they consistently do so by using the handle "art of printing," less as a marker of technological determinism and more as a tool (indeed a weapon) for describing cultural distinctions. Heinrich Bullinger, translated by John Cox, argues predictably that "the art of printing" is "a moste excellent & profitable gift of God giuen vnto vs in these last dayes," but he goes on to claim that this same "art of Printing is reueled by God vnto men [...] that those things which serue the furtherance of a common welth, the knoweledge of historyes, and other good arts and Sciences might perfectly be learned and knowen."[52] European humanism wears printing like a badge. Likewise, in the preface of an English translation of his *Loci Communes* (1583), Petro Vermigli (also known as Peter Martyr) notes that because of the "art of Printing," "the word runneth verie swiftlie into all parts of the world."[53] Thomas Jackson paints a starker picture when he compares the reformation ("our deliuerance from the seruitude of the Romish church") to Israel's deliverance from Egypt, though he notes a key difference: in this case, "God had reuiued the study of tongues, and reuealed the Arte of Printing, a little before our fore-fathers departed out of Babylon, that they should not come away empty, but well furnished to wage warre with their enemies."[54] In the same year, the preface epistle to a book about Burmuda credits "the admirable art of Printing" with the "discouerie and destruction of Poperie," but links that event

---

[52] Heinrich Bullinger, *An Exhortation to the Ministers of Gods Woord in the Church of Christ, That They Set aside All Mutuall Discord, and in These Latter Dayes and Dangerous Times Purely and with One Concent Preache Vnto the World the Onely True Faith in Christe and Amendement of Life* (London, 1575), sig. Iiiiv. STC 4055.5.

[53] Vermigli, *The Common Places of the Most Famous and Renowmed Diuine Doctor Peter Martyr*, sig. a3v-a4r. STC 24669.

[54] Jackson, *The Eternall Truth of Scriptures, and Christian Beleefe, Thereon Vvholly Depending, Manifested by It Owne Light*, sig. Ee3v-Ar. STC 14308.

more broadly with "the manifestation of the truth," the "restoration of learning," and the "diffusion of knowledge."[55] In a translated sermon, Abraham Scultetus ends a list of the ways the present is different from the past by adding "also the inuention of the Art of Printing, which before had ben vtterly vnknowne, and by meanes whereof it came to passe that Doctor Luthers bookes, being dispersed and spread into diuers and most large countries and nations, came into very many mens hands, and were euery where read and diligently studied."[56] In these cases, the relationship between printing and Protestantism is neither reflexive nor inherent but exists as a kind of rhetorically motivated synergy. Scultetus, for instance, appeals to the property of scale ("dispersed and spread ... into very many mens hands") as the mechanism of reformation. Importantly, these examples do not argue for a long-outdated model in which printing fuels the reformation; rather, these narratives gave premodern writers a way to locate themselves in history and distinguish themselves from others. These writers frame the "art of printing" as both cause and effect of European identity.

These mechanisms of distinction located around "the art of printing" grew more explicit over the seventeenth century, still often attached to Protestantism. Thomas Beard clearly connects the dots:

> God also raised vp such a number of bright Starres, learned men in the Church, as no Age euer saw the like: these did not onely refine from Monkish barbarismes, humane learning, but also gaue great light and propagation vnto the truth, which had a long time lyen clouded vnder ignorance and superstition. And to helpe forward this great worke, not long before this time, the Famous Art of Printing was by Gods prouidence found out, as it were of purpose to divulge and spread abroad the most excellent writings of famous men then liuing, which peraduenture otherwise had neuer come to light.[57]

Beard emphasizes a historical rupture, in which the "bright Starres" and "famous men" of the reformation are distinguished from the "barbarismes" of Catholicism. Such rhetoric may be unsurprising in a book titled *Antichrist the pope of Rome*, but what is nevertheless noteworthy is the use of "art of printing" as a factor of historical explanation linked, once more, with the racialized discourse of "barbarism." In the same vein, Samuel Clarke grandly

[55] Silvester Jourdain, *A Plaine Description of the Barmudas, Now Called Sommer Ilands* (London, 1613), sig. A2v. STC 14817.

[56] Abraham Scultetus, *A Secular Sermon* (London, 1618), sig. A3v. STC 22124.

[57] Thomas Beard, *Antichrist the Pope of Rome: Or, the Pope of Rome Is Antichrist Proued in Two Treatises* (London, 1625), sig. Aa3r-v. STC 1657.

observes that "THere were never any former ages which enjoyed the like meanes of knowledge, as we which live at this day do," then he asks rhetorically, "besides the sacred Scriptures in a known tongue, how many volumes of heavenly truths, dropping from the mouthes, and pens, both of ancient and moderne Divines, hath that most excellent, and exquisite Art of Printing conveyed to us?"[58] Arise Evans remarks that "when the Art of Printing was found, and they had liberty to have the Scripture, knowledge is increased among the People."[59] Finally, Nicholas Billingsley's poem about "The Persecution of the English Church after the rising of Martin Luther" likewise imagines coterminous reformations of knowledge and the church:

> THE Christian world appear'd not very clear
> Until the fifteen hundred eighteenth year,
> Wherein God pleased to unbosome night,
> The Art of Printing being brought to light;
> Which furnished the Church with useful books,
> And made them to discerne Religions looks
> From superstition, (as in a mirrour;)
> Substantial Truth, from counterfeited errour.[60]

He then narrates how "sundry men of parts" applied their "Arts" and "strenuously opposed Barbarism." For Billingsley, like the other writers cited above, the "art of printing" is as much a mark of historically situated identity as it is a cause of reformation. The goal of the poem is to define the "English Church," and the hinge of that definition is the "art of printing." Given the apparent media consciousness of these examples, their chief effect is to set themselves, the group to which their writers belong, and even their entire epoch apart.

Not all writers invoke the "art of printing" exclusively in the interest of Protestant polemic. Others more broadly assert the increased number and availability of books and link that increase to another social or cultural phenomenon. Andreas Hyperius, in translation, writes that the "copies of the holy Bookes (by reason of ye newe art of Printing found out by the prouidence of GOD) are in all partes of the worlde solde for little[.]"[61]

---

[58] Samuel Clarke, *A Mirrour or Looking-Glasse Both for Saints and Sinners Held Forth in about Two Thousand Examples* (London, 1654), sig. Y2r-v. Wing C4549.

[59] Arise Evans, *A Rule from Heaven, or, VVholsom Counsel to a Distracted State* (London, 1659), sig. C8r. Wing E3463.

[60] Nicholas Billingsley, *Brachy-Martyrologia, or, A Breviary of All the Greatest Persecutions Which Have Befallen the Saints and People of God from the Creation to Our Present Times* (London, 1657), sig. L2v. Wing B2910.

[61] Hyperius, *The Course of Christianitie*, sig. Mr-v. STC 11755.

These holy books and cheap, including the Bible but not exclusive to it, produce what Hyperius calls "quiet": "a releasement of many troubles." Similarly optimistic, Louis Leroy (also in translation) observes that all the "arts [...] are almost brought to their perfection[,]" improving human knowledge, because "the Art of Printing hath bin a great helpe; and made the encrease thereof much easier."[62] In a preface epistle, William Bradshaw proclaims how, "by that happy Art of Printing, Bookes have multiplyed, swarming continually out of the Presse[,]" making it easier for short books like his to find a public.[63] And Edward Leigh, likewise in an epistle, notes the "numberlesse number of Bookes wherwith in this scribling age the presses are oppressed," then follows up to argue that the "Art of Printing was a happy invention for the propagating of learning[.]"[64] Here, the "art of printing" does not magically or reflexively have an "impact" on culture; rather, the phrase stands for a cluster of knowledge practices, technologies, and relationships that create a lot of books and thus, for these writers, set their culture apart ("their" here refers both to the books and the writers, for they are now identified). The "art of printing" is not a talisman of determinism; it is a token of identity.

Still more capaciously, other writers use "art of printing" with humanism as a backdrop to invoke a reformation in European and English learning. A 1642 broadside addressed to Parliament by the "Masters and Workmen Printers of London" complains that "the State hath been, and still is like to be much disturbed and abused by multitudes of seditious Bookes and Pamphlets daily Printed and published, and the said Art of Printing much debased in workmanship, and otherwise, to the great dishonour of our Nation." This is not how it should be, they argue, because "this Art of Printing much concernes the good both of the Church and Common-wealth, by propagating the Gospel, and advancing all other Arts and Sciences within his Majesties Kingdomes and Provinces."[65] These printing house workers premise their call for changes to the book trade on a claim about the distinct effects of printed books within "his Majesties Kingdomes and Provinces." Like the German/Dutch invention

[62] Louis Leroy, *Of the Interchangeable Course, or Variety of Things in the Whole World and the Concurrence of Armes and Learning* (London, 1594), sig. T5v. STC 15488.

[63] William Bradshaw, *A Discourse of the Sinne against the Holy Ghost* (London, 1640), sig. A3r-v. STC 3515.5.

[64] William Whately, *Prototypes, or, The Primarie Precedent Presidents out of the Booke of Genesis* (London, 1640), sig. A6r. STC 25317.5.

[65] Anonymous, *To the Right Honorable, the Knights, Citizens, and Burgesses, Now Assembled in the High Court of Parliament. The Petition of the Masters and Workmen Printers of London* (London, 1642). Wing T1650A. They go on to ask Parliament to undo longstanding printing patents.

narratives, this broadside identifies a certain nation and people with the "art of printing."

Unsurprisingly, others did the same. The Lutheran historiographer Johannes Sleidanus (translated by Stephen Wythers) states boldly that:

> by ye meanes of the art of printing then inue[n]ted ye which brought with it great co[m]modities, it is vncredible, what a prosperous & desirable progression was made. For since yt time vnto this day the studies haue had in such sort their course, that this our age may compare it self with the most learnedst time that euer were.[66]

The "co[m]modities" of printing have led to a "progression" of knowledge, setting apart "our age" as one of history's most learned. Thomas Brightman agrees, telling how "after the wonderfull art of printing was found out [...] many excellent wits were raysed up to search out the truth."[67] In a treatise on printing, William Ball gesticulates:

> the invention of the Mystery, or Art of Printing may rightly be acknowledged one of the greatest, as an exact and exquisite Instrument, opening to the understanding, not onely all naturall Sciences, but even supernaturall Mysteries; by the meanes whereof the mindes of men have been endowed with many excellent gifts.[68]

Apparently unconsciously, Ball ties the "Mystery" of printing to the "supernaturall Mysteries" it has demystified in the "mindes of men." He goes on to warn, like others we have met, that printing can be abused and its effects corrupted. Samuel Hartlib's imaginary utopian society Macaria is identified with all of printing's best features: there, "the Art of Printing will so spread knowledge, that the common people, knowing their own rights and liberties, will not be governed by way of oppression[.]"[69] In a broadside related to the same complaints raised by the "Masters and Workmen Printers" cited above, the Stationers' Company argues succinctly: "this Art of Printing was the key that opened the doore of knowledge and learning (which is the honour and support of all States and Kingdomes)[.]"[70]

---

[66] Johannes Sleidanus, *A Briefe Chronicle of the Foure Principall Empyres* (London, 1563), sig. Cciiv. STC 19849.

[67] Brightman, *A Revelation of the Apocalyps*, sig. M2v. STC 3754.

[68] William Ball, *A Briefe Treatise Concerning the Regulating of Printing* (London, 1651), sig. A3r. Wing B586.

[69] Samuel Hartlib, *A Description of the Famous Kingdome of Macaria* (London, 1641), sig. Cr-v. Wing H983.

[70] Anonymous, *To the Honourable House of Commons Assembled in Parliament* (London, 1621). STC 16786.10

Each in their own way, these examples forge an identity around and with the "art of printing." The Stationers conjure a European set of nation-states, while Hartlib's utopia is an almost Habermasian public sphere and Ball imagines an illuminated (not to say Enlightened!) group of beneficiaries of printing's scaled-up knowledge dissemination. What makes these appeals to the "art of printing" a form of proto-racialization is that they effect what Bourdieu calls an "embodied social structure," the predicate of cultural distinction.[71] Upstream from the racialized distinctions of modernity is a rhetorically generated identification of Europe with printing technology. This identification takes the form of a cognitive structure that, in Bourdieu's terms, "social agents implement in their practical knowledge of the social world." These structures create "historical schemes of perception and appreciation which are the product of the objective division into classes." In other words, Europe and England are identified with printing, and printing in turn structures European self-perception as civilized, superior, and white. While for Bourdieu the "classes" created by this perception include "age groups, genders, social classes," in this case the division at the root of this embodied social structure is the one between those who have the "art of printing" and those who do not. This division would eventually map onto racial difference.[72] To put the point in the plainer terms of Ta-Nehisi Coates, "race is the child of racism, not the father."[73] In the examples witnessed so far, this distinction is implicit, but as we will see in the next section, it becomes increasingly explicit in the period. The distinction becomes difference.

The European Whiteness of the Art of Printing

When English writers (along with continental writers and writers in Latin) appeal to the art of printing, they imagine it as an apparatus with German and Dutch origins, with divine sanction, and with the capacity to scale and thus reform knowledge and learning across Europe. My claim here is not that this rhetoric of the "art of printing" is itself racist, but more accurately that it contains the seed of an ideology of difference on which modern racism would be premised. Such a view draws on and illustrates Achille Mbembe's broad claim, cited as this chapter's epigraph, that European

---

[71] Bourdieu, *Distinction*, 467. See also Ania Loomba, "Shakespeare and Cultural Difference," in *Alternative Shakespeares*, ed. Terence Hawkes, vol. 2 (New York: Routledge, 1996), 164–91.

[72] See Rezek, "The Racialization of Print."

[73] Ta-Nehisi Coates, *Between the World and Me* (New York: Random House, 2015), 7.

thought has "conceive[d] of identity … in terms of the relation between similar beings." European identity has expressed itself as an "us" and "them" dialectic, rather than a world to which all belong equally. In my argument, as in Mbembe's narrative, the European "us" comes to terms with itself by relation to the "them" of the non-European other. In the case of printing technology, this identity takes the form not (or not yet) of an externalized difference located in the body but of a culturally marked distinction between those who have and use the "art of printing" and those who do not. The art's racework thus functions as a premise for coloniality, cultural superiority, and Eurocentrism.

As we have already seen, premodern writers linked the art of printing with Europe's very identity. This link would grow increasingly strong in the period, even when writers seem to go out of their way to mention it. For instance, Thomas Blundeville paints a picture of Europe's resources:

> the soyle thereof is verie fruitfull both for corne and Wine, and hath manie nauigable Floods stored with plentie of Fish. It hath most excellent Fountaines, and hotte bathes, great mines of Golde, of Siluer, copper, Tinne, Lead, and Iron. The inhabitants doe exercise as well nowe as they haue done in times past the Art military, and it hath manie learned men verie skilful in all sciences, and in Mechanicall artes, they were the inuenters of Artillerie, of Gunpowder, and of the noble Arte of printing, and of making artificiall dials and horologies.[74]

A description that begins with soil ends with ink and the measurement of time (horology).[75] Printing is the only "noble" art in a list that makes Europe Europe. While Blundeville lists the press with other mechanical arts, William Symonds traces its relationship to loftier cultural markers:

> Vpon the ruine of the Empire of Constantinople, the knowledge of the Greeke tongue is brought and spread all ouer the Latin Europe, from whence it had exiled 700. yeeres. About this time was perfected the late inuented laudable art of printing, the art of arts, and science of sciences, a treasure of wisdome and knowledge to be desired. This leaping as it were out of the dennes of darkenes, doth enrich and enlighten the world: vertue contained in infinit bookes, onely found at Paris and Athens, knowne to very few, was by this art manifested to all nations, and kindreds and tongues, and people.[76]

---

[74] Blundeville, *M. Blundevile His Exercises Containing Sixe Treatises*, sig. Kk2r. STC 3146.
[75] The measurement of time has been linked with modernity. Lupton, *Reading and the Making of Time in the Eighteenth Century*; Aleida Assmann, *Is Time out of Joint?: On the Rise and Fall of the Modern Time Regime*, trans. Sarah Clift (Ithaca: Cornell University Press, 2020).
[76] Symonds, *Pisgah Euangelica*, sig. Ff4v. STC 23592.

Symonds connects the dots between the 1453 fall of Constantinople to the Ottoman Empire (itself a key event in the European racial imagination), the European Renaissance, and the "laudable" art of printing, which in turn yields an opposition of light and dark and a vision of Europe as the light to "all nations [...] and people." Thomas Jackson likewise notes that God "revealed the Art of Printing, a little before our fore-fathers departed out of Babylon [i.e., Constantinople]." Printing thus: renewed the face of the earth again, and brought the light of ingenious and sacred Literature forth of the Chaos of Barbarity, obscurity, and fruitless curiosity, wherein it had been long inclosed."[77] Again, the art of printing effects a rhetorical separation between order and chaos, civilization and barbarism, and light and darkness.[78] In another contrast with the classical past, Joannes Jonstonus observes that "we [i.e., Europe] have many helps the Antients wanted. Amongst which the Art of Printing is the chief." As a result, "now in the principall parts of Europe, there are most learned Men."[79] John Trapp makes a similar appeal, writing how God "vouchsafed to mankinde the knowledge of the Art of Printing" and how, "shortly after, there were printed at Paris, Antwerp, Venice, and divers other places, the works of sundry learned men, stirred up by God to fetch the Arts back out of banishment."[80] The pan-European embrace of printing technology makes possible a general return of exiled knowledge. These explicit appeals build on the examples we have already seen, identifying Europe with its possession of the "art of printing.[81]

If printing fashioned Europe's sense of itself – as in a "mirror," in Mbembe' words – then China was the most prominent image reflected. While the controversial question for earlier writers had to do with who (Gutenberg or Fust) and where (Mainz or Haarlem) printing was invented, later writers also invoked the question of whether and to what extent the people of China first possessed the "art of printing." Recall, for instance, Moxon's opening statement in *Mechanick Exercises*: "*I shall say some-what of its Original Invention; I mean here in* Europe, *not of theirs in* China *and other Eastern Countries, who (by general assent) have had it for many hundreds*

[77] Thomas Jackson, *A Collection of the Works of That Holy Man and Profound Divine, Thomas Iackson* (London, 1653), sig. Tv. Wing J88.

[78] See Hall, *Things of Darkness.*

[79] Joannes Jonstonus, *An History of the Constancy of Nature* (London, 1657), sig. F4r. Wing J1016.

[80] Trapp, *A Commentary or Exposition upon the Four Evangelists, and the Acts of the Apostles,* sig. Aaa2v. Wing T2040.

[81] Other examples include Robert Fage, *A Description of the Whole World with Some General Rules Touching the Use of the Globe* (London, 1658), sig. C2v-3r. Wing F83; Thomas Porter, *A Compendious View, or Cosmographical, and Geographical Description of the Whole World* (London, 1659), sig. C4v-5r. Wing P2998A.

of years, though their Invention is very different from ours[.]"[82] Moxon hints at a broad awareness ("by general assent") that printing occurred in China long before it appeared in Europe, and that Chinese language printing worked differently than the hand press with movable type.[83] Adams brilliantly identifies Moxon's claims as "an early version of Edward Said's notion of Orientalism, in which the hegemony of European culture is 'a collective notion identifying "us" Europeans as against all "those" non-Europeans.'"[84] Moxon is careful to distinguish the "art of printing" as a European possession from printing technology more broadly.

In this respect, Moxon is hardly alone. Many writers situated Europe's "art of printing" alongside China's in a variety of ways. In Richard Hakluyt's *Principal Navigations* (1599), we find a "description of China" discussing the "industry of that people." To a longer list, the writer adds "the arte of Printing, albeit their letters be in maner infinite and most difficult" because of the abundance of figures in Chinese script.[85] Peter Heylyn remains agnostic concerning printing's exact origins: "as for Printing, whether Iohn Gertrudenberg learned it of the Chinoys [i.e., Chinese]; or whether good Inventions like good wits do sometimes jumpe, I dare not determine: sure I am that hee first taught it in Europe; and as some say, in the yeare 1440."[86] More confidently, John Speed notes that China "had the Art of Printing many hundred yeares before it was knowne among us," John Trapp that the "Chinois indeed tell us, that they had the Art of Printing long before," and Thomas Porter that "The Art of Printing is more ancient with them [i.e., the Chinese], then in Europe."[87] Thomas Herbert writes that the Chinese people "challenge [i.e., lay claim to] the first art of Printing and inuention of Guns[.]"[88] John Webb lines up Chinese and Christian history by asserting that "The

[82] Moxon, *Mechanick Exercises*, sig. Br-v. See also Misson, "Typography," 92–96.

[83] See Barbier, *Gutenberg's Europe*, 83–105.

[84] Adams, "Inlaid with Inkie Spots of Jet," 93.

[85] Anonymous, *The Principal Nauigations, Voyages, Traffiques and Discoueries of the English Nation Made by Sea or Ouer-Land* (London, 1599), sig. Hhh4v. STC 12626a. See also Mary C. Fuller, *Lines Drawn across the Globe: Reading Richard Hakluyt's Principal Navigations*, McGill-Queen's Studies in the History of Ideas 90 (Montreal: McGill-Queen's University Press, 2023).

[86] Peter Heylyn, *Mikrokosmos A Little Description of the Great World* (Oxford, 1625), sig. Vv3v. STC 13277.

[87] John Speed, *A Prospect of the Most Famous Parts of the Vvorld* (London, 1646), sig. Vv. Wing S4882A; John Trapp, *A Commentary or Exposition upon the Books of Ezra, Nehemiah, Esther, Job and Psalms* (London, 1657), sig. Yy2v. Wing T2041; Porter, *A Compendious View, or Cosmographical, and Geographical Description of the Whole World*, sig. D6r-v. Wing P2998A.

[88] Thomas Herbert Sir, *A Relation of Some Yeares Trauaile Begunne Anno 1626. Into Afrique and the Greater Asia, Especially the Territories of the Persian Monarchie: And Some Parts of the Orientall Indies, and Iles Adiacent* (London, 1634), sig. Dd3v. STC 13190.

Art of Printing [...] had its original among them [i.e., the Chinese peo-ple] about the fiftieth yeare after CHRIST," while another writer calls the people of China a "most curious people, from whom this Western world received their art of Printing, Needle-work, and other rare Sciences; and now doe receive from us that most excellent and supernatural science to know the onely true God, and Jesus Christ whom he hath sent."[89] I quote rather than cite these to emphasize the explicitness with which writers distinguished European from Chinese printing.

Although the above examples attest to China's earlier possession of printing, the last one hints at a dialectic or exchange, in which Europe "received" printing and gives Christianity back in return. However explic-itly, these writers forge a sense of European identity by way of the "art of printing," a phrase that measures similarity and difference alike. Johannes Nieuhof elaborates this dialectic when he writes that the Chinese people:

> have made no small progress in several Sciences, by their early being acquainted with the Art of Printing: for though those of Europe do therein exceed the Chineses, having reduc'd the same to more exactness and certain Method; yet [... the] use of the Printing-Press was much sooner in China than in Europe[.][90]

China had it earlier, but Europe does it better. The Stationers' Company, having declared that "the Mystery and Art of Printing is of publike and great Importance, and ought to be held worthy of extraordinary regard and consideration," notes that "China having had the use of Printing and Guns, long before they were invented in Europe, makes no doubt to mag-nifie her self, as seeing with two Eyes; whereas Europe (as she pretends) sees but with one."[91] The chip on the Stationers' shoulder arises from the implied inferiority of Europe's expertise in printing and guns. Finally and most memorably, Robert Heath defends the claim that "the famous Art of Printing is the worst that ever was invented" in his book of paradoxes (i.e., rhetorical exercises defending a series of paradoxical statements):

> VVHether the Germans first borrowed this Invention from the Chineses, or whether amongst the Germans (who undoubtedly lay best claim to it)

---

[89] J. J., *The Resurrection of Dead Bones, or, The Conversion of the Jewes* (London, 1655), sig. B6r-v. Wing J19; John Webb, *An Historical Essay Endeavoring a Probability That the Language of the Empire of China Is the Primitive Language* (London, 1669), sig. H7v-8r. Wing W1202.

[90] Johannes Nieuhof, *An Embassy from the East-India Company of the United Provinces, to the Grand Tartar Cham, Emperor of China Deliver'd by Their Excellencies, Peter de Goyer and Jacob de Keyzer, at His Imperial City of Peking* (London, 1673), sig. Ssr-v. Wing N1153.

[91] Anonymous, *To the High Court of Parliament: The Humble Remonstrance of the Company of Stationers, London.* (London, 1643), sig. Ar-v. Wing P425.

Iohn Gutenberg the Knight of Mentz, or Iohn Fust a Moguntine, was the first Inventor thereof, it matters not: this is certain, that since the time it was first known experimentally, (which was Anno Salutis 1466) there has been more dissention in Learning and Religion, throughout all Christendom, and more Wars, the necessary Sequels of those Jars, then were known in the Primitive, nay, for all those fourteen hundred years before.[92]

This paradox braids together all the threads of this chapter. Heath wryly invokes the Gutenberg/Fust debate and gestures at the Chinese origins of printing, then asserts (tongue in cheek) that the very spread of learning celebrated by so many writers has in fact yielded "dissention" and "Wars." The break with the "Primitive" past that Bacon and others attribute to the "art of printing" becomes, in this paradox, an open door to conflict and violence. If one sincerely wanted to argue that printing harmed European society, one could hardly do worse than this. I want to emphasize, however, how this passage highlights the extent of Europe's identification with printing's features in distinction to printing's Chinese origins. Heath shows us, in other words, the extent to which printing has become one of the central markers of European identity by way of a relation to and departure from its Chinese past, a temporalization of racial difference that pivots upon a kind of orientalism.

In the mid-seventeenth century, the accumulated associations around the "art of printing," which we have been exploring in this chapter, coalesce into a clear expression of European identity as a form of technological superiority: writers invoke the "art of printing" as a measure of cultural and ethnic difference. Such a connection would culminate, much later, in what we now call modern European whiteness.[93] The sheer number of examples, admittedly tiresome but necessary, shows the extent of this identification. Christian Raue expresses a desire to evangelize the continents of Africa and Asia:

Couldst thou but love the men of Asia and Africa, (as well as thou dost their Sylkes and pretious Stones,) give them the Ebrew, and Arabic bible, teach them thy Art of printing and receave from them their Arabic, and Ethiopic rare Jewells of bookes, what joy would arise in the heart of thy children, and what a thankfull minde wouldst thou finde amongst these ignorant men.[94]

---

[92] Robert Heath, *Paradoxical Assertions and Philosophical Problems Full of Delight and Recreation for All Ladies and Youthful Fancies* (London, 1659), sig. Drff.W ing H1341. On Heath's use of "jars" to mean "dissention," see *OED* "jar n1."

[93] See Painter, *The History of White People*.

[94] Christian Raue, *A Discovrse of the Orientall Tongves* (London, 1649), sig. E111r. Wing R311.

Raue's belief in the power of European printing unspools into colonialist condescension, punctuated by the imagined gratitude of the people of
Asia and Africa. Similarly, Tommaso Campanella writes that the people
of Persia "may indeed be instructed in the Art of Printing, and other Arts,
that are in use among the Christians: to the end they may thereby have the
Christians in admiration, and high esteem."[95] John Ogilby likewise writes
that in Persia, the art of writing is held in great esteem, "they being utterly
ignorant in the Art of Printing" – a backhanded compliment.[96] Johann
Comenius explains how Bohemia (in the modern day Czech Republic)
became part of Europe:

> the art of Printing, lately found out in Germany, began to grow into fre-
> quent use [....] The Bohemians therefore resolving to use this so great a gift
> of God, mostly to salvation of souls, about this time procured the Bible to
> be printed (the first of all Europe again) at Venice, in their Mother tongue:
> A little after, the Copies being dispersed at Noriberg once and again. At last
> setting up a Printing-house at home, they made many impressions, espe-
> cially at Prague, Bolislavia and Kralice in Moravia.[97]

Samuel Collins describes the expansion of printing to Russia: "in the year
of our Lord, 1560. the Art of Printing was brought in amongst them [...]
and a Latin School also was erected[.]"[98] Another writer explains how the
people of Java "know not the Art of Printing, but they paint their own
Characters exactly well, which are rather Figures then Letters."[99] Paul
Rycaut notes that, in the Ottoman Empire, "The Art of Printing [...] is
absolutely prohibited amongst them, because it may give a beginning to
that sublety of Learning which is inconsistent with, as well as dangerous to
the grosseness of their Government, and a means to deprive many of their
livelyhood, who gain their bread only by their Pen[.]"[100]

These examples feature writers coordinating "the art of printing" with
social difference. They imply that Europe's possession of the art sets it
apart among nations and peoples, a clear continuation of the process of

---

[95] Tommaso Campanella, *A Discourse Touching the Spanish Monarchy* (London, 1653), sig. Cc2r.
Wing C401.

[96] John Ogilby, *Asia. Being an Accurate Description of Persia, and the Several Provinces Thereof*
(London, 1673), sig. I4v. Wing O166.

[97] Johann Amos Comenius, *An Exhortation of the Churches of Bohemia to the Church of England*
(London, 1661), sig. Gr. Wing C5507.

[98] Samuel Collins, *The Present State of Russia in a Letter to a Friend at London* (London, 1671), sig. Bv.
Wing C5385.

[99] Adam Olearius, *The Voyages and Travells of the Ambassadors Sent by Frederick, Duke of Holstein, to
the Great Duke of Muscovy and the King of Persia* (London, 1669), sig. Qqq4r. Wing O270.

[100] Paul Rycaut Sir, *The Present State of the Ottoman Empire* (London, 1668), sig. E4v-Fr. Wing R2413.

distinction described earlier. Just as one set of writers negotiated European printing with respect to Chinese printing, another negotiates Europe's distinct possession of printing with others' lack of it. Both sets forge a clear connection between the "art of printing" and the racialized rhetoric of European colonialism. While this rhetoric hardly counts as the only prominent form of premodern racework, its pervasiveness, along with the subsequent ideology of technological superiority in European modernity, merits attention. Printing became white when the "art of printing" manifested itself as European identity.

The Art of Printing, Turning over a New Leaf

This book has combined the study of material texts with scaled philology to argue that books and book technologies shaped premodern English culture in and through language. It is equally true, however, that I have argued that premodern English culture shaped the perception of books and book technologies in and through language. As Jeff Dolven writes, "metaphorical uses of the book ... feed back to affect its material production."[101] Dolven articulates at the level of metaphor what we have just explored as a matter of racialization. The bookish lexicon both expresses and forms a culture, in turn reinforcing that culture's relationship with the books from which the lexicon derives. The process is never simple, rarely linear, always layered, and occasionally legible in the cultural record – as it is in the "art of printing" and indeed all of this book's examples.

I want to return, in conclusion, to Joseph Moxon's explanation of his dictionary of printing terms discussed in Chapter 2. Here again is Moxon's gloss on his glosses (see also Figure 2.1):

> I do not exhibit this as a *Dictionary* so perfect, that all the obstruce Words and Phrases used among *Printers, Letter-cutters* and *Founders* are here exposed [.... S]uch Words and Phrases as have escaped my Consideration, will, I hope, be discovered by some Printer, or others, that may have a kindness for Posterity; not only in this Trade, but in all Trades and Faculties whatsoever: that so a *Dictionary* may in time be completed, that may render so great a number of Words used in *England* by *English-men* intelligible; which now for want of a proper Repository to store them in, seem not only Aliens to our Nation, but barbarous to our Understandings.[102]

---

[101] Dolven, "The Early Modern Book as Metaphor," 532.
[102] Moxon, *Mechanick Exercises*, sig. Ccc2r.

Moxon expresses a desire for a dictionary of all dictionaries – an ency-clopedia – that records and defines the language of "all Trades and Faculties whatsoever." This desire to normalize and externalize all knowledge marks yet another habit of colonialism and its umbrella project, modernity.[103] Given the foregoing discussion of the "art of printing," it is not difficult to recognize the emerging racialization in Moxon's appeal to the disjunction between "Words used in *England* by *English-men*" and words that function as "Aliens to our Nation," not to mention as "barbarous."

At the same time, however, it does not undermine the critique of Moxon's participation in colonialist discourse to observe his keen aware-ness of the relevance of bookish words. Moxon wants to make print-ing house terms accessible to as broad a constituency as possible because the mechanics of knowledge-making matter to "Posterity." He remains deeply sensitive to the intelligibility of printing practices because – then and now, for better and worse – the language of books gives writers and readers a way to locate themselves in the world, indeed to make the world legible. Figurative uses of books provide, as Dolven writes, "a way of understanding how we bear ourselves towards reality."[104] *How the World Became a Book in Shakespeare's England* has gone further, arguing that the premodern vocabularies of books not only expressed that understanding but made it possible.

The emergent whiteness of the "art of printing," by way of Moxon's dictionary, has two related implications for this book's overall argu-ment. The first concerns the nature of the evidence presented. Moxon describes the problem with creating his maximalist dictionary as one of information storage and retrieval. He lacks "a proper Repository to store [the words] in." As it happens, just such a repository now exists: Early English Books Online (EEBO) stores many thousands of image sets and full-text transcriptions, a "kindness for Posterity" if ever there was one. In a peculiar sense, my book is an attempt to realize Moxon's vision of making the bookish lexicon "intelligible," though not the technical lexicon he has in mind. Precisely because it is an archive of printed English texts, however, EEBO normalizes a white, male, literate perspective – the perspective that is also the most immediate beneficiary of the distinction built into the phrase "the art of printing." Even as I have drawn heavily though not exclusively on EEBO, therefore, I have

---

[103] See Chapter 2.
[104] Dolven, "The Early Modern Book as Metaphor," 543.

also taken seriously the mandate for book history research (in Adams's recent words) to "reflect on how it may reinforce, however unintentionally, structures and assumptions guided by whiteness (and maleness) in both research practice and exclusionary behavior."[105] It is my conviction that there are enough premodern divergences and dissonances in the many hundreds of examples cited in this book to decompose such structures and assumptions.

The second implication flows from the first and pertains to the very title and animating intellectual impulses of this book. The "world" that becomes a book is not a universal or neutral one. It is not a *totalized* world, to return to a key term from Chapter 1, and that is precisely the point of demodernizing the symbolic value of books. Like the phrase "Shakespeare's England," which primarily provides a heuristic approximation of the geographical and historical parameters of this project's inquiry, the "world" conjured into existence by the bookish lexicon is, for all its complexity and multifariousness, a function of the same white, male, and literate social formation that grows around "the art of printing." Aware of this, I have done my best to emulate Stephen Best, whose description of research on the black archival past might also be true of the white one made accessible in EEBO: "we call these [archival] objects into being, then, and can feel held by them without owning or being owned in terms of identity, identification, or the need for it all to add up to something in terms of a collective identity."[106] I have tried to hear what is both strange and familiar about the premodern English use of bookish words.

By most accounts, we are now living after the end of what Bruno Latour calls the "modern parenthesis," the two or three centuries of European modernity. If knowledge of the world inside this parenthesis was like reading an encyclopedia – a book symbolizing totality, disembodiment, rationality, and unity – then knowledge outside of it is like reading, say, a quarto *Book of Common Prayer* interleaved with blank pages and bound with another quarto book, marked up and down with marginal annotations, covered with a bespoke binding and fore-edge illustration, and occasionally used by members of a household as a doorstop and devotional object. The book is a whole, but also a set of parts; it can be a totality but also a fragmented assembly. An undercurrent of my argument in this

---

[105] Adams, "'Inlaid with Inkie Spots of Jet,'" 83.
[106] Stephen Best, *None like Us: Blackness, Belonging, Aesthetic Life*, Theory Q (Durham: Duke University Press, 2018), 131.

study is that there is a resemblance but not identity between the premodern world-as-a-book and the postmodern world in which I write. The detotalized book I just conjured has more in common with the internet than either has with the encyclopedia. We must therefore persist in studying the literature and culture of the premodern past to orient ourselves better now. Otherwise, we will find ourselves out of sorts.

Bibliography

Early Texts

Adams, Thomas. *A Commentary or, Exposition Vpon the Diuine Second Epistle Generall, Written by the Blessed Apostle St. Peter.* London, 1633.

Adams, Thomas. *God's Anger; and, Man's Comfort Two Sermons.* London, 1652.

Adams, Thomas. *The Deuills Banket Described in Foure Sermons.* London, 1614.

Alemán, Mateo. *The Rogue: Or The Life of Guzman de Alfarache.* London, 1623.

Alley, William. *Ptōchomuseion [Sic]. The Poore Mans Librarie.* London, 1565.

Alsop, Vincent. *Melius Inquirendum.* London, 1678.

Ames, William. *A Reply to Dr. Mortons Generall Defence of Three Nocent Ceremonies.* Amsterdam, 1622.

Ammianus Marcellinus. *The Roman Historie Containing Such Acts and Occurrents as Passed under Constantius, Iulianus, Iovianus, Valentinianus, and Valens, Emperours.* London, 1609.

Anonymous. *A Counter-Poyson Modestly Written for the Time, to Make Aunswere to the Obiections and Reproches, Wherewith the Aunswerer to the Abstract, Would Disgrace the Holy Discipline of Christ.* London, 1584.

Anonymous. *A Myrroure for Magistrates.* London, 1559.

Anonymous. *A Prymer in Englyshe with Certeyn Prayers [et] Godly Meditations.* London, 1534.

Anonymous. *A Strange Metamorphosis of Man, Transformed into a Vvildernesse Deciphered in Characters.* London, 1634.

Anonymous. *A Supplement to The Morning-Exercise at Cripple-Gate, or, Several More Cases of Conscience Practically Resolved by Sundry Ministers.* London, 1676.

Anonymous. *A Vvord to Lieut. Gen. Cromwel and Two Vvords for the Setling of the King, Parliament and Kingdom.* London, 1647.

Anonymous. *An Exact Abridgement of the Records in the Tower of London from the Reign of King Edward the Second, unto King Richard the Third.* London, 1657.

Anonymous. *Against the Detestable Masse, and More Then Abhominable Popishe Heresie.* London, 1566.

Anonymous. *Biblia the Byble, That Is, the Holy Scrypture of the Olde and New Testament, Faithfully Translated in to Englyshe.* London, 1535.

Anonymous. *Biddle Dispossest, or, His Scripture Perverting Catechism Reformed by Scripture.* London, 1654.

Anonymous. *Caltha Poetarum: Or The Bumble Bee*. London, 1599.

Anonymous. *Certain Most Godly, Fruitful, and Comfortable Letters of Such True Saintes and Holy Martyrs of God*. London, 1564.

Anonymous. *[Dictes or Sayengis of the Philosophhres]*. London, 1477.

Anonymous. *Eikōn Alēthinē. The Pourtraiture of Truths Most Sacred Majesty Truly Suffering, Though Not Solely*. London, 1649.

Anonymous. *Eniaytos Terastios Mirabilis Annus, or, The Year of Prodigies and Wonders Being a Faithful and Impartial Collection of Severall Signs That Have Been Seen in the Heavens, in the Earth, and in the Waters*. London, 1661.

Anonymous. *Funerall Elegies, Vpon the Most Vntimely Death of the Honourable and Most Hopefull, Mr. Iohn Stanhope*. London, 1624.

Anonymous. *Here Begynneth a Lytell Treatyse for to Lerne Englysshe and Frensshe*. London, 1497.

Anonymous. *Here Begynneth a Lytyll Treatyse Schortely Compyled and Called Ars Moriendi*. London, 1491.

Anonymous. *Here Begynneth the Boke Intituled Eracles, and Also of Godefrey of Boloyne*. London, 1481.

Anonymous. *Hier Begynneth the Book Callid the Myrrour of the Worlde*. London, 1481.

Anonymous. *Kaina Kai Palaia Things New and Old, or, A Store-House of Similies, Sentences, Allegories, Apophthegms, Adagies, Apologues, Divine, Morall, Politicall, &c*. London, 1658.

Anonymous. *Lachrymæ Musarum The Tears of the Muses*. London, 1649.

Anonymous. *Lady Alimony, or, The Alimony Lady an Excellent, Pleasant, New Comedy, Duly Authorized, Daily Acted and Frequently Followed*. London, 1659.

Anonymous. *Methinks the Poor Town Has Been Troubled Too Long, or, A Collection of the Several Songs Now in Mode Either at the Court or Theatres*. s.l., 1673.

Anonymous. *Palmerin D'Oliua The Mirrour of Nobilitie, Mappe of Honor, Anotamie of Rare Fortunes, Heroycall President of Loue*. London, 1588.

Anonymous. *Salmacis, Lyrian & Sylvia, Forsaken Lydia, the Rape of Helen, a Comment Thereon, with Severall Other Poems and Translations*. London, 1651.

Anonymous. *The Booke of Meery. Riddles*. London, 1629.

Anonymous. *The Booke of the Common Prayer and Administracion of the Sacramentes, and Other Rites and Ceremonies of the Churche: After the vse of the Churche of England*. London, 1549.

Anonymous. *The Confessyon of the Fayth of the Germaynes Exhibited to the Moste Victorious Emperour Charles the. v*. London, 1536.

Anonymous. *The Decoy Duck: Together with the Discovery of the Knot in the Dragons Tayle Called &c*. London, 1642.

Anonymous. *The Golden Meane Lately Written, as Occasion Serued, to a Great Lord*. London, 1613.

Anonymous. *The. Holie. Bible. Conteynyng the Olde Testament and the Newe*. London, 1568.

Anonymous. *The Morning Exercise [at] Cri[Ppleg]Ate, or, Several Cases of Conscience Practically Resolved by Sundry Ministers*. London, 1661.

Anonymous. *The newe testamente both Latine and Englyshe ech correspondent to the other after the vulgare texte, communely called S. Ieroms.* London, 1538.

Anonymous. *The Principal Nauigations, Voyages, Traffiques and Discoueries of the English Nation Made by Sea or Ouer-Land.* London, 1599.

Anonymous. *The Psalmes of Dauid Truly Opened and Explaned by Paraphrasis, According to the Right Sense of Euerie Psalme.* London, 1581.

Anonymous. *The Spirit of Christ, and the Spirit of the Apostles and the Spirit of the Martyrs Is Arisen, Which Beareth Testimony against Swearing and Oaths.* London, 1661.

Anonymous. *The Treasurie of Auncient and Moderne Times.* London, 1613.

Anonymous. *Theatrum Chemicum Britannicum· Containing Severall Poeticall Pieces of Our Famous English Philosophers, Who Have Written the Hermetique Mysteries in Their Owne Ancient Language.* London, 1652.

Anonymous. *[Thystorye and Lyf of the Noble and Crysten Prynce Charles the Grete Kynge of Frauuce].* London, 1485.

Anonymous. *To the High Court of Parliament: The Humble Remonstrance of the Company of Stationers, London.* London, 1643.

Anonymous. *To the Honourable House of Commons Assembled in Parliament.* London, 1621.

Anonymous. *To the Right Honorable, the Knights, Citizens, and Burgesses, Now Assembled in the High Court of Parliament. The Petition of the Masters and Workmen Printers of London.* London, 1642.

Anonymous. *Two Guides to a Good Life The Genealogy of Vertue and the Nathomy of Sinne.* London, 1604.

Anonymous. *VVits A.B.C. or A Centurie of Epigrams.* London, 1608.

Anthony, Charles. *Gods Presence Mans Comfort: Or, Gods Invisibilitie Manifested unto Mans Capacitie.* London, 1646.

Ascham, Roger. *The Scholemaster or Plaine and Perfite Way of Teachyng Children, to Vnderstand, Write, and Speake, the Latin Tong.* London, 1570.

Attersoll, William. *A Commentarie Vpon the Epistle of Saint Paule to Philemon.* London, 1612.

Austen, Ralph. *The Spirituall Use of an Orchard, or Garden of Fruit-Trees.* Oxford, 1657.

Bacon, Francis. *Essayes Religious meditations. Places of perswasion and disswasion. Seene and allowed.* London, 1597.

Bacon, Francis. *Francis Bacon: The New Organon.* Edited by Lisa Jardine and Michael Silverthorne. Translated by Michael Silverthorne. Cambridge University Press, 2000.

Bacon, Francis. *Franciscy de Verulamio, summi Angliæ cancellarij instauratio magna.* London, 1620.

Bale, John. *The Pageant of Popes Contayninge the Lyues of All the Bishops of Rome, from the Beginning of Them to the Yeare of Grace 1555.* London, 1574.

Ball, William. *A Briefe Treatise Concerning the Regulating of Printing.* London, 1651.

Balzac, Jean-Louis Guez, seigneur de. *Nevv Epistles of Mounsieur de Balzac.* London, 1638.

Bankes, Thomas. *A Verie Godly, Learned, and Fruitfull Sermon against the Bad Spirits of Malignitie, Malice, and Vnmercifulnesse.* London, 1586.

Barker, Peter. *A Iudicious and Painefull Exposition Vpon the Ten Commandements.* London, 1624.

Barlow, William. *An Answer to a Catholike English-Man.* London, 1609.

Barnes, Thomas. *The Court of Conscience: Or, Iosephs Brethrens Iudgement Barre.* London, 1623.

Barry, Lording. *Ram-Alley: Or Merrie-Trickes.* London, 1611.

Basset, Robert. *Curiosities: Or the Cabinet of Nature.* London, 1637.

Bastard, Thomas. *Chrestoleros Seuen Bookes of Epigrames.* London, 1598.

Baxter, Nathaniel. *Sir Philip Sydneys Ouránia That Is, Endimions Song and Tragedie.* London, 1606.

Baxter, Richard. *Richard Baxter's Dying Thoughts upon Phil. I, 23 Written for His Own Life and the Latter Times of His Corporal Pains and Weakness.* London, 1683.

Baxter, Richard. *The Divine Appointment of the Lords Day Proved as a Separated Day for Holy Worship, Especially in the Church Assemblies, and Consequently the Cessation of the Seventh Day Sabbath.* London, 1671.

Beard, Thomas. *Antichrist the Pope of Rome: Or, the Pope of Rome Is Antichrist Proued in Two Treatises.* London, 1625.

Beaumont, Francis, and John Fletcher. *Comedies and Tragedies.* London, 1647.

Beaumont, Francis, and John Fletcher. *Fifty Comedies and Tragedies.* London, 1679.

Becon, Thomas. *A New Postil Conteinyng Most Godly and Learned Sermons.* London, 1566.

Becon, Thomas. *A Pleasaunt Newe Nosegaye Full of Many Godly and Swete Floures.* London, 1543.

Benedetto, da Mantova. *The Benefite That Christians Receiue by Iesus Christ Crucifyed.* London, 1573.

Bernard, Richard. *A Double Catechisme One More Large, Following the Order of the Common Authorized Catechisme, and an Exposition Thereof.* Cambridge, 1607.

Bernard, Richard. *Christian See to Thy Conscience or a Treatise of the Nature, the Kinds and Manifold Differences of Conscience.* London, 1631.

Billingsley, Nicholas. *A Treasury of Divine Raptures.* London, 1667.

Billingsley, Nicholas. *Brachy-Martyrologia, or, A Breviary of All the Greatest Persecutions Which Have Befallen the Saints and People of God from the Creation to Our Present Times.* London, 1657.

Bilson, Thomas. *The Perpetual Gouernement of Christes Church.* London, 1593.

Bloys, William. *Adam in His Innocencie.* London, 1638.

Blundeville, Thomas. *M. Blundevile His Exercises Containing Sixe Treatises.* London, 1594.

Boaistuau, Pierre. *Theatrum Mundi the Theatre or Rule of the World.* London, 1566.

Boethius. *Boecius de Consolacione Philosophie.* London, 1478.

Bourne, Immanuel. *The Anatomie of Conscience Or a Threefold Reuelation of Those Three Most Secret Bookes: 1. The Booke of Gods Prescience. 2. The Booke of Mans Conscience. 3. The Booke of Life.* London, 1623.

Boyle, Robert. *Some Considerations Touching the Vsefulnesse of Experimental Naturall Philosophy.* Oxford, 1663.

Boyle, Robert. *The Excellency of Theology Compar'd with Natural Philosophy (as Both Are Objects of Men's Study).* London, 1674.

Boys, John. *An Exposition of the Festiuall Epistles and Gospels Vsed in Our English Liturgie Together with a Reason Why the Church Did Chuse the Same.* London, 1615.

Boys, John. *An Exposition of the Proper Psalmes Vsed in Our English Liturgie Together with a Reason Why the Church Did Chuse the Same.* London, 1616.

Bradford, John. *The Complaynt of Veritie.* London, 1559.

Bradshaw, William. *A Discourse of the Sinne against the Holy Ghost.* London, 1640.

Brasier, Richard. *A Godly Wil and Confession of the Christian Faythe.* London, 1551.

Brathwaite, Richard. *History Surveyed in a Brief Epitomy.* London, 1651.

Brathwaite, Richard. *The Good Vvife: Or, A Rare One amongst Women.* London, 1618.

Breton, Nicholas. *The Court and Country.* London, 1618.

Brett, Arthur. *A Demonstration How the Latine Tongue May Be Learn't with Far Greater Ease and Speed Then Commonly It Is.* London, 1669.

Bridges, John. *The Supremacie of Christian Princes Ouer All Persons throughout Theor Dominions.* London, 1573.

Brightman, Thomas. *A Revelation of the Apocalyps.* Amsterdam, 1611.

Brinckmair, L. *The Vvarnings of Germany By Wonderfull Signes, and Strange Prodigies Seene in Divers Parts of That Countrey of Germany, Betweene the Yeare 1618. and 1638.* London, 1638.

Brome, Alexander. *Songs and Other Poems.* London, 1664.

Brome, Richard. *A Joviall Crew, or, The Merry Beggars Presented in a Comedie at Drury-Lane, in the Yeer 1641 / Written by Richard Brome.* London, 1652.

Broughton, Hugh. *A Require of Agreement to the Groundes of Divinitie Studie Wherin Great Scholers Falling, & Being Caught of Iewes Disgrace the Gospel: & Trap Them to Destruction.* Middelburg, 1611.

Browne, Edward. *A Description of an Annuall Vvorld.* London, 1641.

Browne, H. *A Map of the Microcosme, or, A Morall Description of Man Newly Compiled into Essayes.* London, 1642.

Browne, Thomas. *The Copie of the Sermon Preached before the Vniversitie at S. Maries in Oxford.* Oxford, 1634.

Browne, Thomas, Sir. *Pseudodoxia Epidemica, or, Enquiries into Very Many Received Tenents and Commonly Presumed Truths.* London, 1646.

Browne, Thomas, Sir. *Religio Medici.* London, 1642.

Buckler, Edward. *A Buckler against the Fear of Death.* London, 1640.

Buckler, Edward. *Midnights Meditations of Death: With Pious and Profitable Observations, and Consolations.* London, 1646.

Bullinger, Heinrich. *An Exhortation to the Ministers of Gods Woord in the Church of Christ, That They Set aside All Mutuall Discord, and in These Latter Dayes and Dangerous Times Purely and with One Concent Preache Vnto the World the Onely True Faith in Christe and Amendement of Life.* London, 1575.

Bunyan, John. *The Resurrection of the Dead and Eternall Judgement.* London, 1665.

Butler, Thomas. *The Little Bible of the Man or the Book of God Opened in Man by the Power of the Lamb*. London, 1649.

Byfield, Nicholas. *A Commentary upon the Three First Chapters of the First Epistle Generall of St. Peter*. London, 1637.

Byfield, Nicholas. *The Rule of Faith, or, An Exposition of the Apostles Creed so Handled as It Affordeth Both Milke for Babes, and Strong Meat for Such as Are at Full Age*. London, 1626.

Cade, Anthony. *A Sermon Necessarie for These Times Shewing the Nature of Conscience*. London, 1639.

Calamy, Edmund. *An Indictment against England Because of Her Selfe-Murdering Divisions*. London, 1645.

Calamy, Edmund. *The Great Danger of Covenant-Refusing, and Covenant-Breaking*. London, 1646.

Calvin, Jean. *An Abridgement of the Institution of Christian Religion Written by M. Ihon Caluin*. London, 1585.

Calvin, Jean. *Foure Godlye Sermons Agaynst the Pollution of Idolatries Comforting Men in Persecutions, and Teachyng Them What Commodities Thei Shal Find in Christes Church*. London, 1561.

Calvin, Jean. *Sermons of Master Iohn Caluin, Vpon the Booke of Iob*. London, 1574.

Calvin, Jean. *The Sermons of M. Iohn Caluin Vpon the Fifth Booke of Moses Called Deuteronomie*. London, 1583.

Campanella, Tommaso. *A Discourse Touching the Spanish Monarchy*. London, 1653.

Carew, Thomas. *Foure Godlie and Profitable Sermons*. London, 1605.

Cartwright, Thomas. *The Second Replie of Thomas Cartwright: Agaynst Maister Doctor Whitgiftes Second Answer, Touching the Churche Discipline*. Heidelberg, 1575.

Caryl, Joseph. *An Exposition with Practicall Observations Continued upon the Eighth, Ninth and Tenth Chapters of the Book of Job*. London, 1647.

Casas, Bartolomé de las. *The Spanish Colonie, or Briefe Chronicle of the Acts and Gestes of the Spaniardes in the West Indies*. London, 1583.

Cavendish, Margaret. *Poems, and Fancies*. London, 1653.

Cavendish, William. *The Country Captaine and the Varietie*. London, 1649.

Chaloner, Edward. *Six Sermons*. London, 1623.

Chapman, George. *Monsieur D'Oliue A Comedie*. London, 1606.

Charron, Pierre. *Of Wisdome*. London, 1608.

Chaucer, Geoffrey. *wHan That Apprill with His Shouris Sote*. London, 1477.

Churchyard, Thomas. *A Pleasaunte Laborinth Called Churchyardes Chance Framed on Fancies, Vttered with Verses, and Writte[n] to Giue Solace to Euery Well Disposed Mynde*. London, 1580.

Cicero, Marcus Tullius. *hEre Begynneth the Prohemye Vpon the Reducynge, Both out of Latyn as of Frensshe in to Our Englyssh Tongue, of the Polytyque Book Named Tullius de Senectute*. London, 1481.

Clare, John. *The Conuerted Iew or Certaine Dialogues Betweene Micheas a Learned Iew and Others, Touching Diuers Points of Religion, Controuerted Betweene the Catholicks and Protestants*, 1630.

Clarke, Samuel. *A Geographicall Description of All the Countries in the Known Vvorld as Also of the Greatest and Famousest Cities and Fabricks Which Have Been, or Are Now Remaining.* London, 1657.

Clarke, Samuel. *A Mirrour or Looking-Glasse Both for Saints and Sinners Held Forth in about Two Thousand Examples.* London, 1654.

Clarke, Samuel. *The Saints Nosegay, or, A Posie of 741 Spirituall Flowers Both Fragrant and Fruitfull, Pleasant and Profitable.* London, 1642.

Cleland, James. *Hērō-Paideia, or The Institution of a Young Noble Man.* Oxford, 1607.

Collins, Samuel. *The Present State of Russia in a Letter to a Friend at London.* London, 1671.

Colman, Walter. *La Dance Machabre or Death's Duell.* London, 1632.

Comenius, Johann Amos. *An Exhortation of the Churches of Bohemia to the Church of England.* London, 1661.

Cooper, Thomas. *The Conuerts First Loue Discerned Iustified, Left and Recouered.* London, 1610.

Cope, Michael. *A Godly and Learned Exposition Vppon the Prouerbes of Solomon.* London, 1580.

Cornwallis, William, Sir. *Essayes.* London, 1600.

Corro, Antonio del. *A Supplication Exhibited to the Most Mightie Prince Philip King of Spain &c.* London, 1577.

Cradocke, Francis. *Wealth Discovered: Or, An Essay upon a Late Expedient for Taking Away All Impositions and Raising a Revenue without Taxes.* London, 1661.

Cragge, John. *A Cabinet of Spirituall Iewells Wherein Man's Misery, God's Mercy, Christ's Treasury, Truth's Prevalency, Errour's Ignominy, Grace's Excellency, a Christian's Duty, the Saint's Glory, Is Set Forth in Eight Sermons.* London, 1657.

Craig, John. *The Mother and the Child A Short Catechisme or Briefe Summe of Religion.* London, 1611.

Crakanthorpe, Richard. *Vigilius Dormitans Romes Seer Overseene.* London, 1631.

Cranmer, Thomas. *An Aunsvvere by the Reuerend Father in God Thomas Archbyshop of Canterbury, Primate of All England and Metropolitane, Vnto a Craftie and Sophisticall Cauillation, Deuised by Stephen Gardiner Doctour of Law, Late Byshop of Winchester Agaynst the True and Godly Doctrine of the Most Holy Sacrament, of the Body and Bloud of Our Sauiour Iesu Christ.* London, 1580.

Crashaw, Richard. *Carmen Deo Nostro, Te Decet Hymnus Sacred Poems.* Paris, 1652.

Crashaw, Richard. *Steps to the Temple Sacred Poems, with Other Delights of the Muses.* London, 1646.

Croll, Oswald. *Philosophy Reformed & Improved in Four Profound Tractates.* London, 1657.

Crowley, Robert. *A Setting Open of the Subtyle Sophistrie of Thomas VVatson Doctor of Diuinitie.* London, 1569.

Culpeper, Thomas. *Morall Discourses and Essayes, upon Severall Select Subjects.* London, 1655.

Culverwel, Nathanael. *Spiritual Opticks, or, A Glasse Discovering the Weaknesse and Imperfection of a Christians Knowledge in This Life.* Cambridge, 1651.

Cumber, John. *A Pleasant Comedie, Called the Tvvo Merry Milke-Maids. Or, the Best Words Weare the Garland*. London, 1620.

Cuningham, William. *The Cosmographical Glasse Conteinyng the Pleasant Principles of Cosmographie, Geographie, Hydrographie, or Nauigation*. London, 1559.

Davenport, Robert. *King Iohn and Matilda a Tragedy*. London, 1655.

Davies, John. *A Scourge for Paper-Persecutors. Or Papers Complaint, Compil'd in Ruthfull Rimes, against the Paper-Spoylers of These Times*. London, 1625.

Davies, John. *Mirum in Modum A Glimpse of Gods Glorie and the Soules Shape*. London, 1602.

Davies, John. *Nosce Teipsum This Oracle Expounded in Two Elegies, 1. Of Humane Knowledge, 2. Of the Soule of Man, and the Immortalitie Thereof*. London, 1599.

Davies, John. *[O Vtinam 1 For Queene Elizabeths Securitie, 2 for Hir Subiects Prosperitie]*. London, 1591.

Davison, Francis. *A Poetical Rapsodie Containing: Diuerse Sonnets, Odes, Elegies, Madrigals, Epigrams, Pastorals, Eglogues, with Other Poems, Both in Rime and Measured Verse*. London, 1611.

Dekker, Thomas. *A Tragi-Comedy: Called, Match Mee in London*. London, 1631.

Dekker, Thomas. *Nevves from Hell Brought by the Diuells Carrier*. London, 1606.

Dekker, Thomas. *Penny-Vvis[e] Pound Foolish*. London, 1631.

Dekker, Thomas. *The Guls Horne-Booke: By T. Deckar*. London, 1609.

Dekker, Thomas. *The Vvonderfull Yeare*. London, 1603.

Deloney, Thomas. *Thomas of Reading. Or, The Sixe Worthy Yeomen of the West*. London, 1612.

Dent, Arthur. *The Plaine Mans Path-Way to Heauen Wherein Euery Man May Clearely See, Whether He Shall Be Saued or Damned*. London, 1606.

Dingley, Robert. *Vox Cæli; or, Philosophical, Historicall, and Theological Observations, of Thunder*. London, 1658.

Donne, John. *Devotions Vpon Emergent Occasions*. London, 1624.

Donne, John. *Iuuenilia or Certaine Paradoxes and Problemes*. London, 1633.

Donne, John. *LXXX Sermons*. London, 1640.

Donne, John. *The First Anniuersarie An Anatomie of the Vvorld*. London, 1612.

Donne, John. *XXVI Sermons*. London, 1661.

Douglas, Robert. *A Phenix, or, The Solemn League and Covenant*. Edinburgh, 1662.

Dove, John. *A Sermon Preached at Pauls Crosse, the 3 of Nouember 1594*. London, 1594.

Dove, John. *An Aduertisement to the English Seminaries, Amd Iesuites Shewing Their Loose Kind of Writing, and Negligent Handling the Cause of Religion, in the Whole Course of Their Workes*. London, 1610.

Downham, George. *Rex Meus Est Deus, or, A Sermon Preached at the Common Place in Christs-Church in the City of Norwich*. London, 1643.

Drayton, Michael. *Ideas Mirrour*. London, 1594.

Du Bartas, Guillaume. *Du Bartas His Deuine Weekes and Workes*. Translated by Josuah Sylvester. London, 1611.

Du Bartas, Guillaume. *Du Bartas His Deuine Weekes and Workes*. London, 1613.

Du Bartas, Guillaume. *The First Day of the Worldes Creation*. London, 1595.

Du Bois, Peter. *Here Begynnethe a Lytyll Treatyse Whiche Is Called the.Xii. Profytes of Trybulacyon*. London, 1499.

Du Laurens, André. *A Discourse of the Preseruation of the Sight: Of Melancholike Diseases; of Rheumes, and of Old Age*. London, 1599.

Du Rosier, Hugues Sureau. *A lamentable discourse of the fall of Hughe Sureau (commonly called Du Rosier) from the truth*. London, 1573.

Dunton, John. *The Art of Living Incognito Being a Thousand Letters on as Many Uncommon Subjects*. London, 1700.

Dunton, John. *The Pilgrims Guide from the Cradle to His Death-Bed with His Glorious Passage from Thence to the New-Jerusalem*. London, 1684.

Durant, John. *Comfort & Counsell for Dejected Soules. Or a Treatise Concerning Spirituall Dejection*. London, 1650.

D'Urfey, Thomas. *The Royalist a Comedy*. London, 1682.

Dury, John. *A Motion Tending to the Publick Good of This Age and of Posteritie*. London, 1642.

Dyke, Jeremiah. *Tvvo Treatises the One of Good Conscicnce; Shewing the Nature, Meanes, Markes, Benefits, and Necessitie Thereof. The Other The Mischiefe and Misery of Scandalls, Both Taken and Given*. London, 1635.

Dymock, Cressy. *An Invention of Engines of Motion Lately Brought to Perfection*. London, 1651.

Eedes, Richard. *Great Salvation by Jesus Christ Tenderd to the Greatest of Sinners and in Particular to Such as Have Been Refusers of It, If God Shall Now at Last Make Them Willing to Receive It*. London, 1659.

Elton, Edward. *An Exposition of the Epistle of St Paule to the Colossians Deliuered in Sundry Sermons*. London, 1615.

Elviden, Edmund. *The Most Excellent and Plesant Metaphoricall Historie of Pesistratus and Catanea*. London, 1570.

Elyot, Thomas. *A Preseruatiue Agaynste Deth*. London, 1545.

Erasmus, Desiderius. *The First Tome or Volume of the Paraphrase of Erasmus Vpon the Newe Testamente*. London, 1548.

Estienne, Henri. *The Stage of Popish Toyes Conteining Both Tragicall and Comicall Partes*. London, 1581.

Euclid. *The Elements of Geometrie of the Most Auncient Philosopher Euclide of Megara*. London, 1570.

Evans, Arise. *A Rule from Heaven, or, VVholsom Counsel to a Distracted State*. London, 1659.

Evans, Edward. *Verba Dierum, or, The Dayes Report of Gods Glory*. Oxford, 1615.

F. H. *An Elogie, and Epitaph, Consecrated to the Ever Sacred Memory of That Most Illustrious, and Incomparable Monarch, Charles, by the Grace of God, of England, Scotland, France, and Ireland, Late King, &c*. London, 1649.

Fage, Robert. *A Description of the Whole World with Some General Rules Touching the Use of the Globe*. London, 1658.

Farindon, Anthony. *LXXX Sermons*. London, 1672.

Fenton, Roger. *A Treatise of Vsurie Diuided into Three Bookes*. London, 1611.

Ferret, John. *Didascaliæ Discourses on Severall Places of the Holy Scriptures.* Amsterdam, 1643.

Feylde, Thomas. *Here Begynneth a Lytel Treatyse Called the Co[n]Traverse Bytwene a Louer and a Jaye.* London, 1527.

Fisher, William. *A Godly Sermon Preached at Paules Crosse the 31. Day of October 1591.* London, 1592.

Fitz-Geffry, Charles. *Deaths Sermon unto the Liuing.* London, 1620.

Fletcher, John. *The Elder Brother a Comedie.* London, 1637.

Fletcher, Phineas. *The Purple Island, or, The Isle of Man.* Cambridge, 1633.

Fletcher, Phineas. *The Way to Blessednes a Treatise or Commentary, on the First Psalme.* London, 1632.

Floyd, John. *The Church Conquerant Ouer Humane Wit.* Saint-Omer, 1638.

Fonseca, Cristóbal de. *Theion Enōtikon, A Discourse of Holy Love, by Which the Soul Is United unto God.* London, 1652.

Fotherby, Martin. *Atheomastix Clearing Foure Truthes, against Atheists and Infidels.* London, 1622.

Foxe, John. *Actes and Monuments.* London, 1583.

Foxe, John. *An Abridgement of the Booke of Acts and Monumentes of the Church.* London, 1589.

Foxe, John. *The Pope Confuted The Holy and Apostolique Church Confuting the Pope.* London, 1580.

Fuller, Thomas. *Ioseph's Partie-Colored Coat.* London, 1640.

Fuller, Thomas. *The Appeal of Iniured Innocence, unto the Religious Learned and Ingenuous Reader in a Controversie Betwixt the Animadvertor, Dr. Peter Heylyn, and the Author, Thomas Fuller.* London, 1659.

Gainsford, Thomas. *The Glory of England, or A True Description of Many Excellent Prerogatiues and Remarkeable Blessings.* London, 1618.

Gardiner, Stephen. *An Explicatio[n] and Assertion of the True Catholique Fayth.* Rouen, 1551.

Garrard, William. *The Arte of Vvarre.* London, 1591.

Gelli, Giovanni Battista. *The Fearfull Fansies of the Florentine Couper.* London, 1568.

Gentillet, Innocent. *A Declaration Concerning the Needfulnesse of Peace to Be Made in Fraunce and the Means for the Making of the Same.* London, 1575.

Glapthorne, Henry. *Wit in a Constable A Comedy.* London, 1640.

Godskall, James. *The Kings Medicine for This Present Yeere.* London, 1604.

Goodman, Godfrey. *The Fall of Man, or the Corruption of Nature, Proued by the Light of Our Naturall Reason.* London, 1616.

Goodwin, John. *Independencie Gods Veritie: Or, The Necessitie of Toleration.* London, 1647.

Goodwin, Philip. *The Evangelicall Communicant in the Eucharisticall Sacrament.* London, 1649.

Gordon, James. *A Treatise of the Vnvvritten Word of God, Commonly Called Traditions.* Saint-Omer, 1614.

Gove, Richard. *The Saints Hony-Comb, Full of Divine Truths.* London, 1652.

Greene, Robert. *Greenes Farewell to Folly*. London, 1591.

Grew, Nehemiah. *The Anatomy of Plants*. London, 1682.

Griffin, Lewis. *Essayes and Characters*. London, 1661.

Guarna, Andrea. *Bellum Grammaticale a Discourse of Great Warand Dissention Betwene Two Worthy Princes, the Noune and the Uerbe, Contending for the Chefe Place or Dignitie in Oration*. London, 1569.

Habington, William. *Castara*. London, 1640.

Hall, John. *A Serious Epistle to Mr. William Prynne*. London, 1649.

Hall, Joseph. *Epistles, the Second Volume*. London, 1608.

Hall, Joseph. *The Vvorks of Ioseph Hall Doctor in Diuinitie, and Deane of Worcester*. London, 1625.

Hall, Thomas. *Chiliasto-Mastix Redivivus, Sive Homesus Enervatus. A Confutation of the Millenarian Opinion*. London, 1657.

Hall, William. *Mortalities Meditation: Or, A Description of Sinne*. London, 1624.

Hamilton, James. *Whereas Some Have given out That by the Act of Councell, Which Explaineth the Confession of Faith Lately Commanded to Be Sworn by His Majestie, to Be Understood of the Confession of Faith*. Edinburgh, 1638.

Hammond, Henry. *Some Profitable Directions Both for Priest & People in Two Sermons Preached before These Evil Times*. London, 1657.

Harding, Thomas. *A Detection of Sundrie Foule Errours, Lies, Sclaunders, Corruptions, and Other False Dealinges, Touching Doctrine, and Other Matters Vttered and Practized by M.Iewel, in a Booke Lately by Him Set Foorth Entituled, a Defence of the Apologie*. Leuven, 1568.

Hardy, Nathaniel. *A Looking-Glasse of Hvmane Frailty Set before Us in a Sermon*. London, 1654.

Hardy, Nathaniel. *Lamentation, Mourning, and Woe Sighed Forth in a Sermon*. London, 1666.

Harington, John. *A Nevv Discourse of a Stale Subiect, Called the Metamorphosis of Aiax*. London, 1596.

Harris, Robert. *Tvvo Sermons: The One Preached before the Iudges of Assize at Oxford. The Other to the Vniuersitie*. London, 1628.

Hart, James. *The Anatomie of Vrines*. London, 1625.

Hartlib, Samuel. *A Description of the Famous Kingdome of Macaria*. London, 1641.

Harvey, Gabriel. *Foure Letters, and Certaine Sonnets*. London, 1592.

Harvey, Richard. *A Theologicall Discourse of the Lamb of God and His Enemies*. London, 1590.

Harvey, Richard. *Philadelphus, or a Defence of Brutes, and the Brutans History*. London, 1593.

Hayman, Robert. *Quodlibets Lately Come Ouer from New Britaniola, Old Newfound-Land Epigrams and Other Small Parcels, Both Morall and Diuine*. London, 1628.

Hayward, John, Sir. *The Second Part of the Sanctuary of a Troubled Soule*. London, 1607.

Heath, Robert. *Paradoxical Assertions and Philosophical Problems Full of Delight and Recreation for All Ladies and Youthful Fancies*. London, 1659.

Herbert, Thomas, Sir. *A Relation of Some Yeares Trauaile Begunne Anno 1626. Into Afrique and the Greater Asia, Especially the Territories of the Persian Monarchie: And Some Parts of the Orientall Indies, and Iles Adiacent.* London, 1634.

Herring, Theodore. *Panacea Christiana, or, A Christians Soueraigne Salue for Euery Soare Deliuered in Two Seuerall Sermons, and Now Digested into One Treatise.* London, 1624.

Heydon, John. *The Harmony of the World Being a Discourse Wherein the Phænomena of Nature Are Consonantly Salved and Adapted to Inferiour Intellects.* London, 1662.

Heylyn, Peter. *Antidotum Lincolniense.* London, 1637.

Heylyn, Peter. *Mikrokosmos A Little Description of the Great World.* Oxford, 1625.

Heywood, Thomas. *Troia Britanica: Or, Great Britaines Troy.* London, 1609.

Hieron, Samuel. *Truths Purchase: Or A Commoditie, Which No Man May Either Neglect to Buie, or Dare to Sell.* Cambridge, 1606.

Hinde, Samuel. *A Free-Vvill Offering, or, a Pillar of Praise with a Thankfull Remembrance for the Receit of Mercies.* London, 1634.

Hoby, Edward. *A Curry-Combe for a Coxe-Combe.* London, 1615.

Hodson, William. *The Divine Cosmographer; or, A Brief Survey of the Whole World Delineated in a Tractate on the VIII Psalme.* Cambridge, 1640.

Hooke, Robert. *Micrographia, or, Some Physiological Descriptions of Minute Bodies Made by Magnifying Glasses.* London, 1665.

Horace. *A Medicinable Morall, That Is, the Two Bookes of Horace His Satyres.* London, 1566.

Hornby, William. *Hornbyes Hornbook Iudge Not Too Rashly, till through All You Looke; If Nothing Then Doth Please You, Burne the Booke.* s.l., 1622.

Howe, John. *The Blessednesse of the Righteous Discoursed from Psal. 17, 15.* London, 1668.

Howell, James. *Londinopolis an Historicall Discourse or Perlustration of the City of London, the Imperial Chamber, and Chief Emporium of Great Britain.* London, 1657.

Huit, Ephraim. *The Anatomy of Conscience, or, The Summe of Pauls Regeneracy.* London, 1626.

Hyperius, Andreas. *The Course of Christianitie.* London, 1579.

J. J. *The Resurrection of Dead Bones, or, The Conversion of the Jewes.* London, 1655.

Jackson, John. *The Booke of Conscience Opened and Read in a Sermon Preached at the Spittle on Easter-Tuesday, Being April 12, 1642 / by John Jackson.* London, 1642.

Jackson, Thomas. *A Collection of the Works of That Holy Man and Profound Divine, Thomas Iackson.* London, 1653.

Jackson, Thomas. *Dauids Pastorall Poeme: Or Sheepeheards Song.* London, 1603.

Jackson, Thomas. *The Eternall Truth of Scriptures, and Christian Beleefe, Thereon Vvholly Depending, Manifested by It Owne Light.* London, 1613.

Jacobi, Joannes. *Here Begynneth a Litil Boke the Whiche Traytied and Reherced Many Gode Thinges Necessaries for the Infirmite & Grete Sekenesse Called Pestilence the Whiche Often Times Enfecteth Vs.* London, 1485.

Jacobus, de Cessolis. *[De Ludo Scachorum].* Bruges, 1474.

James I, King of England. *An Apologie for the Oath of Allegiance.* London, 1609.

Jay, George. *A Sermon Preacht at the Funerall of the Lady Mary Villiers.* London, 1626.

Jeamson, Thomas. *Artificiall Embellishments, or Arts Best Directions How to Preserve Beauty or Procure It.* Oxford, 1665.

Jenkyn, William. *The Blind Guide, or, The Doting Doctor Composed by Way of Reply to a Late Tediously Trifling Pamphlet.* London, 1648.

Jones, Richard. *The Booke of Honor and Armes.* London, 1590.

Jones, Thomas. *Elymas the Sorcerer, or, A Memorial towards the Discovery of the Bottom of This Popish-Plot and How Far His R. Highness's Directors Have Been Faithful to His Honour and Interest, or the Peace of the Nation.* London, 1682.

Jonson, Ben. *The Alchemist.* London, 1612.

Jonstonus, Joannes. *An History of the Constancy of Nature.* London, 1657.

Jonstonus, Joannes. *An History of the Wonderful Things of Nature.* London, 1657.

Jordan, Thomas. *Divinity and Morality in Robes of Poetry.* London, 1660.

Jordan, Thomas. *Jevvels of Ingenuity.* London, 1660.

Jourdain, Silvester. *A Plaine Description of the Barmudas, Now Called Sommer Ilands.* London, 1613.

Kilby, Richard. *The Burthen of a Loaden Conscience: Or the Miserie of Sinne Set Forth by the Confession of a Miserable Sinner.* Cambridge, 1608.

King, John. *A Sermon Preached in Oxon: The 5. of November. 1607.* Oxford, 1607.

King, John. *Lectures Vpon Ionas Deliuered at Yorke.* Oxford, 1599.

Knott, Edward. *Infidelity Vnmasked, or, The Confutation of a Booke Published by Mr. William Chillingworth.* Ghent, 1652.

La Primaudaye, Pierre de. *The Second Part of the French Academie.* London, 1594.

La Tour Landry, Geoffroy de. *[Here Begynneth the Booke Which the Knyght of the Toure Made and Speketh of Many Fayre Ensamples and Thensygnementys and Techyng of His Doughters].* London, 1484.

Lacey, William. *The Iudgment of an Vniuersity-Man Concerning M. VVilliam Chillingvvorth His Late Pamphlet, in Ansvvere to Charity Maintayned.* Saint-Omer, 1639.

Langford, George. *Search the Scriptures. Or, An Enquirie after Veritie.* London, 1623.

Langton, Christopher. *A Uery Brefe Treatise, Ordrely Declaring the Pri[n]Cipal Partes of Phisick.* London, 1547.

Lanyer, Aemilia. *Salue Deus Rex Iudæorum.* London, 1611.

Lassels, Richard. *The Voyage of Italy, or, A Compleat Journey through Italy in Two Parts.* Paris, 1670.

Latimer, Hugh. *Fruitfull Sermons Preached by the Right Reuerend Father, and Constant Martyr of Iesus Christ, M. Hugh Latimer.* London, 1607.

Laurent, Dominican. *This Book Was Compyled [and] Made Atte Requeste of Kyng Phelyp of Fraunce ... Whyche Book Is Callyd in Frensshe. Le Liure Royal That Is to Say the Ryal Book. or a Book for a Kyng.* London, 1485.

Le Petit, Jean François. *A Generall Historie of the Netherlands.* London, 1608.

Lefèvre, Raoul. *hEre Begynneth the Volume Intituled and Named the Recuyell of the Historyes of Troye.* Bruges, 1473.

Legrand, Jacques. *Here Begynneth a Lytell Boke Called Good Maners.* London, 1498.

Leigh, Edward. *A Treatise of Divinity Consisting of Three Bookes*. London, 1646.

Leigh, Edward. *A Treatise of Religion & Learning and of Religious and Learned Men*. London, 1656.

Leighton, William, Sir. *The Teares or Lamentations of a Sorrowfull Soule*. London, 1613.

Leroy, Louis. *Of the Interchangeable Course, or Variety of Things in the Whole World and the Concurrence of Armes and Learning*. London, 1594.

L'Estrange, Roger. *Considerations and Proposals in Order to the Regulation of the Press*. London, 1663.

Lever, Thomas. *A Treatise of the Right Way Fro[m] Danger of Sinne & Vengeance in This Wicked World, Vnto Godly Wealth and Saluation in Christe*. London, 1575.

Lily, William. *A Short Introduction of Grammar*. London, 1607.

Livy. *The Romane Historie*. London, 1600.

Lloyd, Lodowick. *The Tragicocomedie of Serpents*. London, 1607.

Luther, Martin. *A Commentarie of M. Doctor Martin Luther Vpon the Epistle of S. Paul to the Galathians*. London, 1616.

Luther, Martin. *An Exposition of Salomons Booke Called Ecclesiastes or the Preacher*. London, 1573.

Luther, Martin. *The Last Wil and Last Confession of Martyn Luthers Faith*. Wesel, 1543.

Lydgate, John. *Here Begynneth a Lytell Treatyse of the Horse, the Sheep, and the Ghoos*. London, 1495.

Lyly, John. *A Moste Excellent Comedie of Alexander, Campaspe, and Diogenes*. London, 1584.

Lyly, John. *Euphues and His England*. London, 1580.

Lyly, John. *Mother Bombie*. London, 1594.

Lyly, John. *Pappe with an Hatchet*. London, 1589.

Malory, Thomas. *[Le Morte Darthur]*. London, 1485.

Markham, Gervase. *A Health to the Gentlemanly Profession of Seruingmen; or, The Seruingmans Comforts*. London, 1598.

Marprelate, Martin. *Theses Martinianae*. Wolston, 1589.

Martin, Gregory. *A Discouerie of the Manifold Corruptions of the Holy Scriptures by the Heretikes of Our Daies*. Reims, 1582.

Martyn, William. *The Historie, and Liues, of the Kings of England from VVilliam the Conqueror, Vnto the End of the Raigne of King Henrie the Eight*. London, 1615.

Marvell, Andrew. *Mr. Smirke; or, The Divine in Mode*. London, 1676.

Marvell, Andrew. *The Rehearsal Transpros'd*. London, 1672.

Mason, John. *The Turke A Worthie Tragedie*. London, 1610.

Massinger, Philip. *The Maid of Honour*. London, 1632.

Massinger, Philip. *The Picture a Tragaecomaedie*. London, 1630.

Mayhew, R. *Sichah: Or, A Continued Tract of Meditation*. London, 1683.

Melton, John, Sir. *Astrologaster, or, The Figure-Caster*. London, 1620.

Mennes, John. *Recreation for Ingenious Head-Peeces*. London, 1654.

Meres, Francis. *Palladis Tamia Wits Treasury*. London, 1598.

Middleton, Thomas. *The Famelie of Loue*. London, 1608.

Middleton, Thomas. *Your Fiue Gallants*. London, 1608.

Milton, John. *Areopagitica*. London, 1644.

Monson, John, Sir. *A Short Essay of Afflictions*. London, 1647.

Montaigne, Michel de. *Essays*. London, 1613.

Montaigne, Michel de. "Les Essais de Montaigne with Page Images from the Bordeaux Copy." Accessed December 12, 2022. https://artflsrv03.uchicago.edu/philologic4/montessaisvilley/navigate/1/5/9/.

More, Henry. *The Life and Doctrine of Ovr Savior Iesvs Christ*. Ghent, 1656.

More, Thomas. *The Apologye of Syr Thomas More Knyght*. London, 1533.

More, Thomas. *The Co[n]Futacyon of Tyndales Answere Made by Syr Thomas More Knyght Lorde Chau[n]Cellour of Englonde*. London, 1532.

Mornay, Philippe de, seigneur du Plessis-Marly. *A Vvoorke Concerning the Trewnesse of the Christian Religion*. London, 1587.

Morton, Nathaniel. *New-Englands Memoriall*. Cambridge, MA, 1669.

Morton, Thomas. *The Encounter against M. Parsons, by a Revievv of His Last Sober Reckoning, and His Exceptions Vrged in the Treatise of His Mitigation*. London, 1610.

Moryson, Fynes. *An Itinerary*. London, 1617.

Moxon, Joseph. *Mechanick Exercises on the Whole Art of Printing (1683–4)*. Edited by Herbert Davis and Harry Carter. New York: Dover, 1978.

Moxon, Joseph. *Mechanick Exercises, or, The Doctrine of Handy-Works*. London, 1677.

Mulcaster, Richard. *Positions Vvherin Those Primitiue Circumstances Be Examined, Which Are Necessarie for the Training vp of Children, Either for Skill in Their Booke, or Health in Their Bodie*. London, 1581.

Mulcaster, Richard. *The First Part of the Elementarie*. London, 1582.

Münster, Sebastian. *A Treatyse of the Newe India*. London, 1553.

Mynsicht, Adrian von. *Thesaurus & Armamentarium Medico-Chymicum, or, A Treasury of Physick with the Most Secret Way of Preparing Remedies against All Diseases*. London, 1682.

Nash, Thomas. *Nashes Lenten Stuffe*. London, 1599.

Nash, Thomas. *Quaternio or A Fourefold Vvay to a Happie Life*. London, 1633.

Nash, Thomas. *The Apologie of Pierce Pennilesse*. London, 1592.

Nieuhof, Johannes. *An Embassy from the East-India Company of the United Provinces, to the Grand Tartar Cham, Emperor of China Deliver'd by Their Excellencies, Peter de Goyer and Jacob de Keyzer, at His Imperial City of Peking*. London, 1673.

Ochino, Bernardino. *A Tragoedie or Dialoge of the Vniuste Vsurped Primacie of the Bishop of Rome, and of All the Iust Abolishyng of the Same*. London, 1549.

Ogilby, John. *Asia. Being an Accurate Description of Persia, and the Several Provinces Thereof*. London, 1673.

Olearius, Adam. *The Voyages and Travells of the Ambassadors Sent by Frederick, Duke of Holstein, to the Great Duke of Muscovy and the King of Persia*. London, 1669.

Ortelius, Abraham. *An Epitome of Ortelius His Theater of the Vvorld, Vvherein the Principal Regions of the Earth Are Descrived in Smalle Mappes*. Antwerp, 1601.

Otes, Samuel. *An Explanation of the Generall Epistle of Saint Iude*. London, 1633.

Overbury, Thomas, Sir. *Sir Thomas Ouerburie His Wife with New Elegies Vpon His (Now Knowne) Vntimely Death*. London, 1616.

Paradise, John. *Hadadrimmon, Sive, Threnodia Anglicana Ob Regicidium a Sermon on Davids Humiliation for Cutting off the Royal Robe, and Detestation of Cutting off the Royal Head of the Lords Anointed*. London, 1661.

Parker, Martin. *A Briefe Dissection of Germaines Affliction with Warre, Pestilence, and Famine*. London, 1638.

Parker, Robert. *A Scholasticall Discourse against Symbolizing with Antichrist in Ceremonies: Especially in the Signe of the Crosse*. Middelburg, 1607.

Partlicius, Simeon. *A New Method of Physick: Or, A Short View of Paracelsus and Galen's Practice*. London, 1654.

Peacham, Henry. *The Compleat Gentleman*. London, 1622.

Perkins, William. *A Direction for the Government of the Tongue According to Gods Word*. Cambridge, 1593.

Philips, Edward. *Certain Godly and Learned Sermons*. London, 1607.

Pliny, the Younger. *Pliny's Panegyricke: A Speech in Senate*. Oxford, 1645.

Plutarch. *The Lives of the Noble Grecians and Romanes*. London, 1579.

Plutarch. *The Philosophie, Commonlie Called, the Morals*. London, 1603.

Porter, Henry. *The Pleasant History of the Two Angry Women of Abington*. London, 1599.

Porter, Thomas. *A Compendious View, or Cosmographical, and Geographical Description of the Whole World*. London, 1659.

Powel, Gabriel. *The Resolued Christian, Exhorting to Resolution Written, to Recall the Worldling, to Comfort the Faint-Harted, to Strengthen the Faithfull, and to Perswade All Men, so to Runne, That They May Obtaine*. London, 1600.

Powell, Thomas. *The Attourneys Academy, or, The Manner and Forme of Proceeding Practically Vpon Any Suite, Plaint or Action Whatsoever, in Any Court of Record Whatsoever, within This Kingdome*. London, 1623.

Prat, Jos. *The Order of Orthographie: Or, Sixty Sixe Rules Shortly Directing to the True Writing, Speaking, and Pronouncing the English Tongue*. London, 1622.

Preston, John. *A Sermon Preached at the Funerall of Mr. Iosiah Reynel Esquire, the 13. of August 1614*. London, 1615.

Preston, Richard Graham, Viscount. *Angliae Speculum Morale The Moral State of England, with the Several Aspects It Beareth to Virtue and Vice*. London, 1670.

Price, Sampson. *Londons Remembrancer: For the Staying of the Contagious Sicknes of the Plague by Dauids Memoriall*. London, 1626.

Prime, John. *The Consolations of David, Breefly Applied to Queene Elizabeth in a Sermon*. Oxford, 1588.

Puttenham, George. *The Arte of English Poesie*. London, 1589.

Quarles, Francis. *Argalus and Parthenia*. London, 1629.

Quarles, Francis. *Divine Fancies Digested into Epigrammes, Meditations, and Observations*. London, 1633.

Quarles, Francis. *The Loyall Convert*. Oxford, 1644.

R. M. *A President for Young Pen-Men. Or The Letter-Writer*. London, 1615.

Rainolds, William. *A Refutation of Sundry Reprehensions, Cauils, and False Sleightes, by Which M. Whitaker Laboureth to Deface the Late English Translation, and*

Catholike Annotations of the New Testament, and the Booke of Discouery of Heretical Corruptions. Paris, 1583.

Randolph, Thomas. *A Pleasant Comedie, Entituled Hey for Honesty, down with Knavery.* London, 1651.

Rastell, John. *The Pastyme of People.* London, 1530.

Raue, Christian. *A Discovrse of the Orientall Tongves.* London, 1649.

Rawlinson, John. *Fishermen Fishers of Men.* London, 1609.

Raworth, Francis. *Jacobs Ladder, or The Protectorship of Sion, Laid on the Shoulders of the Almighty.* London, 1655.

Raymond of Capua. *Here Begynneth the Orcharde of Syon in the Whiche Is Conteyned the Reuelacyons of Seynt Katheryne of Sene, with Ghostly Fruytes [and] Precyous Plantes for the Helthe of Mannes Soule.* London, 1519.

Reading, John. *Dauids Soliloquie Containing Many Comforts for Afflicted Mindes.* London, 1627.

Revett, Eldred. *Poems.* London, 1657.

Reyner, Edward. *Considerations Concerning Marriage the Honour, Duties, Benefits, Troubles of It.* London, 1657.

Rich, Barnabe. *A Nevv Description of Ireland Vvherein Is Described the Disposition of the Irish Whereunto They Are Inclined.* London, 1610.

Rich, Barnabe. *My Ladies Looking Glasse.* London, 1616.

Rivius, Johann. *Of the Foolishnes of Men in Putting-off the Amendement of Their Liues from Daie to Daie a Godlie and Profitable Treatise for the Present Time.* London, 1582.

Robinson, John. *Tempora Mutantur A Treatise, Theological, Moral, and Historical.* London, 1664.

Rogers, Nehemiah. *A Strange Vineyard in Palæstina in an Exposition of Isaiahs Parabolical Song of the Beloued, Discouered.* London, 1623.

Rolle, Samuel. *Shlohavot, or, The Burning of London in the Year 1666.* London, 1667.

Rowlands, Samuel. *Humors Looking Glasse.* London, 1608.

Rutherford, Samuel. *Christ Dying and Drawing Sinners to Himself.* London, 1647.

Rutherford, Samuel. *The Divine Right of Church-Government and Excommunication: Or a Peacable Dispute for the Perfection of the Holy Scripture in Point of Ceremonies and Church Government.* London, 1646.

Rycaut, Paul, Sir. *The Present State of the Ottoman Empire.* London, 1668.

S. H. *Knaves and Fooles in Folio.* London, 1648.

S. L. *Three Sermons Viz. Davids Tears for His Rebellious Son Absalom, Israels Tears for Abners Fall by Bloudy Joab, Infants Tears for Athaliahs Treason.* London, 1660.

Sampson, William. *Virtus Post Funera Viuit or, Honour Tryumphing over Death.* London, 1636.

Sanderson, Robert. *De Juramento Seven Lectures Concerning the Obligation of Promissory Oathes.* London, 1655.

Sandys, Edwin. *Europæ Speculum. Or, A Vievv or Survey of the State of Religion in the Vvesterne Parts of the World.* The Hague, 1629.

Sandys, Edwin. *Sermons Made by the Most Reuerende Father in God, Edwin, Archbishop of Yorke, Primate of England and Metropolitane.* London, 1585.

Sandys, Miles, Sir. *Prudence the First of the Foure Cardinall Virtues.* London, 1634.

Sanford, John. *Gods Arrowe of the Pestilence.* Oxford, 1604.

Scudéry, Madeleine de. *Clelia, an Excellent New Romance.* London, 1678.

Scultetus, Abraham. *A Secular Sermon.* London, 1618.

Serres, Jean de. *A General Inuentorie of the History of France from the Beginning of That Monarchie, Vnto the Treatie of Veruins, in the Year 1598.* London, 1607.

Serres, Jean de. *The Three Partes of Commentaries Containing the Whole and Perfect Discourse of the Ciuill Warres of Fraunce.* London, 1574.

Settle, Elkanah. *An Elegie on the Late Fire and Ruines of London.* London, 1667.

Shakespeare, William. *A Pleasant Conceited Comedie Called, Loues Labors Lost.* London, 1598.

Shakespeare, William. *Lucrece.* London, 1594.

Shakespeare, William. *Mr. William Shakespeares Comedies, Histories, & Tragedies.* London, 1623.

Shakespeare, William. *Much Adoe about Nothing.* London, 1600.

Shakespeare, William. *Shake-Speares Sonnets.* London, 1609.

Shakespeare, William. *The First Part of the Contention Betwixt the Two Famous Houses of Yorke and Lancaster.* London, 1600.

Shakespeare, William. *The Historie of Troylus and Cresseida.* London, 1609.

Shakespeare, William. *The History of Henrie the Fourth.* London, 1598.

Shakespeare, William. *The Late, and Much Admired Play, Called Pericles, Prince of Tyre.* London, 1609.

Shakespeare, William. *The Second Part of Henrie the Fourth.* London, 1600.

Shirley, James. *Love Tricks, or, The School of Complements.* London, 1667.

Shirley, James. *The Cardinal, a Tragedie.* London, 1652.

Shirley, James. *The Humorous Courtier A Comedy.* London, 1640.

Shirley, James. *The Traytor A Tragedie.* London, 1635.

Sibbes, Richard. *The Excellencie of the Gospell above the Law.* London, 1639.

Sidney, Philip, Sir. *An Apology for Poetry, (or, The Defence of Poesy).* Edited by Geoffrey Shepherd and R. W. Maslen. 3rd ed. Manchester: Manchester University Press, 2002.

Sidney, Philip, Sir. *Sir P.S. His Astrophel and Stella.* London, 1591.

Sidney, Philip, Sir. *The Countesse of Pembrokes Arcadia.* London, 1590.

Sidney, Philip, Sir. *The Defence of Poesie.* London, 1595.

Simson, Patrick. *The Historie of the Church since the Dayes of Our Saviour Iesus Christ, Vntill This Present Age.* London, 1624.

Skelton, John. *Here after Foloweth a Litel Boke Called Colyn Cloute.* London, 1545.

Skelton, John. *Here after Foloweth a Lytell Boke, Whiche Hath to Name, Why Come Ye Nat to Courte.* London, 1545.

Slatyer, William. *The Compleat Christian, and Compleat Armour and Armoury of a Christian, Fitting Him with All Necessary Furniture for That His Holy Profession.* London, 1643.

Sleidanus, Johannes. *A Briefe Chronicle of the Foure Principall Empyres.* London, 1563.

Smith, Henry. *The Christians Sacrifice.* London, 1589.

Smith, Henry. *The Sermons of Maister Henrie Smith.* London, 1593.

Smith, Henry. *The Vvedding Garment.* London, 1590.

Smith, Henry. *Two Sermons, of Ionahs Punishment.* London, 1607.

Smith, Wentworth. *The Hector of Germany. Or The Palsgraue, Prime Elector A New Play, an Honourable History.* London, 1615.

Speed, John. *A Prospect of the Most Famous Parts of the Vvorld.* London, 1646.

Speed, John. *The History of Great Britaine.* London, 1611.

Sprat, Thomas. *The History of the Royal-Society of London for the Improving of Natural Knowledge.* London, 1667.

Stafford, Anthony. *Honour and Vertue, Triumphing over the Grave.* London, 1640.

Stalham, John. *The Reviler Rebuked: Or, A Re-Inforcement of the Charge against the Quakers.* London, 1657.

Stalham, John. *Vindiciæ Redemptionis. In the Fanning and Sifting of Samuel Oates His Exposition upon Mat. 13. 44.* London, 1647.

Steele, Richard. *The Husbandmans Calling Shewing the Excellencies, Temptations, Graces, Duties &c. of the Christian Husbandman.* London, 1668.

Stephens, John. *Essayes and Characters, Ironicall, and Instructiue.* London, 1615.

Sternhold, Thomas. *Psalmes of Dauid in Englishe Metre.* London, 1560.

Sternhold, Thomas. *The Vvhole Boke of Psalmes, Collected into English Metre by Thomas Sternhold, Iohn Hopkins, and Others: Conferred with the Ebrue, with Apt Notes to Syng Them Wyth All.; Newlye Set Foorth and Allowed to Bee Soong of the People Together, in Churches, before and after Moring and Euening Prayer: As Also before and after the Sermon, and Moreouer in Priuate Houses, for Their Godlye Solace and Comfort, Laying Apart All Vngodly Songes and Balades, Which Tend Onely to the Nourishing of Vice, and Corrupting of Youth.* London, 1566.

Stoneham, Mathew. *A Treatise on the First Psalme.* London, 1610.

Stoneham, Mathew. *A Treatise on the First Psalme. By Mathew Stonham. Minister and Preacher in the Cittie of Norwich.* London, 1610.

Stow, John. *The Abridgement of the English Chronicle.* London, 1618.

Stuckley, Lewis. *A Gospel-Glasse, Representing the Miscarriages of English Professors, Both in Their Personal and Relative Capacities.* London, 1667.

Sturm, Johannes. *A Ritch Storehouse or Treasurie for Nobilitye and Gentlemen.* London, 1570.

Swinnock, George. *The Christian-Man's Calling: Or, A Treatise of Making Religion Ones Business.* London, 1662.

Symonds, William. *Pisgah Euangelica.* London, 1605.

T. L. W. *Refractoria Disputatio.* London, 1654.

Talpin, Jean. *A Forme of Christian Pollicie.* London, 1574.

Taylor, Jeremy. *XXVIII Sermons.* London, 1651.

Taylor, John. *A Common Vvhore Vvith All These Graces Grac'd: Shee's Very Honest, Beautifull and Chaste.* London, 1622.

Taylor, John. *An Arrant Thiefe, Vvhom Euery Man May Trust in Vvord and Deed, Exceeding True and Iust. With a Comparison Betweene a Thiefe and a Booke.* London, 1622.

Taylor, John. *Iack a Lent His Beginning and Entertainment with the Many Pranks of His Gentleman-Vsher Shroue Tuesday That Goes before Him, and His Foot-Man Hunger Attending.* London, 1620.

Taylor, John. *Mercurius Nonsencicus*. London, 1648.

Taylor, John. *The Nipping and Snipping of Abuses*. London, 1614.

Taylor, Thomas. *Christs Victorie over the Dragon*. London, 1633.

Thaddaeus, Joannes. *The Reconciler of the Bible*. London, 1655.

Thorpe, William. *The Examinacion of Master William Thorpe Preste*. Antwerp, 1530.

Thrēnoikos The House of Mourning; Furnished with Directions for Preparations to Meditations of Consolations at the Houre of Death. London, 1640.

Throckmorton, Job. *M. Some Laid Open in His Coulers*. La Rochelle, 1589.

Topsell, Edward. *The Historie of Foure-Footed Beastes*. London, 1607.

Torriano, Giovanni. *The Second Alphabet Consisting of Proverbial Phrases Interpreted and Illustrated Where Most Necessary*. London, 1662.

Trapp, John. *A Commentary or Exposition upon the Books of Ezra, Nehemiah, Esther, Job and Psalms*. London, 1657.

Trapp, John. *A Commentary or Exposition upon the Four Evangelists, and the Acts of the Apostles*. London, 1647.

Turner, William. *The Rescuynge of the Romishe Fox*. Bonn, 1545.

Twyne, Thomas. *The Garlande of Godly Flowers*. London, 1574.

Tyndale, William. *The Newe Testament Dylygently Corrected and Compared with the Greke*. Antwerp, 1534.

Tyndale, William. *The Vvhole Workes of W. Tyndall, Iohn Frith, and Doct. Barnes, Three Worthy Martyrs, and Principall Teachers of This Churche of England*. London, 1573.

Vaughan, William. *The Arraignment of Slander Periury Blasphemy, and Other Malicious Sinnes*. London, 1630.

Vaughan, William. *The Golden-Groue Moralized*. London, 1600.

Vermigli, Pietro Martire. *Most Godly Prayers Compiled out of Dauids Psalmes*. London, 1569.

Vermigli, Pietro Martire. *The Common Places of the Most Famous and Renowmed Diuine Doctor Peter Martyr*. London, 1583.

Vicars, John. *A Prospectiue Glasse to Looke into Heauen*. London, 1618.

Vincent, Thomas. *The Wells of Salvation Opened*. London, 1668.

Vines, Richard. *Sermons Preached upon Several Publike and Eminent Occasions*. London, 1656.

Viret, Pierre. *The Christian Disputations*. London, 1579.

Vives, Juan Luis. *A Very Frutefull and Pleasant Boke Called the Instructio[n] of a Christen Woma[n]*. London, 1529.

Wanley, Nathaniel. *The Wonders of the Little World, or, A General History of Man in Six Books*. London, 1673.

Ward, Richard. *Theologicall Questions, Dogmaticall Observations, and Evangelicall Essays, Vpon the Gospel of Jesus Christ, According to St. Matthew*. London, 1640.

Ward, Samuel. *A Coal from the Altar, to Kindle the Holy Fire of Zeale*. London, 1615.

Webb, John. *An Historical Essay Endeavoring a Probability That the Language of the Empire of China Is the Primitive Language*. London, 1669.

Webster, John. *Academiarum Examen, or, The Examination of Academies*. London, 1654.

Westerman, William. *Two Sermons of Assise*. London, 1600.

Westerne, Thomas. *The Flaming Bush. Or, An Embleme of the True Church*. London, 1624.

Whately, William. *Prototypes, or, The Primarie Precedent Presidents out of the Booke of Genesis*. London, 1640.

White, Thomas. *The Middle State of Souls from the Hour of Death to the Day of Judgment*. London, 1659.

Whitehead, George. *The Case of the Quakers Concerning Oaths Defended as Evangelical*. London, 1674.

Whitgift, John. *The Defense of the Aunsvvere to the Admonition against the Replie of T.C.* London, 1574.

Wied, Hermann von. *The Right Institutio[n] of Baptisme*. Ipswich, 1548.

Wilson, Thomas. *A Christian Dictionarie*. London, 1612.

Wilson, Thomas. *A Commentarie Vpon the Most Diuine Epistle of S. Paul to the Romanes*. London, 1614.

Wing, John. *Abels Offering. Or The Earely, and Most Accepted Sacrifice of a Christian*. Vlissingen, 1621.

Wither, George. *Abuses Stript, and Whipt. Or Satirical Essayes*. London, 1613.

Wither, George. *The Modern States-Man*. London, 1653.

Woodward, Ezekias. *A Light to Grammar, and All Other Arts and Sciences*. London, 1641.

Wright, Thomas. *A Treatise, Shewing the Possibilitie, and Conueniencie of the Reall Presence of Our Sauiour in the Blessed Sacrament*. London, 1596.

Young, Robert. *A Breviary of the Later Persecutions of the Professors of the Gospel of Christ Jesus*. Glasgow, 1674.

Younge, Richard. *A Christian Library, or, A Pleasant and Plentiful Paradise of Practical Divinity*. London, 1660.

Younge, Richard. *Sinne Stigmatizd: Or, The Art to Know Savingly, Believe Rightly, Live Religiously*. London, 1639.

Late Texts

Acheson, Katherine O., ed. *Early Modern English Marginalia*. Material Readings in Early Modern Culture. New York: Routledge, 2018.

Acheson, Katherine O. *Visual Rhetoric and Early Modern English Literature*. London: Routledge, 2013.

Adams, Brandi K. "'Inlaid with Inkie Spots of Jet': Early Modern Book History and Premodern Critical Race Studies." In *The Oxford Handbook of the History of the Book in Early Modern England*, edited by Adam Smyth, 81–99. Oxford: Oxford University Press, 2023.

Akhimie, Patricia. *Shakespeare and the Cultivation of Difference: Race and Conduct in the Early Modern World*. Routledge Studies in Shakespeare 29. New York: Routledge, 2018.

Al-Saji, Alia. "Too Late: Fanon, the Dismembered Past, and a Phenomenology of Racialized Time." In *Fanon, Phenomenology, and Psychology*, edited by Derek Hook, Miraj Desai, and Leswin Laubscher, 177–93. London: Routledge, 2022. https://doi.org/10.4324/9781003037132-17.

Amory, Hugh, and David D. Hall, eds. *The Colonial Book in the Atlantic World*. History of the Book in America. Cambridge: Cambridge University Press, 2000.

Anderson, Benedict. *Imagined Communities: Reflections on the Origin and Spread of Nationalism*. Revised edition. London: Verso, 2016.

Andrews, Meghan C. "The Commonplacing of Professional Plays Revisited: Print, Theater, and Early Modern Institutional Exchange." *Shakespeare Quarterly* 73, no. 3 (2022): 199–223.

Arber, Edward, ed. *A Transcript of the Registers of the Company of Stationers of London; 1554–1640 A.D.* 5 vols. New York: Peter Smith, 1950.

Assmann, Aleida. *Is Time out of Joint?: On the Rise and Fall of the Modern Time Regime*. Translated by Sarah Clift. Ithaca, NY: Cornell University Press, 2020.

Bain, Peter, and Paul Shaw. *Blackletter: Type and National Identity*. New York: Princeton Architectural Press, 1998.

Barbier, Frédéric. *Gutenberg's Europe: The Book and the Invention of Western Modernity*. Translated by Jean Birrell. English edition. Malden, MA: Polity, 2017.

Barnard, John, D. F. McKenzie, and Maureen Bell, eds. *The Cambridge History of the Book in Britain. Vol. 4: 1557–1695*. Vol. 4. Cambridge University Press, 2008.

Baron, Sabrina A., Eric N. Lindquist, and Eleanor F. Shevlin, eds. *Agent of Change: Print Culture Studies after Elizabeth L. Eisenstein*. Studies in Print Culture and the History of the Book. Amherst: University of Massachusetts Press, 2007.

Bates, Catherine. *On Not Defending Poetry: Defence and Indefensibility in Sidney's Defence of Poesy*. Oxford: Oxford University Press, 2017.

Belsey, Catherine. "Tarquin Dispossessed: Expropriation and Consent in 'The Rape of Lucrece.'" *Shakespeare Quarterly* 52, no. 3 (2001): 315–35.

Berman, Marshall. *All That Is Solid Melts into Air: The Experience of Modernity*. New York: Simon & Schuster, 1982.

Best, Stephen. *None like Us: Blackness, Belonging, Aesthetic Life*. Theory Q. Durham: Duke University Press, 2018.

Best, Stephen, and Sharon Marcus. "Surface Reading: An Introduction." *Representations* 108, no. 1 (2009): 1–21. https://doi.org/10.1525/rep.2009.108.1.1.

Blair, Ann, and Nicholas Popper, eds. *New Horizons in Early Modern Scholarship*. Baltimore, MD: Johns Hopkins University Press, 2021.

Blake, Liza. "Textual and Editorial Introduction – Margaret Cavendish's *Poems and Fancies*." Accessed December 12, 2022. http://library2.utm.utoronto.ca/poemsandfancies/textual-and-editorial-introduction/.

Blake, N. F. *William Caxton and English Literary Culture*. London; Rio Grande, OH: Hambledon Press, 1991.

Bland, Mark. "The Appearance of the Text in Early Modern England." *Text* 11 (January 1, 1998): 91–154.

Blumenberg, Hans. *The Readability of the World*. Translated by Robert Savage and David Roberts. Signale/Transfer: German Thought in Translation. Ithaca, NY: Cornell University Press, 2022.

Boeckeler, Erika Mary. *Playful Letters: A Study in Early Modern Alphabetics*. Impressions: Studies in the Art, Culture, and Future of Books. Iowa City: University of Iowa Press, 2017.

"Book of Nature." In *Wikipedia*, February 4, 2024. https://en.wikipedia.org/wiki/Book_of_Nature.

Bourdieu, Pierre. *Distinction: A Social Critique of the Judgement of Taste*. Cambridge: Harvard University Press, 1984.

Bourdieu, Pierre. *The Field of Cultural Production: Essays on Art and Literature*. Translated by Randal Johnson. New York: Columbia University Press, 1993.

Bourne, Claire M. L., ed. *Shakespeare / Text: Contemporary Readings in Textual Studies, Editing and Performance*. London: Bloomsbury, 2021.

Bourne, Claire M. L. *Typographies of Performance in Early Modern England*. Oxford: Oxford University Press, 2020.

Bowers, Fredson. *Bibliography and Textual Criticism*. Oxford: Clarendon Press, 1964.

Brayman Hackel, Heidi, Zachary Lesser, and Jesse Lander, eds. *The Book in History, the Book as History: New Intersections of the Material Text: Essays in Honor of David Scott Kastan*. The Beinecke Series in the History of the Book. New Haven: Beinecke Rare Book & Manuscript Library, 2016.

Briggs, Asa, and Peter Burke. *A Social History of the Media: From Gutenberg to the Internet*. 2nd ed. Cambridge: Polity, 2005.

Brown, Georgia. *Redefining Elizabethan Literature*. Cambridge: Cambridge University Press, 2004.

Burke, Victoria E. "Recent Studies in Commonplace Books." *English Literary Renaissance* 43, no. 1 (2013): 153–77. https://doi.org/10.1111/1475-6757.12005.

Butler, Pierce. *The Origin of Printing in Europe*. University of Chicago Studies in Library Science. Chicago: University of Chicago Press, 1940.

Calhoun, Joshua. *The Nature of the Page: Poetry, Papermaking, and the Ecology of Texts in Renaissance England*. Material Texts. Philadelphia: University of Pennsylvania Press, 2020.

Carter, Harry. *A View of Early Typography up to about 1600*. Oxford: Oxford University Press, 1969.

Caswell, Michelle. *Urgent Archives: Enacting Liberatory Memory Work*. 1st ed. Routledge Studies in Archives. Milton: Taylor & Francis, 2021. https://doi.org/10.4324/9781003001355.

Chakravarty, Urvashi. *Fictions of Consent: Slavery, Servitude, and Free Service in Early Modern England*. Philadelphia: University of Pennsylvania Press, 2022.

Chartier, Roger. *The Cultural Uses of Print in Early Modern France*. Translated by Lydia G. Cochrane. Princeton: Princeton University Press, 1987.

Chartier, Roger. *The Order of Books: Readers, Authors and Libraries in Europe Between the Fourteenth and Eighteenth Centuries*. Stanford: Stanford University Press, 1994.

Christian, Lynda G. *Theatrum Mundi: The History of an Idea.* Harvard Dissertations in Comparative Literature. New York: Garland, 1987.

Clanchy, M. T. *From Memory to Written Record: England, 1066–1307.* 3rd ed. Malden, MA: Wiley-Blackwell, 2013.

Coates, Ta-Nehisi. *Between the World and Me.* New York: Random House, 2015.

Cohen, H. Floris. *The Rise of Modern Science Explained: A Comparative History.* Cambridge: Cambridge University Press, 2015.

Cohen, Jeffrey J., and Julian Yates. *Noah's Arkive.* Minneapolis: University of Minnesota Press, 2023.

Cohen, Matt. "Textual Scholarship in the Situation." *Textual Cultures: Texts, Contexts, Interpretation* 15, no. 2 (2022): 1–29.

Cohen, Matt. *The Networked Wilderness: Communicating in Early New England.* Minneapolis: University of Minnesota Press, 2010.

Coker, Cait. "Gendered Spheres: Theorizing Space in the English Printing House." *The Seventeenth Century* 33, no. 3 (July 7, 2018): 323–36. https://doi.org/10.1080/0268117X.2017.1340850.

Coldiron, A. E. B. *Printers without Borders: Translation and Textuality in the Renaissance.* Cambridge: Cambridge University Press, 2015.

Connerton, Paul. *How Modernity Forgets.* Cambridge: Cambridge University Press, 2009.

Cook, Megan L. *The Poet and the Antiquaries: Chaucerian Scholarship and the Rise of Literary History, 1532–1635.* Philadelphia: University of Pennsylvania Press, 2019.

Corns, Thomas N. "The Early Modern Search Engine: Indices, Title Pages, Marginalia and Contents." In *The Renaissance Computer: Knowledge Technology in the First Age of Print*, edited by Neil Rhodes and Jonathan Sawday, 95–105. London, England: Routledge. xi, 2000.

Craig, Hugh. "Shakespeare and Print." *HEAT* 4 (2002): 49–63.

Craig, Hugh, and Brett Greatley-Hirsch. *Style, Computers, and Early Modern Drama: Beyond Authorship.* Cambridge: Cambridge University Press, 2017.

Crain, Patricia. *The Story of A: The Alphabetization of America from The New England Primer to The Scarlet Letter.* Stanford: Stanford University Press, 2000.

Crane, Mary Thomas. *Losing Touch with Nature: Literature and the New Science in Sixteenth-Century England.* Baltimore, MD: Johns Hopkins University Press, 2014.

Cummings, Brian. *Bibliophobia: The End and the Beginning of the Book.* Oxford University Press, 2022.

Cummings, Brian. "The Book as Symbol." In *The Book: A Global History*, edited by Michael F. Suarez and H. R. Woudhuysen, 93–96. Oxford: Oxford University Press, 2013.

Curtius, Ernst Robert. *European Literature and the Latin Middle Ages.* Bollingen Series 36. Princeton: Princeton University Press, 1967.

Dane, Joseph A. *Blind Impressions: Methods and Mythologies in Book History.* Philadelphia: University of Pennsylvania Press, 2013.

Dane, Joseph A. *Out of Sorts: On Typography and Print Culture.* Philadelphia: University of Pennsylvania Press, 2011.

Dane, Joseph A. *The Myth of Print Culture: Essays on Evidence, Textuality, and Bibliographical Method*. Studies in Book and Print Culture. Toronto: University of Toronto Press, 2003.

Dane, Joseph A. *What Is a Book?: The Study of Early Printed Books*. Notre Dame, IN: University of Notre Dame Press, 2012.

Dane, Joseph A, and Alexandra Gillespie. "The Myth of the Cheap Quarto." In *Tudor Books and Readers: Materiality and the Construction of Meaning*, edited by John N. King, 25–45. Cambridge: Cambridge University Press, 2010.

Davis, Natalie Zemon. *Society and Culture in Early Modern France: Eight Essays*. Stanford: Stanford University Press, 1975.

Day, Ronald E. *The Modern Invention of Information: Discourse, History, and Power*. Carbondale: Southern Illinois University Press, 2001.

De Grazia, Margreta. *Hamlet Without Hamlet*. Cambridge: Cambridge University Press, 2007.

De Looze, Laurence. *The Letter and the Cosmos: How the Alphabet Has Shaped the Western View of the World*. Toronto: University of Toronto Press, 2016.

Debray, Régis. "The Book as Symbolic Object." In *The Future of the Book*, edited by Geoffrey Nunberg, 139–51. Berkeley: University of California Press, 1996.

Depledge, Emma. "Paper / Ink." In *Shakespeare / Text*, edited by Claire M. L. Bourne, 383–401. London: Bloomsbury, 2021.

Derrida, Jacques. *Of Grammatology*. Translated by Gayatri Chakravorty Spivak. Fortieth-Anniversary Edition. Baltimore, MD: Johns Hopkins University Press, 2016.

Deutermann, Allison K., and András Kiséry, eds. *Formal Matters: Reading the Materials of English Renaissance Literature*. Manchester: Manchester University Press, 2013.

DeVinne, Theo L. *The Invention of Printing: A Collection of Facts and Opinions Descriptive of Early Prints and Playing Cards, the Block Books of the Fifteenth Century, the Legend of Lourens Janszoon Coster, of Harlem, and the Work of John Gutenberg and His Associates*. Detroit: Gale Research Co., 1969.

Dobranski, Stephen B. *Readers and Authorship in Early Modern England*. Cambridge: Cambridge University Press, 2005.

Dolan, Frances E. *Digging the Past: How and Why to Imagine Seventeenth-Century Agriculture*. Philadelphia: University of Pennsylvania Press, 2020.

Dolven, Jeff. "The Early Modern Book as Metaphor." In *The Oxford Handbook of the History of the Book in Early Modern England*, edited by Adam Smyth, 531–48. Oxford: Oxford University Press, 2023.

Donato, Clorinda, and Robert M. Maniquis, eds. *The Encyclopédie and the Age of Revolution*. Boston: G.K. Hall & Co., 1992.

Dover, Paul M. *The Information Revolution in Early Modern Europe*. Cambridge: Cambridge University Press, 2021.

Drucker, Johanna. "Distributed and Conditional Documents: Conceptualizing Bibliographical Alterities." *MATLIT: Materialidades Da Literatura* 2, no. 1 (November 8, 2014): 11–29.

Drucker, Johanna. *Graphesis: Visual Forms of Knowledge Production.* MetaLABprojects. Cambridge: Harvard University Press, 2014.

Drucker, Johanna. *Inventing the Alphabet: The Origins of Letters from Antiquity to the Present.* Chicago: University of Chicago Press, 2022.

Drucker, Johanna. "Performative Materiality and Theoretical Approaches to Interface." *Digital Humanities Quarterly* 7, no. 1 (July 1, 2013). www .digitalhumanities.org/dhq/vol/7/1/000143/000143.html

Drucker, Johanna. *The Alphabetic Labyrinth: The Letters in History and Imagination.* New York: Thames & Hudson, 1995.

Egan, Gabriel. "'As It Was, Is, or Will Be Played': Title-Pages and the Theatre Industry to 1610." In *From Performance to Print in Shakespeare's England,* edited by Peter Holland and Stephen Orgel, 92–110. Basingstoke, England: Palgrave Macmillan, 2006.

Eggert, Katherine. *Disknowledge: Literature, Alchemy, and the End of Humanism in Renaissance England.* Philadelphia: University of Pennsylvania Press, 2015.

Egginton, William. *How the World Became a Stage: Presence, Theatricality, and the Question of Modernity.* Albany: State University of New York Press, 2003.

Eisenstein, Elizabeth L. *Divine Art, Infernal Machine: The Reception of Printing in the West from First Impressions to the Sense of an Ending.* Material Texts. Philadelphia: University of Pennsylvania Press, 2011.

Eisenstein, Elizabeth L. "Some Conjectures about the Impact of Printing on Western Society and Thought: A Preliminary Report." *The Journal of Modern History* 40, no. 1 (1968): 1–56.

Eisenstein, Elizabeth L. *The Printing Press as an Agent of Change: Communications and Cultural Transformations in Early Modern Europe.* Cambridge: Cambridge University Press, 1979.

Empson, William. *The Structure of Complex Words.* London: Chatto & Windus, 1951.

Erne, Lukas. *Shakespeare and the Book Trade.* Cambridge: Cambridge University Press, 2013.

Estill, Laura. *Dramatic Extracts in Seventeenth-Century English Manuscripts: Watching, Reading, Changing Plays.* Newark: University of Delaware Press, 2015.

Evernden, Lorne Leslie Neil. *The Social Creation of Nature.* Baltimore, MD: Johns Hopkins University Press, 1992.

Fallon, Samuel. *Paper Monsters: Persona and Literary Culture in Elizabethan England.* Material Texts. Philadelphia: University of Pennsylvania Press, 2019.

Fanon, Frantz. *Black Skin, White Masks.* New York: Grove Press, 1968.

Fish, Stanley. *Self-Consuming Artifacts; the Experience of Seventeenth-Century Literature.* Berkeley: University of California Press, 1972.

Fleming, Juliet. *Cultural Graphology: Writing after Derrida.* Chicago: University of Chicago Press, 2016.

Fleming, Juliet. *Graffiti and the Writing Arts of Early Modern England.* Material Texts. Philadelphia: University of Pennsylvania Press, 2001.

Foreman, P. Gabrielle. "Slavery, Black Visual Culture, and the Promises and Problems of Print in the Work of David Drake, Theaster Gates, and Glenn Ligon." In *Against a Sharp White Background: Infrastructures of African American*

Print, edited by Brigitte Fielder and Jonathan Senchyne, 29–61. Madison: University of Wisconsin Press, 2019.

Foucault, Michel. *The Order of Things; an Archaeology of the Human Sciences*. New York: Vintage Books, 1973.

Fraistat, Neil, and Julia Flanders, eds. *The Cambridge Companion to Textual Scholarship*. Cambridge: Cambridge University Press, 2013.

Fuentes, Marisa J. *Dispossessed Lives: Enslaved Women, Violence, and the Archive*. Early American Studies. Philadelphia: University of Pennsylvania Press, 2016.

Fuller, Mary C. *Lines Drawn across the Globe: Reading Richard Hakluyt's Principal Navigations*. McGill-Queen's Studies in the History of Ideas 90. Montreal: McGill-Queen's University Press, 2023.

Fulton, Thomas. *The Book of Books: Biblical Interpretation, Literary Culture, and the Political Imagination from Erasmus to Milton*. Philadelphia: University of Pennsylvania Press, 2021.

Gadd, Ian. "The Use and Misuse of Early English Books Online." *Literature Compass* 6, no. 3 (2009): 680–92. https://doi.org/10.1111/j.1741-4113.2009.00632.x.

Galbraith, Stephen K. "English Literary Folios 1593–1623: Studying Shifts in Format." In *Tudor Books and Readers: Materiality and the Construction of Meaning*, edited by John N. King, 46–67. Cambridge: Cambridge University Press, 2010.

Galey, Alan. *The Shakespearean Archive: Experiments in New Media from the Renaissance to Postmodernity*. Cambridge: Cambridge University Press, 2014.

Gaskell, Philip. *A New Introduction to Bibliography*. Oxford: Clarendon Press, 1972.

Gaukroger, Stephen. *The Emergence of a Scientific Culture: Science and the Shaping of Modernity, 1210–1685*. Oxford: Oxford University Press, 2006.

Gavin, Michael. "How to Think about EEBO." *Textual Cultures* 11, no. 1–2 (2017): 70–105. https://doi.org/10.14434/textual.v11i1-2.23570.

Gellrich, Jesse M. *The Idea of the Book in the Middle Ages: Language Theory, Mythology, and Fiction*. Ithaca, NY: Cornell University Press, 1985.

Gibson, James J. *The Ecological Approach to Visual Perception*. Boston: Houghton Mifflin, 1979.

Gillespie, Alexandra. *Print Culture and the Medieval Author: Chaucer, Lydgate, and Their Books, 1473–1557*. Oxford English Monographs. Oxford: Oxford University Press, 2006.

Gillespie, Alexandra, and Deidre Lynch, eds. *The Unfinished Book*. Oxford: Oxford University Press, 2020. https://doi.org/10.1093/oxfordhb/9780198830801.001.0001.

Gitelman, Lisa. *Always Already New: Media, History, and the Data of Culture*. Cambridge: MIT Press, 2006.

Goldberg, Adele E. *Constructions at Work: The Nature of Generalization in Language*. Oxford: Oxford University Press, 2006.

Grazia, Margreta de. "The Modern Divide: From Either Side." *Journal of Medieval and Early Modern Studies* 37, no. 3 (September 1, 2007): 453–67.

Grazia, Margreta de, and Peter Stallybrass. "The Materiality of the Shakespearean Text." *Shakespeare Quarterly* 44, no. 3 (1993): 255–83. https://doi.org/10.2307/2871419.

Greenblatt, Stephen. *The Swerve: How the World Became Modern*. 1st ed. New York: W.W. Norton & Company, 2011.

Greene, Roland. *Five Words: Critical Semantics in the Age of Shakespeare and Cervantes*. Chicago: University of Chicago Press, 2013.

Greetham, D. C. "Textual Forensics." *PMLA: Publications of the Modern Language Association of America* 111, no. 1 (1996): 32–51. https://doi.org/10.2307/463132.

Greetham, D. C. *Textual Scholarship: An Introduction*. New York: Garland, 1994.

Grier, Miles P. *Inkface: Othello and White Authority in the Era of Atlantic Slavery*. Writing the Early Americas. Charlottesville: University of Virginia Press, 2023.

Guillory, John. *Cultural Capital: The Problem of Literary Canon Formation*. Chicago: University of Chicago Press, 1993.

Guillory, John. "Genesis of the Media Concept." *Critical Inquiry* 36, no. 2 (2010): 321–62. https://doi.org/10.1086/648528.

Guillory, John. "Mercury's Words: The End of Rhetoric and the Beginning of Prose." *Representations* 138, no. 1 (May 1, 2017): 59–86. https://doi.org/10.1525/rep.2017.138.1.59.

Guillory, John. *Professing Criticism: Essays on the Organization of Literary Study*. Chicago: University of Chicago Press, 2022.

Guillory, John. "The Memo and Modernity." *Critical Inquiry* 31, no. 1 (2004): 108–32. https://doi.org/10.1086/427304.

Gumbrecht, Hans Ulrich. *Prose of the World: Denis Diderot and the Periphery of Enlightenment*. English edition. Stanford: Stanford University Press, 2021.

Gumbrecht, Hans Ulrich. *The Powers of Philology: Dynamics of Textual Scholarship*. Urbana: University of Illinois Press, 2003.

Guyer, Benjamin. *How the English Reformation Was Named: The Politics of History, 1400–1700*. Oxford: Oxford University Press, 2022.

Habib, Imtiaz H. *Black Lives in the English Archives, 1500–1677: Imprints of the Invisible*. Aldershot: Ashgate, 2008.

Halasz, Alexandra. *The Marketplace of Print: Pamphlets and the Public Sphere in Early Modern England*. Cambridge Studies in Renaissance Literature and Culture 17. Cambridge: Cambridge University Press, 1997.

Hall, Kim F. *Things of Darkness: Economies of Race and Gender in Early Modern England*. Ithaca, NY: Cornell University Press, 1995.

Hargrave, Jocelyn. "Joseph Moxon: A Re-Fashioned Appraisal." *Script & Print: Bulletin of the Bibliographical Society of Australia and New Zealand* 39, no. 3 (2015): 163–81.

Harrison, Peter. *The Bible, Protestantism, and the Rise of Natural Science*. Cambridge: Cambridge University Press, 1998.

Harvey, David. *The Condition of Postmodernity: An Enquiry into the Origins of Cultural Change*. Oxford: Blackwell, 1989.

Harvey, Elizabeth D., ed. *Sensible Flesh: On Touch in Early Modern Culture*. Philadelphia: University of Pennsylvania Press, 2003.

Haydn, Hiram Collins. *The Counter-Renaissance*. New York: Scribner, 1950.

Hayles, N. Katherine. *How We Became Posthuman: Virtual Bodies in Cybernetics, Literature, and Informatics*. Chicago: University of Chicago Press, 1999.

Hayot, Eric, Anatoly Detwyler, and Lea Pao, eds. *Information: A Reader*. New York: Columbia University Press, 2021.

Healy, Margaret. *Shakespeare, Alchemy and the Creative Imagination: The Sonnets and A Lover's Complaint.* Cambridge: Cambridge University Press, 2011.

Heffernan, Megan. *Making the Miscellany: Poetry, Print, and the History of the Book in Early Modern England.* Philadelphia: University of Pennsylvania Press, 2021.

Heise, Ursula K. *Imagining Extinction: The Cultural Meanings of Endangered Species.* Chicago: University of Chicago Press, 2016.

Heise, Ursula K. *Sense of Place and Sense of Planet: The Environmental Imagination of the Global.* Oxford: Oxford University Press, 2008.

Hellinga, Lotte. *William Caxton and Early Printing in England.* London: British Library, 2010.

Heng, Geraldine. *The Invention of Race in the European Middle Ages.* Cambridge: Cambridge University Press, 2018.

Hobson, Marian, Kate E. Tunstall, and Caroline Warman. *Diderot and Rousseau: Networks of Enlightenment.* SVEC, 2011:04. Oxford: Voltaire Foundation, 2011.

Holsinger, Bruce W. *The Premodern Condition: Medievalism and the Making of Theory.* Chicago: University of Chicago Press, 2005.

Hooks, Adam G. *Selling Shakespeare: Biography, Bibliography, and the Book Trade.* Cambridge: Cambridge University Press, 2016.

Hopper, Paul. "Emergent Grammar." In *The New Psychology of Language: Cognitive and Functional Approaches to Language Structure*, edited by Michael Tomasello, 1:155–75. Mahwah, NJ: L. Erlbaum, 1998.

Houston, Keith. *The Book: A Cover-to-Cover Exploration of the Most Powerful Object of Our Time.* 1st ed. New York: W.W. Norton & Company, 2016.

Hudson, Nicholas, ed. *A Cultural History of Race in the Reformation and Enlightenment.* London: Bloomsbury, 2023.

Jager, Eric. *The Book of the Heart.* Chicago: University of Chicago Press, 2000.

Johns, Adrian. *The Nature of the Book: Print and Knowledge in the Making.* Chicago: University of Chicago Press, 1998.

Jucker, Andreas H., and Irma Taavitsainen, eds. *Historical Pragmatics.* Handbooks of Pragmatics, v. 8. Berlin: De Gruyter Mouton, 2010.

Kalas, Rayna. *Frame, Glass, Verse: The Technology of Poetic Invention in the English Renaissance.* Ithaca, NY: Cornell University Press, 2007.

Kastan, David Scott. *Shakespeare and the Book.* Cambridge: Cambridge University Press, 2001.

Kearney, James. *The Incarnate Text: Imagining the Book in Reformation England.* Material Texts. Philadelphia: University of Pennsylvania Press, 2009.

Kichuk, Diana. "Metamorphosis: Remediation in Early English Books Online (EEBO)." *Literary and Linguistic Computing* 22, no. 3 (June 18, 2007): 291–303. https://doi.org/10.1093/llc/fqm018.

Kiefer, Frederick. *Writing on the Renaissance Stage: Written Words, Printed Pages, Metaphoric Books.* Newark: Associated University Presses, 1996.

King, John N., ed. *Tudor Books and Readers: Materiality and the Construction of Meaning.* Cambridge: Cambridge University Press, 2010.

Knight, Jeffrey Todd. *Bound to Read: Compilations, Collections, and the Making of Renaissance Literature*. 1st ed. Material Texts. Philadelphia: University of Pennsylvania Press, 2013.

Kuskin, William. *Recursive Origins: Writing at the Transition to Modernity*. Notre Dame, IN: University of Notre Dame Press, 2013.

Kuskin, William. *Symbolic Caxton: Literary Culture and Print Capitalism*. Notre Dame, IN: University of Notre Dame Press, 2008.

LaBreche, Ben. "Areopagitica and the Limits of Pluralism." *Milton Studies* 54, no. 1 (2013): 139–60. https://doi.org/10.1353/mlt.2013.0006.

Lakoff, George, and Mark Johnson. *Metaphors We Live By*. Chicago: University of Chicago Press, 2003.

Lamb, Jonathan P. "Ben Jonson's Dead Body: Henry, Prince of Wales, and the 1616 Folio." *Huntington Library Quarterly* 79, no. 1 (March 24, 2016): 63–92. https://doi.org/10.1353/hlq.2016.0001.

Lamb, Jonathan P. "Computational Philology." *Memoria Di Shakespeare. A Journal of Shakespearean Studies* 7 (December 31, 2020). https://doi.org/10.13133/2283-8759/17248.

Lamb, Jonathan P. "Parentheses and Privacy in Philip Sidney's *Arcadia*." *Studies in Philology* 107, no. 3 (2010): 310–35.

Lamb, Jonathan P. *Shakespeare in the Marketplace of Words*. Cambridge: Cambridge University Press, 2017.

Lander, Jesse M. *Inventing Polemic: Religion, Print, and Literary Culture in Early Modern England*. Cambridge: Cambridge University Press, 2006.

Latour, Bruno. *An Inquiry into Modes of Existence: An Anthropology of the Moderns*. Cambridge: Harvard University Press, 2013.

Latour, Bruno. *We Have Never Been Modern*. Cambridge: Harvard University Press, 1993.

Latour, Bruno. "Why Has Critique Run out of Steam? From Matters of Fact to Matters of Concern." *Critical Inquiry* 30, no. 2 (January 1, 2004): 225–48.

Laudan, Larry. *Science and Hypothesis: Historical Essays on Scientific Methodology*. Dordrecht, Holland: D. Reidel, 1981.

Lerer, Seth. "Medieval English Literature and the Idea of the Anthology." *PMLA: Publications of the Modern Language Association of America* 118, no. 5 (October 2003): 1251–60. https://doi.org/10.1632/003081203X68018.

Lesser, Zachary. *Ghosts, Holes, Rips and Scrapes: Shakespeare in 1619, Bibliography in the Longue Durée*. Philadelphia: University of Pennsylvania Press, 2021.

Lesser, Zachary. "Typographic Nostalgia: Play-Reading, Popularity, and the Meanings of Black Letter." In *The Book of the Play: Playwrights, Stationers, and Readers in Early Modern England*, edited by Marta Straznicky, 99–126. Boston: University of Massachusetts Press, 2006.

Lesser, Zachary, and Peter Stallybrass. "The First Literary *Hamlet* and the Commonplacing of Professional Plays." *Shakespeare Quarterly* 59, no. 4 (2008): 371–420.

Levine, Caroline. *Forms: Whole, Rhythm, Hierarchy, Network*. Princeton: Princeton University Press, 2015.

Lewis, C. S. *A Preface to Paradise Lost*. New York: Oxford University Press, 1961.

Little, Arthur L. *White People in Shakespeare: Essays on Race, Culture and the Elite*. Shakespeare and Social Justice. London: The Arden Shakespeare, 2023.

Loomba, Ania. "Shakespeare and Cultural Difference." In *Alternative Shakespeares*, edited by Terence Hawkes, 2:164–91. New York: Routledge, 1996.

Love, Harold. "Early Modern Print Culture: Assessing the Models." *Parergon* 20, no. 1 (2003): 45–64. https://doi.org/10.1353/pgn.2003.0071.

Love, Harold. *Scribal Publication in Seventeenth-Century England*. Oxford: Clarendon Press, 1993.

Lupton, Christina. *Knowing Books: The Consciousness of Mediation in Eighteenth-Century Britain*. Material Texts. Philadelphia: University of Pennsylvania Press, 2012.

Lupton, Christina. *Reading and the Making of Time in the Eighteenth Century*. Baltimore, MD: Johns Hopkins University Press, 2018.

MacDonald, Joyce Green, ed. *Race, Ethnicity, and Power in the Renaissance*. Madison, NJ: Fairleigh Dickinson University Press, 1997.

MacGeddon [pseud. Randall McLeod], R. "An Epilogue: Hammered." In *Negotiating the Jacobean Printed Book*, edited by Pete Langman, 137–99. London: Routledge, 2016.

Maguire, Laurie. *The Rhetoric of the Page*. Oxford: Oxford University Press, 2020.

Mak, Bonnie. *How the Page Matters*. Studies in Book and Print Culture Series. Toronto: University of Toronto Press, 2011.

Mann, Jenny C. *The Trials of Orpheus: Poetry, Science, and the Early Modern Sublime*. Princeton: Princeton University Press, 2021.

Marotti, Arthur F. *Manuscript, Print, and the English Renaissance Lyric*. Ithaca, NY: Cornell University Press, 1995.

Marotti, Arthur F., and Michael D. Bristol, eds. *Print, Manuscript, & Performance: The Changing Relations of the Media in Early Modern England*. Columbus: Ohio State University Press, 2000.

Martin, Craig. *Subverting Aristotle: Religion, History, and Philosophy in Early Modern Science*. Baltimore, MD: Johns Hopkins University Press, 2014.

Maruca, Lisa. *The Work of Print: Authorship and the English Text Trades, 1660–1760*. Literary Conjugations. Seattle: University of Washington Press, 2007.

Maruca, Lisa, and Kate Ozment. "What Is Critical Bibliography?" *Criticism* 64, no. 3/4 (Summer/Fall ///Summer/Fall2022 2022): 231–36. https://doi.org/10.1353/crt.2022.a899716.

Masten, Jeffrey. *Queer Philologies: Sex, Language, and Affect in Shakespeare's Time*. Material Texts. Philadelphia: University of Pennsylvania Press, 2016.

Mbembe, Achille. *Critique of Black Reason*. Translated by Laurent Dubois. Durham: Duke University Press, 2017.

McCarthy, Erin A. *Doubtful Readers: Print, Poetry, and the Reading Public in Early Modern England*. Oxford: Oxford University Press, 2020.

McGann, Jerome. "Philology in a New Key." *Critical Inquiry* 39, no. 2 (January 1, 2013): 327–46. https://doi.org/10.1086/668528.

McGrath, Alister E. *Historical Theology: An Introduction to the History of Christian Thought*. London: Wiley-Blackwell, 2012.

McKenzie, D. F. *Bibliography and the Sociology of Texts*. Cambridge: Cambridge University Press, 1999.

McKenzie, D. F. *Making Meaning: "Printers of the Mind" and Other Essays*. Edited by Peter D. McDonald and Michael F. Suarez. Amherst: University of Massachusetts Press, 2002.

McKitterick, David. *Print, Manuscript and the Search for Order, 1450–1830*. Cambridge: Cambridge University Press, 2003.

McLeod, Randall. "Information on Information." *Text* 5 (1991): 241–81.

McLuhan, Marshall. *The Gutenberg Galaxy; the Making of Typographic Man*. Toronto: University of Toronto Press, 1962.

McLuhan, Marshall. *Understanding Media: The Extensions of Man*. 1st MIT Press ed. Cambridge: MIT Press, 1994.

Merchant, Carolyn. *Autonomous Nature: Problems of Prediction and Control from Ancient Times to the Scientific Revolution*. New York: Routledge, 2016.

Merchant, Carolyn. *Reinventing Eden: The Fate of Nature in Western Culture*. 2nd ed. New York: Routledge, 2013.

Merchant, Carolyn. *The Death of Nature: Women, Ecology, and the Scientific Revolution: A Feminist Reappraisal of the Scientific Revolution*. 1st ed. San Francisco: Harper & Row, 1980.

Miller, Julia. *Books Will Speak Plain: A Handbook for Identifying and Describing Historical Bindings*. Ann Arbor: The Legacy Press, 2010.

Misson, James. "Typography." In *The Oxford Handbook of the History of the Book in Early Modern England*, edited by Adam Smyth, 310–27. Oxford: Oxford University Press, 2023.

Mitchell, Dianne. "The Absent Lady and the Renaissance Lyric as Letter." *English Literary Renaissance* 49, no. 3 (September 2019): 304–29. https://doi .org/10.1086/704507.

Needham, Paul. "Haec Sancta Ars: Gutenberg's Invention as a Divine Gift." *Gazette of the Grolier Club* 42 (1990): 101–20.

Newcomb, Lori Humphrey. *Reading Popular Romance in Early Modern England*. New York: Columbia University Press, 2002.

Newman, Harry. *Impressive Shakespeare: Identity, Authority and the Imprint in Shakespearean Drama*. New York: Routledge, 2019.

Nichanian, Marc, and Narine Jallatyan. "Philology from the Point of View of Its Victims." *Boundary 2* 48, no. 1 (February 1, 2021): 177–206. https://doi .org/10.1215/01903659-8821473.

Nicholson, Catherine. "Algorithm and Analogy: Distant Reading in 1598." *PMLA: Publications of the Modern Language Association of America* 132, no. 3 (2017): 643–50.

Nunberg, Geoffrey. "Farewell to the Information Age." In *The Future of the Book*, edited by Geoffrey Nunberg, 103–38. Berkeley: University of California Press, 1996.

Nunberg, Geoffrey. "Information, Disinformation, Misinformation." In *Information: A Historical Companion*, edited by Ann Blair, Paul Duguid, Anja-Silvia Goeing, and Anthony Grafton, 496–502. Princeton: Princeton University Press, 2021.

Oliveira, Vanessa Machado de. *Hospicing Modernity: Facing Humanity's Wrongs and the Implications for Social Activism*. Berkeley: North Atlantic Books, 2021.

Ong, Walter J. *Orality and Literacy: The Technologizing of the Word*. London: Routledge, 2002.

Painter, Nell Irvin. *The History of White People*. New York: W.W. Norton & Company, 2011.

Parker, Patricia A. *Inescapable Romance: Studies in the Poetics of a Mode*. Princeton: Princeton University Press, 1979.

Partington, Gill, and Adam Smyth, eds. *Book Destruction from the Medieval to the Contemporary*. New Directions in Book History. New York: Palgrave Macmillan, 2014.

Pasanek, Brad. *Metaphors of Mind: An Eighteenth-Century Dictionary*. Baltimore, MD: Johns Hopkins University Press, 2015.

Peters, John Durham. "Information: Notes Toward a Critical History." *Journal of Communication Inquiry* 12, no. 2 (1988): 9–23. https://doi.org/10.1177/019685998801200202.

Peters, John Durham. *Speaking into the Air: A History of the Idea of Communication*. Chicago: University of Chicago Press, 1999.

Pettegree, Andrew. *The Book in the Renaissance*. New Haven: Yale University Press, 2010.

Piper, Andrew. *Book Was There: Reading in Electronic Times*. Chicago: University of Chicago Press, 2012.

Piper, Andrew. *Dreaming in Books: The Making of the Bibliographic Imagination in the Romantic Age*. Chicago: University of Chicago Press, 2009.

Piper, Andrew. *Enumerations: Data and Literary Study*. Chicago: University of Chicago Press, 2018.

Pollock, Sheldon. "Future Philology? The Fate of a Soft Science in a Hard World." *Critical Inquiry* 35, no. 4 (2009): 931–61. https://doi.org/10.1086/599594.

Popper, Karl. *The Logic of Scientific Discovery*. London: Routledge, 2002.

Popper, Nicholas. "The Knowledge of Early Modernity: New Histories of Sciences and the Humanities." In *New Horizons in Early Modern Scholarship*, edited by Ann Blair and Nicholas Popper, 131–49. Baltimore, MD: Johns Hopkins University Press, 2021.

Postman, Neil. *Amusing Ourselves to Death: Public Discourse in the Age of Show Business*. New York: Penguin Books, 1986.

Price, Leah. "From the History of a Book to a 'History of the Book.'" *Representations* 108, no. 1 (November 1, 2009): 120–38.

Price, Leah. *What We Talk about When We Talk About Books*. New York: Basic Books, 2019.

Principe, Lawrence M. "Virtuous Romance and Romantic Virtuoso: The Shaping of Robert Boyle's Literary Style." *Journal of the History of Ideas* 56, no. 3 (1995): 377–97. https://doi.org/10.2307/2710032.

"Quantum Physics: The Quantum Atom." *Nature* 498, no. 7452 (June 1, 2013). https://doi.org/10.1038/498021a.

Quijano, Aníbal. "Coloniality and Modernity/Rationality." *Cultural Studies* 21, no. 2–3 (March 1, 2007): 168–78. https://doi.org/10.1080/09502380601164353.

Ramos, Eduardo. "Philology and Racist Appropriations of the Medieval." *Literature Compass* 20, no. 7–9 (2023): e12734. https://doi.org/10.1111/lic3.12734.

Razzall, Lucy. *Boxes and Books in Early Modern England: Materiality, Metaphor, Containment.* Cambridge: Cambridge University Press, 2021.

Reid, Pauline. *Reading by Design: The Visual Interfaces of the English Renaissance Book.* Toronto: University of Toronto Press, 2019.

Remien, Peter. *The Concept of Nature in Early Modern English Literature.* Cambridge: Cambridge University Press, 2019. https://doi.org/10.1017/9781108654906.

Rezek, Joseph. "The Racialization of Print." *American Literary History* 32, no. 3 (September 1, 2020): 417–45.

Rhodes, Neil. *Common: The Development of Literary Culture in Sixteenth-Century England.* Oxford: Oxford University Press, 2018.

Richards, William. *Wallography, or, The Britton Describ'd.* London, 1682.

Roberts, Colin H., T. C. Skeat, and Colin H. Roberts. *The Birth of the Codex.* London: Published for the British Academy by the Oxford University Press, 1983.

Robertson, Kellie. *Nature Speaks: Medieval Literature and Aristotelian Philosophy.* The Middle Ages Series. Philadelphia: University of Pennsylvania Press, 2017.

Robinson, Solveig C. *The Book in Society: An Introduction to Print Culture.* Peterborough, Ontario: Broadview Press, 2014.

Rosa, Hartmut. *Social Acceleration: A New Theory of Modernity.* New Directions in Critical Theory. New York: Columbia University Press, 2013.

Round, Phillip H. *Removable Type: Histories of the Book in Indian Country, 1663–1880.* Chapel Hill: University of North Carolina Press, 2010.

Said, Edward W. *Humanism and Democratic Criticism.* Columbia Themes in Philosophy. New York: Columbia University Press, 2004.

Sawday, Jonathan. *Blanks, Print, Space, and Void in English Renaissance Literature: An Archaeology of Absence.* Oxford: Oxford University Press, 2023.

Schalkwyk, David. "Giving Intention Its Due?" *Style* 44, no. 3 (2010): 311–27.

Scott, Charlotte. *Shakespeare and the Idea of the Book.* Oxford Shakespeare Topics. Oxford: Oxford University Press, 2007.

Sellew, Philip. "Red Letter Bible." In *The Oxford Companion to the Bible,* edited by Bruce M. Metzger and Michael D. Coogan. Oxford: Oxford University Press, 1993. www.oxfordreference.com/display/10.1093/acref/9780195046458.001.0001/acref-9780195046458-e-0589.

Shapin, Steven. *A Social History of Truth: Civility and Science in Seventeenth-Century England.* Science and Its Conceptual Foundations. Chicago: University of Chicago Press, 1994.

Shapin, Steven. *Leviathan and the Air-Pump: Hobbes, Boyle, and the Experimental Life: Including a Translation of Thomas Hobbes, Dialogus Physicus de Natura Aeris by Simon Schaffer.* Princeton: Princeton University Press, 1985.

Shapin, Steven. *The Scientific Revolution.* 2nd ed. Chicago: University of Chicago Press, 2018.

Sherman, William H. *Used Books: Marking Readers in Renaissance England*. Philadelphia: University of Pennsylvania Press, 2008.

Shore, Daniel. *Cyberformalism*. Baltimore, MD: Johns Hopkins University Press, 2018.

Silva, Denise Ferreira da. *Toward a Global Idea of Race*. Borderlines, v. 27. Minneapolis: University of Minnesota Press, 2007.

Silva, Denise Ferreira da. *Unpayable Debt*. On the Antipolitical, v. 1. London: Sternberg Press, 2022.

Silverman, Gillian. "Neurodiversity and the Revision of Book History." *PMLA: Publications of the Modern Language Association of America* 131, no. 2 (2016): 307–23.

Simon, David Carroll. *Light without Heat: The Observational Mood from Bacon to Milton*. Ithaca, NY: Cornell University Press, 2018.

Simon, Margaret. "Glossing Authorship: Printed Marginalia in Aemilia Lanyer's Salve Deus Rex Judaeorum." *Renaissance Papers*, 2017, 125–38.

Siskin, Clifford, and William Warner, eds. *This Is Enlightenment*. Chicago: University of Chicago Press, 2010.

Smith, Emma. *Portable Magic: A History of Books and Their Readers*. First American edition. New York: Alfred A. Knopf, 2022.

Smith, Helen. "'A Man in Print?' Shakespeare and the Representation of the Press." In *Shakespeare's Book: Essays in Reading, Writing and Reception*, edited by Richard Meek, Jane Rickard, and Richard Wilson, 59–78. Manchester: Manchester University Press, 2008.

Smith, Ian. *Black Shakespeare: Reading and Misreading Race*. Cambridge: Cambridge University Press, 2022.

Smith, Ian. *Race and Rhetoric in the Renaissance: Barbarian Errors*. 1st ed. Early Modern Cultural Studies. New York: Palgrave Macmillan, 2009.

Smith, Margaret M. "Black Letter." In *The Oxford Companion to the Book*. Oxford University Press, January 1, 2010. www.oxfordreference.com/display/10.1093/acref/9780198606536.001.0001/acref-9780198606536-e-0588.

Smith, Steven B. *Modernity and Its Discontents: Making and Unmaking the Bourgeois from Machiavelli to Bellow*. New Haven: Yale University Press, 2016.

Smyth, Adam. *Material Texts in Early Modern England*. Cambridge: Cambridge University Press, 2018.

Smyth, Adam. *The Oxford Handbook of the History of the Book in Early Modern England*. Oxford: Oxford University Press, 2023.

Sperrazza, Whitney. *Anatomical Forms: The Science of the Body in Early Modern Women's Poetry*. Philadelphia: University of Pennsylvania Press, Forthcoming.

Sperrazza, Whitney. "Knowing Mary Wroth's Pamphilia." *Journal for Early Modern Cultural Studies* 19, no. 3 (2019): 1–35. https://doi.org/10.1353/jem.2019.0027.

Spires, Derrick R. "On Liberation Bibliography: The 2021 BSA Annual Meeting Keynote." *The Papers of the Bibliographical Society of America* 116, no. 1 (2022): 1–20. https://doi.org/10.1086/717066.

Starks-Estes, Lisa S. *Violence, Trauma, and Virtus in Shakespeare's Roman Poems and Plays: Transforming Ovid*. New York: Palgrave Macmillan, 2014.

Stenner, Rachel. *The Typographic Imaginary in Early Modern English Literature.* Material Readings in Early Modern Culture. New York: Routledge, 2019.

Stern, Tiffany. *Documents of Performance in Early Modern England.* Cambridge: Cambridge University Press, 2009.

Stern, Tiffany. "'On Each Wall and Corner Poast': Playbills, Title-pages, and Advertising in Early Modern London." *English Literary Renaissance* 36, no. 1 (2006): 57–89. https://doi.org/10.1111/j.1475-6757.2006.00072.x.

Strawson, Galen. *Locke on Personal Identity: Consciousness and Concernment.* Princeton Monographs in Philosophy. Princeton: Princeton University Press, 2011.

Swann, Elizabeth L. *Taste and Knowledge in Early Modern England.* Cambridge: Cambridge University Press, 2020.

Tanselle, G. Thomas. "The Concept of Format." *Studies in Bibliography* 53 (2000): 67–115.

Tatlock, John S. P. "The Epilog of Chaucer's 'Troilus.'" *Modern Philology* 18, no. 12 (1921): 625–59.

Taylor, Charles. *Modern Social Imaginaries.* Public Planet Books. Durham: Duke University Press, 2004.

Taylor, Diana. *The Archive and the Repertoire: Performing Cultural Memory in the Americas.* Durham: Duke University Press, 2003.

Taylor, Victor E., and Charles E. Winquist, eds. *Postmodernism: Critical Concepts.* 4 vols. Routledge Critical Concepts. New York: Routledge, 1998.

Thompson, Ayanna. *The Cambridge Companion to Shakespeare and Race.* Cambridge: Cambridge University Press, 2021.

Tillyard, E. M. W. *The Elizabethan World Picture.* London: Chatto & Windus, 1943.

Traub, Valerie, ed. *The Oxford Handbook of Shakespeare and Embodiment: Gender, Sexuality, and Race.* Oxford: Oxford University Press, 2016.

Traugott, Elizabeth Closs, and Richard B. Dasher. *Regularity in Semantic Change.* Cambridge Studies in Linguistics 96. Cambridge: Cambridge University Press, 2002.

Trettien, Whitney. *Cut/Copy/Paste: Fragments from the History of Bookwork.* Minneapolis: University of Minnesota Press, 2022.

Trettien, Whitney. "Title Pages." In *Book Parts*, edited by Dennis Duncan and Adam Smyth, 39–49. Oxford: Oxford University Press, 2019.

Tribble, Evelyn B. *Margins and Marginality: The Printed Page in Early Modern England.* Charlottesville: University Press of Virginia, 1993.

Tuer, Andrew White. *History of the Horn-Book.* New York: Arno Press, 1979.

Tycz, Katherine M. "Material Prayers and Maternity in Early Modern Italy: Signed, Sealed, Delivered." In *Domestic Devotions in Early Modern Italy*, edited by Maya Corry, Marco Faini, and Alessia Meneghin, 244–71. Leiden: Brill, 2019.

Wall-Randell, Sarah. *The Immaterial Book: Reading and Romance in Early Modern England.* Ann Arbor: University of Michigan Press, 2013.

Walsham, Alexandra. *The Reformation of the Landscape: Religion, Identity, and Memory in Early Modern Britain and Ireland.* Oxford: Oxford University Press, 2011.

Warner, Michael. *The Letters of the Republic: Publication and the Public Sphere in Eighteenth-Century America.* Cambridge: Harvard University Press, 1990.

Warren, Michelle R. "Introduction: Relating Philology, Practicing Humanism." *PMLA: Publications of the Modern Language Association of America* 125, no. 2 (2010): 283–88.

Werner, Sarah. *Studying Early Printed Books, 1450–1800: A Practical Guide.* Hoboken, NJ: Wiley Blackwell, 2019.

West, William N. *Common Understandings, Poetic Confusion: Playhouses and Playgoers in Elizabethan England.* Chicago: The University of Chicago Press, 2021.

White, Roger M. *The Structure of Metaphor: The Way the Language of Metaphor Works.* Oxford: Blackwell, 1996.

Williams, Raymond. *Keywords: A Vocabulary of Culture and Society.* New York: Oxford University Press, 1985.

Wilson, Robert. *Martine Mar-Sixtus.* London, 1591.

Wisecup, Kelly. *Assembled for Use: Indigenous Compilation and the Archives of Early Native American Literatures.* The Henry Roe Cloud Series on American Indians and Modernity. New Haven: Yale University Press, 2021.

Wootton, David. *The Invention of Science: A New History of the Scientific Revolution.* 1st U.S. ed. New York: Harper, an imprint of HarperCollinsPublishers, 2015.

Woudhuysen, H. R. *Sir Philip Sidney and the Circulation of Manuscripts, 1558–1640.* Oxford: Clarendon Press, 1996.

Ziolkowski, Jan. "'What Is Philology': Introduction." *Comparative Literature Studies* 27, no. 1 (1990): 1–12.

Index